SUCCESSFUL WRITING AT WORK

Philip C. Kolin

University of Southern Mississippi

D. C. HEATH AND COMPANY

Lexington, Massachusetts   Toronto

Cover photograph by Harry Wilks/STOCK, BOSTON

International Standard Book Number: 0-669-03507-6

Library of Congress Catalog Card Number: 81-81600

To
Eric, Kristin, and Janeen
Julie and Loretta
and
MARY

Preface

Successful Writing at Work has been designed for use in technical, business, professional, and occupational writing courses. Its approach is practical, emphasizing that communications skills are essential for career advancement and that writing is not separate from, but a vital part of, the job. Throughout, students are given detailed guidelines for writing.

Teachers will find the following features especially useful:

- The book contains a wide range of examples taken from sources such as student papers, business correspondence, governmental reports, and magazine articles. Since knowing what not to do is sometimes the first step in learning what to do, students will also find examples of poor writing with comments on its faults.
- Letters, instructions, and reports are frequently described from the point of view of the intended audience. For example, students learn what personnel directors want to see in a résumé and what executives want to see in an abstract. Students are encouraged to perform audience analysis as a part of the writing process.
- Numerous, detailed exercises follow each chapter, allowing instructors to test students' mastery of every major concept presented in the text. An instructor's guide, with answers to most of the exercises, is also available.
- Topics proceed from the less complex to the more difficult. Thus, students learn the fundamentals of writing before they are asked to write memos, letters, or reports. From these shorter assignments, they move to more difficult ones, such as the preparation of instructions and questionnaires.
- Readers are addressed from points of view appropriate to the subject under study. In the first four chapters, they are seen as students preparing for careers, then in Chapter 5, as graduates who are looking for

positions. In Chapter 6 and in many later chapters, they are addressed as employees who must meet the needs of their employers.

A brief survey of the chapters suggests how these special features are incorporated throughout the book.

Section I emphasizes the essentials of writing. Chapter 1 identifies and illustrates the basic concepts of audience, purpose, message, and style. It then explains how these concepts relate to occupational writing. Chapters 2 and 3 discuss words and sentences—spelling, diction, punctuation, economy, and clarity.

Section II deals with business correspondence. Chapter 4 establishes the importance of selecting the appropriate format, language, and tone. From the student's perspective, Chapter 5, which covers the job search, may be the most important in the book. It shows how to prepare a placement file, write a résumé and letter of application, anticipate interviewers' questions, and accept or decline a job. For greater teaching flexibility, I have included letters of application and résumés suitable for students with varying degrees of experience. Chapter 6 examines the varieties of business correspondence and their appropriate contexts. It provides effective strategies for writing many types of letters.

The four chapters in Section III cover techniques for gathering and summarizing information. Chapter 7 takes students on a guided tour of the library, showing them how to locate printed and audio-visual materials and then how to document what they have found. This chapter also contains an annotated appendix of useful reference works.

Once students have located material, they may need to summarize it. Chapter 8, therefore, explains how to write summaries and abstracts and how to take careful minutes.

Chapter 9, which deals solely with questionnaires, provides practical advice on restricting a topic, constructing valid and reliable questions, selecting informants, organizing responses, and reporting results.

Chapter 10 suggests ways of devising visuals and explains how to introduce them, coordinate them with written commentary, and draw conclusions from them.

In Section IV students are encouraged to apply the skills they have learned in Section III to more complex writing assignments. Chapter 11 approaches the writing of instructions as a process in which students must select language, graphics, and details appropriate for a given audience. Chapter 12 outlines the principles common to all short reports and then discusses specific types. (Instructors will find the discussion of unusual-occurence reports especially detailed and helpful.) Finally, students are cautioned about the legal implications of what they write and are given advice on avoiding legal pitfalls.

The preparation of a long formal report is explained in Chapter 13, which reprints, as a model, a very readable report from an industrial research journal. Chapter 14 focuses on the importance of audience analysis in oral communications. It offers practical advice on using the telephone, handling impromptu conversations and technical briefings, and constructing and delivering formal talks.

I am grateful to many friends who gave helpful criticism as I wrote this book. They include David and Linda Goff, Ed Wheeler, and Mark Winchell, all of the University of Southern Mississippi; Ovid Vickers of East Central Junior College; Robert O. Wyatt of Middle Tennessee State University; Nancy Evans, formerly of the C. V. Mosby Company; and Gerry Hundscheid and Al Parish of the Hercules Company.

I am especially indebted to three reviewers who meticulously read and improved the manuscript. Mary Alice Griffin of Valdosta State College offered her expertise in all matters, especially in correspondence; John S. Harris of Brigham Young University provided helpful comments throughout the project; and Ronald Strahl of Indiana University/Purdue University at Indianapolis was instrumental in directing the final shape of the book. My thanks also to Al Phillips, in the Office of the General Counsel at Raytheon Company, and to my editors, Holt Johnson and Gordon Lester-Massman of D. C. Heath and Company, for their advice, thoroughness, and many profitable suggestions.

The University of Southern Mississippi generously provided research funds, and Mrs. Ann Sykes typed several drafts of the manuscript with exceptional dedication and skill.

Finally, I thank my wife, Janeen L. Kolin, for patiently reading and evaluating every word I wrote.

Philip C. Kolin

Contents

SECTION III. GATHERING AND SUMMARIZING INFORMATION

SECTION IV. INSTRUCTIONS AND REPORTS

SUCCESSFUL
WRITING AT WORK

SECTION I

BACKGROUNDS

Getting Started: Writing and Your Career

What are you going to do with the skills you are learning in your major? Perhaps you are preparing for a career in a health care agency as a nurse, respiratory therapist, or dental hygienist. Maybe you want to be a law enforcement officer working with a crime-detection unit or tackling a city's traffic problems. Possibly your studies are leading you to a career in forestry, ecology, or agriculture. Or maybe you are enrolled in a program that will prepare you for a position as an executive secretary, computer operator, salesperson, office manager, or accountant. Whatever your major, it will give you the facts and the practical know-how that you want and need for your career.

You need an additional skill, however, to ensure a successful career—that is, you must be able to write clearly about the facts, procedures, and problems of your job. Writing is a part of every job. In fact, prior to securing a job, your first contact with an employer is through your letter of application, which determines a company's first impression of you. And the higher you advance in an organization, the greater the amount of writing you will be doing.

Offices and agencies contain numerous visible reminders of the importance of writing—"in" and "out" boxes, file cabinets, typewriters, word processors, and photocopiers. Why? Writing keeps business moving. It allows individuals working for a company to communicate with one another and with the customers and clients they must serve if the company is to stay in business. Written communications include memos, letters, order forms, records, questionnaires, and reports. This book was written to show you, step by step, how to write these and other job-related communications easily and well.

Chapter 1 presents basic questions that you as a writer must answer. The chapter also gives information about the characteristics of on-the-job writing.

▶ The Key to Effective Writing

Effective writing on the job is carefully planned, thoroughly researched, and clearly presented. Whether you send a routine memo to a co-worker or a special report to the president of the company, each written assignment requires you to ask the following four questions:

1. *Who* will read what I write? (Identify your *audience*.)
2. *Why* should they read what I write? (Establish your *purpose*.)
3. *What* do I have to say to them? (Formulate your *message*.)
4. *How* can I best achieve my purpose? (Select your *style*.)

The *who? why? what?* and *how?* do not function independently; they are all related. You write for a specific audience (1) with a clearly defined purpose in mind (2) about a topic your readers need to understand (3) in language appropriate for the occasion (4). Once you answer the first question, you are off to a good start toward answering the three others. Now let us examine each of these four questions in more detail.

Identifying Your Audience

Knowing *who* makes up your audience is your most important function as a writer. Once you have identified your audience, you will be able to aim your message at its specific needs. Remember, not all audiences have the same needs. What has to be said to one group may not necessarily have to be said to all.

Look at the American Heart Association posters reproduced in Figs. 1.1, 1.2, and 1.3. The message—smoking is dangerous to health—is the same in each poster. But note how different details have been selected in order to reach three different audiences effectively. The poster in Fig. 1.1 emphasizes problems especially troublesome to a teenager: red eyes, bad breath, discolored teeth, unattractive hair. The message at the top of the poster plays on two meanings of the word "heart": (1) smoking can harm the heart, and (2) it can interfere with a romance. The audience for Fig. 1.2 is pregnant women; the warning focuses on the health of both mother and unborn child. Figure 1.3 is directed toward fathers: Will the father's story (and his life) be permanently interrupted? The three posters show how the needs and interests of three different audiences control the kinds of details chosen by the copywriter.

These posters reveal the variety of details writers can select from when they must reach separate audiences. On your job you may have to communicate with many different audiences—customers, supervisors, government inspectors, accountants, engineers. The members of each audience will have differing backgrounds and expectations. For each you will have to consider the following questions:

Fig. 1.1 No-smoking poster aimed at teenagers.

Fig. 1.2 No-smoking poster directed at pregnant women.

© Reprinted with permission of the American Heart Association.

© Reprinted with permission of the American Heart Association.

Fig. 1.3 No-smoking poster appealing to fathers.

© Reprinted with permission of the American Heart Association.

1. *How much technical knowledge of my field does my audience have?* Are you writing to individuals who are familiar with all the technical procedures you know? Or are you addressing an employer or customer who, however intelligent, is not an expert in your field and cannot be expected to know the facts? *Most often you will be writing to people who do not know as much about a job as you do.* Such individuals need more background information, definitions of terms, and explanatory visuals than does a technically skilled audience.
2. *How many people will make up my audience?* Is it just one individual (the nurse on the next shift, the desk sergeant) or many (all the users of a product manufactured by my company)? The more diverse your audience, the less technical must be your discussion.
3. *Why should my audience read my work?* Is it a part of my readers' routine duties? Am I offering them something beyond the ordinary? How will they benefit? Must I provide extra motivation to maintain their interest?
4. *What should they do after reading my work?* Should they file it for future reference, review it and send it along to another office, use it as the basis for a recommendation, get back to me, act on it at once? If you are uncertain about the needs of your audience, do not be afraid to ask, if circumstances permit.

There will be times, of course, when you cannot identify all the members of your potential audience. In such cases assume that you have a general audience and keep your message as simple as possible.

Establishing Your Purpose

By knowing *why* you are writing to readers, you will be better able to meet their needs. Knowing your purpose will help you determine exactly what you can and must say. Since your purpose controls the amount and order of information, state it clearly at the beginning of every letter or report. Start writing with such an opening firmly fixed in mind: "I am writing to inform you about four changes in your owner's manual." "This report has been written to review the water supply problems at Bear Harbor and to recommend a solution." The major goal of job-related writing is to inform—through letters, instructions, reports. But job-related writing can also sell (yourself in a letter of application, a specific product in a sales letter), make recommendations, question respondents, or solve problems. The following preface to a pamphlet on architectural casework details contains a model statement of purpose suited to a particular audience:

> This publication has been prepared by the Architectural Woodwork Institute to provide a source book of conventional details and uniform detail terminology. For this purpose a series of casework detail drawings, . . . representative of the best industry-wide practice, has been prepared and is presented here. By supplying both architect and woodwork manufacturer with a common authoritative reference, this work will enable architects and woodworkers to communicate in a

common technical language. . . . It is hoped that besides serving as a basic reference for architects and architectural draftsmen, it will be an effective training tool for the beginning draftsman-architect-in-training. It should also be a valuable aid to the project manager in coordinating the work of many draftsmen on large projects.[1]

After reading the preface, readers will have a clear sense of why they should read the casebook and what to do with the material they find in it.

Formulating Your Message

Your message is the sum of *what* facts, responses, and recommendations you put into writing. Some messages will consist of one or two sentences: "Do not touch; wet paint." "Order #756 was sent this afternoon by parcel post. It should arrive at your office by March 21." At the other extreme, messages may extend over twenty or thirty pages. Messages may carry good news or bad news. They may deal with routine matters, or they may handle changes in policy, special situations, or unexpected problems. Consider the message of the following excerpt from a section on "Tips on Communication," included in a metropolitan telephone book. The message provides factual information about a change in mailing policy, informing the general public about acceptable and unacceptable sizes of first-class and third-class mail:

New Size Standards for Domestic Mail

NONSTANDARD MAIL

The following material is considered nonstandard mail. First-class mail weighing one ounce or less and single piece third-class mail weighing two ounces or less which

1. Exceeds any of the following:
    (a) Height—6⅛ inches
    (b) Length—11½ inches
    (c) Thickness—¼ inch
2. Has a height to length ratio which does not fall between 1:13 and 1:25 inclusive.

In the near future, a surcharge will be assessed on each piece of nonstandard mail in addition to the applicable postage and fees.

NEW MINIMUM SIZES

Effective November 30, 1978, all mail must be at least .007 of an inch thick and mail which is ¼ inch or less in thickness must be

1. At least 3½ inches in height and at least 5 inches long.
2. Rectangular.

---

[1] Reprinted by permission of Architectural Woodwork Institute.

The message above is appropriate for a general audience. Readers are given neither less nor more information than is required. However, employees of the U.S. Postal Service or individuals working in mail rooms of large companies or in mail-order houses need more detailed instructions. Because of their specialized work, these individuals need to consult the *Postal Service Manual.*

Selecting Your Style

Your style determines *how* well your messages are received. Style is concerned with the individual words and sentences you choose to write. Again, you must consider the audience. If all your readers are specialists in your field, you may safely use the technical language and symbols of your profession. Your audience will be familiar with such terminology and will expect you to use it. Nonspecialists, however, will be confused and annoyed if you write to them in the same way. As mentioned before, each group has different needs; your words, and the amount of detail you include, will vary with the audience. The average consumer, for example, will not know what a *pitometer* is; by writing "volume control on a radio," you will be using language that the general public can understand.

Here are two descriptions of *heparin*, a drug used to prevent blood clots. The first example appeared in a reference work for physicians. It shows how technical vocabulary and sophisticated descriptions are appropriate (and necessary) for that particular audience:

Technical Style

HEPARIN SODIUM INJECTION, USP ℞
Description: Heparin Sodium Injection, USP is a sterile solution of heparin sodium derived from porcine intestines, standardized for use as an anticoagulant, in water for injection with sodium chloride, if needed for isotonicity, and may contain 1% benzyl alcohol as a preservative.

Actions: Heparin inhibits reactions which lead to the clotting of blood and the formation of fibrin clots both in vitro and in vivo. Heparin acts at multiple sites in the normal coagulation system. Small amounts of heparin in combination with antithrombin III (heparin co-factor) can prevent the development of a hypercoagulable state by inactivating activated Factor X, preventing the conversion of prothrombin to thrombin.

Dosage and administration: Heparin sodium is not effective by oral administration and should be given by deep subcutaneous (intrafat i.e., above iliac crest or into the abdominal fat layer) injection, by intermittent intravenous injection, or intravenous infusion. The intramuscular route of administration should be avoided because of the frequent occurrence of hematoma at the injection site.[2]

---

[2] Copyright © 1979 *Physicians' Desk Reference*, published by Medical Economics Company, Inc., at Oradell, New Jersey 07649.

The following alternative description of heparin is more appropriate for patients who are receiving the drug in a hospital. Note how in this nontechnical style common words have replaced highly technical ones. Comments about the origin and composition of the drug are also excluded, because the audience does not need them.

Nontechnical Style

Heparin dissolves the blood clots already in the legs and also stops new clots from forming. Since heparin cannot be absorbed by the body from the stomach or the intestines, it is not given in a capsule or tablet. Instead, it is injected into the vein or muscle. After several days, when the danger of clotting is reduced, the heparin is gradually discontinued, and another medication that can be taken by mouth is started.

▶ Functions of Job-Related Writing

The following five functions of job-related writing tell you what kind of writing you will produce after you successfully answer the *who? why? what?* and *how?* just discussed.

Providing Practical Information

On-the-job writing requires a practical "Here's what I can do for you" approach. One such practical approach is "action-oriented." In this kind of job-related writing the writer instructs someone to do something—check cost estimates, make a service more economical, call a customer, test for bacteria, read a blueprint, participate in a conference, operate a computer, or buy a product. Another practical goal of job-related writing is to have someone "understand" something—why a mistake was made, how a problem was solved, what procedures were used. For example, a manufacturer might send letters to customers explaining a product recall.

The following description of Energy Efficiency Ratio combines both the "action-oriented" and "understanding" approaches of practical writing:

Whether you are buying window air-conditioning units or a central air-conditioning system, consider the performance factors and efficiency of the various units on the market. Before you buy, determine the Energy Efficiency Ratio (EER) of the units under consideration. The EER is found by dividing the BTU's (units of heat) that the unit removes from the area to be cooled by the watts (amount of electricity) the unit consumes. The result is usually a number between 5 and 12. The higher the number, the more efficiently the unit will use electricity. You'll note that EER will vary considerably from unit to unit of a given manufacturer, and from brand to brand. As efficiency is increased, you may find the purchase price is higher; however, operating costs will be lower. Remember, a good rule to follow is to choose the equipment with the highest EER. That way you'll get efficient equipment and enjoy operating economy.[3]

Giving Facts, Not Impressions

Writing on the job is concerned largely with those things that can be seen, heard, felt, tasted, or smelled. The emphasis is on facts rather than the writer's feelings. The following discussion by a group of scientists about the sources of oil spills and their impact on the environment is an example of objectivity. It describes events and causes without anger or tears. Imagine how much emotion could have been packed into this topic by the residents of the south Texas coast as they watched large amounts of oil being washed ashore in the summer of 1979.

> The most critical impact results from the escapement of oil into the ecosystem, both crude oil and refined fuel oils, the latter coming from sources such as marine traffic. Major oil spills occur as a result of accidents such as blowout, pipeline breakage, etc. Technological advances coupled with stringent regulations have helped to reduce the chances of such major spills; however, there is a chronic low level discharge of oil associated with normal drilling and production operations. Waste oils discharged through the river systems and practices associated with tanker transport dump more significant quantities of oils into the ocean, compared to what is introduced by the offshore oil industry. All of this contributes to the chronic low-level discharge of oil into world oceans. The long-range cumulative effect of these discharges is possibly the most significant threat to the ecosystem.[4]

Relying on Visuals to Convey Information

On-the-job writing makes frequent use of visuals, such as tables, charts, photographs, diagrams, and drawings, to clarify and condense information. A visual can play an important role in a work environment, as shown by the illustration in Fig. 1.4. Included in an employee handbook, the illustration could remind readers about correct lifting procedures and thereby help prevent injuries.

A great deal of information about the growth and diversity of commercial TV stations is condensed in Table 1.1. Consider how many words a writer would need in order to supply the data contained in the table. Note, too, how easily the numbers can be read when they are arranged in columns. It would be far more difficult to decipher them if they were printed like this: Commercial TV stations in operation: 1965, Total 586, VHF 487, UHF 99; 1966, Total 598, VHF 491, UHF 107, and so forth.

---

[3] Reprinted by permission of New Orleans Public Service, Inc.

[4] *The Offshore Ecology Investigation* (Galveston, Tex.: Gulf Universities Research Consortium, 1975), p. 4.

Fig. 1.4 Use of visual to convey information.

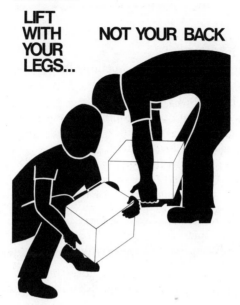

© National Safety Council, Chicago.

Table 1.1 Commercial TV stations in operation

Year	Total	VHF	UHF
1965	586	487	99
1966	598	491	107
1967	620	497	123
1968	648	504	144
1969	675	506	169
1970	690	508	182
1971	696	511	185
1972	699	510	189
1973	700	511	189
1974	705	513	192
1975	711	513	198
1976	710	513	197
1977	728	517	211
1978	727	516	211
1979	732	516	216
1980	746	517	229

Source: Reprinted, with permission, from the *1981 Broadcasting Cable Yearbook.*
Note: The number of stations is as of Jan. 1 of the year noted.

In addition to the visuals mentioned above, use the following graphic devices within your letters and reports to make your writing easier to understand:

- HEADINGS (such as The Key to Effective Writing, Functions of Job-Related Writing)
    - Subheadings to divide major sections into parts
        1. Providing Practical Information
        2. Giving Facts, Not Impressions
- Numbers within a paragraph, or even a line, such as (1) this, and (2) this, and (3) also this
- Different types of s p a c i n g
- CAPITALIZATION (as in the word HEADINGS)
- *Italics* (indicated in typed copy by <u>underscoring</u>)
- Asterisks * to * separate * items * or to *note key items
- Bullets (raised periods like those before each entry in this list)

Such devices will help you organize, arrange, and emphasize your material. Keep in mind, though, that such devices must be used carefully and with moderation. They should be used only where they can help you to accomplish your purpose more quickly and clearly and not just to dress up a letter or report.

Giving Accurate Measurements

Much of your work will depend on measurements—acres, calories, centimeters, degrees, dollars and cents, grams, percentages, pounds, square feet, units. Readers will look carefully at the kinds of measurements you record. Numbers are clear and convincing. An architect depends on specifications to accomplish a job; a nurse must record precise dosages of medications; a sales representative keeps track of the number of customers visited; and an electronics technologist has to monitor antenna patterns and systems. The following discussion of mixing colored cement for a basement floor would be useless without the quantities it supplies:

The inclusion of permanent color in a basement floor is a good selling point. One way of doing this is by incorporating commercially pure mineral pigments in a topping mixture placed to a 1-inch depth over a normal base slab. The topping mix should range in volume between 1 part portland cement, 1¼ parts sand, and 1¼ parts gravel or crushed stone and 1 part portland cement, 2 parts sand and 2 parts gravel or crushed stone. Maximum size gravel or crushed stone should be ⅜ inch. Mixing of cement and pigment is done before aggregate and water are added and must be very thorough to secure uniform dispersion and the full color value of the pigment. The proportion varies from 5 to 10 percent of pigment by weight of cement, depending on the shade desired. If carbon black is used as a pigment to obtain grays or black, a proportion of from ½ to 1 percent will be adequate. Manufacturers' instructions should be followed closely and care in cleanliness, placing and finishing must be regarded as essential. Colored topping mixes are available from some suppliers of ready mixed concrete.[5]

Stating Precise Responsibilities

Job-related writing, since it is directed to a specific audience, must make absolutely clear what it expects of, or can do for, that audience. Misunderstandings waste time and cost money. Directions on order forms, for example, should indicate how and where information is to be listed and how it is to be routed and acted on. The following kinds of directions appear on typical job-related forms.

- Include agency code numbers in the upper-right corner.
- Items 1 through 16 of this form should be completed by the injured employee or by someone acting on his or her behalf, whenever an injury is sustained in the performance of duty. The term injury includes occupational disease caused by the employment. The form should be given to the employee's official superior within 48 hours following the injury. The official superior is that individual having responsible supervision over the employee.
- The Journal Tape from each cash register is to be removed on a daily basis. Record the register number and date on the exterior of the Journal Tape as it is removed. Place each day's Journal Tapes, along with the corresponding day's Cashier's Balance Sheets and bank deposit records, in a small bag, i.e. 10 lb. bag. Record the date on the face of this bag and staple it closed.[6]

Other kinds of job-related writing deal with the writer's responsibilities rather than the reader's. For example, "Tomorrow I will have a meeting with the district sales manager to discuss (1) July's sales, (2) the possibility of expanding our Madison home market, and (3) next fall's production schedule. I will send you a report of our discussion by August 3, 1982." In a letter of application for a job, writers should conclude by asking for an interview and clearly inform a prospective employer when they are available for an interview—weekday mornings, only on Monday and Tuesday afternoons, or any time after February 15.

▶ How This Book Will Work for You

This book is based on the belief that writing will substantially influence your career. Effective writing can help you to obtain a job, perform your duties successfully, and be promoted for your efforts. Guidelines and examples

---

[5] Reprinted by permission from *Concrete Construction Magazine,* World of Concrete Center, 426 South Westgate, Addison, Illinois 60101.

[6] Reprinted by permission from *A&P Store Management Manual,* NCR 2125.

found in this book emphasize the progress you can make in your career by acquiring effective writing skills. Specifically, *Successful Writing at Work* will

1. Describe the function and format of a variety of job-related communications.
2. Show you how to write each type of communication.
3. Teach you how to supply an audience with the information it must have.

The way the book is organized can reflect realistically your own progress in writing—taking you from being a student to becoming an employee. Chapters 2 and 3 present the basics of writing you must master if you are to advance in your profession. From the basics, the book discusses how you should write a business letter (Chapter 4) and a letter of application and résumé for a job (Chapter 5) and then turns to the letters you will write once you get a job (Chapter 6). In your job you will be responsible for gathering and summarizing information (Chapters 7–10). And, most important, you will have to report your findings both in writing (Chapters 11–13) and orally (Chapter 14). In your writing this term, you can evaluate step by step your progress toward fulfilling your professional goals.

Another useful feature of this book is that it frequently represents the view of the audience (prospective employer, customer, supervisor, questionnaire respondent) receiving the work you write. Each type of communication is discussed in terms of what diverse readers will be looking for. In Chapter 5, for example, a letter of application and comments appropriate at an interview are discussed in the light of what personnel directors seek when they recruit new employees. In Chapter 6 your readers are customers or agencies from whom you are ordering merchandise or to whom you have supplied merchandise or services. In Chapter 8, which deals with summaries, your reader is a busy executive who does not have the time to read a twenty-page article and will rely on your two hundred-word summary of it instead. Each of these readers represents a different challenge. The insights you will gain from this book about readers' needs should prove extremely useful. With these insights, you will be able to prepare yourself psychologically for the writing assignments you will encounter in business and industry. You will also learn how to manage your own writing resources to your best advantage.

▶ Exercises

1. What is your desired career field? Make a list of the kinds of writing you think you will encounter (or perhaps already have encountered) in this career.

2. Make a list of the kinds of writing you have done in a history or English class or for a laboratory or shop course.

3. Compare your lists for questions 1 and 2 above. How do the two types of writing differ?

4. Bring to class a set of printed instructions, a sales letter, or a brochure. Comment on how well the printed material answers the following questions:
   (a) Who is the audience?
   (b) Why was the material written?
   (c) What is the message?
   (d) How is the language used appropriate for the audience?

5. Cut out a newspaper ad that contains a drawing or photograph. Bring it to class together with a paragraph (75–100 words) describing how the message of the ad is directed to a particular audience and commenting on why the illustration was selected for that audience.

6. Pick one of the following topics and write two descriptions of it. In the first description use technical vocabulary. In the second use language suitable for the general public.
   (a) blood   (b) telephone   (c) trees
   (d) carburetor   (e) muscle   (f) bread
   (g) water   (h) protein   (i) computers
   (j) cement   (k) nylon   (l) money

7. Select one article from a daily newspaper and one article from either a professional journal in your major field or one of the following journals: *Advertising Age, American Journal of Nursing, Construction Equipment, Food Service Marketing, Journal of Forestry, Journal of Soil and Water Conservation, National Safety News, Nutrition Action, Office Machines, Park Maintenance, Scientific American, Today's Secretary.* State how the two articles you selected differ in terms of audience, purpose, message, and style.

8. Compose a letter to a local business asking for a contribution of goods, services, or funds for a worthwhile cause. Indicate why it should give.

9. Read the following article and identify its audience (technical or general), purpose, message, and style.

Microwaves

From a wireless phone line to a super-fast
kitchen oven, this first cousin to radio waves is fast becoming
the wave of the future.

Much of the world around us is in motion. A wave-like motion. Some waves are big like tidal waves and some are small like the almost unseen footprints of a waterstrider on a quiet pond. Other waves can't be seen at all, such as an idling truck sending out vibrations our bodies can feel. Among these are electromagnetic waves. They range

Raytheon Magazine (Winter 1981), pp. 22–23. Reprinted by permission.

from very low frequency sound waves to very high frequency X-rays, gamma rays, and even cosmic rays.

Energy behaves differently as its frequency changes. The start of audible sound—somewhere around 20 cycles per second—covers a segment at the low end of the electromagnetic spectrum. Household electricity operates at 60 hertz (cycles per second). At a somewhat higher frequency we have radio, ranging from shortwave and marine beacons, through the familiar AM broadcast band that lies between 500 and 1600 kilohertz, then to citizen's band, FM, television, and up to the higher frequency police and aviation bands.

Even higher up the scale lies visible light with its array of colors best seen when light is scattered by raindrops to create a rainbow.

Lying between radio waves and visible light is the microwave region—from roughly one gigahertz (a billion cycles per second) up to 3000 gigahertz. In this region the electromagnetic energy behaves in special ways.

Microwaves travel in straight lines, so they can be aimed in a given direction. They can be *reflected* by dense objects so that they send back echoes—this is the basis for radar. They can be *absorbed,* with their energy being converted into heat—the principle behind microwave ovens. Or they can *pass through* some substances that are transparent to the energy—this enables food to be cooked on a paper plate in a microwave oven.

Microwaves for Radar

World War II provided the impetus to harness microwave energy as a means of detecting enemy planes. Early radars were mounted on the Cliffs of Dover to bounce their microwave signals off Nazi bombers that threatened England. The word radar itself is an acronym for *RAdio Detection And Ranging.*

Radars grew more sophisticated. Special-purpose systems were developed to detect airplanes, to scan the horizon for enemy ships, to paint finely detailed electronic pictures of harbors to guide ships, and to measure the speeds of targets. These were installed on land and aboard warships. Radar—especially shipboard radar—was surely one of the most significant technological achievements to tip the scales toward an Allied victory in World War II.

Today, few mariners can recall what it was like before radar. It is such an important aid that it was embraced universally as soon as hostilities ended. Now, virtually every commercial vessel in the world has one, and most larger vessels have two radars: one for use on the open sea and one, operating at a higher frequency to "paint" a more finely detailed picture, for use near shore.

Microwaves are also beamed across the skies to fix the positions of aircraft in flight, obviously an essential aid to controlling the movement of aircraft from city to city across the nation. These radars have also been linked to computers to tell air traffic controllers the altitude of planes in the area and to label them on their screens.

A new kind of radar, phased array, is now being used to search the skies thousands of miles out over the Atlantic and Pacific oceans. Although these advanced radars use microwave energy just as ordinary radars do, they do not depend upon a rotating antenna. Instead, a fixed antenna array, comprising thousands of elements like those of a fly's eye, looks everywhere. It has been said that these radars roll their eyes instead of turning their heads.

High-speed Cooking

During World War II Raytheon had been selected to work with M.I.T. and British scientists to accelerate the production of magnetrons, the electron tubes that generate microwave energy, in order to speed up the production of radars. While testing some new, higher-powered tubes in a laboratory at Raytheon's Waltham, Massachusetts plant, Percy L. Spencer and several of his staff engineers observed an interesting phenomenon. If you placed your hand in a beam of microwave energy, your hand would grow pleasantly warm. It was not like putting your hand in a heated oven that might sear the skin. The warmth was deep-heating and uniform.

Spencer and his engineers sent out for some popcorn and some food, then piped the energy into a metal wastebasket. The microwave oven was born.

From these discoveries, some 35 years ago, a new industry was born. In millions of homes around the world, meals are prepared in minutes using microwave ovens. In many processing industries, microwaves are being used to perform difficult heating or drying jobs. Even printing presses use microwaves to speed the drying of ink on paper.

In hospitals, doctors' offices, and athletic training rooms, that deep heat that Percy Spencer noticed is now used in diathermy equipment to ease the discomfort of muscle aches and pains.

Telephones without Cable

The third characteristic of microwaves—that they pass undistorted through the air—makes them good messengers to carry telephone conversations as well as live television signals—without telephone poles or cables—across town or across the country. The microwave signals are beamed via satellite or by dish reflectors mounted atop buildings and mountaintop towers.

Microwaves take their name from the Greek *mikro* meaning very small. While the waves themselves may be very small, they play an important role in our world today: in defense; in communications; in air, sea, and highway safety; in industrial processing; and in cooking. At Raytheon the applications expand every day.

2

Writing: Words

Words are the most basic units of writing. They are like bricks out of which you construct larger structures. If your words are wrong, misleading, or inappropriate, then so too will be the letters, forms, and reports you fashion from those words. Chapter 2 discusses some of the most common problems writers face with words and offers some suggestions on how to avoid or repair ineffective word use. Specifically, after reading this chapter, you will know more about:

1. Spelling words correctly
2. Matching the right word with the right meaning
3. Selecting precise words
4. Correcting the faulty use of pronouns
5. Avoiding jargon and slang words

▶ Spelling Words Correctly

Your written work will be judged on how you spell. A misspelled word may seem like a small matter, but on an employment application, incident report, or letter, it stands out to your discredit. Readers will inevitably wonder about your other skills if your spelling is incorrect.

Your professional work places a double duty on you as a speller. You must learn to spell correctly the technical terms of your field as well as the common words of the English language. The following suggestions can help to improve your spelling:

1. Keep a college-level dictionary at your desk (not on a shelf where you have to reach for it) and use it. Better yet, buy a small pocket dictionary and carry it with you.

2. Also keep on your desk a specialized dictionary or manual that lists technical vocabulary.

3. Make a list of the words you have the most trouble spelling. Write them down in a small spiral notebook for easy reference. You can also place in this notebook any new and difficult words you encounter.

4. Double-check your spelling before submitting your work.

The chances are that many of the words you have trouble spelling are the same words that cause others difficulty. Alerting you to the following five danger areas may help you to spot words that are tricky to spell.

1. *Silent letters.*

a*c*quaint	fas*c*inate	lei*s*ure
ai*s*le	for*e*arm	man*e*uver
as*c*end	ga*u*ge	min*i*ature
*c*holesterol	hemorr*h*age	mor*t*gage
code*i*ne	hyg*i*ene	n*e*utral
colum*n*	knapsnack	vacu*u*m
diaphrag*m*	lik*e*ly	We*d*nesday

2. *Use of* ei *and* ie. *In general,* i *before* e, *except after* c.

ie	*ei*	*exceptions*
believe	ceiling	ancient
cashier	conceive	conscience
chief	deceive	deficient
experience	perceive	financier
yield	receive	society

3. *Double consonants.* Many words double a consonant when a verb changes from present to past tense (prefer / preferred) or when the root form changes from verb to noun (occur / occurrence).

admit / admitted / admittance
commit / committed / *but* commitment
omit / omitted
plan / planning
repel / repelling / repellent
write / written / *but* writing

4. *Prefixes and suffixes.* When adding a prefix *(un-, il-, mis-),* do not change the spelling of the word to which it is attached.

*il*logical
*mis*spell
*un*necessary

Watch out for the following suffixes:

-able	*-iable*	*-ible*
acceptable	appreciable	audible
dependable	justifiable	combustible
noticeable	negotiable	edible
profitable	reliable	eligible
serviceable	variable	visible

5. *Plurals.*
   (a) When a word ends in *y*, add *-ies* if the *y* follows a consonant: apology / apologies; army / armies; history / histories; library / libraries; party / parties. If the word ends in *y* and the *y* follows a vowel, add *s:* bay / bays; toy / toys; turkey / turkeys.
   (b) Words that end in *f* or *fe sometimes* change these letters to *v* before adding *-es:* calf / calves; half / halves; knife / knives; life / lives; leaf / leaves; self / selves; shelf / shelves; wife / wives.
   (c) Nouns ending in *o* after a vowel form their plurals by adding *s:* patio /patios; stereo / stereos; studio / studios; zoo / zoos. When the *o* follows a consonant, add *-es* to form the plural: echo / echoes; hero / heroes; potato / potatoes; tomato / tomatoes. *Exceptions:* lasso / lassos; piano / pianos; tobacco / tobaccos.
   (d) Some nouns do not form their plural by adding *-s* or *-es.* Instead, they use an older kind of plural (ox / oxen; child / children), or they indicate a change in number in the middle of a word rather than at the end (foot / feet; tooth / teeth), or they use a foreign plural (criterion / criteria; curriculum / curricula; phenomenon / phenomena; syllabus / syllabi). Some nouns for animals are the same for both singular and plural: fish, deer, sheep, snipe. Finally, some words are "false" plurals; they end in *s*, leading you to think that they are plural. These words, however, are always singular in meaning and are never spelled without the final *s:* economics, measles, pants, pediatrics, scissors.

▶ Matching the Right Word with the Right Meaning

The English language contains many common words that are frequently mistaken for each other because they are pronounced alike but spelled differently. These words are called homonyms. *Meat* (food) and *meet* (to greet) are examples. When a dispatcher orders employees to keep overtime to a "bear" minimum, no reference to a grizzly is intended; rather, *bear* has been confused with *bare*. Similarly, the mechanic who writes on a work order to "idol" down a car has confused *idol* (religious image) with *idle* (a verb meaning to slow down).

The words in the following list frequently are mistaken for one another. By studying their correct spelling, part of speech, and meaning, you will save yourself time and embarrassment.

accept (to receive); *except* (to omit, to exclude)

advice (a recommendation—noun); *advise* (to counsel—verb)

affect (to change, to influence—verb); *effect* (a result—noun; to bring about—verb)

ascend (to climb); *assent* (to agree to, to concur)

beside (next to—The book is beside the bed); *besides* (in addition to— Besides Joan and Jack, who will go?)

brake (to stop—verb; a mechanism to halt a vehicle—noun); *break* (to split, to fracture)

breath (air inhaled—noun); *breathe* (to inhale air—verb)

bullion (gold bars); *bouillon* (broth)

canvas (cloth—noun); *canvass* (to take a poll—verb)

cent (one penny); *scent* (a smell); *sent* (past tense of the verb to send, cause to go)

cite (to document—verb); *site* (place, building location—noun); *sight* (vision, something seen—noun)

coarse (rough—adjective); *course* (class, plan—course of action—noun, or agreement, as in *of course*—adverb)

complement (something that completes—noun; to add to—verb—The green rug complements your curtains.); *compliment* (to praise, to flatter—verb—I compliment you on your sense of color.)

elicit (to gather information—verb); *illicit* (illegal—adjective)

fair (just or attractive—adjective; exhibition, carnival—noun); *fare* (food on a menu, price charged to travel—noun)

hare (rabbit); *hair* (covering on the scalp)

hear (to listen—verb); *here* (in this place—adverb)

imply (to suggest); *infer* (to draw a conclusion)

it's (contraction of it + is—the apostrophe replaces the *i* of *is* in it + is); *its* (possessive pronoun—The ship lost its anchor.)

lay (to put something down); *lie* (to recline, to sleep)

Present	*Past*	*Past participle*
lay	laid	laid
lie	lay	lain

(The man laid the package down; he then lay down on the couch.)

lose (to misplace something—verb); *loose* (not tight—adjective)

may be (two-word verb phrase—I may be at home tonight if I do not have to be at the office.); *maybe* (one-word adverb meaning perhaps—Maybe it will snow tomorrow.)

pair (two, a couple—noun); *pare* (to cut with a knife—verb); *pear* (a fruit—noun)

peace (calm, no war); *piece* (a portion)

personal (private—adjective); *personnel* (staff of people working for a company—noun)

perspective (a sight the eye beholds—noun); *prospective* (expectant, waiting for something to happen—adjective—Prospective employees must furnish employers with references.)

plain (simple, not fancy—adjective; an open field—noun); *plane* (airplane—noun; to make smooth and level—verb)

prescribe (to order medications); *proscribe* (to prohibit)

precede (to go ahead—An arrest precedes a conviction); *proceed* (to carry on with something, to continue—The laboratory technician proceeded with the test after the coffee break.)

principal (main, chief—adjective, *or* head of a school—noun); *principle* (a policy or belief—The principal reason for the democratic principles in the Constitution is to protect human rights.)

stationary (not moving—adjective); *stationery* (memos, letters, envelopes—noun—The *-er* could remind you of the *-er* in pap*er*.)

straight (not bent or crooked—adjective); *strait* (a narrow body of water—Strait of Magellan—noun, *or* something confining—straitjacket—adjective)

than (a conjunction used in comparisons—It's bigger than both of us.); *then* (an adverb of time—Then we went home.)

their (a plural possessive pronoun—Where is their house?); *there* (a place—adverb—Go over there); *they're* (they are—two words, a pronoun and a verb—They're happy in their new jobs.)

two (the number); *to* (the preposition meaning toward); *too* (also—conjunction, *or* excessive—adverb—There is too much slack in the lines.)

ware (purchased goods—noun); *wear* (to dress—verb); *where* (place—pronoun)

weather (state of the atmosphere—noun); *whether* (if—conjunction—I don't know whether she plans to attend.)

week (seven days in a row—noun); *weak* (not strong, infirm—adjective)

who's (contraction of who is—Who's next for promotion?—the apostrophe is the place holder for the *i* of *is*); *whose* (possessive pronoun—Whose book is this?)

you're (contraction of you + are); *your* (possessive pronoun—You're going to like their decision; they're in agreement with your ideas.)

▶ Selecting Precise Words

Writing that is exact and clear can save an employer much time and money. It will save you frustration and unnecessary explanations. Precise writing gets the job done right the first time. You can be precise, though, only if your words are. After all, your words take the place of the references they describe. Your words must answer clearly such questions as

- How big?
- How much?
- What color?
- How many?
- Who?
- Where?
- When?

To write precisely, use specific words rather than vague ones. For example, "Smith-Corona portable blue electric typewriter, Coronet Super 12" is clearer than "piece of office equipment." Words such as *aspect, condition, creature, factor, nice, thing,* and *work* raise more questions than they answer. Is a "nice" house made of brick or covered with aluminum siding? Does it have gas or electric heat? Will you find it in the city, suburbs, or the country? Here is another example of the advantage of using exact words:

General: Adequate storage retains the product for some time.

Specific: If refrigerated at 32°F (0°C) and covered with crushed ice, fresh fish may be stored up to three days.

Unlike the first sentence, the second sentence provides helpful, practical information.

There is a wide range between "general" and "specific." In Table 2.1 note that the vague, general terms in the far left column gradually become more precise as you proceed to the right.

How can you be sure that your words are precise, that they are specific and not vague? Follow two simple procedures after you have written a rough draft and before you submit the final copy:

Table 2.1 The range between general and specific terms

General			*Specific*
vehicle	truck	pickup	Dodge wide cab
medication	injection	barbiturate	Seconal 100 mg.
food	protein	poultry	Chicken Kiev
residence	house	cottage	Tudor cottage
official	federal agent	USDA inspector	Mary Whitton
reasonable	inexpensive	bargain	20 percent off from $500 sale price
circumstance	disaster	storm	Hurricane Frederic

1. *Circle all your nouns.* Do they point to a specific person, place, or object? Could your reader see and separate that person, place, or object from all others like it? If so, you have a specific word. If readers or listeners cannot quickly identify an object, person, or place from your description, you have used a general word.
2. *Underline all your adjectives.* Do they tell readers the exact color, size, texture, quantity, or quality you want to convey? Adjectives like *bad, fantastic, good, great, interesting, numerous, serious,* or *small* will not help your audience see vividly or measure accurately. Next, see if you need every adjective you have underlined. A noun or verb may render some adjectives unnecessary; the adjective or adverb could repeat what the noun or verb has already said—for example, "shout loudly" (shouts are loud), "a big Saint Bernard" (such dogs are big), "a small 3″ × 5″ card" (is there a large 3″ × 5″ card?).

▶ Correcting the Faulty Use of Pronouns

Another kind of vagueness comes from the faulty use of pronouns. When you use a pronoun whose antecedent (the person, place, or object the pronoun is referring to) is unclear, you risk confusing your reader. Here are some examples of unclear pronoun references, with correct revisions following:

Unclear: After the plants are clean, we separate the stems from the roots and place them in the sun to dry. (Is it the stems or the roots that lie in the sun?)

Revision: After the plants are clean, we separate the stems from the roots and place the stems in the sun to dry.

Unclear: The park ranger was pleased to see the workers planting new trees and installing new benches. This will attract more tourists. (The trees or the benches?)

Revision: The park ranger was pleased to see the workers planting new trees and installing new benches, for the new trees will attract more tourists.

Unclear: When Bill talked with his boss, he became angry. (Who became angry, Bill or his boss?)

Revision: When he talked with his boss, Bill became angry.

You can correct faulty pronoun references by replacing the unclear pronoun with the noun it stands for. The reader will then know exactly which word is the subject or object of the sentence. Another way to correct misleading pronouns is to rewrite the sentence.

▶ Avoiding Jargon and Slang Words

Jargon

Jargon is shop talk, the specialized vocabulary of a particular occupation. Jargon includes, for example, an *IPPB* (Intermittent Positive Pressure Breathing) *machine* in respiratory therapy, or *hard water* (water containing more than 85.5 parts per million of calcium carbonate) in geology. Such technical terms are necessary, but should be used only when the following three conditions are met:

1. The audience understands jargon and expects the writer to use it.
2. A technical term or phrase conveys a precise idea that could not be adequately described with a common word or phrase.
3. The kind of form or report you are completing requires jargon—for example, a patient record in a hospital, a specification sheet, or a legal description.

The word *jargon* has another meaning besides the legitimate technical language of a profession. More often, it refers to phony, inflated, and uselessly complex language. Jargon is a label attached to pompous words (pseudoscientific jawbreakers) some writers use instead of the much more simple, natural, and direct vocabulary their readers could better understand and value. Jargon is language that puts on airs; it reeks of the stuffiness found in some business letters (see pp. 72–74). People who favor jargon dislike pleasantly clear and direct verbs. For the unassuming verb *get,* they substitute *procure;* for *simplify* or *ease,* they choose (or *elect,* in jargon) *facilitate;* rather than *join* or *connect,* they prefer to *interface.* Here are three characteristics of jargon, together with suggestions for doing away with it:

1. Pompous words. Use short, serviceable words instead of pompous expressions ("verbiage" in jargon). Your readers will appreciate your clarity and your honesty. Cut a three-word smoke-screen phrase (scholastic achievement profile) to one simple word (transcript); aquatic support system to lifejacket.

2. Use of -ize and -ation words. Avoid words such as finalize (for conclude); hypothesize, energize, personalize, conceptualize (for think); mortuize (for bury); visualize (for see); utilize (for use); verbalization (for statement); conflagration (for fire); democratization (for democracy); socialization (for acceptance); precipitation (for rain, sleet, or snow); illumination (for light); institutionalization (for company policy).

3. Excessive and unclear abbreviations. Do not use abbreviations which, while they may be understood by professionals in your field, will confuse readers unfamiliar with such shorthand. For example, if a nurse told patients that they would have to be NPO (initials indicating that patients are to have nothing by mouth) for a GB vis. (X-ray of the gallbladder), the patients would certainly be baffled and perhaps terrified. The writer of the following letter to Ann Landers sums up the situation well:

Dear Ann Landers: The growing tendency to call everything by initials is extremely irritating. I've discussed this with others and find that I am not alone.

It wasn't so bad when there were just a few, such as the CIO, the AFL and the CIA. Now we have the IRS, the ERA, the IUD, the NAACP, HEW, MIT, ORT and DNA.

Where I work, quarterly meetings are mandatory. We must sit and listen for an hour and a half to talk like this: "The IAM met with the TQA and discussed the YTD. We must now check back with the IRA and do something about the LTC." I become thoroughly confused trying to sort out the meaning of the initials.

What's more, I feel like a fool because I don't know what's going on. Will you please tell those double-dome intellectuals to call things by their names and not assume that because THEY know what all the initials mean, everybody else does?—Abbreviated into Oblivion in Kalamazoo

Dear Kal.: IOU warm thanks for writing such an OK letter. I am printing it PDQ.[1]

Slang

All of us use slang expressions and words when we talk to our friends. It is a sign that we are comfortable with the people we know best. Slang, however, is out of place in professional communication, written or oral. Slang is playful, irreverent, and sometimes vulgar—qualities not appreciated in business communication. You need not be a stuffed shirt, but don't be too casual, either. Here are examples of slang terms to avoid in your professional writing; a more formal equivalent is given in parentheses.

bread (money)
bull (nonsense, exaggeration)
cool it (relax)
dude (man)
far out, way out (exceptional)
get on your case (check up on someone)
pad (house, apartment)
rip off (steal)
uptight (uncomfortable; tense)

---

[1] *Hattiesburg American,* May 18, 1980. Reprinted by permission of Ann Landers and Field Newspaper Syndicate.

The following poem laments, with numerous examples, the invasion of slang into our language.

Remember when hippie meant big in the hips,
And a trip involved travel in cars, planes, and ships?
When pot was a vessel for cooking things in,
And hooked was what grandmother's rugs may have been
When fix was a verb that meant mend or repair,
And be-in meant merely existing somewhere?
When neat meant well-organized, tidy, and clean,
And grass was a ground cover, normally green?
When groovy meant furrowed with channels and hollows,
And birds were winged creatures, like robins and swallows
When fuzz was a substance, real fluffy, like lint,
And bread came from bakeries and not from the mint?
When roll meant a bun, and rock was a stone,
And hang-up was something you did with the phone?
It's groovy, man, groovy, but English it's not.
Methinks that our language is going to pot.

Anonymous

▶ Exercises

1. The following sentences contain misspelled words. Find these words and correct them.
   (a) The forman did not find our performence acceptible on the new equipment.
   (b) Unusual occurance reports help safety commitees make thier decesions.
   (c) If the carburator is not adjusted proparly, the timing will be alwrong.
   (d) Students must recieve twenty-five hours of instruction to become familar with trafic control problems.
   (e) Only the patients family is admited to ICU.
   (f) To describe the suspect's physical apparance, aquaint your self with the correct descripters.
   (g) Eat high nutriant foods containing protiens, carbohidrates, and sufficeint ruffage.
   (h) Unflammable liquids could be dangerus.
   (i) Some freindly newly weds occupyed the bridel suit.
   (j) These architectural designs are unexpensive.
   (k) According to City Ordnance 67, combustables cannot be storred on open shelfs.
   (l) I will have a zerox copy of the order preparred for you.
   (m) We have printed new calandars with pictures of wild turkies and deers on them.
   (n) Gasaline prices will reach a cieling before autum.
   (o) We were orderl to precede with our work, all though the storm threatened to close the black top road leading toward home.

2. Select the appropriate word in the following sentences and briefly explain your choice.
   (a) My new listings book is larger (then / than) last year's.
   (b) All new (personnel / personal) reported to pick up (there / their) identification cards.
   (c) Regardless of (it's / its) price, buy the property so the firm does not (lose / loose) it. We must (attain / obtain) it.
   (d) She kept her (stationary / stationery) on the desk where she could easily reach it (beside / besides) her typewriter.
   (e) The fabric was (course / coarse) and cheap, and the buyer refused to (choose / chose) it.
   (f) Please (except / accept) this (complementary / complimentary) offer with our best wishes.
   (g) The (principle / principal) reason given was that our test scores were (to / too) low and the superintendent was afraid none of us would (pass / past) the test.
   (h) Corn grows well on the flat (plains / planes) of Illinois.
   (i) Smoking (affects / effects) blood pressure.
   (j) Our squad had to (sight / cite) every violation so that it could be reported in the district commander's log.
   (k) The doctor (proscribed / prescribed) no more smoking for the overweight patient.
   (l) Unusually hot days in March often cause a lot of bad (weather / whether).
   (m) (Its / It's) possible to find a (peace / piece) of material in the shop.
   (n) The applicant (who's / whose) credentials were so suitable for our position took another job working for a (pare / pair) of attorneys.

3. The following sentences contain vague and abstract words. Replace them with concrete ones. The first sentence has been done for you.
   (a) The individual saw the occurrence.

   The police officer from the second district saw the young boy steal Ms. Saliba's purse.

   (b) Three factors disturbed the crew when it had to deliberate.
   (c) The case she outlined sounded interesting.
   (d) Circumstances dictated that we follow another course of action in handling this matter.
   (e) The nature of the area is such that alternative measures must be sought.
   (f) It happened this week.
   (g) The materials were incomplete; we found defects, too.
   (h) The causes of the action seemed to be good.
   (i) The phenomenon she discussed happened occasionally in our area.
   (j) The individual sought an immediate solution to the problem.

4. Rewrite the following sentences to correct faulty pronoun references.
   (a) The head nurse ordered the aide and the technician to help the patient in Room 334. She came at once.
   (b) The boss sent four different memos to the maintenance department about the problems with refuse on the weekends. They really made an impact on the department.
   (c) As Barbara saw Mary, she shouted with joy.
   (d) The filter was placed over the vent, but it was too small.
   (e) The machine had to be primed and oiled regularly, which insured a quick start.
   (f) An all-purpose battery would be better in this car than an expensive one.
   (g) The white mice were placed in the new cages, and they were to be cleaned daily.
   (h) Mr. Martin told Mr. Jones that he had found his glasses.
   (i) A check-up is important for good health. That is something you want to have.
   (j) Fourteen recruits joined the force in the months of July, August, and September. They will not be forgotten.

5. The following paragraph contains jargon. Rewrite the paragraph and replace the jargon with precise and appropriate words.

> It has been verified conclusively by this writer that our institution must of necessity install more bicycle holding racks for the convenience of students, faculty, and staff. These parking modules should be fastened securely to walls outside strategic locations on the campus. They could be positioned there by work crews or even by the security forces who vigilantly patrol the campus grounds. There are many students in particular who would value the installation of these racks. Their bicycles could be stationed there by them, and they would know that safety measures have been taken to ensure that none of their bicycles would be apprehended or confiscated illegally. Besides the precaution factor, these racks would afford users maximized convenience in utilizing their means of transportation when they have academic business to conduct, whether at the learning resource center or in the instructional facilities.

3

Writing: Sentences

The way in which you construct sentences can determine whether you succeed or fail in writing. Sentences show readers how well, or poorly, you combine words to express thoughts. If your sentences are unclear, immature, crowded with excess baggage, or illogical, readers will question your powers of reasoning and action. Employers will certainly not reward or retain writers who embarrass them and cost the company money.

Chapter 3 supplies you with the fundamentals needed to write effective sentences. If you study the chapter carefully, you will learn to

1. Construct and punctuate sentences correctly.
2. Write clear sentences that say what you mean.
3. Use sentences that are economical and easy to read.

▶ Writing and Punctuating Sentences

A sentence is a complete thought that is expressed by a subject and a verb and that makes sense and can stand alone. The first step toward success in writing sentences is learning to recognize the differences between phrases and clauses.

The Difference Between Phrases and Clauses

A *phrase* is a group of words that does not contain a subject and a verb; phrases cannot stand alone to make sense. Phrases cannot be sentences.

in the park   *No subject:* Who is in the park?
                                               No verb: What was done in the park?

for every patient in intensive care	***No subject:*** Who did something for every patient?
	No verb: What was done for the patients?

A *clause* does contain a subject and a verb, but—*and this is important*—not all clauses are sentences. Only independent clauses can stand alone as sentences. Here is an example:

       subject   verb   object
The president closed the college.

A dependent (or subordinate) clause also contains a subject and a verb, but does not make complete sense and cannot stand alone. Why? A dependent clause contains a subordinating conjunction—*after, although, as, because, before, even though, if, since, unless, when, where, while*—at the beginning of the clause. Such conjunctions subordinate the clause in which they appear and make the clause dependent for meaning and completion on an independent (or main) clause.

> After
> Before
> Because   the president closed the college
> Even though
> Unless

"After the president closed the college" is not a complete thought. This dependent clause leaves us in suspense. It needs to be completed with an independent clause telling us what happened "after."

     dependent clause   independent clause
                               subject   verb   phrase
After the president closed the college,   we   played   in the snow.

Sentence Fragments

Complete sentences do not leave the reader hanging in midair, wondering who did something, how it was done, or under what conditions it was done. An incomplete sentence is called a *fragment*. Fragments are phrases or dependent clauses. They either lack a verb or a subject or have broken away from an independent (main) clause. A fragment is isolated; it needs an overhaul to supply missing parts to turn it into an independent clause or to glue it back to the independent clause from which it became separated.

You can avoid writing sentence fragments by following a few rules. (In the next few pages, incorrect examples are preceded by a minus sign; corrected versions, by a plus sign.)

1. *Every sentence must have a subject telling the reader who does the action.*

    − Being extra careful not to spill the water. (Who?)
    + The aide was extra careful not to spill the water.

2. *Every sentence must have a complete verb.* Watch especially for verbs ending in *-ing*. They need another verb (some form of *to be* or *have*) to make them complete.

> − The woman in the blue uniform. (What did she do?)
> + The woman in the blue uniform directed traffic.
> − The machine running in the computer department. (Did what?)

You can change the last fragment into a sentence by supplying the correct form of the verb.

> + The machine *is* running in the computer department.
> + The machine *runs* in the computer department.

Or you can revise the entire sentence, adding a new thought.

> + The machine running in the computer department handles all new accounts.

3. *Do not detach prepositional phrases* (beginning with *at, by, for, in, to, with,* and so forth) *from independent clauses.* Such phrases are not complete thoughts and cannot stand alone. Correct the error by leaving the phrases attached to the sentence to which they belong.

> − By three o'clock the next day. (What was to happen?)
> + The supervisor wanted our reports by three o'clock the next day.
> − For every patient in intensive care. (What was done?)
> + Nurses kept hourly reports for every patient in intensive care.

4. *Do not use a subordinate clause as a sentence.* To avoid this kind of sentence fragment, simply join the two clauses (the dependent clause with the subordinating conjunction, and the independent clause) with a comma—*not* a period or semicolon.

> − Unless we agreed to the plan. (What would happen?)
> − Unless we agreed to the plan; the project manager would discontinue the operation. (A semicolon cannot set off the subordinate clause.)
> + Unless we agreed to the plan, the project manager would discontinue the operation.
> − Because safety precautions were taken. (What happened?)
> + Because safety precautions were taken, ten construction workers escaped injury.

Sometimes subordinate clauses appear at the end of a sentence. They may be introduced by a subordinate conjunction, an adverb, or a relative pronoun *(that, which, who).* Do not separate these clauses from the preceding independent clause with a period, thus turning them into fragments.

> − Some of the new employees selected the high-risk option in their policy. While others did not.
> + Some of the new employees selected the high-risk option in their policy while others did not. (The *while* subordinates the clause, and therefore that clause cannot stand alone.)

− An all-volunteer fire department posed some problems. Especially for
  residents in the southern part of town.
+ An all-volunteer fire department posed some problems, especially for
  residents in the southern part of town.

(The word *especially* qualifies *problems,* referred to in the independent
clause.)

The Comma Splice

Writing fragments involves using only bits and pieces of complete sentences.
Another common error that some writers commit involves just the reverse
kind of action. They weakly and wrongly join two complete sentences (independent clauses) with a comma as if those two sentences were really only one
sentence. This error is called a *comma splice.* Here is an example:

− Gasoline prices have risen by 10 percent in the last month, we will drive the
  car less often.

Two independent clauses (complete sentences) exist:

Gasoline prices have risen by 10 percent in the last month.
We will drive the car less often.

A comma alone lacks the power to separate independent clauses.

Four Ways to Correct Comma Splices

1. *Remove the comma separating two independent clauses and replace it with a period.* Then capitalize the first letter of the first word of the newly rein-
   stated sentence.

   + Gasoline prices have risen by 10 percent in the last month. We will drive the
     car less often.

2. *Delete the comma and insert a semicolon.*

   + Gasoline prices have risen by 10 percent in the last month; we will drive the
     car less often.

   The semicolon is an effective and forceful punctuation mark when the
   two independent clauses are closely related—that is, when they announce
   contrasting or parallel views, as the two following examples reveal:

   + The union favored the new legislation; the company opposed it. (contrasting
     views)
   + Night classes help the college and the community; more students can take
     more credit hours. (parallel views)

3. *Insert a coordinating conjunction* (and, but, for, yet) *after the comma.* Together, the conjunction and the comma properly separate the two independent clauses.

+ Gasoline prices have risen by 10 percent in the last month, <u>and</u> we will drive the car less often.

4. *Rewrite the sentence* (if it makes sense to do so). Turn the first independent clause into a dependent clause by adding a conjunction; insert a comma and add the second independent clause.

+ <u>Because</u> gasoline prices have risen by 10 percent in the last month, we will drive the car less often.

(Of the four ways to correct the comma splice, the last example is the most suitable for the sample sentence, because the price of gasoline affects how much a car is driven.)

How Not to Correct Comma Splices

Some writers mistakenly try to correct comma splices by inserting a conjunctive adverb *(also, consequently, furthermore, however, moreover, nevertheless, therefore)* after the comma.

− Gasoline prices have risen by 10 percent in the last month, consequently we will drive the car less often.

But because the conjunctive adverb *(consequently)* is not as powerful as the coordinating conjunction *(and, but, for)*, the error is not eliminated. If you use a conjunctive adverb—*consequently, however, nevertheless*—insert a semicolon or a period before it, as the following examples show:

+ Gasoline prices have risen by 10 percent in the last month; consequently, we will drive the car less often.
+ Gasoline prices have risen by 10 percent in the last month. Consequently, we will drive the car less often.

▶ Sentences that Say What You Mean

Your sentences should say exactly what you mean—without double-talk, misplaced humor, or nonsense. Sentences are composed of words and word groups that influence each other. Like molecules, they bump and rub into each other, exerting a strong reciprocal influence. The kinds of errors discussed in this section can be eliminated if you remind yourself to read your sentences to see how one group of words fits into and relates to another.

Logical Sentences

Sentences should not contradict themselves or make outlandish claims. The following examples contain such errors; note how easily the suggested revisions handle the problem.

Illogical: Chicago is the largest city on the seacoast of Lake Michigan. (The seacoast borders the sea, not the lake; the writer made the wrong association.)

Revision: Chicago is the largest city on the shore of Lake Michigan.

Illogical: The president's order establishes a new precedent for our time. (A precedent is something that has already been established; hence it cannot be new.)

Revision: The president's order will establish a precedent.

Illogical: Steel roll-away shutters make it possible for the sun to be shaded in the summer and to have it shine in the winter. (The sun is far too large to shade; the writer meant that a room or a house, much smaller than the sun, could be shaded with the shutters.)

Revision: Steel roll-away shutters make it possible for owners to shade their living rooms in the summer and to admit sunshine during the winter.

Contextually Appropriate Words

The right words show that you have made the correct choices for your subject matter. Here are some illustrations of sentences containing inappropriate words, together with suggested revisions:

Inappropriate: The building materials need to be explained in small, concrete steps. (The writer was thinking of "concrete" in terms of teaching; the context, though, encourages the reader to picture cement stairs.)

Revision: The building materials need to be explained separately and carefully.

Inappropriate: The members of the Nuclear Regulatory Commission saw fear radiated on the faces of the residents. (The word "radiated" is obviously ill-advised; use a neutral term.)

Revision: The members of the Nuclear Regulatory Commission saw fear reflected on the faces of the residents.

Inappropriate: The game warden is shooting for an increase in the number of nonresident licenses this year.

Revision: The game warden hopes to increase the number of nonresident licenses this year.

Correct Modifiers

A *modifier* is a word, phrase, or clause that describes, limits, or qualifies the meaning of another word or word group. A modifier can consist of one word (a *green* car), a prepositional phrase (the man *in the telephone booth*), a relative clause (the woman *who won the marathon*), or an *-ing* or *-ed* phrase (*walking three miles a day,* the man was in good shape; *seated in the first row,* we saw everything on stage).

A *dangling modifier* is one that cannot logically modify any word in the sentence.

- When answering the question, his notebook fell off the table.

To correct the error, insert the right subject after the *-ing* phrase.

+ When answering the question, he knocked his notebook off the table.

You can also turn the phrase into a subordinate clause:

+ When he answered the question, his notebook fell off the table.
+ His notebook fell off the table as he answered the question.

A *misplaced modifier* illogically modifies the wrong word or words in the sentence. The result is often comical.

- Hiding in the corner, growling and snarling, our guide caught the frightened cub. (Is our guide growling and snarling in the corner?)
- All travel requests must be submitted by employees in green ink. (Are the employees covered in green ink?)

The problem with both of the examples above is word order. The modifiers are misplaced because they are attached to the wrong words in the sentence. Correct the error by moving the modifier where it belongs.

+ Hiding in the corner, growling and snarling, the frightened cub was caught by our guide.
+ All travel requests by employees must be submitted in green ink.

Misplaced modifiers may also be corrected by recasting the sentence.

+ While the frightened cub was hiding in the corner, growling and snarling, our guide caught it.
+ Our guide caught the growling and snarling, frightened cub, which was hiding in the corner.

Note that each "correct" version has a slightly different emphasis; the choice depends on the aspect of the situation you wish to stress.

▶ Lean and Clean Sentences

Keeping Sentences Short

How long should your sentence be? The answers to this question vary, depending on the educational level of your audience and the subject you are writing about. Be guided by one rule, however: Write so that it is easy for your reader to understand you. Generally, the longer the sentence, the more difficult it is to understand. Most readers have very little trouble with sentences ranging from eight to fifteen words. On the other hand, readers find sentences over twenty to twenty-three words much more difficult. As a general rule, keep your sentences under twenty words in order to reach most readers; yet write like a mature and professional individual. To stay within that comfortable range, follow these two guidelines:

1. *Do not write a string of short, choppy sentences that read like a grade school reader.* Sentences like the following reflect an immature style of writing:

   Secretaries have many responsibilities. Their responsibilities are important. They must answer telephones. They must take dictation. Sometimes the speaker talks very fast. Then the secretary must be quick to transcribe what is heard. Words could be missed. Secretaries must also type letters. This will take a great deal of time and concentration. These letters are copied and filed properly for reference.

   Such writing can be improved by combining the short, choppy sentences with connective words (italicized in the revision below).

   Secretaries have many important responsibilities. *These* include answering telephones and taking dictation. *When* a speaker talks rapidly, the secretary will have to transcribe quickly *so* that no words are omitted. *Among the most demanding* of their duties are typing letters accurately *and then* making copies of them and filing those copies properly for future reference.

2. *Avoid complex, lengthy sentences that pile one clause on another.* The following sentence is too long for readers to understand, even the second time through:

   The planning committeee decided that the awards banquet should be held on May 15 at 6:30, since the other two dates (May 7 and May 22) suggested by the hospitality committee conflict with local sports events, even though one of those dates could be changed to fit our needs.

   Why is the following revision easier to read and understand?

   The planning committee has decided to hold the awards banquet on May 15 at 6:30. The other dates suggested by the hospitality committee—May 7 and May 22—conflict with two local sports events. Although the date of one of those sports events could be changed, the planning committee still believes that May 15 is our best choice.

The Difference Between Active and Passive Voice

"Voice" refers to whether the subject of a sentence performs the action or receives it. In the active voice a subject performs the action and so appears in the first (and subject) part of the sentence. In the passive voice the subject becomes the recipient of the action and no longer occupies the first part of the sentence, but now appears in the last part or is even omitted.

Active voice: The recruiting staff made three visits.

Passive voice: Three visits were made by the recruiting staff.

Passive voice: Three visits were made.

In sentence 1 the writer stresses the actions of the staff. In sentence 2 and especially in 3 the writer is more interested in the number of visits than in who made them.

When to Use the Active Voice

The active voice is often more forceful and direct than is the passive voice. It also requires fewer words than the passive voice (except when the subject is deleted entirely as in sentence 3 above). Sentence 2 contains two more words than are in sentence 1: "were" and "by." These extra words show how passives are formed. Sentences in the passive voice introduce the preposition *by*, add some form of the verb *to be*, and change the form of the main verb to a participle.

Since both the active and the passive voices have advantages, use both in your work. The active voice has the following characteristics:

1. The active voice gives instructions authority and clarity.

   Active: Remove the hex nut.
   Passive: The hex nut should be removed.

   Active: Wear protective eyeglasses.
   Passive: Protective eyeglasses should be worn.

2. The active voice can eliminate awkwardness.

   Active: I completed two years of technical training.
   Passive: Two years of technical training were completed by me.

   Active: Ms. Rodgers spoke about the new design.
   Passive: The new design was spoken about by Ms. Rodgers.

3. The active voice lets readers know that another person, not a machine, is writing to them in letters and reports.

   Active: The tour director arranged the plans for your travel.
   Passive: Plans have been arranged for your travel.

   Active: I can make an appointment for you.
   Passive: An appointment can be made for you.

You will find that using sentences in the active voice will make your letters and reports easier to read and to follow. The active voice shows exactly who is in charge and who has accomplished certain tasks.

When to Use the Passive Voice

Scientists often use the passive voice in order to emphasize the experiment or the procedure rather than the individual performing it. They believe that references to "I" detract from the objectivity of the work. Many scientists would prefer the second of the following two sentences:

Active: The biologist performed the experiment three times in forty-eight hours.

Passive: The experiment was performed three times in forty-eight hours.

Clearly, some contexts call for the "I" and the active voice in reporting scientific data. But the passive voice does have its advantages when you are writing about a process—changing hydrogen and oxygen into water, for example—when the emphasis is not on the human actor, but on the changes brought about through scientific law.

The passive voice also serves the following useful functions:

1. The passive voice can be used when the actor is unknown.

   The car was stolen at noon. (The thief's identity is not known.)

   The practice was started in 1955. (Who started it?)

   Monthly house payments are scaled down during the first five years of the mortgage. (By whom?)

2. The passive voice can be used when the object is more important for the reader than is the actor.

   The injection of insulin was given at 6:30 A.M.

   Pieces of the bullet were found in the dining room wall.

   The generator was periodically inspected.

3. The passive voice can be used as a business strategy when anonymity is necessary or when emphasis on the subject has unfavorable moral implications. Compare these two sentences:

   Mr. Jones fired the mechanic.

   The mechanic was fired.

   The first sentence emphasizes the fact that it was Mr. Jones who dismissed the mechanic; the second sentence does not even mention Mr. Jones. Sometimes for legal reasons a person's identity must be kept secret:

   The juvenile was arraigned in court.

   The suspect's identity was not revealed by the police.

   The pilot's license was suspended by the Board.

Cutting Out Unnecessary Words

Too many individuals in business and industry think that the more words they use, the better their work will be. Nothing could be more self-defeating. The best occupational writing is direct and lean. Your readers are busy, and unnecessary words slow them down. Make every word go to work; when a word takes up space and gives no meaning, cut it. Cut out any words you can from your sentences; if the sentence still makes sense and reads correctly, you have eliminated wordiness.

The phrases on the left should be replaced with the precise words on the right:

Wordy	*Concise*
at a slow rate	slowly
at an early date	early
at the point where	where
at this point in time	now
bring to a conclusion	conclude; end
brings together	combines; joins
by means of	with
come to terms with	agree; accept
due to the fact that	because
expresses an opinion that	believes
feels quite certain about	believes
for the length of time that	while
for the period of	interval
for the purpose of	to
in an effort to	to
in such a manner that	so
in the area / case / field of	in
in the event that	if
in the neighborhood of	approximately
looks something like	resembles
serves the function of	functions as
shows a tendency to	tends
take into consideration	consider
take under advisement	consider
takes place in such a manner	occurs
with reference to	regarding
with the result that	so

The following tips will help you eliminate other kinds of wordiness just as easily:

1. Replace a wordy phrase or clause with a one- or two-word synonym.

   Wordy: The college has parking zones for different areas for people living on campus as well as for those who do not live on campus and who commute to school.

   Revision: The college has different parking zones for resident and commuter students. (Twenty words of the original wordy sentence—everything after "areas for"—have been reduced neatly to four words: "resident and commuter students.")

   Wordy: Many banks use a system of tubes which move small items by means of air pressure from one place to another.

Revision: Many banks use pneumatic tubes to send small items from one place to another. (Using the phrase "pneumatic tubes" will save many words and identify the system more precisely—provided, of course, that your reader knows what pneumatic tubes are.)

2. Combine sentences beginning with the same subject or ending with an object that becomes the subject of the next sentence.

Wordy: I asked the inspector if she were going to visit the plant this afternoon. I also asked her if she would come alone.

Revision: I asked the inspector if she were going to visit the plant alone this afternoon.

Wordy: Homeowners want to buy low-maintenance plants. These low-maintenance plants include the ever-popular holly and boxwood varieties. These plants are also inexpensive.

Revision: Homeowners want to buy such low-maintenance and inexpensive plants as holly and boxwood. (This revision combines three sentences into one, condenses twenty-four words into fourteen, and joins three related thoughts into one tightened sentence.)

Another kind of wordiness comes from using redundant expressions. Being redundant means that you say the same thing twice, only in different words. "Fellow colleague," "component parts," and "corrosive acid" are phrases that contain this kind of double speech; a fellow is a colleague, a component is a part, and acid is corrosive. Redundant expressions are uneconomical and can be classified as clichés. The suggested revisions on the right are preferable to the redundant phrases on the left:

Redundant	*Concise*
basic necessities	needs
cease and desist	stop
close proximity	close
each and every	all
exposed opening	opening
fair and just	fair
final conclusions / final outcome	conclusions / outcome
first and foremost	primarily
full and complete	full
passing fad	fad (a fad always passes)
personal opinion	opinion
tried and true	honest

Adding a prepositional phrase can sometimes contribute to redundancy. The italicized words below are redundant because of the unnecessary qualification they impose on the adverb or adjective. Delete the italicized phrases:

audible *to the ear*	hard *to the touch*
bitter *in taste*	honest *in character*
fly *in the air*	light *in weight*

orange *in color*	soft *in texture*
quickly *with haste*	tall *in height*
rectangular *in shape*	twenty *in quantity*
second *in sequence*	visible *to the eye*
short *in duration*	wise *in intelligence*

Certain combinations of verbs and adverbs are also redundant. Again, the italicized words should be deleted.

advance *forward*	open *up*
cancel *out*	plan *ahead*
circle *around*	prove *conclusively*
close *off*	refer *back*
connect *together*	repeat *again*
funnel *through*	

Watch for repetitious material within a sentence. Sometimes one part of a sentence needlessly duplicates another part, or a second sentence may repeat the first.

Redundant: The post office hires part-time help, especially around the holidays, to handle the large amounts of mail at Christmas time. ("Especially around the holidays" means the same thing as "at Christmas time.")

Revision: The post office often hires part-time help to handle the large amounts of mail at Christmas time.

Redundant: The fermenting activity of yeast is due to an enzyme called zymase. This enzyme produces chemical changes in yeast. (The second sentence says vaguely what the first sentence says precisely; delete it.)

Revision: The fermenting activity of yeast is due to an enzyme called zymase.

Redundant: To provide more room for employees' cars, the security department is studying ways to expand the employee parking lot. (The first phrase says nothing that the reader does not know from the independent clause; cut the phrase.)

Revision: The security department is studying ways to expand the employee parking lot.

Chapter 3 has presented information on using correct and effective sentences. By following the guidelines in the chapter, you will become a better writer in your profession. "How to Write Clearly," the following article by Edward T. Thompson, can serve as a review of much material in this chapter and of the previous chapter as well. Thompson is the editor-in-chief of *Reader's Digest,* a well-known magazine that often clarifies and condenses a great deal of information. His advice, therefore, carries the force of experience and success.

How to write clearly

By Edward T. Thompson

Editor-in-Chief, Reader's Digest

International Paper asked Edward T. Thompson to share some of what he has learned in nineteen years with Reader's Digest, a magazine famous for making complicated subjects understandable to millions of readers.

If you are afraid to write, don't be.

If you think you've got to string together big fancy words and high-flying phrases, forget it.

To write well, unless you aspire to be a professional poet or novelist, you only need to get your ideas across simply and clearly.

It's not easy. But it *is* easier than you might imagine.

There are only three basic requirements:

First, you must *want* to write clearly. And I believe you really do, if you've stayed this far with me.

Second, you must be willing to *work hard*. Thinking means work—and that's what it takes to do anything well.

Third, you must know and follow some *basic guidelines*.

If, while you're writing for clarity, some lovely, dramatic or inspired phrases or sentences come to you, fine. Put them in.

But then with cold, objective eyes and mind ask yourself: "Do they detract from clarity?" If they do, grit your teeth and cut the frills.

Follow Some Basic Guidelines

I can't give you a complete list of "dos and don'ts" for every writing problem you'll ever face.

But I can give you some fundamental guidelines that cover the most common problems.

1. Outline what you want to say.

I know that sounds grade-schoolish. But you can't write clearly until, *before you start,* you know where you will stop.

Ironically, that's even a problem in writing an outline (i.e., knowing the ending before you begin).

So try this method:

- On 3″×5″ cards, write—one point to a card—all the points you need to make.
- Divide the cards into piles—one pile for each group of points *closely related to each other*. (If you were describing an automobile, you'd put all the points about mileage in one pile, all the points about safety in another, and so on.)

Reprinted by permission of International Paper Company.

- Arrange your piles of points in a sequence. Which are most important and should be given first or saved for last? Which must you present before others in order to make the others understandable?
- Now, *within* each pile, do the same thing—arrange the *points* in logical, understandable order.

There you have your outline, needing only an introduction and conclusion.

This is a practical way to outline. It's also flexible. You can add, delete or change the location of points easily.

2. Start where your readers are.

How much do they know about the subject? Don't write to a level higher than your readers' knowledge of it.

CAUTION: Forget that old—and wrong—advice about writing to a 12-year-old mentality. That's insulting. But do remember that your prime purpose is to *explain* something, not prove that you're smarter than your readers.

3. Avoid jargon.

Don't use words, expressions, phrases known only to people with specific knowledge or interests.

Example: A scientist, using scientific jargon, wrote, "The biota exhibited a one hundred percent mortality response." He could have written: "All the fish died."

4. Use familiar combinations of words.

A speech writer for President Franklin D. Roosevelt wrote, "We are endeavoring to construct a more inclusive society." F.D.R. changed it to "We're going to make a country in which no one is left out."

CAUTION: By familiar combinations of words, I do *not* mean incorrect grammar. *That* can be *un*clear. Example: John's father says he can't go out Friday. (Who can't go out? John or his father?)

5. Use "first-degree" words.

These words immediately bring an image to your mind. Other words must be "translated" through the first-degree word before you see the image. Those are second/third-degree words.

First-degree words	Second / third-degree words
face	visage, countenance
stay	abide, remain, reside
book	volume, tome, publication

First-degree words are usually the most precise words, too.

6. Stick to the point.

Your outline—which was more work in the beginning—now saves you work. Because now you can ask about any sentence you write: "Does it relate to a point in the outline? If it doesn't, should I add it to the outline? If not, I'm getting off the track." Then, full steam ahead—on the main line.

7. Be as brief as possible.

Whatever you write, shortening—*condensing*—almost always makes it tighter, straighter, easier to read and understand.

Condensing, as *Reader's Digest* does it, is in large part artistry. But it involves techniques that anyone can learn and use.

- *Present your points in logical ABC order:* Here again, your outline should save you work because, if you did it right, your points already stand in logical ABC order—A makes B understandable, B makes C understandable and so on. To write in a straight line is to say something clearly in the fewest possible words.
- *Don't waste words telling people what they already know:* Notice how we edited this: "Have you ever wondered how banks rate you as a credit risk? ~~You know, of course, that it's some combination of facts about your income, your job, and so on. But actually,~~ Many banks have a scoring system. . . ."
- *Cut out excess evidence and unnecessary anecdotes:* Usually, one fact or example (at most, two) will support a point. More just belabor it. And while writing about something may remind you of a good story, ask yourself: "Does it *really help* to tell the story, or does it slow me down?"

   (Many people think *Reader's Digest* articles are filled with anecdotes. Actually, we use them sparingly and usually for one of two reasons: either the subject is so dry it needs some "humanity" to give it life; or the subject is so hard to grasp, it needs anecdotes to help readers understand. If the subject is both lively and easy to grasp, we move right along.)
- *Look for the most common word wasters:* windy phrases.

Windy phrases	Cut to . . .
at the present time	now
in the event of	if
in the majority of instances	usually

- *Look for passive verbs you can make active:* Invariably, this produces a shorter sentence. "The cherry tree *was* chopped down by George Washington." (Passive verb and nine words.) "George Washington *chopped* down the cherry tree." (Active verb and seven words.)
- *Look for positive / negative sections from which you can cut the negative:* See how we did it here: "The answer ~~does not rest with carelessness or incompetence. It lies largely in~~ having enough people to do the job."
- Finally, to write more clearly by saying it in fewer words: when you've finished, stop.

▶ Exercises

1. Punctuate the following sentences correctly.
   (a) Cooking can kill many bacteria in food, it cannot kill them all.
   (b) Bass fishing attracts many tourists to the lake. Not just during the summer but also during the fall.
   (c) No new accounts will be opened today, therefore the credit office is closed.

(d) The Land Rover is popular with sports enthusiasts partly because it is economical. And partly because it is so rugged.

(e) The patient received an injection for pain, however, he said that it did not help.

(f) Because real estate values soared; many buyers were unable to own their own homes. Which angered them.

(g) The college is offering five sections of Business English this term, many of them are in the late afternoon and night.

(h) The sales manager had to prepare her report by that afternoon. Because the buyer wanted to review it before the conference tomorrow;

(i) The buses left for Dayton punctually. On the hour and on the half.

2. The following sentences are contradictory or contain words that are inappropriate for the context. Rewrite these sentences to correct the errors.

   (a) In metric terms, our new olympic swimming pool is twenty-five feet long.

   (b) His report discusses the differences in jogging between the United States and Great Britain.

   (c) The operator fed the load onto the truck using a hydraulic fork.

   (d) Sampling all of the residents of Cherry Hill, we found that 25 percent wanted the zoning laws to remain the same, 40 percent wanted them modified to include multiple family housing, and the other 45 percent wanted changes in housing and transportation.

   (e) The watch commander was happy to report that convictions exceeded arrests.

   (f) The local committee threw its spirited support behind the opposition to the new liquor laws.

   (g) The nonsoluble retaining wall will let in only a small amount of water.

   (h) New drilling techniques make it possible to create oil faster.

   (i) The applicant did not plan ahead and was, therefore, ready for the interviewer's questions.

   (j) Health food stores take a great interest in nuts.

3. Rewrite the following sentences to correct dangling and misplaced modifiers.

   (a) When preparing school papers, your dictionary will be a great aid.

   (b) Using the Heimlich Maneuver, a bolus of food will be forced out of a person's airway.

   (c) We purchased a new model from the salesclerk with adjustable arms.

   (d) Topped with a tasty hollandaise sauce, the waiter brought us a delicious salad.

   (e) Allowing for a 3 percent margin for error, the specifications arrived on the builder's desk this morning.

   (f) Before turning the patient, intravenous solutions are given.

   (g) The bank almost closed before we got there.

   (h) Fastened securely, the officer left the compound.

(i) The show dog ran away from the trainer with a leash around his neck.

(j) All travel requests must be submitted by employees in triplicate.

(k) The meal is prepared by the chef delicately seasoned with oregano.

(l) Almost maintenance-free, the housekeeper liked the new electric broom.

(m) Before placing the specimen under the microscope, proper care has to be taken.

(n) About the size of a quarter, most Americans did not like the new Susan B. Anthony dollar.

(o) My neighbor went to see the dentist with a huge cavity.

(p) Turning the machine counterclockwise, the springs were loosened.

4. The following sentences contain wordy expressions. Rewrite these sentences to make them leaner.

(a) Due to the fact that the bus was late, we did not get home until after midnight.

(b) In an effort to correct some health violations, we fixed the refrigerator in such a way that it would not cause us any more trouble.

(c) You will have to connect together the terminals with the assistance of a Phillips screwdriver.

(d) In terms of our ability to meet the demands of those individuals living in the Thames district, all that we can articulate adequately at this date on the calendar is that every effort will be made to find appropriate work crews to find, gather, and remove the refuse left by the storm.

(e) Our manager is very supportive of our efforts to expand our line of coats, hats, shirts, pants, blouses, dresses, and socks for young children between the ages of two weeks and one year.

(f) For the length of time that the powder is left around the edges of the room, you might want to check the walls and doors.

(g) The patient's arm was soaked in warm water with the result that she felt much better and in such a way that the doctor discharged her.

5. The following sentences contain redundancies. Rewrite these sentences to remove unnecessary repetition.

(a) It was a foreign import.

(b) The owner's car was light azure blue in color and a convertible in the model.

(c) The president told them to terminate the plan and end it.

(d) A student delivered an oral talk to fellow classmates.

(e) The crew was traveling and in transit; therefore, it could not be reached.

(f) The troops advanced forward even when they were confronted face-to-face with hazardous dangers, staring them in the eyes.

(g) The chemistry major had to reread the chapter on bonding again.

Exercises

(h) The chief canceled our leaves when the mayor requested additional, ~~further~~ officers.

(i) The clamp was connected ~~together~~ with the hose.

(j) After explaining the new policy, the office manager centered her discussion around the ways of implementing ~~and carrying out~~ that policy in our routine, ~~daily activities~~.

(k) When the technician walked into the room, the patient was ~~really~~ bleeding profusely.

(l) She came to her final conclusion after referring ~~back~~ to the occurrence report.

(m) ~~Although~~ the diamond was oval in shape, it still ~~would~~ satisfy the buyer.

(n) First ~~and foremost~~, the guests received a complimentary bottle of wine, ~~which did not cost them a cent~~.

(o) He received personalized ~~and individual~~ care.

(p) A knife, tent, and food supplies are ~~basic~~ necessities on an outdoor ~~camping~~ trip in the woods.

(q) The report will specifically and ~~exclusively~~ deal with urban problems affecting the city.

(r) The ~~local,~~ neighborhood commission gave sufficient ~~and adequate~~ reasons for letting the carpenter work independently, ~~and use her own resources~~.

(s) They have legal recourse ~~as promised~~ by the law.

SECTION II

CORRESPONDENCE

4

Letter Writing: Some Basics

Letters are the most likely kind of written work that will be expected of you in your job. Because letters are so important, Chapters 4, 5, and 6 are devoted exclusively to ways of writing letters effectively. Chapter 4 introduces the entire process and provides some guidelines, definitions, and strategies common to letter writing.

▶ The Importance of Letters

A letter can be defined as a formal or informal written message carefully planned and prepared, addressed to a specific audience, and having a clearly announced function. Letters are not telegrams, lists, or computer printouts. Letters are more formal than the memos that are written to people who work in your office. They are both a personal and professional means of communication. Effective letters clearly announce their purpose and are written in complete sentences in a style that (1) follows an appropriate format, (2) courteously addresses the reader, and (3) selects the most precise and useful terms.

Companies annually spend millions of dollars writing letters. The average business letter now costs between five and ten dollars to compose, dictate, type, proofread, mail, and file. Not surprisingly, many companies own computerized typewriters that allow them to send a letter across the country in a few minutes. But even with such machines, firms need people to write and proofread the letters. Numerous firms offer their employees seminars on how to write clear and appropriate letters. The skill of good letter writing can be learned and can lead the writer to advancement and rewards.

Why are letters so important to the employer and the employee? Letters represent the public image of the company and the writer. They influence people favorably or unfavorably. Basically, letters serve the following five functions:

1. *Letters provide information.* They can inform clients about a new policy, a change in time for deliveries, an alteration in procedures, a new product, or a new service. They can also give instructions and outline in a clear, unemotional way the facts that the company thinks are important.
2. *Letters prompt action.* They can collect money from overdue accounts, alter a city ordinance, speed the shipment of new parts, initiate a policy, call a meeting, change a grade, or waive a requirement.
3. *Letters establish goodwill.* They can thank someone, convey congratulations, answer a complaint, settle an account satisfactorily, or provide a recommendation.
4. *Letters sell.* They can sell a product, a service, or the writer's own skills.
5. *Letters follow up on telephone conversations.* They can also provide documentation for oral agreements.

Letters accomplish all these goals by following certain conventions. These conventions are the ways in which businesses and their readers expect letters to be written. This chapter will show you how to write an effective letter and will provide examples for you to study.

▶ Typing and Proofreading Letters

The first thing a reader notices about a letter is how the words and paragraphs are arranged on the page. A letter should look neat, clean, and professional to tell the reader that the work, service, or skill the writer promises to deliver will be done in the same way. Strikeovers (crossing out one letter by putting another letter on top of it), messy erasures that leave the paper bare in one spot, blotches of liquid corrector smeared across the page, handwritten changes inserted to correct errors—all look unprofessional and interfere with the reader's attempt to get the message quickly and accurately.

The way in which a letter is typed on the page significantly affects the visual impression it makes. You can avoid crowded or lopsided letters if you take a few minutes to estimate the length of the message before you type it. You do not want to start a brief letter at the top of the page and leave three-fourths of the page blank. Plan to start near the center of the page. Also avoid cramming everything onto one page; sometimes you will have to use a second sheet. A letter that is squeezed onto one page will deprive the reader of necessary and pleasant white space.

Specific typing instructions are included later in the chapter. Here are a few general hints. Leave generous margins of approximately 1½ inches all around your letter. Have more white space at the top than at the bottom, and watch right-hand margins in particular, since it is easy to exceed their limits. Shorter letters may require wider margins than longer letters, but don't exceed a margin of 1½ inches on the right-hand side.

Be especially careful about the typewriter you use. Make sure that all the keys work and that none of them produces a broken or half letter. Clean your keys and buy a new ribbon so that your typed letter will not be fuzzy or messy.

Proofread everything that has your name on it, even if you did not type it. You cannot blame a typist for work for which you are responsible. Typographical errors can be costly and embarrassing. If you want to tell a steady customer that "the order will be hard to fill" and you type instead that "the order will be hard to bill," confusion will result. Poor typing and proofreading can also lead to omissions (the "ill arrived" for "the bill arrived"), transpositions ("hte" for "the," "nad" for "and," "fra" for "far," "sti" for "its"), or omitted words ("the market value of the was high").

Proofreading is reading in slow motion. Here are seven ways to proofread effectively. You may want to combine all of them to ensure accuracy.

1. Read the letter backwards.
2. Read the letter from the start to the finish aloud. Pronounce each word carefully to make yourself more aware of typographical errors or omitted words.
3. Place your finger under each word as you read the letter silently.
4. Have a friend read the letter. Four eyes are better than two.
5. Have your friend read the original copy of the letter aloud while you follow the typed copy.
6. If you have the time, proofread the letter the following day.
7. Never proofread when you are tired and avoid reading large amounts of material in one sitting.

▶ Letter Formats

Letter format refers to the way in which you type a letter—where you indent and where you place certain kinds of information. A number of letter formats exist. Two of the most popular in the business world are the full block format (Fig. 4.1) and the semiblock format (Fig. 4.2). Either form is acceptable, but to be safe, find out your employer's preference.

The full block style is the easiest to use because all information in the letter is typed flush against the left-hand margin. You will not have to worry about indenting paragraphs or aligning dates with signatures. For these reasons the full block form is preferred by many businesses. Figure 4.1 shows a full block letter typed on letterhead stationery (specially printed stationery giving a company's name, address, telephone number, and sometimes the names of its chief executives or the company symbol or design). The use of letterhead stationery eliminates the need to type the writer's inside address.

Fig. 4.1   Full block format.

oii

RICHARD E. FELTS
Chairman Emeritus

CAMERON E. WILLIAMS, CPCU
Chairman

RICHARD L. PHILLIPS, CPCU
First Vice Chairman

Ohio Insurance Institute / 620 EAST BROAD STREET, P.O. BOX 632, COLUMBUS, OHIO 43216 / PHONE (614) 228-1593

JOHN C. WINCHELL, CPCU ,
President

NOREEN R. WILLS
Vice President,
Public Information

ALAN V. RINARD, CPCU
Vice President,
Research & Education

CAROLINE KASLER
Assistant Vice President,
Education & Research

April 2, 1982

Ms. Molly Georgopolous, C.P.A.
Business Manager
Diversified Industries
3400 South Madison
Akron, OH 44324

*Everything is
lined up
against the
left-hand
margin*

Dear Ms. Georgopolous:

As I promised in our telephone conversation this afternoon,
I am enclosing a study of the Ohio financial responsibility
law. I hope that it will help you in your survey.

I wish to emphasize again that probably 95 percent of all
individuals who are involved in an accident do obtain
reimbursement for hospital and doctor bills and for damages
to their automobiles. If individuals have insurance, they
can receive reimbursement from their own carrier. If they do
not have insurance and the other driver is uninsured and
judged to be at fault, the State Bureau of Motor Vehicles
will revoke that party's driver's license and license plates
until all costs for injuries and damages are paid.

Please call upon me again if I may be of help to you.

Sincerely yours,

John C. Winchell

John C. Winchell, President

JCW/pck

Encl.

Letterhead reproduced by permission.

Fig. 4.2   Semiblock format.

Inside address, dateline, complimentary close, and writer's name indented

7239 East Daphne Parkway
Mobile, AL 36608
July 30, 1982

Mr. Travis Boykin, Manager
Scandia
703 Hardy Street
Hattiesburg, MS 39401

Dear Mr. Boykin:

The name of your store is listed in the <u>Annual Catalog</u> as the closest distributor of Copenhagen products in my area. I would appreciate knowing if you currently stock the Crescent pattern of model 5678 and how much you charge per model number. I would also like to know if you have special prices per box order.

Also, could you give me directions on how to get to your shop from Mobile and what hours you are open.

I look forward to hearing from you.

Sincerely yours,

Arthur T. McCormack

Arthur T. McCormack

On plain stationery, the inside address is typed flush with the left-hand margin, directly above the date.

The semiblock style, by contrast, has the writer's address (if it is not imprinted on a letterhead), date, complimentary close, and the signature at the right-hand side of the letter. The typist must make a number of adjustments to align the date with the complimentary close and must remember to go back to the left side to note any enclosures with the letter.

If your letter runs to a second page (and it may not do this often), use a sheet of plain white bond paper rather than company letterhead. About six lines, or 1½ inches from the top of the page, type the recipient's name on the left-hand side, a simple Arabic 2 in the center, and the date of the letter on the right-hand side. Do it like this:

Patricia Riordan–Sanchez   2   April 30, 1982

Alternatively, put "Page 2" and the date directly under the recipient's name on the left-hand side.

▶ Parts of a Letter

A letter can contain many parts to communicate its message. Those parts marked with an asterisk are found in every letter you will write. Figure 4.3 contains a sample letter displaying all the parts discussed below. Note where each part is placed in the letter.

*Date line

Where you place the month, day, and year depends on the format you are using. If you are using the block style, the dateline is flush with the left-hand margin. If you are using the semiblock style, the date can be placed at the center point, centered under a company letterhead, or flush with the right-hand margin.

Spell out the name of the month in full; type out "September" and "March" rather than abbreviating to "Sept." or "Mar." Most frequently the dateline is typed this way: November 14, 1981. The military and other gov-

Fig. 4.3   A sample letter, full block format.

Writer's address	**Madison and Moore, Inc.** **Professional Architects** **7900 South Manheim Road** **Crystal Springs, NE 71003**

Date line

December 10, 1981

Inside address

Ms. Paula Jordan
Systems Consultant
Broadacres Development Corp.
12 East River Street
Detroit, MI 48001

Salutation

Dear Ms. Jordan:

Subject line

SUBJECT: Request for alternate duplex plans, No. 32134a

Body of letter

Thank you for your letter of December 2, 1981. I have discussed your request with the officials in our Planning Department and have learned that the forms we used are no longer available.

In searching through my files, however, I have come across the enclosed catalog from a Nevada firm that might be helpful to you. This firm, Nevada Designers, offers plans very similar to the ones you are interested in, as you can tell from the design on page 23 of their catalog.

I hope this will help your project and I wish you success in your venture.

Complimentary close

Sincerely yours,

Company name

MADISON AND MOORE, INC.

Signature

William Newhouse

Writer's name and title

William Newhouse
Office Manager

Stenographic identification

WN/kpl

Enclosure

Enclosure: Catalog

Carbon copy to

cc. Planning Department

ernmental agencies, however, may ask you to date correspondence with the day followed by month and year (14 November 1981), with no commas separating the day, month, and year.

*Inside Address

The inside address, which is the same address that goes on the envelope, is placed against the left-hand margin in both full block and semiblock formats. It contains the name, title (if any), company, street address, city, state, and zip code of the person or company to which you are writing. If possible, try to write to a specific individual. You will get off to a bad start if you do not spell that person's name right; don't put Anderson for Andersen, Kean for Keen, or MacDermott for McDermott.

Single space the inside address, but do not use a comma at the end of the lines. The name of the individual, together with a courtesy title such as Mr., Ms., Dr., Professor, goes on the first line. When writing to a woman, use Ms. unless she expressly asked to be called Mrs. or Miss. A woman's marital status should not be an issue. The initials M.D., Ph.D., or D.P.H. should not be added after you use Dr. Use either Janice Howell, M.D. or Dr. Janice Howell, not Dr. Janice Howell, M.D. Some common initials indicating a person's position or occupation are R.N. (registered nurse), M.T. (medical technologist), P.A. (professional architect), and C.P.A. (certified public accountant). Place these initials after the individual's name, separated by a comma: Charles Barton, R.N. Any military titles (captain, corporal), academic ranks (professor, assistant professor), or religious designations (reverend, father, sister) should be written out in full and the first letter capitalized.

If the individual to whom you are writing holds an office or has a title within the company, put a comma after the person's name, followed by the title: Ms. Kathy Buel, President. Use the courtesy title Ms. and capitalize the "P" in President. If the title contains more than one word, put the title on the next line: Mr. Henry Gerald / Director of Computer Services. If you do not know the individual's name or if you are writing to an entire corporation or section of a company, put the department or company name on one line and the street address on the next line: Public Relations Department / The Doulet Brace Company / 1343 Jackson Street / Chicago IL 60624.

The last line of the inside address contains the city, state, and zip code. Table 4.1 lists the official U.S. Postal Service abbreviations—two capital letters without a period—for the states and territories of the United States. Acceptable abbreviations for the provinces of Canada are listed below the table. Pay special attention to those abbreviations beginning with the same letter. For example, mail going to Jackson, Mississippi (MS), could go astray if a letter without a zip code used the same abbreviation for Michigan (MI). Also note the difference between AR (Arkansas) and AK (Alaska).

Table 4.1 U.S. Postal Service Abbreviations

U.S. state / territory	Abbreviation	U.S. state / territory	Abbreviation
Alabama	AL	Montana	MT
Alaska	AK	Nebraska	NE
Arizona	AZ	Nevada	NV
Arkansas	AR	New Hampshire	NH
American Samoa	AS	New Jersey	NJ
California	CA	New Mexico	NM
Colorado	CO	New York	NY
Connecticut	CT	North Carolina	NC
Delaware	DE	North Dakota	ND
District of Columbia	DC	Ohio	OH
Florida	FL	Oklahoma	OK
Georgia	GA	Oregon	OR
Guam	GU	Pennsylvania	PA
Hawaii	HI	Puerto Rico	PR
Idaho	ID	Rhode Island	RI
Illinois	IL	South Carolina	SC
Indiana	IN	South Dakota	SD
Iowa	IA	Tennessee	TN
Kansas	KS	Trust Territories	TT
Kentucky	KY	Texas	TX
Louisiana	LA	Utah	UT
Maine	ME	Vermont	VT
Maryland	MD	Virginia	VA
Massachusetts	MA	Virgin Islands	VI
Michigan	MI	Washington	WA
Minnesota	MN	West Virginia	WV
Mississippi	MS	Wisconsin	WI
Missouri	MO	Wyoming	WY

Canadian province	Abbreviation	Canadian province	Abbreviation
Alberta	AB	Nova Scotia	NS
British Columbia	BC	Ontario	ON
Labrador	LB	Prince Edward Island	PE
Manitoba	MB	Quebec	PQ
New Brunswick	NB	Saskatchewan	SK
Newfoundland	NF	Yukon Territory	YT
Northwest Territories	NT		

*Salutation

The greeting part of your letter, or the salutation, is a written equivalent to
"Hello" or "It's a pleasure to talk with you." The salutation is typed flush
against the left-hand margin in both the full block and semiblock formats.
Begin with "Dear," a convention showing respect for your reader, and then

follow with a courtesy title, the reader's last name, and a colon (Dear Mr. Brown:). A comma is reserved for an informal letter. If you are not sure of the sex of the reader, type *Dear Terry Banks,* using the reader's full name. When writing to a group made up of both sexes, use *Dear Ladies and Gentlemen* rather than the sexist *Dear Sir.* And finally, if you are on a first-name basis with your reader, using his or her last name would be awkward; simply type *Dear Bill,* or *Dear Sue.*

Subject Line

The subject line, preceded by the word "subject" in capital letters, can be placed two spaces below the salutation, flush with the left-hand margin:

```
Dear Mr. Hogan:

SUBJECT: Repair of model 7342
```

Or it can be moved to the right-hand side of the letter, on the same line with the salutation:

```
Dear Mr. Hogan:                    SUBJECT: Repair of model 7342
```

The subject line provides a concise summary of the letter (something like a title), or it lists account numbers, order notations, policy identifications, or referral numbers so that the reader can at once check the files and see what the status of your account or policy is. Your most recent letter can then be placed accurately in your file.

*Body of the Letter

The body of a letter contains the message. In the full block format paragraphs are not indented; in the semiblock format paragraphs may or may not be indented five spaces. Whichever style you choose, single space within the paragraph, but double space between paragraphs.

Excessively long paragraphs can make the reader work too hard finding ideas buried in them. On the other hand, short, choppy, one-sentence paragraphs that follow one on top of the other give an impression of spotty, incomplete coverage. Most paragraphs in a letter usually run from three to eight typed lines (forty to sixty words, or three to six sentences). Readers appreciate short sentences (under twenty words) because they are easier to understand and convey information quickly and clearly.

*Complimentary Close

The complimentary close appears two spaces below the body of the letter: flush with left-hand margin in the full block format and at the center point, aligned with the date, for the semiblock format. As the term suggests, the complimentary close ends the letter in a polite way. Your close should be appropriate for the reader. For most business correspondence, the standard close is *Sincerely yours, Sincerely,* or *Respectfully.* Capitalize only the first word of the complimentary close, and follow the entire close with a comma.

*Signature

The typed signature appears four spaces below the complimentary close, either on the left side (full block format) or at the center point (semiblock format). You need four spaces between the typed name and the close so that your name, when you write it out, will not look squeezed in. Never forget to sign your name, just as it is typed. Your name not only indicates who you are, but also verifies that the contents of your letter have your approval. An unsigned letter indicates carelessness or, worse, indifference.

Some firms like to have the company name as well as the employee's name in the signature section. If so, type the company name in capital letters two spaces below the complimentary close, and then sign your name as was just explained. Add whatever title you have underneath your typed name. Here is an example:

```
Sincerely yours,

THE FINELLI COMPANY

Robert Jones
Robert Jones
Cover Coordinator
```

Stenographic Identification

When a letter is typed for you, the typist's initials are placed two spaces below your typed signature. The typist's (stenographer's) initials are typed in lowercase letters and follow your initials, which are typed in capital letters. The notation WBT/vgh, for example, means that Winnie B. Thompson's letter was typed by Victor G. Higgins. The company thus has a record in its files of who dictated the letter and who typed it. Never list any initials if you typed your own letter.

Enclosure(s) Line

The enclosure line is typed two spaces beneath the stenographic initials or your typed signature if you typed your own letter. This line informs the reader that some materials (brochures, diagrams, forms, job description, plans) are being sent with your letter. You can type the word "Enclosure" in full or abbreviate it to "Encl." Most writers indicate briefly what is being enclosed (Encl. Incident report; Encl. Résumé) or at least give the number of enclosures (Encl. 3).

Initials for Carbon Copy

The initials "cc." (typed with no space between them) indicate that a letter has been duplicated. Type the initials two spaces below the enclosure line. Because so many businesses today copy their letters, using some kind of photocopying technique, the initials "xc." (Xerox copy) may replace "cc."

Letters are copied and sent to a third party for a variety of reasons. An individual may want to know what has happened:

    cc. John Bandy

or another department in your firm may be interested in your letter

    cc. Service Dept.

Often letters are copied without the knowledge of the reader. Such copies are called "blind carbon copies." But professional courtesy dictates that you tell the reader that a copy of your letter is being sent to someone else.

▶ Addressing an Envelope

When addressing an envelope, use a standard $9\frac{1}{2}'' \times 4\frac{1}{8}''$ white envelope or, as most firms use when they mail statements, an envelope measuring $6\frac{1}{2}'' \times 3\frac{5}{8}''$, with a window (a transparent cellophane opening) showing the customer's address. Because mail is sorted now by scanning machines, the Postal Service has established regulations concerning envelope size. In particular, avoid small, invitation-sized envelopes and odd-shaped ones. Review the regulations listed in Chapter 1, p. 7, on proper envelope sizes. The Postal Service now recommends using all capitals and no punctuation on the envelope.

Outside Address

An envelope has two parts—the outside address and the return address, as in Fig. 4.4. The outside address, the same as the reader's inside address on your letter, should be typed and centered on the envelope. Leave at least one-half inch of white space between the last line of address and the bottom of the envelope. Do not run your address to the very end of the envelope. Never exceed five lines for an address, and make sure that all lines of the address are lined up. If an individual's address contains both a street address and an apartment, room, or suite number, put all this information on the same line:

Fig. 4.4   The envelope.

```
THOMAS ADDINGTON    ⎫
45 SIMMONS APT 2B   ⎬  Return address
MEDVALE VT 05402    ⎭




                        ⎧ MS PATRICIA BARNES
                        ⎪ OFFICE MANAGER
    Outside address    ⎨  COURTESY MOTORS
                        ⎪ 1700 LAKEWOOD STREET
                        ⎩ POTSDAM NY 13676
```

809 TROUP STREET APT 7B. If individuals do not live at an address permanently, you will have to send the letter in care of (C/O) the permanent resident:

```
MS MARY JANE TRUAX
C/O MS FAYE JELINICK
33 WEST 91ST STREET
NEW YORK NY 10072
```

Always use a zip code, even if a letter is going to someone in your city, because a letter with a zip code will arrive at its destination sooner.

Return Address and Special Instructions

The return address is your address. It should appear at the upper left-hand side of the envelope (not on the flap), single spaced, and without any courtesy title. Sometimes special mailing directions are required. In such cases one of the following designations is added to the envelope.

- **Hold for Arrival:** Individuals may be away on business or on vacation, and you want to make sure that the letter finds them on their return. Perhaps, too, you are writing to someone who will arrive at a hotel or firm after your letter does. The notation "hold for arrival" will ensure that your letter is not returned or thrown away.
- **Personal** or **Confidential:** This designation indicates that only the individual to whom you are writing should open and read your letter. Otherwise, the letter will be considered routine business correspondence.

- **Attention:** An attention line clearly earmarks your letter for someone's special handling. The attention line is particularly helpful when you have been dealing regularly with one section, office, or individual in a large company—credit department, parts warehouse, or statistics office. An attention line also helps a company sort and route its mail faster.
- **Please Forward:** This designation asks that your letter be sent on to a new address after an individual has moved.

All such special instructions, except the attention line, are placed at the top left, two spaces below the outside address. The attention line is typed on the second line of the outside address. Figure 4.5 shows the proper format.

Fig. 4.5   Envelopes with special notations.

```
KATHY KOOPERMAN
769 EAST 45TH STREET
BALTIMORE MD 21224




                       THE PLACEMENT OFFICE
                       ATTENTION MS FAYE GLADSTONE
                       EAST CENTRAL COMMUNITY COLLEGE
                       BALTIMORE MD 21228
```

```
GARY ALLEN
WILCOX LABS
73 DUNWITTY LANE
ST PAUL MN 55476

PLEASE HOLD FOR ARRIVAL


                       MS NANCY PARKER
                       THE HANRAHAN COMPANY
                       C/O THE WILTSHIRE HOTEL
                       BARCLAY SQUARE
                       NEW YORK NY 10031
```

▶ Making a Good Impression on Your Reader

We have discussed the mechanical requirements your letter must fulfill. Now we will discuss the content of your letter—what you say and how you say it. Writing letters means communicating to influence your readers—not to alienate or antagonize them. Keep in mind that writers of effective letters are like successful diplomats, in that they represent both the company they work for and themselves.

To write an effective letter, first put yourself in the reader's position. What kinds of letters do you like to receive? You would at once rule out letters that are vague, sarcastic, pushy, or condescending. You want letters addressed to you to be respectful, businesslike, and considerate of your needs and requests. If you have questions, you want them answered honestly and courteously. And you do not want someone to waste your time with a long, puffy letter when a few well-chosen sentences would have done the job much better.

What do you as a writer have to do to send such effective letters? Adopt the "you attitude"; in other words, signal to readers that they are the most important ingredient in your letter. Incorporating this "you attitude" means that you should be able to answer "yes" to these two questions: (1) Will my readers receive a positive image of me? (2) Have I chosen words that convey both my respect for the readers and my concern for their questions and comments? The first question deals with your overall view of readers. Do your letters paint them as clever or stupid, practical managers or spendthrifts? The second question deals with specific language conveying your view of the reader. Words can burn or soothe. Choose them carefully.

The following four guidelines will help you make a good impression on your readers.

1. Never forget that your reader is a real person.   Avoid writing cold, impersonal letters that sound as if they were punched out by a computer or tape-recorded on a telephone. Let the readers know that you are writing to them as individuals. Neglecting this rule, a large clinic sent its customers this statement: "Your bill is overdue. If you pay it by the 15th of this month, no one except the computer will know that it is late." Similarly, abandoning the personal approach, a general during the Korean War once sent this order to his soldiers: "All troops will have a Merry Christmas."

The letter below violates every rule of personal and personable communications:

```
It has come to our attention that policy number #342q765r has been
delinquent in payment and is in arrears for the sum of $302.35. To
keep the policy in force for the duration of its life, a minimum
payment of $50.00 must reach this office by the last day of the
month. Failure to submit payment will result in the cancellation
of the aforementioned policy.
```

There is no sense in the example above of one individual writing to another, of a customer with a name, personal history, or specific needs. Revised, this letter contains the necessary personal (and human) touch.

> We have not yet received your payment for your insurance policy (#342q765r). By sending us your check for $50.00 within the next three weeks, you will keep your policy in force and can continue to enjoy the financial benefits and emotional security it offers you.

The benefits to the particular reader are stressed, and the reader is addressed directly to feel like a valued customer.

2. Keep the reader in the forefront of your letter. Make sure that the reader's needs control the letter. This is the essence of the "you attitude." No one likes people who talk about themselves all the time. What is true about conversation is equally true of letters. Stress the "you," not the "I." Again, try to find out about your readers. Here is a letter that forgets about the reader:

> I think that our rug shampooer is the best on the market. Our firm has invested a lot of time and money to ensure that it is the most economical and efficient shampooer available today. We have found that our customers are very satisfied with the results of our machine. We have sold thousands of these shampooers, and we are proud of our accomplishment. We hope that we can sell you one of these fantastic machines.

The letter above talks the reader into boredom by spending all its time on the machine, the company, and the sales success. Readers are interested in how they can profit from the machine, not in how much profit the company makes from selling it. To win the confidence of the readers, the writer needs to show how they will find the product useful, economical, and worthwhile at home or at work. Here is a reader-centered alternative:

> Our rug shampooer would make cleaning your motel rooms easier for you. It is equipped with a heavy-duty motor that will handle your 200 rooms with ease. Moreover, that motor will give heavily trafficked areas, such as the lobby or hallways, a fresh and clean look you can be proud of.

3. Be courteous and tactful. However serious the problem or the degree of your anger at the time, refrain from turning your letter into a punch through the mails. Capture the reader's goodwill, and the rewards will be greater for you. Some words can create a bad taste in the reader's mouth—*I demand, you have failed, you contend, we reject, you allege, you must, you lied*—and the list could go on. Words that emphasize the "you attitude" avoid offensive language. Compare the discourteous sentences on the left with the courteous alternatives on the right:

Discourteous	*Courteous*
We must discontinue your service unless payment is received by the date shown.	Please send us your payment so that your service will not be interrupted.
You completely misunderstood my letter.	Evidently my letter did not make clear . . .
Your claim that our product was defective on delivery is outlandish.	We are sorry to learn that you were dissatisfied with the way our product arrived.
The rotten coil you installed caused all my trouble.	The trouble may be caused by a malfunctioning coil.
You are sadly mistaken about the warranty.	We are sorry that the warranty did not explain the service costs better.
The new dishwasher you sold me is third-rate and you charged first-rate prices.	Since the dishwasher is still under warranty, I hope that you can make the repairs easily.

4. Be neither boastful nor meek.   These two strategies—one based on pride and the other on humility—often lead inexperienced letter writers into trouble. On the one hand, they believe that a forceful statement will make a good impression on the reader. Or, perhaps they feel that a cautious and humble approach will be the least offensive way to earn the reader's respect. Both paths are wrong.

Aggressive letters, filled with boasts, rarely appeal to readers. Letters should radiate confidence without sounding as if the writer had written a letter of self-recommendation. Letters should let the facts speak directly and pleasantly for themselves. The sentences on the left boast; those on the right capture confidence with grace.

Boastful	*Graceful*
You will find me the most diplomatic employee you ever hired.	Much of my previous work has been in answering and adjusting customer complaints.
The Sun and Sea unqualifyingly promises the nicest rooms on the Coast.	Each room at the Sun and Sea has its own private bath and bar refrigerator.
I have performed that procedure so many times I can do it in my sleep.	I have performed all kinds of IV therapy as part of standard procedure.
The Check-Pack offers you incomparable customer convenience.	The Check-Pack gives you a free safe-deposit box.

At the other extreme, some writers stress only their own inadequacy. Their attitude as projected in their letters is "I am the most unworthy person who ever lived, and I would be eternally grateful if you even let my letter sit on your desk, let alone open it." Readers will dismiss such writers as pitiful, unqualified weaklings. Note how the meek sentences on the left are rewritten more positively on the right.

Meek	*Positive*
I know that you have a busy schedule and do not always have time to respond, but I would be appreciative if you could send me your brochure on how to apply Brakelite.	Please send me your brochure on how to apply Brakelite.
The season is almost over I know, but could you possibly let me know something about rates for the rest of the summer.	I am interested in renting a cabin in late August (24–30) and would like to know about your rates for that week.
I will be grateful for whatever employment opportunities you could kindly give me.	I will welcome the opportunity to discuss my qualifications with you.

▶ Using the Most Effective Language in Your Letters

For many people, the hardest problem about writing letters is putting their ideas into the right language. Three simple suggestions can help. Your words should be (1) clear, (2) concise, and (3) contemporary.

1. Be clear. Clarity obviously is the most important quality of a business letter. If your message cannot be understood easily, you have wasted your time. Confusion costs time and money. Plan what you are going to say—what your objective is—by taking a few minutes to jot down some questions you want answered or some answers to questions asked of you. Doing this will actually save you time.

Choose precise details appropriate for your audience. In choosing exact words, answer the reader's five fundamental questions—who? what? why? where? and how? Supply concrete words, facts, details, numbers. On the left are some examples of vague sentences that will puzzle a reader because necessary details are missing. These sentences have been rewritten on the right, with exact words replacing unclear ones.

Vague	*Clear*
Please send me some brochures to share with my fellow workers.	Please send me fourteen brochures on the new salt substitute to share with my fellow dietitians.

You can expect an appraisal in the next few weeks.	You will receive an estimate on the installation of a new 50,000 BTU air conditioning unit no later than July 12.
One of our New York stores carries that product.	Our store at 856 East Fifth Avenue sells the entire line of Texworld gloves.
I would like some information about your scheduling policies to Rio de Janeiro.	Please let me know if Pan Am has a morning flight for Rio de Janeiro and how far in advance reservations would have to be made for that flight.
The fee for that service is nominal.	The fee for caulking the five windows on the first floor will be $25.

Sometimes a writer will use exact language and still confuse the reader. This can happen when a letter contains highly technical terms that are familiar only to specialists in the field. It is wise to avoid jargon in your general correspondence; never use it to impress readers with your vocabulary. The following letter is indecipherable because the writer did not take the time to consider the reader's background and explain the housing situation in understandable terms:

Dear Mr. Johnson:

Thank you for your letter about relocating to Monroe. We do have one improved parcel where part of your amortization could be secured through a wraparound mortgage. The owner wants to know if you have sufficient monetary implementation capability.

When the realtor's jargon is replaced by words easily understood by the buyer, the letter reads as follows:

Dear Mr. Johnson:

Thank you for informing us you want to move to Monroe. We do have a two-story frame house in a beautiful neighborhood. Part of your monthly payment on it can be handled through owner financing. The owner would like to know if you have a sufficient down payment (10%).

2. Be concise. "Get to the point" is one of the most frequent commands in the business world. A concise letter does not ramble; instead, it is easy to read and to act on. Ask yourself these two questions: (1) What is the main message I want to tell my reader? (2) Does every sentence and paragraph stick to the main point? The secret to efficient correspondence is to get to the main point at once:

I am pleased to inform you that your order will be delivered by
July 26.

I am writing to confirm the figures we discussed in our telephone
conversation last Wednesday.

I am requesting an extension of two weeks in paying my note.

Please accept our apologies for the damaged Movak shipped to you
last week.

Enclosed is the report you asked our accountant to prepare. It
does contain the new figures on the Manchester store you wanted.

Many letter writers get off to a deadly slow start by repeating, often word
for word, the contents of the letter to which they are responding:

Poor:
I have your letter of March 23 before me in which you ask if our
office knows of any all—electric duplexes for rent less than five
years old and that would be appropriate for senior citizens. You
also ask if these duplexes are close to shopping and medical
facilities.

Better
Thank you for your letter of March 23. Our office does rent all—
electric duplexes suitable for senior citizens. We have two
units, each renting for $275 a month, that are four blocks from
the Mendez Clinic and two blocks from the Edgewater Mall.

Another way to write a concise letter is to include only material that is
absolutely relevant. In a letter complaining about inadequate or faulty telephone service, mentioning color preferences for extension telephones would
be inappropriate. In a request for some information on transferring credits
from one college to another, do not ask about intramural sporting activities.

Finally, make sure that your letter is not wordy (review the pertinent sections of Chapter 3, pages 37–43). By taking a few minutes to revise your letters before they are typed, you can write shorter, more direct letters.

3. Be contemporary.   Being contemporary does not mean you should
use in your letters the slang expressions you hear all around you ("I had a
tire ripped off"; "He is a cool dude"; "That rejection was a bummer"). Reserve that language for conversations with your friends. Nor should you go
to the other extreme and become too stiff and formal. Sound friendly and
natural. Business letters today are upbeat, simple, and direct. They are not
loaded down with expressions tarnished with age or rust. A business letter is
readable and believable; it should not be old-fashioned and flowery.

Often individuals are afraid to write because they fear that they will not
sound important. They resort to using phrases that remind them (and the

reader) of legalese—language that smells of contracts, deeds, and starched collars. The following list of words and phrases on the left contains musty expressions that have crept into letters for years; the list on the right contains modern equivalents.

Musty Expression	*Modern Equivalent*
aforementioned	previous
at this present writing	now
I am in receipt of	I have
attached herewith	enclosed
at your earliest possible date	soon
I beg to differ	I disagree
we beg to advise	we are certain that
I am cognizant of	I know
contents duly noted	we realize
forthwith	at once
hereafter, heretofore, hereby	(drop these three "h's" entirely)
humbly request	I ask
immediate future	soon
in lieu of	instead of
in reference to yours of the 10th	your letter of the 10th
kindly advise	let us know
please be advised that	you should know that
pending your reply	until I hear from you
per our conversation	when we spoke
prior to	before
we regret to inform you that	we are sorry that
remittance	payment
remuneration	cost, salary, pay
rest assured that	be confident that
same (as in "your letter arrived and I have same")	I have your letter
thanking you in advance	thank you
the undersigned / the writer	I
under separate cover	I'm also sending you
the wherewithal	the way
your humble servant	I look forward to helping you
yours of recent date	your recent letter
your communication	your phone call, your memo, your order, your conversation in my office

Figure 4.6 contains a flowery letter from Roger Hayes to his English teacher. Note how many old-fashioned, pompous expressions he uses. Figure 4.7 contains a modern translation of the same letter.

If you can be clear, concise, and contemporary, your letters will be well written and well received. These three C's will establish your reputation as a competent writer whose letters are easy to understand and easy to answer courteously and promptly.

Fig. 4.6   A flowery letter with stilted, old-fashioned language.

23 Babson Court
Chicago, IL 60648
May 1, 1982

Professor Bernard Jackson
Department of English
Harrison College
Chicago, IL 60649

Dear Professor Jackson:

Please accept my humblest apologies for being absent on the 25th when
your examination was in progress. As you requested at the commencement
of the term, I am cognizant of my responsibility to advise you about the
cause of my absence. Herewith is an explanation to that effect.

I am sorry to inform you that my automobile was impaired due to the fact
that one of the tires was punctured when I was on my way to your
classroom. Please be advised that I took every precaution to avoid this
puncture but the burden of travel made such attention on my part
ineffective. Lest you doubt my excuse, I herewith enclose a copy of my
indebtedness to a local repairman for road service. My situation was
such that I was forced to accompany him to his place of employment.
Accordingly, I thereby failed to attend your class.

The aforementioned disruption in my schedule will not occur again this
term. But I beg permission to take the examination in question at your
earliest possible convenience. Pending your reply, this writer will
diligently prepare for said examination.

At this present point in time, I wish to express my sincerest gratitude
to you and eagerly anticipate our future meeting.

Your dedicated student,

Roger Hayes

Roger Hayes

Encl.

Fig. 4.7   A clear and concise translation of Roger's letter.

23 Babson Court
Chicago, IL 60648
May 1, 1982

Professor Bernard Jackson
Department of English
Harrison College
Chicago, IL 60649

Dear Professor Jackson:

I am sorry that I missed your examination last Tuesday (April 25), but I
do have a valid excuse. On my way to class, I had a flat tire, and I had to
go with the mechanic when he repaired it. A copy of his bill is enclosed.

I would appreciate your letting me take a make-up examination, and I
will come to your office during your office hour on Monday to discuss
this with you.

Sincerely yours,

Roger Hayes

Roger Hayes

Encl.

► Twenty Questions Letter Writers Should Ask Themselves

Here is a checklist of twenty questions to ask yourself. They deal with the format, style, and content of your letter. If you can answer each one satisfactorily, you are off to a good start at communicating with your reader.

1. Does my letter look neat and professional?
2. Have I followed one typing model (either the full block or semiblock) consistently?
3. Are my margins wide enough—1½ inches all the way around?
4. Did I spell every word, including the reader's name, correctly?
5. Have I corrected every typographical error?
6. Did I tell the reader exactly why I am writing?
7. Have I begun each sentence with "I," or have I injected the "you attitude" into my letter?
8. Are my words clear and precise?
9. Is my letter free from flowery and stuffy language?
10. Do I get my message across politely?
11. Have I answered the reader's questions without including irrelevant material?
12. Have I eliminated unnecessary repetition?
13. Are all my figures—costs, policy numbers, model types, dates—correct?
14. Have I included all important information—dates, quantities, locations, names, costs, references to previous orders or letters?
15. Does my last paragraph sum up my letter appropriately?
16. Have I chosen an appropriate complimentary close?
17. Did I sign the letter?
18. Have I indicated an enclosure line if I am sending something with the letter?
19. Is my return address on the envelope?
20. Does the reader's name and address on the envelope match identically with the inside address?

► Exercises

1. What kind of letters do you receive addressed to you at home? At your work? Write a paragraph about one of these kinds of letters, indicating why it was sent to you and what it wanted you to do.

2. Find two business letters and identify the various parts of a letter discussed in this chapter.

3. Bring to class a letter following the full block format and one written in the semiblock style.

4. Find a letter that is addressed to "Dear Customer," "Postal Patron," or "Dear Homeowner" and rewrite this form letter making it more personal.

5. Correct the following inside addresses:

   (a) Dr. Ann Clarke, M.D.
       1730 East Jefferson
       Jackson, MI. 46759

   (b) To: Tommy Jones
       Secretary to Mrs. Franks
       Donlevey Labs
       Cleveland, O. 45362

   (c) Debbie Hinkle
       432 Parkway
       N.Y.C. 10054

   (d) Mr. Charles Howe, Chairman, Acme Pro.
       P.O. Box 675
       1234 S.e. Boulevard
       Gainesville, Flor. 32601

   (e) Alex Goings, man.
       Pittfield Industries
       Longview, TEXAS 76450

   (f) ATTENTION: G. Yancy
       Police Academy
       1329 Tucker
       N.O., La. 70122

   (g) David and Mahenny
       Lawyers
       Dobbs Build.
       L.A. 94756

6. Write appropriate inside addresses and salutations to (a) a woman who has not specified her marital status; (b) an officer in the armed forces; (c) a professor at your school; (d) an assistant manager at your local bank; (e) a member of the clergy; (f) your postmaster.

7. Which of the following complimentary closes is suitable for a business letter to someone you have never written to before and do not know?

Yours,	Cordially,
Gratefully yours,	Blissfully,
Sincerely,	Thankfully yours,
Faithfully,	Yours truly,

8. Find and correct the typographical errors in the following letter:

   Dear MR. Jones;

   I am very much enterested in finding a copy of your most recent brochure on nutrition. I am najoring in foodscience at Westgatte

Community Colledge and would appreicate obtainning some
infornation about your polcies and procedurs in the disrtibution
of hot lucnchs in teh elemantery grades. Your extenaive operatiom
in this area has been priased for its thoroghness.

If you have any copies of this borchure, or other instructons I
mihgt see, I would like to use them in my class repotrs. With yoor
permision, I would like to shafe these materials with my
homeeconomics calss.

Sincerly yours,

J. P. Allen

J. P. Allen

9. Rewrite the following sentences to make them more personal.
   (a) It becomes incumbent upon this office to cancel order #2394.
   (b) Management has suggested the curtailment of parking privileges.
   (c) ALL USERS OF HYDROPLEX: Desist from ordering replacement
       valves during the period Dec. 19–29.
   (d) The request for a new catalog has been honored; it will be shipped
       to same address soon.
   (e) Unless circumstances prevent operation, repair crews will report on
       schedule for thoroughfare maintenance.
   (f) Perseverance and attention to detail have made this writer important
       to company in-house work.
   (g) The Director of Nurses hereby notifies staff that a general meeting
       will be held Monday afternoon at 3:00 P.M. sharp. Attendance is
       mandatory.
   (h) Reports will be filed by appropriate personnel no later than the
       scheduled plans allow.
   (i) Company guidelines prevent awarding benefits to policy holder
       #2838y0.

10. The following sentences are discourteous, boastful, excessively humble,
    vague, or do not reflect the "you attitude." Rewrite them to correct these
    mistakes.
    (a) Something is obviously wrong in your head office. They have once
        more sent me the wrong model number. Can they ever get things
        straight?
    (b) My instructor wants me to do a term paper on safety regulations at
        a small factory. Since you are the manager of a small factory, send
        me all the information I need at once. My grade depends heavily on
        all this.
    (c) It is apparent that you are in business to rip off the public.
    (d) I was wondering if you could possibly see your way into sending me
        the local chapter president's name and address, if you have the time,
        that is.

(e) I have waited for my confirmation for two weeks now. Do you expect me to wait forever or can I get some action?

(f) Although I have never attempted to catalog books before, and really do not know my way around the library, I would very much like to be considered at some later date convenient to you for a part-time afternoon position.

(g) May I take just a moment of your valuable time to point out that our hours for the next three weeks will change and we trust and pray that no one in your agency will be terribly inconvenienced by this.

(h) Your application has been received and will be kept on file for six months. If we are interested in you, we will notify you. If you do not hear from us, please do not write us again. The soaring costs of correspondence and the large number of applicants make the burden of answering pointless letters extremely heavy.

(i) My past performance as a medical technologist has left nothing to be desired.

(j) Credit means a lot to some people. But obviously you do not care about yours. If you did, you would have sent us the $49.95 you rightfully owe us three months ago. What's wrong with you?

(k) The Sunnyside Police Force alerts all residents of the Parkway Heights section that parking violations have been noticed and cautions vehicle owners that these violations will be strictly enforced. If a vehicle is ticketed twice in a month period, said vehicle will be towed away. Vehicle owners will then have to reclaim their property at the police garage.

11. Rewrite the following letter to eliminate old-fashioned and stilted language.

Dear Mr. Wellington:

I am in receipt of yours of the 25th and thank you for same. Regarding your solicitation for information on our rocking chairs, model 542a, please be advised that under separate cover we are forwarding you a brochure with pertinent details for your perusal. For your information as well, I shall herewith quote the exact remittance necessary for each unit: $79.95. Shipping and handling payments should be remitted as well.

I eagerly await your reply and beg to advise you that quantities are indeed limited.

Thanking you in advance for your patronage.

Humbly yours,

J. alfred Stone

J. Alfred Stone

12. Write a business letter to one of the following individuals and submit an appropriate envelope with your letter:
    (a) Your mayor, asking for an appointment
    (b) Your college president, stressing the need for more parking spaces
    (c) The local water department, asking for information about fluoride
    (d) The editor of a weekly magazine, asking permission to reprint an article in a school newspaper
    (e) The author of an article you have read recently, telling why you like or dislike the views presented
    (f) The disc jockey at a local radio station, asking for more songs by a certain group.

5

How to Get a Job: Résumés, Letters, Applications, Interviews, and Evaluations

Obtaining a job today involves a lot of hard work. Before your name is added to the payroll, you will have to do more than simply walk into a personnel office and fill out an application form. Furthermore, finding the *right* job takes time. And finding the right person to fill that job also takes time for the employer. From the employer's viewpoint, the stages in the search for a valuable employee include the following:

1. Deciding on what duties and responsibilities go with the job and determining the qualifications the future employee should possess.
2. Advertising the job.
3. Reading and evaluating résumés and letters of application.
4. Having candidates complete application forms.
5. Requesting further proof of the candidates' skills—letters of recommendation, transcripts.
6. Interviewing selected candidates.
7. Offering the job to the best-qualified individual.

Sometimes these steps are interchangeable, especially steps 4 and 5, but generally speaking, employers go through a long and detailed process to select employees.

The job seeker will have to know how and when to give the employer all the kinds of information the steps above require. As a job seeker you will also have to follow a certain schedule in your search for a job. The following procedures will be required of you:

1. Analyzing your strengths and restricting your job search.
2. Preparing a dossier (placement file).
3. Looking in the right places for a job.
4. Constructing a résumé.

5. Writing a letter of application.
6. Filling out a job application.
7. Going to an interview.
8. Accepting or declining a job.

Your timetable should match that of your prospective employer.

Chapter 5 shows you how to begin your job search and how to prepare appropriate letters that are a part of the job-search process. You will have to write a letter of application, letters requesting others to write recommendations for you, letters thanking employers for interviews, and letters accepting or declining a position. In addition to discussing each of these kinds of letters, this chapter shows you how to assemble the supporting data—dossiers, résumés—that employers request. You will also find some practical advice on how to handle yourself at an interview. The chapter concludes with the kinds of evaluations—of self and others—that you can expect to write once you have worked on your job.

The eight steps of your job search are arranged in this chapter in the order in which you are most likely to proceed when you start looking for a job. By reading about these stages in sequence, you will have the benefit of going through a dry run of the employment process itself.

▶ Analyzing Your Strengths and Restricting Your Job Search

Individuals who advise students about how to get a job have isolated two "fatal assumptions" that job seekers hold. If you assume the following two points, chances are that you will not be very successful in your job search. These two assumptions are stated quite well by Lewis E. Patterson and Ernest M. Schuttenberg (*College Board Review*, Fall 1979, p. 15).

1. I should remain loose (vague) about what I want so I'm free to respond to any opportunity.
2. The employer has the upper hand in the whole process.

The first "fatal assumption" will disqualify you for any position for which your major has prepared you. Your first responsibility is to identify your professional qualifications. Employers want to hire individuals with highly developed, refined skills and training. Your education and experience will help you to identify and emphasize your marketable skills. Make an inventory of your accomplishments in your major and then decide which specialty within your chosen career appeals to you most. If you are enrolled in a criminal justice program, do you want to be a corrections officer, a security official, or a member of the local police force? If you are in a nursing program, do you want to work in a large hospital, a nursing home, a state health agency; what kinds of patients do you want to care for—geriatric, pediatric, psychiatric? If your major is foodscience, do you want to be a caterer or a restaurant owner, or would you rather work for an industrial or hospitality employer? Ask yourself, Where do I want to work and why?

Avoid applying for positions for which you are either overqualified or underqualified. If a position requires ten years of on-the-job experience and you are just starting out, you will only waste the employer's time by applying. On the other hand, if you have two or three years of experience in the food industry, for example, you would not apply for a position that calls for someone who has no training.

The second "fatal assumption"—assuming that the employer controls the entire job-search process—is equally misleading. To a large extent, you can determine whether you are a serious contender for a job by the letters you write and the self-image you present. Even in today's highly competitive job market, you can secure a suitable job if you keep in mind that the basic purpose of all job letters is to sell yourself. Employers almost always have a shortage of good, qualified employees.

▶ Preparing a Dossier

The job placement office (sometimes called the career center) at your school will assist you by providing counseling; notifying you of available, relevant jobs; and arranging on-campus interviews. The job placement office will also help you establish your dossier, sometimes referred to as your placement file.

The dossier, a French word for a bundle of documents, is your own personal file that is stored at the placement office. This file contains information about you that substantiates and supplements the facts you will list in your résumé and letter of application. Your dossier should contain your letters of recommendation; copies of these letters are made and sent out to prospective employers, thus relieving those who have recommended you of writing an original letter each time you apply for a job. You may also want to include unsolicited letters—those awarding you a scholarship, praising you as the employee of the month (or year), or honoring you for some community service. Be very selective about these kinds of letters; you do not want to crowd your dossier with less important items that will compete for attention with your academic recommendations. The dossier also contains biographical information, a listing of your job experiences, and your transcript(s). You may ask that your dossier be sent to an employer, or employers may request it themselves if you have listed the placement office address on your résumé.

The most important part of your dossier is the letter-of-recommendation section. Whom should you ask to recommend you? Your present or previous employer is a logical choice, but be cautious here. If your employer knows that your education is preparing you for another profession, or if you are working at a part-time job while you are in school, you should obtain a letter of recommendation to be included in your dossier. If you are happily and successfully employed and are looking for a new position only for advancement or better salary, you may not want to tell your present employer you are searching for a new job. If another employer is interested in you, you have the right to request the prospective employer to respect your confidence until you become an active (and also a leading) candidate. At that point you should be happy to have your current employer consulted for a reference. On the other hand, if you are at loggerheads with your current employer and want very much to find a new, more suitable position, you need to prepare the prospective employer as honestly and professionally as you can with the least damage to yourself. No sure solution exists.

By all means ask two or three of your professors to be references. Choose teachers who know your work, have graded your papers, and have supervised you in field work or laboratory activities. Superiors who knew your work in the military are also likely candidates. Never include a letter from a member of the clergy or your family or from a neighbor. Objectivity is lost here.

Make sure that you ask permission of these individuals before you list them as references. Not only is this a courtesy, but also it will then give them time to write an appropriate letter for you. In a letter or in person, stress how much a strong letter of support means to you and find out if they are willing to write such a letter. It is important to stress that you need a strong letter of recommendation; a general or weak one will hurt your chances in your job search. As a help to your references, tell them what kind of jobs you are applying for and keep them up to date about your educational and occupational achievements. Figure 5.1 shows a sample letter requesting an individual to serve as a reference.

You have a legal right to see these letters of recommendation. But if you have read your recommendations, that fact is noted on the dossier. Some employers feel that if the candidates see what is written about them, the writers of the letters of recommendation will be less frank and unwilling to volunteer critical information. If you waive your right to see the letters written about you, you must sign an appropriate form, a copy of which is then given to the individual recommending you. Keep in mind, too, that some individuals may refuse to write a letter that they know you will see; they may prefer absolute confidentiality. Fig. 5.2 shows a confidential evaluation form. Before you make any decision about seeing your letters, get the advice of your instructors and your placement counselor.

Do not wait to establish your dossier until you begin applying for jobs. Most placement offices recommend that candidates set up their dossiers at least three to six months before they begin looking for jobs. Thus you will ensure that your letters of recommendation are on file and that you have benefited from the placement office's services. In counseling you, the placement office will ask that you complete a confidential questionnaire about your geographic preferences, salary expectations, and the types of positions for

Fig. 5.1 Request for a letter of recommendation.

5432 South Kenneth Avenue
Chicago, IL 60651
March 30, 1982

Mr. Sunny Butler
Manager, A&P Supermarket
4000 West 79th Street
Chicago, IL 60652

Dear Mr. Butler:

As you may recall, I was employed at your store from September 1980 through August 1981. During the school year, I worked part time as a stock boy and relief cashier, while in the summer months I was a full-time employee in the produce department, helping to fill in while Bill Dirksen and Vivian Rogers were away on their vacations.

I enjoyed my work at A&P, and I learned a great deal about ordering stock, arranging merchandise, and assisting customers.

This May I expect to receive my A.A. degree from Moraine Valley Community College in retail merchandising. I have already begun preparing for my job search for a position in retail sales. Would you be kind enough to write a letter of recommendation for me in which you mention what you regard as my greatest strengths as one of your employees? If you agree, I will send you a letter of recommendation form from the Placement Office at Moraine Valley. Your letter will then become a part of my permanent placement file.

I look forward to hearing from you. I thought you might like to see the enclosed résumé, which shows what I have been doing since I left A&P.

Sincerely yours,

Robert B. Jackson

Robert B. Jackson

Encl. Résumé

Fig. 5.2   A letter-of-recommendation form.

Return this form to:

**OFFICE OF CAREER DEVELOPMENT & PLACEMENT
VALDOSTA STATE COLLEGE**
Valdosta, Georgia 31601

CONFIDENTIAL EVALUATION

TO THE CANDIDATE: (type in)

Candidate's   Name of
Full Name_____ Reference_____
　　　　first　　　middle　　　last
Courses under this instructor (title, quarter, year) or Period of employment_____

_____

Today's date_____ Your (anticipated) date of graduation_____ Degree program_____

TO THE TEACHER OR EMPLOYER:

Please note that this is a confidential evaluation. The candidate has waived his or her right of access to this evaluation. We shall appreciate both a rating and a statement regarding the candidate's suitability for employment. Your evaluation will become a permanent part of his or her placement record which is made available to employers and graduate schools. *Do not show it to the candidate.* Also, *please type* this form if possible. Blue ink does not duplicate clearly. Once this form is on file you may refer future requests concerning this candidate to the Career Development & Placement Office for a reply.

Indicate degree of acquaintance with candidate:

Length of acquaintance:_____

☐ Know personally

☐ Know as a student

☐ Know only as a member of a large class

☐ Know as an employee

	Unable to Observe	Excellent	Above Average	Average	Below Average	Poor
Appearance						
Academic Performance (within subject (s) under your supervision)						
Promptness in assignments; regularity of attendance						
Ability to communicate: Orally						
In Writing						
Initiative						
Leadership						
Social qualities (congeniality, interest in others)						
Promise in _____(specify field)						
Suitability for graduate school						

STATEMENT: (Please elaborate on the above and comment on any other appropriate points. This statement is considered an important part of the total evaluation.)

Signature_____

Title & Dept._____

Institution or Organization_____

Date:_____   Address_____

Reprinted by permission of Office of Career Development and Placement, Valdosta (Georgia) State College.

which you are qualified. With this information on hand, the placement office will be better prepared to assist you.

Some placement offices will charge a nominal fee for their services, while others provide their services free of charge.

▶ Looking in the Right Places for a Job

One way to search for a job is to simply send out a batch of letters to companies you want to work for. But how do you know what jobs, if any, these companies have available, what qualifications they are looking for, and what application procedures and deadlines they want you to follow? Avoid these uncertainties by knowing where to look for a job and knowing what a specific job requires. Such information will make your search easier and, in all likelihood, more successful. Here are a number of sources to consult:

1. Do not overlook the obvious—the newspaper. Look at local newspapers as well as papers with a wide circulation: the *New York Times*, the *Chicago Tribune*, the *Los Angeles Times*, the *New Orleans Times–Picayune*, the *Cleveland Plain Dealer*. The Sunday editions advertise positions available all over the country. The ads you find may list the name, address, and phone number of the company seeking employees or may be blind, that is, listing only a post office box to conceal the employer's identity.
2. Investigate openings listed in professional journals in your major. The *American Journal of Nursing*, for example, carries notices of openings arranged by geographic location in each of its monthly issues.
3. Visit your college's placement office. Counselors keep an up-to-date file of available positions and can also tell you when a firm's recruiter will be on campus to conduct interviews. They can also help you locate summer and part-time work, both on and off campus.
4. Check with your state and local employment offices. They also have a current file of positions and offer some counseling (free of charge). Some educational television stations even broadcast information (qualifications, salary) about positions on file at a state employment office. If you are interested in working for the U.S. government, visit a Civil Service Commission Office, a Federal Job Information Center, or any government agency. Get the addresses from the white pages of your phone book.
5. Visit the personnel department of a company or agency to see if there are any current openings or if any vacancies are anticipated. Often you will be given an application to fill out, or your name will be placed on a list.
6. Let your friends, neighbors, and professors know that you are looking for a job. They may hear of something and can notify you. Better yet, they may recommend you for the position—with a phone call, a trip to the personnel department (if they also work for the company), or a letter.

A respected employee can open the door for you. John D. Erdlen and Donald H. Sweet, experts on the job search, cite the following as a primary rule of job hunting: "Don't do anything yourself you can get someone with influence to do for you."

7. Write to the Chamber of Commerce. Although not a placement center, the Chamber of Commerce can give you the names and addresses of employers likely to hire individuals with your qualifications, as well as information about these companies to use in a letter of application or at an interview.

8. Register with a professional employment agency. Some agencies list two kinds of jobs—those that are found for the applicant free of charge (the employer pays the fee) and those for which the applicant pays a fee. Sometimes that fee can be stiff—for example, a percentage of your annual salary. Employment agencies often find out about jobs through channels already available to you. Before turning your search over to a professional employment agency, however, make sure that you have exhausted all the previously mentioned services.

► Preparing a Résumé

The résumé, sometimes called a data sheet or vita, is a factual and concise summary of your qualifications for the job. It is not your life's history or an emotional autobiography; nor is it a transcript of your college work. The résumé is a one- (no more than two-) page outline accompanying your letter of application for a job. Résumés are never sent alone. You may, however, bring one with you to an interview. The main function of the résumé is to present your qualifications accurately and quickly so that a busy personnel manager or department head will want to interview you. The résumé should make a good first impression.

What You Exclude from a Résumé

Preparing a résumé involves skills highly valued in any job—neatness; the ability to organize, summarize, and persuade; and most important, a sense of proportion. Knowing what to exclude from a résumé is as important as what to include. Here is information to exclude from your résumé:

1. Salary demands or expectations
2. Preferences for work schedules, days off, or overtime
3. Comments about fringe benefits
4. Travel restrictions
5. Your photograph
6. Any handicaps you may have
7. Comments about your family, spouse, or children
8. Your sex, race, religion, ethnic background

Each of these is irrelevant or—numbers 5, 6, 7, and 8—illegal. Save any questions or preferences you have for the interview. The résumé should be written appropriately to get you that interview.

What You Include in a Résumé

What should you include on your résumé? Both experienced candidates and recent graduates with limited experience ask this question. The dangers involve including too much or putting in too little. If you have years of experience and have recently returned to school, you may risk flooding your prospective employer with too many details. You cannot possibly include every detail of your job(s) for the last ten or twenty years. Therefore, you must be selective and emphasize those skills and positions most likely to earn you the job. Figure 5.3 shows a résumé from an individual who had years of job experience before she returned to school.

Many job candidates who have spent most of their lives in school are faced with the other extreme—not having much job experience to put down. The worst thing to do is to write "none" for experience. Even part-time or summer jobs or work done at school for a library, science laboratory, or for buildings and grounds shows a prospective employer you are responsible and knowledgeable about the obligations of being an employee. Figure 5.4 shows a résumé from a student with very little job experience; Fig. 5.5 shows one from a student with a few years of experience.

Parts of a Résumé

Name, Address, Phone

Center this information at the top of the résumé. Capitalize all the letters of your name to make it stand out. But do not capitalize every letter of your address. Include a zip code and telephone number with a proper area code so a prospective employer can call you for an interview. If you live in a dormitory, it is wise to list both your home and school addresses. (It is perfectly acceptable to list two phone numbers if one of them is where you receive messages during the day and the other in the evening.)

Career Objective Statement

The first step in the job process is to prepare a career objective statement. Such a statement involves self-evaluation and will influence everything else you list. You should ask yourself four basic questions: (1) What kind of job do I want? (2) What kind of job am I qualified for? (3) What kinds of skills do I possess? and (4) What kinds of skills do I want to learn? Do not apply for a position that requires years of experience you lack or demands skills you do not possess. On the other hand, do not give the impression that you will take anything. Define your job goal precisely so that prospective employers can measure your experience and education against their needs. Do not simply

Fig. 5.3   Résumé from individual with ten years' job experience.

RÉSUMÉ

ANNA C. CASSETTI

6457 South Blackstone

Ft. Worth, Texas 76119

817–234–5657 (Home)
817–432–7211 (Office)

CAREER OBJECTIVE: Full–time sales position with large real estate office in the Phoenix or Tucson area with specific opportunities in real estate appraisals and tax counseling.

EXPERIENCE:

1981–present — Real estate agent, MacMurray Real Estate, Haltom City, Texas; working in small office (two salespersons plus broker) with limited listings, sold individually $550,000 in residential property and appraised both residential and commercial listings.

1975–1980 — Teller, Dallman Federal Savings and Loan, Inc., Ft. Worth. Responsible for supervising, training, and coordinating activities of six full–time tellers and two part–time ones. Promoted to Chief Teller, March 1978.

1975 (Jan. – May) — Tax consultant, H&R Block, Westover Hills, Texas, office.

1972–1973 — Salesperson, Cruckshank's Hardware Store, 7542 Montrose Drive, Ft. Worth.

1968–1972 — U.S. Navy, honorably discharged with rank of Petty Officer, Third Class. Served as stores manager.

EDUCATION:

1974–1980 — Awarded B.S. degree in real estate management from Texas Christian University, Ft. Worth. Completed thirty–three hours in business and real estate courses with a concentration in real estate finance, appraising, and property management. Wrote a pamphlet on appraisal procedures as part of supervised training program in my last term.

1973 (Sept. – Dec.) — Diploma in Basic Income Tax Preparation earned after completing intensive ten–week course offered through H&R Block's Ft. Worth office (Westover Hills, Texas).

Fig. 5.3 (continued)

84–85 Eastern H.S.
85–86 BSU Tipp. Valley
86 – Present

Anna C. Cassetti, page 2

Education 1980 ND
Summer 1985–1986 B.SU
1985–1980–1983 TU

1969–1970   Attended U.S. Navy's Supply Management School, U.S. Naval Base, San Diego, California. Applied principles of stores management at Newport Naval Base.

Work Related Activities
Summer 1992–1993
Summer Park Program

PERSONAL: Social Security Number: 329-35-9465
     Texas Realtor's License: 756a2737

Feb 1992 – present church youth

HOBBIES   Member, Financial Committee, Grace Presbyterian
  AND   Church, Ft. Worth. Have also worked with Junior
INTERESTS: Achievement advising teenagers in business management. Enjoy golfing.

Summer 1993
Purdue calculus Project

REFERENCES:

My complete dossier is available from the Texas Christian University College Placement Office, Ft. Worth, Texas 76119. In it are letters from the following individuals:

Dr. Peter Murcheson
Department of Business
Texas Christian University
Ft. Worth, TX 76119
817-266-1003

Mrs. Patricia Albertson
Controller
Dallman Federal Savings and Loan
7858 South Broadway
Ft. Worth, TX 76109
817-266-7301

Mrs. Gladys Mates
Vice-President
Dallman Federal Savings and Loan
7858 South Broadway
Ft. Worth, TX 76109
817-266-7301

Mr. Pat MacMurray
Broker, MacMurray Real Estate
1732 Main Street
Haltom City, TX 77832
817-993-4201

Fig. 5.4 **Résumé from student with little job experience.**

RÉSUMÉ

ANTHONY H. JONES

73 Allenwood Boulevard

Santa Rosa, California 95401

707–464–6390

CAREER OBJECTIVE: Full–time position as a layout/paste–up artist with commercial publishing house.

EDUCATION:

1978–1980   Will receive A.S. degree in June from Santa Rosa Junior College, majoring in industrial graphics illustration with a specialty in layout design. Completed more than forty hours in design principles, layout and lettering, graphic communications, and photography. Am very familiar with both layout techniques and electromechanical illustration. Major projects included assisting layout editors at McAdam Publishers during an apprenticeship program completed in May 1980 and writing a detailed report on the kinds of designs, photographs, and art work used in two local magazines–<u>Living in Sonoma County</u> and <u>Real Estate in Sonoma County</u>. Made Dean's List in 1980 with a GPA of 3.4.

1974–1978   Attended Santa Rosa High School. Took electives in drawing, photography, and industrial arts. Did art work for student magazine, <u>Thunder</u>.

EXPERIENCE:

1979–1980   Part–time salesperson at Buchman's Department Store while attending Santa Rosa Junior College full time. Duties included assisting customers in sporting goods and appliance departments. Also assisted Sport Shop manager with displaying merchandise.

PERSONAL: Age 21   Height 5'8"   Weight 147 lbs

REFERENCES:

Mr. Albert Kim
Art Department
Santa Rosa Junior College
Santa Rosa, California 95401
(707) 464–6300

Ms. Margaret Feinstein
Layout Editor
McAdam Publishers
Santa Rosa, California 95410
(707) 453–8699

little experience

Fig. 5.5   Résumé from student with some job experience.

RÉSUMÉ

MARIA H. LOPEZ

1725 Brooke Street

Miami, Florida 32701

305-372-3429

CAREER OBJECTIVE: Full-time position assisting dentist in providing dental health care and counseling and performing preventive dental treatments; especially interested in learning more about pedodontics.

EDUCATION:

August 1979–
June 1981

Will receive A.S. degree in dental hygiene from Miami–Dade Community College in May. Have completed nine courses in oral pathology, dental materials and specialties, peridontology, and community dental health. Currently enrolled in clinical dental hygiene program. Am familiar with procedures and instruments used with oral prophylaxis techniques. Subject of major project was on proper nutrition for preschoolers. Minor area of interest is psychology (twelve hours completed). GPA is 3.2. Expect to take the American Dental Assistants' Examination on June 2.

1972–1976

Miami North High School. Took electives in electronics and secretarial science.

EXPERIENCE:

April 1977–
July 1979

Full-time ward clerk on the pediatrics unit at St. Francis Hospital (Miami Beach). Duties included ordering supplies, maintaining records, transcribing orders, and greeting and assisting visitors.

June 1976–
April 1977

Secretary–receptionist, Murphy Construction Company, 1203 Francis, Miami; did light typing, filing, and mailing in small office (three secretaries).

Summers
1974–1975

Water Meter Reader, City of Hialeah, Florida.

PERSONAL:

Health: Excellent   Bilingual (Spanish/English)

HOBBIES
AND
INTERESTS:

Swimming, reading (especially in applied psychology), and tennis. Have done volunteer work for church day–care center.

Fig. 5.5 (continued)

Maria H. Lopez, page 2

REFERENCES:

The following individuals have written letters of recommendation for me. Their letters are in my placement file, which is available from the Placement Center, Miami-Dade Community College, Medical Center Campus, Miami, FL 33127.

Sister Mary James
Head Nurse, Pediatric Unit
St. Francis Hospital
10003 Collins Avenue
Miami Beach, FL 33141
305-432-5113

Professor Mitchell Pellborne
Department of Dental Hygiene
Miami-Dade Community College
Medical Center
Miami, FL 33127
305-421-3872

Mildred Pecos, D.D.S.
9800 Exchange Avenue
Miami, FL 33167
305-421-1039

Mr. Jack Murphy
Owner, Murphy Construction
1203 Francis Street
Miami, FL 33157
305-421-6767

say "sales work" or "law enforcement." Instead, concentrate on specific immediate and long-range goals within your chosen career. For example: "Full-time position with urban police force eventually allowing me to gain experience in correctional counseling"; "Management trainee in personnel department providing opportunity for professional growth and advancement in insurance counseling"; "Full-time position as staff nurse on medical-surgical unit with opportunity for team nursing"; "Receptionist position in attorney's office answering phones, taking messages, and greeting clients." Demonstrate to your prospective employer your current level of competence and show, through a statement of objective, your willingness to advance in the organization. The order of these next two categories—education and experience—can vary. If experience is your best selling point, list it before education, as in Fig. 5.3. List education first if you are short on job experience, as in Fig. 5.4.

Education

In listing your educational experiences, begin with your most recent education, and list everything significant since high school. Indicate when you received your latest degree, diploma, or certificate or when you expect to receive it. You need not list every school if you have transferred frequently. Do indicate your major and minor in college work, but remember, a résumé is not a transcript. Do not simply list a series of courses. Your goal is to convince your prospective employer that you have special abilities. Simply listing standard courses will not set you apart from hundreds of other applicants taking similar courses across the country. Mention the number of credit hours you have completed and then indicate by title or subject area the most relevant courses in your major.

Try to avoid vague titles such as Science I or Nursing IV. Instead, concentrate on the kinds of skills you learned. For example, "took 30 hours in planning and development courses specializing in transportation and land use and community facilities and in field methods where gathering, interpreting, and writing survey data were required." Or state that "24 hours in my major included courses in business marketing, management, and materials in addition to 12 hours in business law." Also note any laboratory, field work, internship, or cooperative educational experiences. They are important to an employer looking for someone with previous practical experience. List your GPA (grade point average) only if it is 3.0 or above and your rank in class only if you are in the top 35 percent. Otherwise, indicate your GPA in just your major or during your last term, if it is above 3.0.

Also list any academic honors you have won (dean's list, department awards, school honors, scholarships, grants, or honorable mentions). Indicate membership in any honor societies in your major, because such participation will show that you are professionally active. You also should mention military schools, institutes or special workshops, or company-sponsored seminars you have attended. If you have attended many of these kinds of learning programs, do not list your high school. Applicants with limited educational experience may include their high school, the date of graduation, and, if helpful, any special training related to their current work (shops, labs, trips) and any honors. As a rule, though, high school activities should be deemphasized.

Experience

This is the most important category for many employers. It shows them that you have held jobs before and that you are responsible. Beginning with your most recent position, include both full- and part-time work, and list the dates, company name, titles you held, and major responsibilities. Do not mention why you left a job. Give the most attention to your latest, most relevant position. If it happens to be your second position, keep the correct order, but spend more time on it. Do not discuss jobs that you held eight or nine years ago; either just list the places of employment or do not mention them at all.

In describing your position, emphasize any responsibility you had that involved handling money, other employees, or customer accounts, services, or programs. Prospective employers are interested in your leadership abilities, financial shrewdness, and tact in dealing with the public. They are also favorably impressed by promotions you may have earned. Use strong, active language to pinpoint your duties (*managed, supervised, organized, directed, trained, arranged, handled, maintained, calculated, operated, prepared, wrote, performed*). Don't just say you worked for a newspaper—your prospective employer will not know if you wrote editorials, took ads, or delivered papers. Perhaps you were an assistant to the ads editor and were responsible for arranging and verifying copy. Say so. That sounds impressive. Rather than saying that you were a secretary, indicate that you wrote business letters, organized files, prepared schedules for part-time help in a large office (twenty-five people), or assisted the manager in preparing accounts. Of course, do not inflate your role to the point of calling a receptionist a "communications consultant" or a waitress a "foodservice manager."

If you have held many jobs, which ones should you list, and which ones should you omit? As a general rule, indicate whatever positions are most relevant for the job you are seeking. Your summer job as a lifeguard who knew life-saving techniques may help you in getting a position as a respiratory therapist. Waiting on tables is good experience for candidates who want to obtain a position with a hospitality chain or a foodservice organization. Do not forget jobs you may have had at school—stacking books in the library, typing for a teacher, cleaning buildings, tutoring. Employers are not impressed by babysitting or lawn-mowing jobs, however, unless you can relate those duties to your present search.

If you have had several jobs in the last ten or twenty years, list only those in which your responsibilities were significant and relevant to your present search for a job. Avoid stringing out five or six temporary jobs (each under three months). Combine all of them into one brief statement or omit them. Remember, space is at a premium in your résumé. If you have been a housewife for ten years and reared three children before you returned to school or the job market, list these factors and note why you are reentering the business world. Indicate the management skills you developed in running a household.

Personal (Optional)

Federal employment laws prohibit discrimination on the basis of sex, race, national origin, age, or religion, so you should omit references to these subjects. (Of course, some employers in following the guidelines of affirmative action ask minority candidates to identify themselves.) You will have to determine whether listing such personal details as height, weight, health, or marital status will enhance your prospects for a job. The trick is to know your would-be employer and to profit from that employer's preferences. For example, if you are applying for a sales position requiring extensive travel, your putting down that you are single would inform the employer that you do not have family obligations to worry about. Moreover, if you are applying for a position in a child day-care center or one as a teacher's aide, the fact that you have children may be important to your employer. Other pertinent personal details include any foreign languages you speak or any special licenses and certificates you hold. For example, if you are bilingual in Spanish, Vietnamese, or French and are applying for a position in customer relations work, list that fact. It will be a drawing card for your employer. If you have already passed nursing state boards or have a pilot's license, state that by indicating your appropriate license numbers. Ultimately, common sense dictates that you reveal only personal information that is required or that underscores your qualifications for the job.

Hobbies or Interests (Optional)

This category is of least value to a prospective employer, *if there is no connection between it and the rest of your résumé.* Of course, if a pastime, sport, or hobby has a direct bearing on the kind of job you are applying for or the kinds of subjects you studied in school, then by all means list and briefly describe it. For example, the following activities may be appropriate for careers listed after them: weight lifting for construction work; photography for advertising; volunteer work for nursing or social work; travel for the hospitality industry; gardening for a horticultural position; civic work for law enforcement.

References

You can inform readers of your résumé that you will provide references on request or that they can obtain a copy of your dossier from your placement center; or you can list the names, titles, addresses, and telephone numbers of three or four individuals directly on your résumé. Prospective employers can then write to you, ask for your dossier, or directly write or call the individuals whose names have been given. Listing the names of your references is useful only when they are well known or belong to the same profession in which you are seeking employment. In these cases you profit from the magic a recognizable name or title gives you.

Typing Your Résumé

Employers look for three virtues in a résumé: (1) eye appeal, (2) correctness, and (3) consistency. If a résumé is carefully prepared, employers will predict that the work you do for them will be done the same way. A résumé can make that first good impression for you; a poorly prepared résumé assures you that you will not get a second chance.

Your résumé should be typed on good-quality 8½″ × 11″ white bond paper. Avoid exotic colors. Use only one side of the paper. If you have a lot of experience to condense, consider using a photocopy reducer that allows you to put a great deal of information on a large sheet and then reduces the size of that sheet. Avoid the twin dangers of crowding information all over the page or of leaving huge, highly conspicuous chunks of white space at the bottom and sides. A crowded résumé suggests that you cannot summarize; a résumé with too many blank spaces points to a lack of achievements. You should have white space between categories and for margins to emphasize certain points and to make reading your résumé easier. Study Figs. 5.3, 5.4, and 5.5 again. Type a number of rough drafts to experiment with spacing. Better yet, hire a professional typist and explain how you want your résumé to look.

Unlike your letter of application, the résumé is not retyped for each job you apply for. Your prospective employers will not expect an original copy, but they do expect a professional-looking copy. Never send a carbon, mimeographed, or thermafax copy. Rather than photocopying your résumé, use the services of a professional printer, who for a relatively modest fee will phototypeset your résumé, giving it a highly professional look.

Because you are supplying a copy of your résumé, a single error in it would appear each time you sent it out. Therefore, proofread your résumé to make sure it is letter-perfect. Figure 5.6 contains a poorly prepared résumé and reasons why it is bad. Figure 5.7 shows a résumé evaluation form used by six experts from business, industry, and education who judged student résumés done for a workshop at the University of Colorado, Boulder. After you complete your résumé, evaluate it according to the ten criteria on the form.

▶ Writing a Letter of Application

Together with your résumé, you send your prospective employer a letter of application, one of the most important pieces of correspondence you may ever write. Its goal is to get you an interview and ultimately the job. Letters

Fig. 5.6 A poor résumé.

RÉSUMÉ

JAMES L. McPHERSON
33 North Platte Road *Poor alignment*
Noland, New Mexico *No zip code*
No telephone number

Spelling
PERSONNEL

Age: 22yrs. 5 mos. *Spelling* Wieght: 156 lbs
Not needed { Marital Status: Engaged   Height: 5'10 *Abbreviation*
Religion: Presbyterian   Health: O.K. *Slang*

CAREER OBJECTIVE: I like to work outdoors and
Poor Typing   want to get any suitable job *Too broad*
in the forrestry industry.

Spelling
EDUCATION:

1977–1980   Attended Noland Junior College,
Noland, N.M. 84546. I took courses
Listing courses at random in English, Outdoor Recreation,
says nothing about specific Forrest Surveying, Forrest *Spelling*
skills   Management, Forest Economics,
Park Administration, Human
Spelling Rolations, Recreation
Margin   Maintenance, Communication, and
Mathematics, and Science. I did
better my secondyear than my *Typing*
first. In my English and
Communications courses I wrote papers and
Spelling delivered sppeeches about
the forrest. Also, I went on *Margin*
two or three lengthy field trips in
the north. *What skills did he learn?*

1977   I attended Noland Junior College
part time *Why a separate entry?*

Hyphen
1976   I graduated from Noland High *missing*
School where I played basket-
ball my third year and fourth year.
I also was the team co-captain.
Vague phrase Helped out with The Torch.
What is it?

Fig. 5.6 **(continued)**

Underscore	EXPERIENCE:	
	1976–1977 *Doing what?*	Worked for Walgreen's. Address: 754 South Loma Blvd. Also I joined
	Abbreviation	the (N. Mexico) National Guard. We were sent to Ft. Carson for our basic training. *Why mention Ft. Carson? What does he do in the Guard?*
Capitalize	Hobbies:	I like swimming, jogging, and water polo.

REFERENCES:

Mr. Henry R. Pepeer	Dr. John Lyons	Alice McPherson
P.O. Box 768	Noland Junior College	33 N. Platte
Noland, N.M.	Noland, N.M.	Noland, N.M.
What relationship to McPherson?	*What department?*	*Relative is not an impartial reference*

you write in applying for jobs should be personable, professional, and persuasive—the three P's, something to remember. Knowing how the letter of application and résumé work together and how they differ can give you a better idea of how to begin your letter.

How the Letter and Résumé Differ

The résumé is a compilation of facts—a record of dates, important courses, names, places, addresses, and jobs. You will have your résumé duplicated, and you will send a copy to each prospective employer. Your letter of application, however, is much more personal. You must write a new, original letter to each prospective employer. Photocopied letters of application say that you did not care enough, that you did not want to spend the time and energy to answer the employer's ad personally. Whereas your résumé is intended for all readers, each letter of application should be tailored to a specific job It should respond precisely to the kinds of qualifications the employer seeks. The letter of application is a sales letter emphasizing and applying the most relevant details (of education, experience, and talents) on your résumé. In short, the résumé contains the raw material that the letter of application transforms into a finished and highly marketable product—you!

Fig. 5.7   Evaluating a résumé.

	not on résumé				
1. Clarity of job objective	☐	very unclear			extremely clear
		1	2 3 4		5

1. Clarity of job objective

not on résumé ☐

very unclear — extremely clear

1   2   3   4   5

2. Essence of educational information

not on résumé ☐

too much or too little information — extremely concise and informative

1   2   3   4   5

3. Description of job experience with skills emphasis

not on résumé ☐

poor description of skills — excellent description of skills

1   2   3   4   5

4. Additional positive information that supports job objective

not on résumé ☐

irrelevant additional information — very supportive additional information

1   2   3   4   5

5. Correctness of typing, spelling, and grammar

poorly written and typed — well written and typed

1   2   3   4   5

6. Organization

poorly organized — extremely well organized

1   2   3   4   5

7. Ease of reading (layout)

very difficult to read — very easy to read

1   2   3   4   5

8. Quality of reproduction (paper, print)

poor quality — excellent quality

1   2   3   4   5

9. Attractiveness

not attractive — very attractive

1   2   3   4   5

10. Overall rating

poor résumé — excellent résumé

1   2   3   4   5

Journal of Employment Counseling, 16, (September 1979):156. Copyright 1979 American Personnel and Guidance Association. Reprinted with permission.

Résumé Facts You Exclude from a Letter of Application

The letter of application does not simply repeat the details listed in your résumé. In fact, the following details belong only on your résumé and should not be restated in the letter: (1) personal data about height, weight, and license or certificate numbers, (2) the names of all your courses in your major, (3) your hobbies, and (4) the names and addresses of your references. Duplicating these details in your letter gives no new information to help persuade prospective employers that you are the individual they are seeking.

Finding Information About Your Prospective Employer

One of the best ways to sell yourself to future employers is to demonstrate that you have some knowledge of their company. A number of years ago, a college was looking for an instructor and was pleased with one candidate who referred to the college's specific courses by their numbers in her letter of application. This individual went to the profitable trouble of reading the college's catalog before applying. Do a little similar homework; investigate the job and the company. You can sometimes obtain information from the company itself by writing for brochures, descriptions, and schedules a number of months before you actually apply. Check with the Chamber of Commerce. Ask people who work in the company. Except in response to a blind ad, write directly to the individual responsible for hiring—the personnel officer, the supervisor, the director of nurses, the district manager. You can call the company and ask the switchboard operator to give you the name of this individual.

How Application Letters Are Written

The letter of application should be typed neatly on a plain white sheet of good bond paper, 8½″ × 11″. Make sure that your typewriter works perfectly and that the type does not appear faded. Proofread meticulously; a spelling error here will harm your chances. Avoid abbreviations ("thru" for "through," "nite" for "night") and slang expressions. Don't forget the "you attitude." Employers are not impressed by boastful proclamations ("I am the most efficient and effective repairman," "I am a natural-born nurse"). One student wrote that he needed the job to pay tuition and repay a car loan. The employer was not impressed. Another applicant spent so much time on advantages to her that she forgot the employer entirely: "I have worked with this kind of equipment before, and this experience will give me the edge in running it. Moreover, I can more quickly adjust to my working environment."

The best letters of application are to the point and are readable. Keep in mind that employers will receive many letters and that yours will have to compete for their time. Don't waste it. A letter of application should not exceed one page; it is to your advantage to make it shorter. On the other hand, you should not write a telegraphic message—two or three sentences. But you should strive for brevity and clarity. Emphasize your qualifications; don't let them get lost in a sea of words. A three-paragraph letter will be sufficient for most candidates. Figure 5.8 contains a model letter—Maria Lopez's application for a job. Compare her letter with her résumé (Fig. 5.5). Then compare her letter with the letter in Fig. 5.9, written by Anthony Jones, who has no

Fig. 5.8   Letter of application from student with some job experience.

1725 Brooke Street
Miami, FL 32701
May 14, 1981

Dr. Marvin Hendrady
Suite 34
Medical/Dental Plaza
839 Causeway Drive
Miami, FL, 32701

Dear Dr. Hendrady:

Mr. Mitchell Pellborne, my clinical instructor at Miami—Dade Community
College, informs me that you are looking for a dental hygienist to work
in your northside office. I am writing to apply for that position. Next
month, I will graduate with an A.S. degree in the dental hygienist
program at Miami—Dade Community College, and I will take the American
Dental Assistants' Examination in early June. I could begin work any
time after June 15.

I have successfully completed all course work and clinical programs in
oral hygiene, anatomy, and prophylaxis techniques. During my clinical
training, I received intensive practical instruction from a number of
local dentists, including Dr. Mildred Pecos. Since your northside
office specializes in pedodental care, you might find the subject of my
major project—proper nutrition for preschoolers—especially relevant. I
have also had some related job experience in working with children in a
health care setting. For a year and a half, I was employed as a ward clerk
on the pediatric unit at St. Francis Hospital, and my experience in
greeting patients, filling out forms, and assisting the nursing staff
would be useful to you. I enclose a résumé containing more detailed
information about me and my experience.

I would welcome the opportunity talk with you about the position and my
interest in pedodontics. I am available for an interview any time after
2:30 until June 13. After that date, I could come to your office any time
at your convenience.

Sincerely yours,

Maria H. Lopez

Maria H. Lopez

Encl. Résumé

Fig. 5.9   Letter of application from student with little job experience.

my address 1717 North Tyland

73 Allenwood Boulevard
Santa Rosa, CA 95401
May 25, 1980

Ms. Jocelyn Nogasaki
Personnel Manager
Megalith Publishing Company
1001 Heathcliff Row
San Francisco, CA 94123

Dear Ms. Nogasaki:

I am writing to apply for the layout editor position you advertised in
the May 25 edition of the San Francisco Chronicle. Early next month, I
will receive an A.S. degree in industrial graphics illustration from
Santa Rosa Junior College and will be available to start work the week of
June 15.

I have successfully completed more than forty credit hours in courses
directly related to layout design. In these courses, I have acquired
skills in draftsmanship, reproduction processes, and production
techniques. You might like to know that many of the design patterns of
Megalith publications were used as models in my graphic communications
and photographic technology classes. My studies have also led to
practical experience at McAdam Publishers, as part of my Santa Rosa
apprenticeship program. Working at McAdam's, I was responsible for
assisting the design department in photo research and in the preparation
of mockups. Other related experience I have had includes artwork and
proofreading for the student magazine, Thunder. As you will note on the
enclosed résumé, I have also had experience in displaying merchandise at
Buchman's Department Store.

I would appreciate the opportunity to discuss my qualifications with
you. Through June 12 I will be available for an interview daily after
2:00 p.m., and after that date at any time that suits your convenience.

Sincerely yours,

Anthony H. Jones

Anthony H. Jones

Encl. Résumé

relevant job experience; see his résumé, Fig. 5.4. He must rely mainly on his educational training.

The first paragraph of your application letter is your introduction. It should answer four questions: (1) why you are writing, (2) where or how you learned of the job, (3) what your most important qualification is for the job, and (4) when you are able to begin the job. Begin your letter by stating directly that you are writing to apply for a job. Do not say that you "want to apply for the job," for such an opening raises the question "Why don't you then?" And do not start off in an unconventional or annoying way: "Are you looking for a dynamic, young, and talented photographer?" Do not begin with a question; be more positive and professional. If you learned of the job through a newspaper or journal, make sure that you underscore the title:

> I am applying for the foodservice manager position you advertised
> in the May 10 edition of the <u>Los Angeles Times</u>.

If you learned of the job from a professor, friend, or employee at the firm, state that fact also. Do not waste the employer's time and your space on the page by repeating verbatim the words of the advertisement. Next, indicate your chief qualification—you will soon graduate with an A.A. in foodservice, you have worked in the large restaurant of a major hotel chain, or you have ten years experience managing a cafeteria. Select one fact that justifies your suitability for the job. Also state when you are available to start.

The second paragraph of your application letter emphasizes your education and work background. Recent graduates with little work experience will, of course, spend more time on their education, but even if you have much experience, do not forget your education. Stress your most important educational accomplishments. Do not dwell on being a nurse's aide three years ago when you have nearly completed a degree program to be an R.N. Being a busboy is good experience, but do not let that job overshadow your current work as a management trainee for a large hotel chain. Employers want to know what skills and expertise your education has given you and how those skills apply to a particular job. Simply saying that you will graduate with a degree in criminal justice does not explain how you, unlike all the other graduates of a criminal justice program, are best qualified for the job. Indicate that in thirty-six hours of course work you have specialized in industrial security and that you have twelve hours in business and communications. That says something specific. Rather than boasting that you are qualified, give the facts to prove it. If your GPA is relatively high or if you have won an award, mention that. Do not worry about stating an important fact in both your letter and résumé.

After you discuss your educational qualifications, turn to your job experience. The best letters show how the two are related. Employers like to see a continuity between a candidate's school and job experience. Provide that link by showing how the jobs you have held have something in common with your major—in terms of responsibility, research, customer relations, community service. Say that your course work in data processing helped you to be a better programmer for your previous employer, that your summer jobs for the local park district allowed you to reinforce your studies in human services.

Above all, the second paragraph of your application letter must relate your education and experience directly to the employer's job. Tell exactly how your school work and job experience qualify you to function and advance in the job advertised. Here, your homework on what the company is like should pay off. Note in Fig. 5.8 how Maria Lopez uses her knowledge of Dr. Hendrady's specialty to her advantage; in Fig. 5.9 Anthony Jones profitably emphasizes how he gained his knowledge of and respect for Megalith publications.

The second paragraph may run to six or seven sentences. You might want to spend three sentences on your educational qualifications and three on your job experience; or perhaps your work experiences are so rich that you will spend four sentences on them. At any rate, do not neglect education for experience or vice versa. Refer to your résumé, and do not forget to say that you are including it with your letter.

The third paragraph has three functions: (1) to emphasize once again your major qualification, (2) to ask for an interview, and (3) to indicate when you are available for an interview. Paragraph three is short—about three sentences. End gracefully and professionally. Don't leave the reader with just one weak sentence: "I would like to have an interview at your convenience." Such a sentence does nothing to sell you. Say that you would appreciate talking with the employer further to discuss your qualifications. Then mention your chief talent. Indicate your interest in the job and give the times you are available for an interview. If you are going to a professional meeting where the employer might be present, or if you are visiting the employer's city, say so. Below are some poor ways to close the letter:

Pushy:	I would like to set up an interview with you. Please phone me to arrange a convenient time. (That's the employer's prerogative, not yours.)
Too Informal:	I do not live too far from your office. Could we meet for coffee sometime next week. (Turn this around. Say that since you live nearby, you will be available for an interview.)
Too Humble:	I know that you are busy, but I would really like to have an interview. (Say you would like to discuss the job further.)
Introduces New Subject:	I would like to discuss other qualifications you have in mind for the job. (How do you know what they might be?)

▶ Filling Out a Job Application

At some point in your job search, you will be asked to complete a prospective employer's application form. A recruiter may hand you a job application form at a campus interview, or you may be mailed a form in response to your letter of application. Most often, though, you will be given an application to complete when you are at the employer's office.

Application forms vary tremendously. But they all ask you to give information about your education, military service, present and previous employment, references, general state of health, and reasons for wanting to work for the company or agency. Since these topics overlap those on your résumé, bring the résumé with you to the employer's office to make sure you omit nothing important. Some forms even require you to attach your résumé. But *under no circumstances* attach a résumé to a blank form instead of filling the form out. Employers want their own forms completed by job seekers.

The following general guidelines can help you to complete an application form:

1. Read the instructions before you begin.
2. Answer all the questions. Some forms instruct you to put N/A (not applicable) rather than leave a space blank.
3. Print neatly, using a dark, preferably black, ball-point pen. Do not use a felt-tip pen; what you write will smear. And do not write with a pencil.
4. Double-check numbers—social security, driver's license, area codes, registration numbers, union certificates.
5. Do not write in spaces marked "For Office Use Only."
6. Check spelling and punctuation.
7. Be as neat as you can. Do not write over the lines or in the margins or insert asterisks indicating further clarification. If necessary, attach a separate sheet of paper if you need more room to answer a question. Make sure that your name and the specific question appear on the attached sheet.
8. Be truthful. Don't say you can type seventy words a minute when you have trouble with forty.
9. Be as precise as possible. For "previous experience," do not just say "construction worker"; indicate "building inspector," "mason," "carpenter."
10. When asked about salary expectations, avoid extremes. If you have done your homework, you will have a sense of the established range. Do not put "minimum wage"; an employer has to give you that anyway.
11. Many applications ask you to comment on your training and education, giving you one or two inches of space for your answer. Fill the blank space with facts, not padding. Giving just one or two small details will not sell your talents and only points to your lack of self-expression and confidence. Many employers, including the federal government, rank prospective employers on the basis of their answers to such a question. So, as a rule of thumb, provide as much relevant information as space allows, and make sure that you are positive, not negative, about your previous position and employer.
12. Sign the application, verifying that what you have written is true and complete. Your signature is essential if you must have a security clearance

or if the company has to release any of the information you have provided or obtain your permission to find out more about you.

Individuals desiring to work for one of the many branches of the United States government complete a "Personal Qualifications Statement." That form contains many of the kinds of questions you can expect future employers to ask you. The government, like so many employers, expects job candidates to have done their homework. The first question asks the applicant to identify the desired job by title and number—information readily available from a civil service or governmental agency. Since the federal government is the largest employer in the nation, many users of this book will complete this form. You can obtain a copy of the form from a Federal Job Information Center.

Figure 5.10 contains an application form similar to ones used by private companies. This form asks applicants to give reasons for leaving previous jobs and also requires them to write a "personal essay" stating why the company should hire them. Both of these questions will require tact and thought. If you were fired from a past job, it is not to your advantage to simply state the fact. Indicate further relevant information, such as that the industry suffered a recession. More frequently, though, your reasons for leaving a job will be financial, educational, or geographic. You may have received a better offer, decided to return to school, or planned to move to another town.

Writing the personal essay will require that you convince the employer of your sincerity and qualifications. In doing so, do not dwell on what the company can do for you. Concentrate on how your previous experience and education will help your employer; emphasize, too, your willingness to learn new techniques and skills on the job. Do not be afraid to cite specific accomplishments; your success will depend on it.

▶ Going to an Interview

An interview can be challenging, threatening, friendly, or chatty; sometimes it is all of these. By the time you arrive at the interview stage, you are far along in your job search. Basically, there are two kinds of interviews. One is a screening interview, to which numerous applicants have been invited so that a company can narrow down the candidates; campus interviews are screening interviews. The other kind of interview is known as a line interview, to which the employer invites only a few select applicants to the company's office.

Preparing for an Interview

An interview gives the employer a chance to see how you look, act, and *react*. Once in a while interviewers intentionally create stressful situations for you, such as inviting you to smoke and not providing an ashtray. But most em-

Fig. 5.10   Job application form.

APPLICATION FOR EMPLOYMENT

Date_____

PERSONAL INFORMATION

SS#_____

Name _____
            Last   First   Middle

Present address   _____

Phone no. _____

            Height_____Weight_____Hair color_____

                                                                    Eye color _____

            If related to anyone in our employ
            state name, relationship, and position_____

EMPLOYMENT DESIRED

        Position applying for_____ or _____

EDUCATIONAL BACKGROUND

Name and location of school	Years attended	Date graduated	Subjects studied
High school			
College			
Other			

In case of emergency, notify:

_____
Name   Address   Phone number

Fig. 5.10   (continued)

EMPLOYMENT RECORD

Former employer	Address	Salary & position	Reason for leaving	Dates employed

REFERENCES

Give the names of three persons not related to you whom you have known for at least one year:

Name	Address	Business	Years acquainted

Why did you leave your last job ? Expand your answer above.

_____

_____

_____

PERSONAL ESSAY

Please state why you feel we should hire you for the position desired, including any qualifications not mentioned above.

_____

_____

_____

_____

_____

_____

DO NOT WRITE BELOW THIS LINE—FOR OFFICE USE ONLY

Date interviewed _____ By _____

General appearance _____

Attitude _____

Personality _____

Date hired (if any) _____

Salary _____

Position _____

ployers do not want to trick you. They want to see how well you can talk about yourself and your work; they also want to see how well you listen and respond to their answers. Interviewers expect applicants to be nervous, but you can free yourself of some anxiety if you know what to expect.

Interviews can last half an hour or extend to two or three days. Most often, though, an interview will last about one hour. It has been estimated that the applicant will do about 80 to 90 percent of the talking. Since you will be asked to speak at length, make the following preparations before your interview:

1. Do your homework about the employer—types of services provided, location of offices, contributions to the field or the community.
2. Review the technical skills most relevant for the job. You might want to reread sections of a textbook, study some recent journal articles, or talk to a professor or employee you know from the company.
3. Prepare a brief (one- or two-minute) review of your qualifications to deliver orally should you be asked about yourself.
4. Bring your résumé with you. Your interviewer will have a copy on the desk, so you can be sure that its contents will be the subject of many questions. Be able to elaborate and supplement what is on your résumé. Any extra details or information that bring your résumé up to date ("I received my degree last week"; "I'll get the results of my state board examinations in one week") will be appreciated.

Questions to Expect at an Interview

You can expect questions about your education, job experience, and personal style. An interviewer will ask you questions about courses, schools, technical skills, and job goals. An interviewer will want to discover your good points as well as your bad ones. A common strategy is to postpone questions about your bad points until near the end of the interview. Once a relaxed atmosphere has been established, the interviewer thinks that you may be less reluctant to talk about your weaknesses. The following fifteen questions are typical of those you can expect from interviewers:

1. Tell us something about yourself. (Here, your one-minute oral presentation of yourself comes in handy.)
2. Why do you want to work for us? (Recall any job goals you have and apply them to the job under discussion.)
3. What qualifications do you have for the job? (Mention educational achievements in addition to any relevant work experience.)
4. What could you possibly offer us that other candidates do not have? (Say "enthusiasm" in addition to educational achievement.)
5. Why did you attend this school? (Be honest—location, costs, programs.)

6. Why did you major in "X"? (Do not simply say financial benefits; concentrate on both practical and professional benefits. Be able to state career objectives.)

7. Why did you get a grade of "C" in a course? (Do not hurt your chances of being hired by saying you could have done better if you tried; that response shows a lack of motivation most employers find unacceptable. Explain what the trouble was and mention that you corrected it in a course in which you made a B or an A.)

8. What extracurricular activities did you participate in while in high school or college? (Indicate any duties or responsibilities you had—handling money, writing memos, coordinating events; if you were not able to participate in such activities, tell the interviewer that a part-time job, or community or church activities, or commuting a long way to school each day prevented your participating. Such answers sound better than saying that you did not like sports or fraternities or clubs in school.)

9. Did you learn as much as you wanted from your course work? (This is a loaded question. Indicate that you learned a great deal but now look forward to the opportunity to gain more practical skill, to put into practice the principles you have learned; say that you are never through learning enough about your major.)

10. Why was your summer job important? (Highlight things you learned, people you helped, employers you pleased.)

11. What is your greatest strength? (Being a team player, cooperation, willingness to learn, ability to grasp difficult concepts easily, taking criticism easily, and profiting from criticism are all appropriate answers.)

12. What is your greatest shortcoming? (Be honest here and mention it, but then turn to ways in which you are improving. Do not dwell on your weaknesses, but do not keep silent about them. Saying "none" to this kind of question is as inadvisable as rattling off a list of wrongdoings.)

13. How much did you earn at your last job and what salary do you expect in working for us? (Some job counselors advise interviewees to lie about their past salaries in order to get a larger one from the future employer. But if the prospective employer checks your last salary and finds that you have lied, you lose. It is better to round off your last salary to the nearest thousand. As far as present salary is concerned, if you did your homework you should have a sense of the salary range.)

14. Why did you leave your last job? (Usually you will have educational reasons—"I returned to school full time." Or you will have received a better offer. *Never attack your previous employer. This only makes you look bad.*)

15. Is there anything else you want to discuss? (Here is your opportunity to end the interview with more information about yourself. You might take time to reiterate a strength of yours, to correct an earlier answer, or to indicate your desire to work for the company.)

Of course, you will have a chance throughout the interview to ask questions, too. Do not forget important points about the job—responsibilities, security, and chances for promotion. You will also want to ask about salary (but do not dwell on it), fringe benefits, days off, vacations, and bonuses. If you spend time on these subjects, especially during the first part of the interview, you tell the interviewer that you are more interested in the rewards of the job than in the duties and challenges it offers. Do not go to the interview with dollar signs flashing in your eyes.

There are some questions that the interviewer cannot legally ask you. Questions about your age, marital status, ethnic background, race, or any physical handicaps violate equal opportunity employment laws. Even so, some employers may disguise their interest in these subjects by asking you indirect questions about them. A question such as, "Will your husband care if you have to work overtime?" or "How many children do you have?" could probe into your marital life. Confronted with such questions, it is best to answer them positively ("My home life will not interfere with my job," "My husband understands that overtime may be required") rather than bristling defensively, "It's none of your business if I have a husband."

There are some other interview "dos" and "don'ts." Go to the interview alone. Dress appropriately for the occasion. Speak slowly and distinctly; do not nervously hurry to finish your sentences, and never interrupt or finish an interviewer's sentences. Refrain from chewing gum, smoking, rolling a pencil, or tapping your foot against the floor or a chair. Maintain eye contact with the interviewer; do not sheepishly stare at the floor or the desk. Body language is equally important. Do not fold your arms—that's a signal indicating you are closed to the interviewer's suggestions and comments. And one last point: *Be on time.* If you are unavoidably delayed, telephone to apologize and set up another interview.

The Follow-up Letter

After the interview, it is good strategy to send a follow-up letter thanking the interviewer for his or her time and interest in you. The letter will keep your name fresh in the interviewer's mind. Do not forget that this individual interviewed other candidates, too, some of them probably on the same day as you. In your follow-up letter, you can reemphasize your qualifications for the job by showing how they apply to conditions described by the interviewer; you might also ask for some further information to show your interest in the job and the employer. You could even refer to a detail, such as a tour or film that was part of the interview. A sample follow-up letter appears in Fig. 5.11.

▶ Accepting or Declining a Job

Even if you have verbally agreed to take a job, you still have to respond formally in writing. Your letter will make your acceptance official and may even be included in your permanent personnel file. Accepting a job is easy. Make this communication with your new employer a model of clarity and diplomacy. Respond to the offer as soon as possible (certainly within two

Fig. 5.11   A follow-up letter.

2739 East Street
Latrobe, PA 17042
September 12, 1981

Mr. Jack Wong
Personnel Manager
Transatlantic Steel Company
1334 Ridge Road N.E.
Pittsburgh, PA 17122

Dear Mr. Wong:

I enjoyed talking with you last Wednesday and learning more about the
security officer position available at Transatlantic Steel. It was
especially helpful to take a tour of the plant's north gate section to
see the problems it presents for the security officer stationed there.

As I told you, my training in surveillance electronics has prepared me
to operate the sophisticated equipment Transatlantic has installed at
the north gate. I was happy that Mr. Rawson took time to show me this
equipment.

I shall look forward to receiving the brochure about Transatlantic's
employees' services. Would it also be possible for you to include a copy
of the newsletter introducing the new security equipment to the
employees?

Thank you for considering me for the position. I look forward to hearing
from you.

Sincerely yours,

Mary LeBorde

Mary LeBorde

weeks). Often a time limit is specified. A sample acceptance letter appears in Fig. 5.12. In the first sentence tell the employer that you are accepting the job, and refer to the date of the letter offering you the position. Indicate when you can begin the job. Then mention any pleasant associations from your interview or any specific challenges you are anticipating. That should take no more than a paragraph. Do not douse your letter with lavish praise for the employer or the job.

In a second paragraph express your plans to fulfill any further requirements for the job—going to the personnel office, taking a physical examination, having a copy of a certificate or license forwarded, sending a final transcript of your college work. A final one-sentence paragraph might state that you are looking forward to starting your new job.

Refusing a job requires tact. You are obligated to inform an employer why you are not taking the job. Since the employer has spent time interviewing you, respond with courtesy and candor. For an example of a refusal letter, see Fig. 5.13.

Do not bluntly begin with the refusal. Instead, prepare the reader for bad news by starting with a complimentary remark about the job, the interview, or the company. Then move to your refusal and supply an honest but not elaborate explanation of why you are not taking the job. Many students cite educational opportunities, work schedules, geographic preference, health reasons, or better, more relevant professional opportunities. End on a friendly note; you may be interested in working for this company in the future.

▶ Employment Evaluations

Even after you have been hired and have been working at your job for a while, you may be expected to write convincingly about your qualifications for that job. Many companies and agencies annually require their employees to fill out self-evaluation forms as part of a routine review used in deciding promotions and salary increases. In the past, employee evaluations were handled by supervisors and administrative personnel. Today, many companies ask employees to grade themselves in addition to having supervisors do an assessment. The two evaluations are then compared, and employees are given the opportunity to see and respond to what their supervisors have written about them. Employees may also be asked to evaluate their supervisors. The days of accountability are here, making it important for employees to know how to evaluate themselves and others effectively.

What kinds of questions can you expect your employer to ask? Here are a few of the most common:

1. What are your current duties?
2. How well do you perform them?
3. What improvements can you make?

Fig. 5.12   Letter accepting a job.

73 Park Street
Evansville, WI 53536
June 30, 1982

Ms. Melinda A. Haas
Manager, Weise's Department Store
Janesville Mall
Janesville, WI 53545

Dear Ms. Haas:

I am pleased to accept the position of assistant controller that you
offered me in your letter of June 23. There will be no problem with
starting on July 15. I look forward to helping Ms. Meyers in the business
office. In the next few months I know that I will learn a great deal about
Weise's.

I will make an appointment for early next week with the Personnel
Department to discuss travel policies, salary payment schedules, and
insurance coverage.

I am eager to start working for Weise's.

Sincerely yours,

John Dubinski

John Dubinski

Fig. 5.13   Letter refusing a job.

345 Melba Lane
Bellingham, WA 98225
March 8, 1982

Ms. Gail Buckholtz
Assistant Editor
The Everett News
Everett, WA 98421

Dear Ms. Buckholtz:

I enjoyed meeting you and the staff photographers at my recent interview for the photography position at the News. Your plans for the special weekend supplements are very exciting, and I know that I would have enjoyed my assignments greatly. But because I have decided to continue my education part-time at Western Washington University in Bellingham, I have accepted a position with the Bellingham American. Not having to commute to Everett every day will give me more time for my studies and also my free-lance work.

Thank you for your kind offer and for the time you and the staff spent explaining your plans to me. I wish you success with the supplements.

Sincerely yours,

George Alexander

George Alexander

4. What would you like to accomplish in the next year?
5. Where would you rank yourself in comparison with others in your department or on your floor?
6. What special contributions have you made to the company (or agency) in the last year?
7. Why do you deserve a raise or a promotion?

Before you answer such questions, keep in mind that your readers know you are automatically prejudiced in your behalf; objectivity, therefore, will be deemed a virtue. Rather than simply saying that you are invaluable or that you are a hard worker, tell your employer why you hold this view of your work. Give relevant facts—cite how many customers you visited and sold products to, mention any exceptional services you performed for clients. Indicate how your work benefited the company and your fellow employees. Did you make any suggestions that improved services or schedules? If your supervisor praised your work, cite his or her comments and give dates. Keep your assessment short and to the point. Also make sure that your comments about your accomplishments directly pertain to your assigned duties. At the other extreme, do not sell yourself short by saying that you did what was expected of you or that you accomplished what you were told. Tell your reader how you carried out routine tasks with skill and to the benefit of the company. A credible answer to question 3 would indicate that you have made a mistake, but would also indicate what you have done to correct it and to ensure that it will not occur again.

When asked to evaluate your supervisor, be objective. Avoid cheap shots or any attempts to get even for grievances. Questions of leadership, honesty, respect, and clarity in explaining job goals are usually found on evaluations of one's supervisors. Respond according to these criteria with facts and with honesty.

Your employer may supply you with a form (or checklist) for your evaluation of yourself and/or your supervisor. Or you may be instructed to write a formal letter of assessment. In either case, proofread what you write carefully for spelling and punctuation. You may also want to make a copy for your own records.

▶ Exercises

1. Make a list of your marketable job skills. To do this, first concentrate on the specialized kinds of skills you learned in your major or on your job (e.g., giving injections, fingerprinting, preparing specialized menus, keeping a ledger book, operating a computer). Write down as many of these skills as you can think of; then organize them into three or four separate categories that reflect your major abilities.

2. Compile a list of local employers for whom you would like to work. Get their names, addresses, phone numbers, and the names of the managers

or personnel officers. Select one company and write a profile about it—location, services, kinds of products or services offered, number of employees working for it, clients served, types of schedules used.

3. Tell your college placement office when you will begin your job search. The office will almost certainly give you some forms to complete. Bring these forms to class and discuss the kinds of questions they contain and the most effective ways to answer them.

4. Obtain some letter-of-recommendation forms from your placement office. Write a sample letter to a former or current teacher and/or employer, asking for a recommendation. Tell this individual what kinds of jobs you will be looking for and politely mention how a strong letter would help you in your job search. Make sure that you bring this individual up to date about your educational progress and any employment you have had since you worked for him or her.

5. Determine what is wrong with the following sentences in a letter of application. Rewrite them to eliminate any mistakes, to focus on the "you attitude," or to make them more precise.
   (a) Even though I have very little actual job experience, I can make up for it in enthusiasm.
   (b) My qualifications will prove that I am the best person for your job.
   (c) I would enjoy working with your other employees.
   (d) This letter is my application for any job you now have open or expect to fill in the near future.
   (e) Next month, my family and I will be moving to Detroit, and I must get a job in the area. Will you have anything open?
   (f) If you are interested in me, then I hope that we make some type of arrangements to interview each other soon.
   (g) Your ad specified that you wanted someone who was familiar with food sanitation techniques, worked for at least one year in industry, and had at least thirty hours in course work at a community college in foodscience. I am the very person you are looking for.
   (h) I have not included a résumé since all pertinent information about me is in this letter.
   (i) My GPA is only 2.5, but I did make two B's in my last term.
   (j) I hope to take state boards soon.
   (k) Your company, or so I have heard through the grapevine, has excellent fringe benefits. That is right up my alley, so I am applying for a position which you may advertise.
   (l) I am writing to ask you to kindly consider whether I would be a qualified person for the position you announced in the newspaper.
   (m) I have made plans to further my education.
   (n) My résumé speaks for itself.
   (o) I could not possibly accept a position which required weekend work, and night work is out, too.

(p) In my own estimation, I am a go-getter, an eager beaver, so to speak.

(q) My last employer was dead wrong when he let me go. I think he regrets it now.

(r) When you arrange an interview time, give me a call. I am home every afternoon after four.

(s) A friend of mine who works for you told me that you are thinking of hiring some extra help around the holidays. I am interested.

(t) Seeing that I have been active in student activities, you will certainly rate me as a good risk in your office.

6. Why is the following letter ineffective? Rewrite it to make it more precise and appropriate.

```
Apartment 32
Jeggler Drive
Talcott, Arizona

Monday

Bob Rand
Production Supervisor
Jellco
Capitol City, Arizona

Dear Sir:

I am writing to ask you if your company will consider me for the
position you announced in the newspaper yesterday. I believe that with
my education (I have an associate degree) and experience (I have worked
four years as a freight supervisor), I could fill your job.

My school work was done at two junior colleges, and I took more than
enough courses in business management and modern packaging. In fact,
here is a list of some of my courses: Supervision, Materials
Management, Work Experience in Management, Business Machines, Loading
and Landing Tactics, Introduction to Packaging, Art Design, Modern
Business Principles, and Small Business Management. In addition, I
have worked as a loading dock supervisor for the last two years, and
before that I worked in the military in the Quartermaster Corps.

Please let me know if you are interested in me. I would like to have an
interview with you at the earliest possible date, since there are some
other firms also interested in me, too.

Sincerely yours,

George D. Milhous
```

7. Request an application form for employment from a local store, hospital, government agency, or contractor. Bring the form to class and be prepared to discuss the best ways of completing it.

8. Rewrite this follow-up letter to make it more professional.

Dear Mr. Gage:

It was good talking to you yesterday. The job is even more attractive than I thought. I had no idea that the salary was in the $15,000 to $16,000 range. That is excellent money for someone starting out.

I am sorry that I did not know the answers to your questions on the use of the new telex machines. After checking with my instructor, Dr. Patricia Holmes, I can give you a full and complete answer now. If you would like me to put it in writing, please let me know, and I shall be happy to oblige you. I do not want you to think that I am not properly trained.

I am really excited about working for your company. And I am staying glued to the phone in the hopes that you will give me that call that will start me on a great career.

9. Which of the following would belong on your résumé? Why?
   (a) student I.D. number
   (b) social security number
   (c) the zip codes of your references' addresses
   (d) a list of all your English courses in college
   (e) section numbers of the courses in your major
   (f) statement that you are divorced
   (g) subscriptions to journals in your field
   (h) the titles of any stories or poems you published in a high school literary magazine or newspaper
   (i) your GPA
   (j) foreign languages you studied
   (k) years you attended college
   (l) the date you were discharged from the service
   (m) names of the neighbors you are using as references
   (n) your religion
   (o) job titles you held
   (p) your summer job as a waitress
   (q) your telephone number
   (r) your license number for your car
   (s) the reason you changed schools
   (t) your current status with the National Guard
   (u) your child's name
   (v) the name of your major professor in college
   (w) your work for the Red Cross
   (x) hours a week you spend reading science fiction
   (y) the title of your last term paper in your major
   (z) the name of the agency or business where you worked last

10. From the Sunday edition of your local newspaper, clip ads for two or three jobs you are qualified to fill and then write a letter of application for one of them.

11. Write a résumé to go along with the letter you wrote for exercise 10 above.

12. Write a letter to a local business inquiring about summer employment. Indicate that you can work only for one summer and that you will be going back to school by September 1.

13. Indicate what is wrong with the following career objective statements and rewrite them to make them more precise and professional.
    (a) Job in a dentist's office.
    (b) Position with a safety emphasis.
    (c) Desire growth position in large department store.
    (d) Am looking for entry position in health sciences with an emphasis on caring for older people.
    (e) Position in sales with fast promotion rate.
    (f) Want a job working with semiconductor circuits.
    (g) Job in agriculture.
    (h) I would like a position in fashion, especially one working with modern fashion.
    (i) Desire a good-paying job, hours: 8–4:30, with double pay for extra time. Would like to stay in the Omaha area.
    (j) Insurance adjuster.
    (k) Computer operator in large office.
    (l) Personal secretary.
    (m) Job with preschoolers.
    (n) Full-time position with hospitality chain.
    (o) Cashier with financial institution; interested in position that promises growth and advancement within company.
    (p) I want a career in nursing.
    (q) Police work, particularly in suburb of large metropolitan area.
    (r) A job that lets me be me—a creative designer.
    (s) Desire fun job selling cosmetics.
    (t) Any position for qualified dietitian.
    (u) Although I have not made up my mind about which area of forestry I shall go into, I am looking for a job that offers me training and rewards based upon my potential.

6

Types of Business Correspondence

Chapter 6 discusses six of the most common types of business correspondence that you will be expected to write on the job:

1. Memos
2. Order letters
3. Letters of inquiry
4. Special request letters
5. Sales letters
6. Customer relations letters

These six kinds of correspondence will introduce you to a variety of formats and a number of writing techniques. Generally speaking, memos, the least formal type of correspondence, convey brief notes or instructions; order, inquiry, and special request letters give and request information using widely differing formats; sales letters require a careful review of your product or service and a convincing argument for your reader; and customer relations letters are vital to company image and customer satisfaction.

▶ Memos

Memorandum is a Latin word signifying that something is to be remembered. The Latin meaning points to the memo's chief function—to record information of immediate importance that could otherwise easily be overlooked or forgotten in the busy world of work. Memos are usually written by and for individuals within your company or agency, although sometimes memos are sent to persons outside your firm. Memos allow a business or agency to communicate with itself in its day-to-day operations.

Function and Format of Memos

Memos have a variety of functions. They are written to ask or to respond to questions affecting daily work. They can notify employees about the date of a meeting or the main points raised at that meeting. They can inform readers about appointments, policies, or new procedures. They can alert the staff to a forthcoming order and any special problems in handling it. Or they can provide some last-minute figures necessary to honor a customer's request, confirm what has been decided in telephone or in face-to-face conversations, and offer suggestions or recommendations.

Memos vary in format. Some companies use half sheets of paper, whereas others employ long, $8\frac{1}{2}'' \times 11''$ paper. Some firms have their names (letterhead) on their memos as in Fig. 6.1, and other companies rely on a standard memo form, as in Fig. 6.2.

Memos versus Letters

As you can see, memos look different from letters. They are more streamlined and less formal. Memos do not have a salutation, complimentary close, or signature line (although some writers put their initials after their names). The easily recognized parts of memos—the *to, from, subject,* and *date* lines— are appropriate for their function as speedy messengers of company business. Sometimes memos are handwritten and refer to the reader by his or her first name (if you are on a first-name basis with the individual). Memos are shorter than letters; an average memo may be only a few sentences long, sometimes a few paragraphs long, but rarely more than one page. Unlike a letter, the memo does not have to arouse a reader's interest in the subject; your reader is a fellow employee. Since memos are written to save time and money, they are sent through interoffice mail or are hand carried. When you send a memo to specific individuals within a firm, you can list all these individuals after the "TO:" and then put a check after the name of the individual who will receive a copy of your memo, as in Fig. 6.1. Keep in mind that memos are often composed in haste and are written on the spot under the pressure of a deadline; you may have little time to revise and polish sentences as you would for a formal business letter.

Writing Memos

You cannot be careless when writing memos. Clarity and accuracy are just as important in a memo as they are in a letter. Here are a few suggestions on writing effective memos:

1. Memos should cover only one topic. Three or four different subjects in one memo will confuse the reader. For example, in one memo do not say that the parts department will be closed on Saturday, the new valves have

Fig. 6.1 Memo on letterhead stationery.

BILL'S CATERING SERVICE
56 North Jones
Canton, Ohio 45307

TO: Bill Torance, Marge Adcox, ✓   DATE: November 23, 1981
Mildred Dressel, Alice Ricks,
Carlos Fernandez, Phebe   SUBJECT: Management Training
Sullivan   Seminar Review

FROM: Roger Blackmore

I attended the Management Training Seminar (November 19–20), as you
requested, and here is a list of the major points made by the director,
Jack Lowery.

(1) The individual conducting the training sessions should always talk
    in a loud voice so that the trainees can hear him or her.

(2) The main purpose of the training session should always be announced
    so that the trainees can focus on a specific set of topics.

(3) Instructors should allow at least a ten–minute break for each two-
    hour session. This will increase the trainee's attention span and
    allow for better learning.

(4) The easiest tasks should be assigned first, and more complicated
    ones should follow.

(5) The instructor should provide feedback to the trainees at the end of
    each major section completed.

I will be happy to meet with you later to discuss these points in detail.
These training techniques could help our orientation program. Let me
know when it would be convenient for you to talk about these points.

Fig. 6.2   Standard memo form without any letterhead.

TO: All RN's

FROM: Margaret Wojak, Director of Nurses *m\w*

DATE: August 12, 1981

SUBJECT: RN identity patches

Effective September 1, 1981, all RN's will have the choice of wearing
their caps or an identity patch. Patches should be sewn on the upper
right arm of lab coats or uniforms so that staff and patients can easily
identify you as an RN. Those RN's wishing to wear identity patches may
obtain them for one dollar apiece at the Health Uniforms Shop directly
across from the hospital on Ames Street. Call me at extension 732 if you
have any questions.

---

arrived, and part number #34666r is being discontinued. Write three separate
memos.

2. Memos should follow a logical order.   Begin by telling your reader
what you will discuss in your memo and how you will discuss it. Perhaps you
will first mention a cause of a problem before you offer a solution; or you
might begin with a chronological sequence of events. Indicate that you are
dividing your topic into subcategories and then label them with letters or
numbers.

3. Memos must be clear if they are to work.   Date and subject lines
must be precise. Do not simply list the day of the week; give the date as well.
Some companies have adopted the military practice of indicating the precise
time of the day—for example, 1400 hours instead of 2:00 P.M. A subject line
should always be completed; it is the title of your memo. Vague descriptions,
such as "New Policy," "Operating Difficulties," "Time Change," "Salary," do
not identify your message accurately. A specific subject line also helps readers
to file your memo.

4. Memos should be concise and to the point.   But do not get carried
away in your desire to be concise. Memos are not telegrams. A memo in this

style may be confusing: "Pkg. rec'd 8/4 w/o prop. wrap. Must reshp. asap. Call rec. dept. re error." A better way of saying the same thing is: "The package was received 8/4, but without the proper wrapping. It must be reshipped as soon as possible. Please call the receiving department about the error." If you use an abbreviation, make sure your readers understand its meaning.

5. Memos should exclude irrelevant details. If you have to write a memo about a meeting you attended, supply only the major points raised at that meeting, as in Fig. 6.1. Do not waste time describing the room where the meeting was held, how much time was spent on socializing, or where you went to lunch. A memo about how many cartons of your product were used last year, for example, need not describe where they were stored or if they were stocked properly. Sometimes your response to a memo will be asked for at the bottom of the memo; a simple yes or no answer or a brief description will suffice. In such instances writing another memo is also useless. Write your response on the original memo and return it to the sender.

6. Memos should be functional. A memo is useless if it is sent to the shipping department to handle a certain package with special care twenty-four hours after that package has been delivered. In order to be functional, memos must be timely and to the point. Do not send a memo announcing a meeting two hours before it is to take place. Rather, send the memo two or three days before the scheduled meeting, and be sure to state the time, place, and subject of the meeting.

A special kind of memo is the phone message, illustrated in Fig. 6.3 (page 128). This kind of message is easy to write as long as you do so while the information is fresh in your mind. Write the message as it is being dictated on the phone; you will thus be able to get the caller's name, message, and required action straight. Check the appropriate boxes and make sure that the message is delivered.

▶ Order Letters

Order letters are straightforward notices informing a seller that you want to purchase a product or service—perhaps some articles of clothing, replacement parts for an intricate machine, or large quantities of various food. To make sure that you receive exactly what you want, your letter must be clear, precise, and accurate. Double-check the seller's brochure, catalog sales list, or agency manual before you write your order letter. It is a waste of time to write to Sears Roebuck for a product available only from J.C. Penney's.

Order letters address the following five points:

1. *Description of the product or service.* Specify the name, model or stock number, quantity, color, weight, height, width, size, or any special features that separate one model from another, e.g., chrome as opposed to cop-

Fig. 6.3   A telephone message.

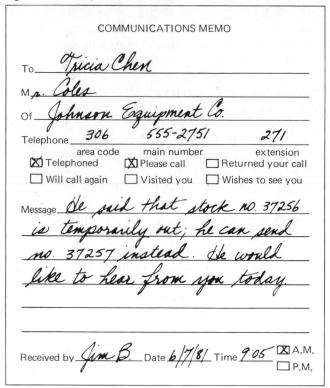

COMMUNICATIONS MEMO

To *Tricia Chen*

M. *Coles*

Of *Johnson Equipment Co.*

Telephone *306*   *555-2751*   *271*
  area code   main number   extension

☒ Telephoned   ☒ Please call   ☐ Returned your call
☐ Will call again   ☐ Visited you   ☐ Wishes to see you

Message *He said that stock no. 37256 is temporarily out; he can send no. 37257 instead. He would like to hear from you today.*

Received by *Jim B.* Date *6/7/81* Time *9:05* ☒ A.M.
                                          ☐ P.M.

per handles. Make your order letter easy to read by itemizing when you order more than one product. Typing the products or materials in tabular form will set them apart and allow the seller an opportunity to check off each item as it is being prepared for shipment.

2. *Price of the product or service.* Indicate precisely the price per unit, per carload, per carton, and then multiply that price for the number you are ordering. For example, ask for "twelve units @ $5 a unit." Do not put down the cost of one product ($5) for the dozen products you are requesting. You will receive only one.

3. *Shipping instructions.* Do you want the product sent by first-class or fourth-class mail, Federal Express, railway express? Specify any special handling instructions—Do not fold; Use hand stamp; Refrigerate or pack in dry ice; Ship to the Production Department.

4. *Date needed.* Is there a rush date?

5. *Method of payment.* Businesses with good credit standing are sent a bill. Individuals, however, may be required to pay beforehand. If so, are you enclosing a check or money order? Is the product to arrive COD (cash on delivery), or are you using a charge card? In the latter case, specify which card, and include your charge account number. Will you be paying in in-

stallments? State how much you are including and when and how the balance is to be paid.

Orders can be considered external or internal. An external order is sent to an individual or company you do not work for or with. You will refer to the five points just discussed and use a letter or sometimes a form provided by the company from which you are ordering the product. Figure 6.4 shows a sample order letter; Fig. 6.5 shows a sample order form furnished by the supplier.

An internal order, often called a *requisition,* asks one individual or department or section of your company to supply another section with necessary materials, equipment, service, or publications. A letter is not necessary for an internal order; instead, use a memo or a specially provided form such as the one illustrated in Fig. 6.6 (page 132), showing how a unit secretary in a hospital orders supplies for the floor.

▶ Letters of Inquiry

A letter of inquiry asks for information about a product, service, publication, or procedure. As a customer, you have occasion to ask for catalogs, names of stores in your town selling a special line of products, and the price, size, and color of a particular object. Businesses are eager to receive such inquiries and will answer them swiftly because they promise a future sale. Another example of a letter of inquiry might be a letter asking how much time can elapse before an insurance policy premium must be paid. Since questions like these directly affect cash flow, you can expect a speedy reply.

Figure 6.7 (page 133) illustrates a letter of inquiry. Addressed to a real estate office managing a large number of apartment complexes, Jackson Brown's letter follows the three basic rules for an effective inquiry letter. It

1. States exactly what information the writer wants.
2. Indicates clearly why the writer must have this information.
3. Specifies when the writer must have the information.

Whenever you request information, be sure to supply appropriate stock and model numbers, pertinent page numbers, or exact descriptions. You might even clip and mail the advertisement describing the product you want. Vague or general letters delay a response to you. Had Jackson Brown written the following letter to Acme, he would not have helped his family move. "Please send me some information on housing in Roanoke. My family and I plan to move there soon." Such a letter does not indicate whether he wants to rent or buy, whether he is interested in a large apartment or small one, furnished or unfurnished, where he would like it to be located, the price he is willing to pay. Similarly, a letter asking a firm to "Send me all the information you have on microwave ovens" might bring back a detailed service manual when the writer simply wanted prices of the top-selling models.

Fig. 6.4   An order letter.

DAVIS CONSTRUCTION COMPANY
1200 South Devon
Millersville, Pennsylvania 17321

August 1, 1981

E. F. Wonderlic and Associates
820 Frontage Road
P.O. Box 7
Northfield, IL 60093

Dear E. F. Wonderlic:

Please send us by first–class mail the following materials as listed in
your 1981 catalog entitled "Personnel Forms for Testing, Selection,
Administration, and Evaluation":

#P–4	Personnel Interviewer's Guide	25 copies for	$10.00
#P–5	Health Questionnaire	100 copies for	24.00
#EA–4	Personnel Application Forms	25 copies for	12.00
#ATS–6	Health History	1 sample copy for	1.50
			$47.50

When you mail these forms, send them to the Personnel Department in care
of my attention. Please send these forms within the next ten days and
telephone me collect if there will be any delay.

A check for one half the amount ($23.75) is enclosed and the balance will
be paid upon receipt of the materials.

Sincerely yours,

THE DAVIS CONSTRUCTION COMPANY

Roberta Youngblood

Roberta Youngblood
Personnel Department

Encl. Check #3467 for $23.75

Fig. 6.5   An order form supplied by seller.

HULTON-DANSEN HOUSEWARES, INC.
Remington, Iowa 52643

SHIP
ORDER
TO

PLEASE
PRINT

NAME___JANIS TAYLOR_____ DATE___11/5/81___

ADDRESS___1347 WALSH ST._____

CITY___MILWAUKEE_____

STATE___WISCONSIN_____ ZIP___53202___

NOTE: PRINT COMPLETE INFORMATION. DON'T FORGET TO GIVE SIZE, COLOR, ETC., IF THERE IS A CHOICE!

Catalog number	Quantity	Name of Item, Size, and Color	Price each	Amount
G 2732	2	AIR CONDITIONER COVERS	2.98	5 96
G 9170	4	TAPE (YELLOW)	1.99	7 96
H 1885	1	DELUXE BATTERY CHARGER	12.50	12 50

Postage and Handling Charges if Your Order is:

Under $2.00—Add 25c	$ 7.01 to $ 9.00—Add $1.50
$2.01 to $3.00—Add 60c	$ 9.01 to $11.00—Add $1.75
$3.01 to $5.00—Add $1.10	$11.01 to $13.00—Add $1.95
$5.01 to $7.00—Add $1.30	Over $13.00—Add $2.35

TOTAL 26 42

New Jersey Residents Add 5% Sales Tax

PLEASE NO COD'S 2 35

TOTAL 28 77

TOTAL ENCLOSED (CHECK OR MONEY ORDER)

CHARGE TO MY: (PLEASE CHECK ONE)

X MASTER CARD   VISA

ACCOUNT NUMBER 3 2 5 9 2 8 5 3 6 5 6 4 7 9 6 8

INTERBANK NUMBER 1 0 0 6   CARD EXPIRES 10 82

MASTER CARD ONLY (4 digits above your name)   MO.   YR.

Janis Taylor

SIGNATURE

Fig. 6.6   An internal order form.

COUNTY GENERAL HOSPITAL
DEPARTMENTAL PURCHASE REQUISITION

Department _Nursing 7E_

Date _1/16/80_

Completed by
Receiving Dept.

Quantity	Unit	Cat. number	Item description	Price unit	Extension
1 box	10	758A329	Spiral notebook		
1	1	916D572	Downey Fabric Softener		
1	1	389A183	Ivory Snow		
2 boxes	10	523E617	Hall markers with room numbers		

Fm. No. CGH 1222   Requested by: _J. Jones, Unit Secretary_

▶ Special Request Letters

A particular kind of inquiry letter is not routine sales correspondence. Making a special demand, such letters are called special request letters. These letters can ask, among other things, (1) a company for information that you as a student will use in a paper, (2) an individual for a copy of an article or a speech, or (3) an agency for facts that your company needs to prepare a proposal or sell a product. The person or company being asked for help stands to gain no financial reward for supplying this information; the only reward is the goodwill such a response creates.

Make your request clear and easy to answer. One department store manager made it very easy for customers to assess how courteously they were treated when they wanted to exchange some merchandise. In his letter to these customers, he included the following request: "Perhaps you would take a moment and list on the back of this page any remarks or suggestions you might have regarding our service and/or merchandise. (You will note that a self-addressed, postage-paid envelope is enclosed for your convenience.)"

Fig. 6.7   A letter of inquiry.

403 South Main Street
Kingsport, TN 37721
March 2, 1982

Mr. Fred Stonehill
Property Manager
Acme Property Corporation
Main and Broadway
Roanoke, VA 24015

Dear Mr. Stonehill:

Please let me know if you will have any two-bedroom furnished apartments
available for rent during the months of June, July, and August. I am
willing to pay up to $250 a month plus utilities. My wife, one-year-old
son, and I will be moving to Roanoke for the summer so that I can attend a
course at Virginia Western Community College. If possible, we would
like to have an apartment within two or three miles of the college. We do
not have any pets.

I would appreciate hearing from you within the next two weeks. My phone
number is (606) 273-8957.

If you have any vacancies, we can drive to Roanoke to look at them and, if
they are satisfactory, give you a deposit to hold an apartment for us.

Sincerely yours,

Jackson Brown

Jackson Brown

Supply readers with addressed, postage-paid envelopes and a telephone number where you can be reached for questions.

Saying "please" and "thank you" will help you get the information you want. Also, do not expect your reader to write the paper or proposal for you. Asking for information is quite different from asking readers to organize and write it for you. Follow these seven points when asking for information in an unsolicited letter:

1. State who you are and why you are writing.
2. Indicate clearly your reason for requesting the information.
3. Give the reader precisely and succinctly the questions you want answered. List, number, and separate the questions.
4. Specify exactly when you need the information. Allow sufficient time—at least three weeks.
5. Offer to forward a copy of your report, paper, or survey in gratitude for the help you were given.
6. Indicate that you will secure whatever permissions are necessary if you reprint or publish the materials you ask for or, if necessary, that you will keep the information confidential.
7. Thank the reader for helping.

Figure 6.8 gives an example of an unsolicited letter that follows these suggestions.

▶ Sales Letters

A sales letter is written to persuade the reader to buy a product, try a service, support some cause, or participate in some activity. A sales letter can also serve as a method of introducing yourself to potential customers. You have already received numerous sales letters from military recruiters, local banks and merchants, charitable organizations, and campus groups. Sales letters face a lot of competition that you will have to overcome.

To write an effective sales letter, you have to do three things:

1. Identify and limit your audience.
2. Find out exactly what the needs of this group are.
3. Determine precisely what you want your readers to do after reading your sales letter.

These three points require that you do adequate homework about both your audience and the product or service you are selling.

In deciding whom you want to reach, you will also be investigating the needs of your audience. Do you want to write a letter to all the nurses in your state district nurses' association or only the pediatric nurses at a particular hospital? Are you writing to all homeowners who purchased aluminum siding from your company in the last three years or in the last three months? Some-

Fig. 6.8   A special request letter.

234 Springdale Street
Rochester, NY 14618
March 25, 1982

Ms. Victoria Stanton
Research Director
Creative Marketing Concepts
198 Madison Avenue
New York, NY 10016

Dear Ms. Stanton:

A third-year student at Monroe College in Rochester, I am preparing a
term paper on the topic "Current Marketing Practices." As part of my
research for this paper, I am writing a brief overview of marketing
practices for the past fifty years. Could you please send me the
following pamphlets:

1. "A History of Marketing in the United States"
2. "Creative Marketing Comes of Age"

I would appreciate receiving these materials by April 17 and would be
pleased to send you a copy of my paper in late May. Creative Marketing
Concepts will, of course, be fully cited in the bibliography.

Thank you for your assistance. I shall be looking forward to hearing
from you.

Sincerely yours,

Julie Lester

Julie Lester

times a sales letter will be duplicated and sent to hundreds of readers; sometimes you may write to only one reader. Some helpful considerations in audience selection are occupation, age, consumer needs or habits, geographic location, and memberships. Your employer may have a mailing list that you should consult. Once you have selected those who should receive your letter, you have made a great deal of headway in knowing what you will say to that audience.

The "you attitude" is crucial. A sales letter is not written to provide a detailed set of instructions or elaborate explanations about a product. That kind of information comes after the sale. Nor is a sales letter written to proclaim the merits of your company. Here is a safe rule to follow: Don't boast or be a bore. The sales letter is written to persuade readers to buy, support, or join. Everything in the letter should be directed toward that goal. Appeal to readers' emotions, pocketbooks, or self-images. Entertain, amuse, coax, inform, or flatter the reader. The central question is, What are we trying to do for you, our customer? Ask yourself that question before you begin writing.

Sales letters follow a time-honored and workable plan of development; that is, each sales letter follows what can be called the "four A's":

1. Gets the reader's *attention*
2. Highlights the product's *appeal*
3. Shows the customer the product's *application*
4. Ends with a specific request for *action*

These four parts may be handled in less than four paragraphs. Holding a sales letter down to one page or less will keep the reader's attention. Television commercials and ads in magazines provide useful models of this fourfold approach to the customer. The next time you see one of these ads, try and identify the "four A's."

Getting the Reader's Attention

Your opening sentence is crucial. If you lose readers here, you will have lost them forever. A typical television commercial has thirty to sixty seconds to sell viewers; your first sentence has about two to five seconds to catch the readers' attention and prompt them to read on. That first sentence is bait on a hook. It must show readers how their problems could be solved, their profits increased, or their pleasures enriched. The reader's attitude will be "What's in this for me?"

Avoid an opening that is flat, vague, or lengthy. Beginning with a statement such as "I have great news for you" tells the readers nothing. They are more likely to toss your letter away if it does not contain something personally relevant in the first sentence. Tell them what that news is by selecting something that will appeal to their wallets, their emotions, or their chances to look better in the eyes of others. A letter for a pesticide that begins: "The cockroach could become the next endangered species if a California manufacturer has his way" offers some interesting, specific news. Keep your opening short, one or two sentences at most. Do not lose readers before you have had an opportunity to convince them.

The following five techniques are a few of the many ways to begin a sales letter. Each technique requires you to adapt it to your product or service.

1. Asking a question. Mention something that readers are vitally concerned about that is also relevant to your product or service. Look, for example, at the opening question in Fig. 6.9 (page 138). Avoid such general questions as "Are you happy?" or "Would you like to make money?" Use more specific questions. For example, an ad for a home-study training course in crime investigation and identification asked readers "Are you promotable? Are you ready to step into a bigger job?" And an ad for Air Force Reserve Nursing asked nurses if they were "looking for something 30,000 feet out of the ordinary?" These are precise questions relevant to the offers they introduce. Similarly, sales letters beginning with "Could you use $100?" or "Will you be wearing the latest jewelry at this year's Christmas party?" zero in on one particular desire of the reader. Since your main goal is to persuade readers to continue reading your letter, choose a question that they will want to see answered.

2. Employing a "how to" statement. This is one of the most frequently used openers in a sales letter. The reason for its success is simple—the letter promises to tell readers something practical and profitable. Here are some effective "how to" statements: "We can show you how to increase all your plant growth up to 91%." "Here is how to save $50.00 on your next vacation." "This is how to provide nourishing lunches on less than fifty cents a person." These "how to" statements attract the readers' attention by introducing a subject that promises rewards and then shows how to gain those rewards.

3. Using flattery. Appeal to a reader's ego. But readers are not naive; they will be suspicious of false praise. Select some compliment that affects the reader professionally or that praises the reader for some specific actions. A sales letter for a school supply shop was sent to every new member of a campus sorority announcing, "You've made the right choice in joining Delta Zeta. Now, let us make the right choice in helping you select your supplies this term."

4. Offering a free gift. Everyone likes to receive something for nothing or to boast about a bargain. Often you can lure readers further into your letter by telling them that there is a sale going on and that they can save a lot of money or that they can get the second product free, or at cost, or at half price if they purchase the first one at full price. The American Garden Guild promises prospective customers, "We'll give you three books for $1.00 and a free Tote Bag to put them in . . . with membership." An automobile dealer promises $50.00 to every customer who test drives a new car. A local realtor tempts customers to see lots for sale with, "Enclosed please find a coupon worth $10.00 in gas for seeing Deer Run Trails Estates."

Fig. 6.9   A sales letter.

MOSBY
TIMES MIRROR

THE C. V. MOSBY COMPANY · 11830 WESTLINE INDUSTRIAL DRIVE, ST. LOUIS, MISSOURI 63141

314-872-8370 · CABLE ADDRESS "MOSBYCO"

Dear Doctor:

After you look it up, do you really know which drug is best for YOUR patient . . . and WHY?

It all depends on where you look. If you consult standard "cookbook" guides to current drug therapy, you'll have only the personal opinions of one or two physicians on which drug they prefer to treat a specific disease.

However, if you consult the new DRUGS OF CHOICE 1980–1981, you'll have an authoritative, critical, unbiased appraisal of all drugs in current use, written specifically to support and verify your selection of the optimum drug for a specific patient in a particular clinical situation.

DRUGS OF CHOICE is the only drug therapy book which recognizes that you alone can fit drug and patient together, and thus gives you all the facts necessary to assist you in that "fitting." Dr. Modell and his 45 eminent contributors discuss all drugs available for a particular condition, based on their specialized knowledge and experience, substantiated by selected references. You will note revision updating in every chapter, particularly those on diuretics and drugs for cardiac arrhythmias.

You'll find a more complete description of the new DRUGS OF CHOICE 1980–1981 on the specially prepared brochure enclosed, including table of contents, distinguished contributors, and 54 timesaving tables. Take a moment now to examine it; then examine the book itself for 30 days at our expense. Just complete the examination certificate and return it to us in the postage–paid envelope provided.

Each time you sign a prescription, you, and you alone, endorse the safety and quality of the drug prescribed. If you're going to look it up, you want the whole story. And only one book offers you that . . . DRUGS OF CHOICE 1980–1981. Can you afford to be without it?

Sincerely,

William J. DeRoze

William J. DeRoze
for The C. V. Mosby Company

WJD:ne

Letter adapted courtesy The C.V. Mosby Company.

5. Using a comparison. Compare your product or service with conventional or standard products or procedures. Scriptomatic Addressing Systems persuasively begins with: "Address mail fives times faster than typing with Scriptomatic's new Model 5, a complete addressing system designed for home or office use." A jacket firm told police officers that if they purchased a coat, they were really getting three jackets in one, since their product had a lining for winter and another lining used for greater visibility at night.

Calling Attention to the Product's Appeal

Once you have aroused the reader's attention, introduce the product or service. Make it so attractive, so necessary, and so profitable that the reader will want to buy or use the product or service. Persuade readers to want to see it, touch it, and ultimately own or use it. Don't lose the momentum you have gained with your introduction by boring the reader with petty details, flat descriptions, elaborate inventories, or trivial boasts. Appeal to the reader's intellect or emotions while at the same time introducing the product. In Fig. 6.9 Mosby Company's mass-mailing letter appeals to the physician's professional requirements for an up-to-date book. Here is an emotional appeal by the Gulf Stream Fruit Company:

> Can you, when you bite into an orange, tell where it was grown? If it tastes better than any you have ever eaten . . . full of rich, golden flavor, brimming with juice, sparkling with sunshine . . . then you know it was grown here in our famous Indian River Valley where we have handpicked it, at the very peak of its flavor, just for your order.[1]

From a leading question, the sales letter moves to a vivid description of the product, name of the supplier, and the customer's ability to recognize how special both the product and he or she is to the Gulf Stream Fruit Company. Using another kind of appeal, the manufacturers of Tree Saw show how their product can decrease customers' fears and increase their safety.

> The greatest invention since the ladder, and a lot safer. With the Tree Saw, you can cut branches thirty feet above the ground. No need to call in a tree surgeon. And you don't have to risk your life on a shaky ladder. Just toss the beanbag weight of the flexible Tree Saw over a branch. Pull on each end of the control rope to make a clean cut. Spring pruning is quick and safe with this perfect tool.[2]

Showing the Customer the Product's Application

The third part of your sales letter lets the readers know how and why the product is worthwhile for them. Here is the place where you give evidence of the value of what you are selling. You have to be careful, though, that you do

---

[1] "Gifts from Gulf Stream" Oct. 1980, Gulf Stream Fruit Company, Ft. Lauderdale, Florida. Reprinted by permission.
[2] Reprinted courtesy Green Mountain Products, Inc., Norwalk, Conn.

not overwhelm readers with facts, statistics, detailed mechanical descriptions, or elaborate arguments. The emphasis is still on the use of the product and not on the product itself or the company that manufactures or sells it. The shift from your company to your prospective customer is essential to any sale. The sales letter in Fig. 6.9 emphasizes the importance of the physician's role in prescribing drugs: "You alone can fit drug and patient together." The following Fisher-Price Toys sales message is addressed to parents who are worried about children damaging a phonograph. Note how the details about the phonograph are all related to that reader-centered issue.

> Fisher-Price knows that children begin to appreciate music at a very early age. Usually, a little before they fully appreciate how to handle delicate things like tone arms and fragile records. That's why we designed our new phonograph with lots of features other record players don't offer. To assure that this phonograph can take the toughest treatment young music lovers can hand out and keep playing in fine tune year after year
>
> 1. There's a real, replaceable diamond needle that lasts five times longer than a sapphire needle.
> 2. The needle cartridge actually retracts when the tone arm is forced down, to prevent deep scratches.
> 3. The tone arm is solidly constructed so it can be pulled and tugged and still work smoothly.
> 4. The detachable case cover is specially designed to gently guide the tone arm back in place even if the cover is slammed shut.
> 5. The phonograph's 4″ speaker provides a nice clear sound. And there are just two simple controls for volume and record speed (33 and 45 rpm) plus a built-in storage space for the electrical cord.
>
> So you can see, the Fisher-Price Phonograph is not a toy. It's a really dependable piece of audio equipment that's made especially for children. So you, and they, can relax and enjoy its wonderful sound for years to come. And that should be music to your ears.[3]

What evidence should you use to convince the reader? Concentrate on descriptions of the product or service that emphasize convenience, usefulness, and economy. Any special features or changes in the product or service that make it more attractive for the customer should be mentioned. For example, an ad for a greenhouse manufacturer stressed that in addition to using its structure just for a place to grow plants, customers would also find it a "perfect sun room enclosure for year 'round 'outdoor' activities, gardening or leisure health spa."

Testimonials—endorsements from previous customers as well as from specialists—may also convince readers to respond favorably to your letter. Rather than saying that hundreds of customers are satisfied with your product, get two or three of those happy customers to allow you to quote them in

---

[3]Reprinted courtesy Waring & LaRosa, Inc., and Fisher-Price Toys, Inc.

your letter. A large nursing home published residents' compliments about the food and care to show that it was a good place to live. A private boarding school printed a brief biography (with now and then pictures) of a successful graduate to prove that the school inspires students to leadership. A roach powder tells customers that its product is used at the White House. You might also cite any awards, honors, accreditations, or citations that your product or service has won.

Worth mentioning also are warranties, guarantees, services, or special considerations that will make the customer's life easier or happier. One store advises readers: "As usual, there is no charge for local deliveries when purchases are over $100." Tell the reader that labor and parts are good for a year, two years, or however long they last. Emphasize that you will refund the price if the customer is not completely satisfied. Do you have your own repair crew? Tell customers that they do not have to wait for parts or that you will loan them a replacement if they do.

You may be obligated to mention costs in your letter. Postpone discussion of them until the reader has been shown how appealing and valuable the product is. Of course if price is a key selling point, it should be mentioned early in the letter. Readers will react more favorably to costs after they have seen the reasons why the product or service is useful. Do not bluntly state the cost. Relate prices, charges, or fees to the benefits provided by the services or products to which they apply. After giving the price per can of its insecticide, the manufacturer tells readers that "one can covers up to a nine-room residence, plus one can for basement or garage." Customers then see how much they are getting for their money. An electric-blanket ad tells customers that it costs only four cents a night to be warm and comfortable. That sounds more inviting than just listing the cost of the blanket as $30. A dealer who installs steel shutters does not tell readers the exact price of the product, but does indicate that they will save money by buying it: "Virtually maintenance free, your Reel Shutters also offer substantial savings in energy costs by reducing your loss through radiation by as much as 65% ... and that lowers your utility bills by 35%." Keep costs tied to the reader's profit.

Ending with a Specific Request for Action

This last section of your letter is vital. If the reader ignores your request for action, your letter has been written in vain. Tell readers exactly what you want them to do and make it easy and pleasurable to do it. Do you want them to fill out a postcard ordering your product, send for a brochure, come into your store, take a test drive, participate in a meeting? Indicate clearly the actions you want readers to take. Tell them if they have to sign an order blank or merely initial it. Is there an enclosed stamped envelope for their convenience? When do they have to notify you? Is there a deadline for taking advantage of a sale price or bonus? "Come to our store tomorrow between 10 A.M. and 10 P.M. to get your free lounge chair with the purchase of any bedroom suite." As with price, link the benefits the customers will receive to their responses. "Respond and be rewarded" is the basic message of the last section of your letter. Note that in Fig. 6.9 the call to action is made in the next-to-last paragraph, but is followed by a brief reminder of the significance of the action. Fig. 6.10 shows a call-to-action statement in the last paragraph. The letter urges readers to act immediately in order to receive the free installation.

▶ Customer Relations Letters

Much business correspondence deals explicitly with promoting and maintaining friendly working relations. Such correspondence, known as customer relations letters, includes thank-you letters, congratulation letters, follow-up letters, complaint letters, adjustment letters, and collection letters. All such letters show how you and your company regard the people with whom you do business. Customer relations letters must reveal a sensitivity to customers' needs, whether you are communicating about something pleasant (a promotion, an award, a business favor) or something unpleasant (a defective piece of machinery, spoiled goods, or unpaid bills). The words you choose and the order in which you present information will determine the success or failure of a customer relations letter. As you read this section, keep in mind the two basic principles captured in the words "the customers always write":

1. Customers will write about how they would like to be or have been treated—to thank, to complain, to request an explanation.
2. Customers have certain rights that you must respect in your correspondence with them. They deserve a prompt and courteous reply, whether they are correct or not. If you refuse their request, they deserve to know why; if they owe you money, you should give them an opportunity to explain and a chance, up to a point, to set up a payment schedule.

Thank-You Letters

A thank-you letter tells someone how much that person's acts or words have meant to you. In the business world thank-you letters show that the writer is a responsible individual who values human relations. Even if you have already expressed your gratitude in person or over the telephone, a letter further underlines your thoughtfulness and courtesy.

Obviously, you will not write a thank-you letter for every kindness shown you or your firm. Reserve a letter for the special occasions when an individual or company does something extra—something that did not have to be done or that was especially helpful. Thank-you letters also figure significantly in a job search. The individuals who write your letters of recommendation, as well as the prospective employers who interview you, deserve thank-you letters.

Fig. 6.10   A letter with a call-to-action statement.

FAITHFUL ANSWERING SERVICE
4300 South Wabash
Lincoln, Oregon 97407

September 27, 1981

Ms. Katherine Eubanks
Eubanks Pest Control
18 West Gannon Drive
Lincoln, OR 97411

Dear Ms. Eubanks:

How much business do you lose when your telephone rings and you are not there to answer it? A prospective client or steady customer might call one of the other twenty-two exterminators listed in the Lincoln Yellow Pages.

You will never miss a call if you use the Faithful Answering Service. Our courteous and experienced operators are on duty twenty-four hours a day, every day of the year. They are prompt, too. Your telephone will be answered before the caller hears the third ring.

You tell us when we are needed by simply calling us and giving us your identifying code number. We will be there to take messages or to transfer calls to any number you give us. When you are out of the office, a quick call to us can save you extra trips, time, and gas. Your customers will also be happier, knowing that you can be reached whenever they need you to solve their pest problems.

All this convenience and peace of mind can be yours for less than $.80 a day. And if you act by October 4, you can have the Faithful service installed free of charge and save the $15.00 installation fee. We promise to have your phone connected within three days after we hear from you.

I urge you to call us at 657-3434 by October 4. You can call us at any time, day or night. Don't forget, we are here twenty-four hours a day.

Sincerely yours,

Samuel Heywood

Samuel Heywood, Owner

11 contains a thank-you letter to Mr. Butler, to whom Robert Jackson wrote (in Chapter 5) for a reference. Also review the letter on p. 114 to a prospective employer after the candidate has been interviewed.

Thank-you letters should be a joy to write. Your main concerns are (1) being specific about what you liked and (2) explaining why you are grateful. Begin with a simple, direct statement of gratitude identifying what has pleased you. Indicate how and when this service was provided. Mention the names of individuals responsible for the work and why their work was so extraordinary. Also indicate why this service deserves special thanks—that is, how the action helped you or how it applies to your company.

The letter in Fig. 6.12 illustrates an apt thank-you letter. A local merchant thanks a glass company for the exceptional service she received. When

Fig. 6.11　A thank-you letter.

5432 South Kenneth Avenue
Chicago, IL 60651
April 30, 1982

Mr. Sunny Butler
Manager, A&P Supermarket
4000 West 79th Street
Chicago, IL 60652

Dear Mr. Butler:

Thank you very much for writing a letter of recommendation to be included in my dossier at the Placement Office at Moraine Valley Community College. I appreciate your taking the time to do this, and I am especially grateful for the many kind things you said you had included in your letter. Your high praise of my work for A&P will certainly help me in finding a job in retail sales.

Once again, thank you for your recommendation. I will let you know how my job search goes.

Sincerely yours,

Robert B. Jackson

Robert B. Jackson

Fig. 6.12   A thank-you letter.

GRANGER HARDWARE STORE
20 N.E. Hasse Road
Fair View, New Jersey 02386

February 25, 1982

Mr. Rudolph Della Sinta
Manager, Dole Glass Company
Manners Highway
Kensington, NJ 02384

Dear Mr. Della Sinta:

I want to thank the Dole Glass Company for giving me outstanding service
last Sunday night, February 23. My store's front plate glass window (21
feet by 12 feet) was smashed by some flying debris. Your regular crew,
Paula Romero and Tim Tulley, were at my store thirty minutes after I
phoned them late Sunday night. They quickly cleared away the glass and
measured my window. Realizing that the plates they had on their truck
would not fit my window, they drove all the way back to your Devonshire
warehouse to locate a suitable piece. They could have waited until the
next day to do this, but they returned and installed the new glass window
in record time.

Their service was exceptional. It allowed me to open my store on Monday
morning for business as usual. If your crew had not worked so quickly and
made that extra trip, I would have been forced to board up my store and
close on Monday to have the repairs made.

I have the highest opinion of Dole Glass and the two employees who came
to my store two days ago.

Sincerely yours,

Barbara Stovall-Granger

Barbara Stovall—Granger
Owner

---

the Dole Glass Company has any need of hardware parts, it will certainly be favorably disposed to order from Granger Hardware because of Ms. Stovall-Granger's kind and welcome thank-you letter.

Congratulation Letters

When you put your praise into a letter, you show considerable thoughtfulness. You could call the individual on the telephone or speak to him or her in person to extend your congratulations. But a letter shows that you have taken the extra effort. This personal touch also says far more than a greeting card with a printed message. Your attention and courtesy will rarely go unnoticed and will create goodwill.

The occasions for such letters, in both your business and personal life, are many. In the business world you might congratulate someone for (1) being promoted, (2) opening a new business or expanding an existing one, or (3) being honored for an accomplishment (for example, having the highest sales record of the month or year, completing a course in cardiac life support, or becoming a broker). When you honor someone for a distinction, you also honor the company the individual represents. In your own community you create goodwill by congratulating someone for being elected to public office, serving on a charitable or civic committee, or receiving an award or medal. In addition to complimenting people for professional or civic achievements, you will also be called on to congratulate individuals for engagements, marriages, births, graduations, and anniversaries.

Congratulatory letters must arrive at the right time. Write as soon after the accomplishment as you can. Good news travels fast; acknowledging the individual's honor quickly shows that you are keeping track of events and are eager to express your congratulations. A late letter will say that you did not have the time to write (that the news was not very important to you) or that you belatedly joined everyone else in sending your good wishes.

Keep your letters short and sincere. But a one-sentence letter—"Please accept my congratulations on being promoted"—is inappropriate. A letter this short looks as if you sent it not because you were sincerely interested in the individual, but because you felt that you must write something.

You need not write four or five long paragraphs. A long congratulatory letter with flowery language and repeated backslapping smacks of insincerity. Excessive praise is doubtful praise, as the following letter suggests:

Dear Ms. Bozanich:

I would like to take this opportunity to extend my warmest congratulations on your being justly promoted to branch manager at the Powersville store.

The Jordan Company could not have picked a more qualified woman or a less selfish person to take on this heavy

responsibility. This is a post I know you will fill with
distinction. Your years of rewarding experience in the field have
finally paid off richly and well, as they should have. I know that
you will continue to perform the same high caliber work in your
new office as you did in the field. We are lucky to have your able,
proven leadership as we approach a new fiscal year.

Once again, please kindly accept my heartiest congratulations
for your new well-deserved honor.

Sincerely,

Robert Mayer

Robert Mayer

The trite phrases in this letter ("take this opportunity," "could not have
picked a more qualified woman," "paid off richly," "same high caliber work,"
"we are lucky to have your able, proven leadership," "well-deserved honor")
ring hollow. The writer obviously overdid the praise.

A sincere yet brief letter of congratulation praises one or two significant
points of the individual's accomplishment. The following two paragraphs
provide a suitable "translation" of the verbose, flowery letter above:

Dear Ms. Bozanich:

Please accept my congratulations on being promoted to branch
manager of the Powersville store. Your work in the field for the
Jordan Company will profit you and us in your new job.

I wish you great success as branch manager.

Sincerely,

Robert Mayer

Robert Mayer

This next congratulatory letter selects a few details, including the place where
the writer learned of the reader's achievement, to show the writer's sincere
interest:

Dear Mr. Goshin:

Congratulations on your new title of Certified Insurance
Counselor just announced in the <u>Midtown Financial Record</u>. It

certainly is an honor to be among only three thousand agents in
the country who can sign C.I.C. after their name.

You have our best wishes for continuing success in your
insurance business.

Sincerely yours,

Jenifer Rodriguez

Jenifer Rodriguez

One last point about congratulatory letters: Do not use them to sell a
product or service. By calling attention to your company's services, you reveal
that your supposed congratulations are only a gimmick.

Follow-up Letters

A business follow-up letter is sent by a company after a sale to thank the customer for buying a product or using a service and to ask the customer to buy
more products and use more services in the future. A business follow-up letter is, therefore, a combination thank-you note and sales letter. The letter in
Fig. 6.13 is sent to customers soon after they have purchased an appliance
and offers them the option of a continued maintenance policy. The letter in
Fig. 6.14 shows how an income tax preparation service attempts to obtain repeat business. Both of these letters follow certain helpful guidelines:

1. They begin with a brief and sincere expression of gratitude for having
   served the customer.
2. They discuss the benefits (advantages) already known to the customer.
   Then, they transfer the company's dedication to the customer from the
   product or service already sold to a new or continuing sales area.
3. They end with a specific request for future business.

Occasionally a follow-up letter is sent to a good customer who, for some
reason, has stopped doing business with the company. Perhaps the customer
has closed an account of long standing, no longer comes to the store, discon-
tinues a subscription, or fails to send in an order for a product or service.
Such a follow-up letter should try to find out why the faithful customer has
stopped doing business and to persuade that customer to resume business
dealings. Study the letter in Fig. 6.15, in which Jim Margolis first politely inquires whether Mr. Janeck has experienced a problem and then urges him to
come back to the store.

Complaint Letters

Each of us at some time has been frustrated by a defective product, inadequate service, or incorrect billing. Usually our first response is to write a letter

Fig. 6.13   A follow-up letter.

SOUTHERN APPLIANCE COMPANY

February 9, 1982

Mr. John H. Abbott
5634 Desire
New Orleans, Louisiana 70211

Dear Mr. Abbott:

   We are pleased that you have chosen a Southern appliance. To help ensure your satisfaction, this appliance is backed by Southern warranty. At the same time, we realize that you bought the appliance to serve you not just for the period of the warranty, but for many, many years. That's why the purchase of a Southern Maintenance Agreement at this time is one of the wisest investments you can make.

   A Southern Maintenance Agreement provides savings benefits many cost-conscious customers such as yourself want and look for today. It helps extend the life of the appliance by means of an annual, on-request <u>preventive maintenance</u> check-up. And if you need service, <u>it provides for as many service calls as necessary for repairs due to normal use—at no extra charge to you</u>.

   All this coverage is now available to you at a special introductory price. This price takes into consideration the warranty coverage you have remaining. Act now, by completing the enclosed form, and begin enjoying peace of mind today.

                              Sincerely,

                              SOUTHERN APPLIANCE CO.

                              Carole Brown

                              Carole Brown
                              Sales Representative
                              588-9681
                              Extension 285

Fig. 6.14   A follow-up letter.

TAYLOR TAX SERVICE
Highway 10 North
Mobile, Alabama 36613

December 1, 1980

Ms. Laurie Pavlovich
345 Jefferson Parkway
Mobile, AL 36602

Dear Ms. Pavlovich:

Thank you for using our services in February of this year. We were honored to help you prepare your 1979 federal and state income tax returns. Our goal is to save you every tax dollar to which you are entitled. If you ever have any questions about your return, we are open all year long to help you.

We are looking forward to seeing you again next year. The new federal tax laws, which go into effect January 1, will change the type of deductions you can declare. These changes might appreciably increase the size of your return. Our consultants have studied these new laws and are ready to explain them to you and apply them to your return.

Another important tax matter influencing your 1980 returns will be any losses you suffered because of Hurricane Frederic, which hit the Gulf Coast three months ago. Our consultants are specially trained to assist you in filing proper damage claims with your federal and state returns.

To make using our services even easier next year, we have started an appointment policy for your convenience. Please feel free to call us at 884-3457 or 885-7853 as soon as you have received all your forms in order to set up your own appointment. We are waiting to serve you any day of the week from 8:00 A.M. to 9:00 P.M.

You can depend on us to help you with all your income tax needs.

Sincerely yours,

TAYLOR TAX SERVICE

J. P. Sanders
Manager

Fig. 6.15   A follow-up letter.

BROADWAY CLEANERS
Broadway at Davis Drive
Baltimore, Maryland 21228

April 3, 1982

Mr. Edward Janeck
34 Brompton Lane
Apartment 143
Baltimore, MD 21227

Dear Mr. Janeck:

You have given us the privilege of taking care of your cleaning needs for
more than three years now. It has been our pleasure to see you in the
store each week and to clean your shirts, slacks, and coats to your
satisfaction. Since you have not come in during the last month, we are
concerned that we may have in some way disappointed you. We hope not,
because a valuable and loyal customer such as you allows us to stay in
business.

If there is something wrong, please tell us about it. We welcome any
suggestions on how we can serve you better. Our goal is to have a
spotless reputation in the eyes of our customers.

The next time you need some garments cleaned, won't you please bring
them to us, along with the enclosed coupon worth $2.50 off our services.
We look forward to seeing you again—soon.

Sincerely yours,

BROADWAY CLEANERS

Jim Margolis

Jim Margolis, Manager

dripping with juicy insults. But a hate letter rarely gets results and can in fact hurt the writer and create an unfavorable image of the company being represented. A letter of complaint is a delicate one to write.

A letter of complaint is written for more reasons than just blowing off steam. You want some action taken. By adopting the right tone, you increase your chances of getting what you want. Do not call the reader names, hurl insults, refuse to do business with the company again. Register your complaint courteously and tolerantly. Companies want to be fair to you in order to keep you as a satisfied customer and correct defective products so that other customers will not be inconvenienced. The "you attitude" is especially important here.

An effective letter of complaint can be written by an individual consumer or by a company. Figure 6.16 shows Michael Trigg's complaint about a defective fishing reel; Fig. 6.17 expresses a restaurant's dissatisfaction with an industrial dishwasher. Present your case logically, and provide enough detail to obtain a speedy settlement. To accomplish this objective, follow these five steps.

1. Begin with a detailed description of the product or service. Give the appropriate model numbers, size(s), quantity, color. Indicate when and where (specific address) you purchased it, and also how much warranty time remains. If you are complaining about a service, give the name of the company, the frequency of the service, the personnel providing it, and their exact duties.

2. State exactly what is wrong with the product or service. Precise information will enable the recipient to understand and act on your complaint. How many times did the machine work before it stopped, what parts were malfunctioning, what parts of a job were not done or were done poorly, and when did all this happen? Stating that "the brake shoes were defective" tells very little about how long they were on your car, how effectively they may have been installed, or what condition they were in when they ceased functioning safely. Reach some conclusion, even if you qualify your remarks with words like "apparently," "possibly," or "seemingly" when you describe the difficulty.

3. Briefly describe the inconvenience you have experienced. Your comments in this section of the letter of complaint show that your problems were directly caused by the defective product or service. If you purchased a calculator and it broke down during a mathematics examination, say so (but do not blame the calculator company if you failed the course). Were you forced to postpone a luncheon because the caterer was late, did you have to pay a mechanic to fix your car when it was stalled on the road, did you have to take time away from your other chores to clean up a mess made by a leaky new dishwasher, did you have to buy a new fishing reel?

Fig. 6.16   A complaint letter from a consumer.

17 Westwood
Magnolia, MA 02171
September 15, 1981

Mr. Ralph Montoya
Manager, Customer Relations Department
Smith Sports Equipment
Tulsa, OK 74109

Dear Mr. Montoya:

On August 31, 1981, I purchased a Smith reel, model #191, at the Uni–Mart
Store on Marsh Avenue in Magnolia. The reel sold for $24.95 plus tax.
Since the reel is not working effectively, I am returning it to you under
separate cover.

I had made no more than five casts with the reel when it began to
malfunction. The button that releases the spool and allows the line to
cast will not spring back into position after casting. In addition, the
gears make a grinding noise when I try to retrieve the line. Because of
these problems, I was unable to continue my participation in the
Gloucester Fishing Tournament.

I want a new reel to be sent to me free of charge in place of the defective
one I returned. I would also like to know what was wrong with this
defective reel.

I shall appreciate your handling my claim as quickly as possible.

Sincerely yours,

Michael Trigg

Michael Trigg

Fig. 6.17   A complaint letter from a business.

THE LOFT
Cameron and Dale
Sunnyside, California 91793

June 17, 1982

Customer Relations Department
Superflex Products
San Diego, CA 93141

Dear Customer Relations Department:

On September 15, 1981, we purchased a Superflex industrial dishwasher, model number 5634a, at the Hillcrest Store at 3452 Broadway in Sunnyside, for $2,000. In the last three weeks, our restaurant has had repeated problems with this machine. Three more months of warranty remain on this machine.

The machine does not complete a full cycle; it stops before the final rinsing and thus leaves the dishes still dirty. It appears that the cycle regulators are not working properly because they refuse to shift into the next necessary gear. Attempts to repair the machine by the Hillcrest crew on June 3, 12, and 16 have been unsuccessful.

Our restaurant has been greatly inconvenienced. The kitchen team has been forced to sort, clean, and sanitize utensils, dishes, pans, and pots by hand. Moreover, our expenses for proper detergents have increased.

We want your main office to send another repair crew at once to fix this machine. If your crew is unable to do this, we want a discount worth the amount of warranty life on this model to be applied to the purchase of a new Superflex dishwasher. This amount would come to $400.00, or 20 percent of the original purchase price.

Please answer our claim as soon as you can. Thank you.

Sincerely yours,

Emily Rashon

Emily Rashon
Manager

4. Indicate precisely what you want done.   Do not simply write that you "want something done" or that "the situation should be corrected." State that you want your purchase price refunded, your model repaired or replaced, or a completely new crew provided. Maybe you want only an apology from the company for some discourteous treatment. If you are asking for damages, state your request in dollars and cents, and include a copy of any bills resulting from the problem. Perhaps you had to rent a car, were forced to pay a janitorial service to clean up, or had to rent equipment at a higher rate because the company did not make its deliveries as promised.

5. Ask for prompt handling of your claim.   Ask that an answer be provided to any question you may have (such as finding out where calls came from that you were billed for but did not make). And ask that your claim be handled as quickly as possible.

Adjustment Letters

Adjustment letters tell customers dissatisifed with a product or service how their claim will be settled. Adjustment letters should reconcile the differences that exist between a customer and a firm and restore the customer's confidence in that firm.

Rather than ignoring or quarreling with complaint letters, most companies view answering them as being good for business. Many large firms maintain separate claims and adjustment departments just to handle disappointed customers. By writing to complain about a product or service, the customer alerts your company to a problem that can be remedied to avoid similar complaints in the future. Customers who have taken the time to put complaints in writing obviously regard them as important; they want and deserve a reply. If you do not answer the customer's letter politely, you stand to lose a lot of business—not just the customer's business, but also that of his or her friends, family, and associates, who will all have been told about your unreliable and discourteous company.

An effective adjustment letter requires diplomacy; be prompt, courteous, and decisive. Do not brush the complaint aside in hopes that it will be forgotten. Delay will only make the customer angrier. Investigate the complaint quickly and determine its validity by checking previous correspondence, warranty statements, guarantees, and your firm's policies on merchandise and service. In some cases you may even have to send returned damaged merchandise to your firm's laboratory to determine who is at fault.

A noncommittal letter signals the customer that you have failed to investigate the claim or are stalling for time. Do not resort to vague statements like the following:

- We will do what we can to solve your problems.
- A company policy prohibits our returning your purchase price in full.
- Your request, while legitimate, will take time to process.

- We will act on your request with your best interest in mind.
- While we cannot now determine the extent of an adjustment, we will be back in touch with you.

Customers want to be told that they are right; or if they cannot get what they want, they will demand to know why, in the most explicit terms. At the other extreme, do not overdo an apology by saying that the company is "completely at fault" or that "such shoddy merchandise is inexcusable." An expression of regret need not jeopardize all future business dealings. If you make your company look too bad, you risk losing the customer permanently. A begrudging tone will destroy the goodwill created by your refund or replacement.

Adjustment Letters that Tell the Customer "Yes"

If investigation reveals the customer's claim to be valid, you must write a letter saying "Yes, you are right; we will give you what you asked for." Such a letter is easy to write if you remember a few useful suggestions. You want customers to realize that you sincerely agree with them—not to feel as if you are reluctantly granting their request. The two examples of adjustment letters saying "yes" show you how to write this kind of correspondence. The first example, Fig. 6.18, says "yes" to Michael Trigg's letter in Fig. 6.16. You might want to reread the Trigg complaint letter to see what problems Ralph Montoya faced when he had to write to Mr. Trigg. The second example of an adjustment letter that says "yes" is in Fig. 6.19. It responds to a customer who has complained about an incorrect billing. The following four steps will help you write a "yes" adjustment letter:

1. Admit immediately that the customer's complaint is justified and apologize.   Simply state that you are sorry and thank the customer for writing to inform you.

2. State precisely what you are going to do to correct the problem.   Are you going to cancel a bill, return a damaged camera in good working order, repaint a room, enclose a free pass, provide a complimentary dinner, or give the customer credit toward another purchase? Do not postpone the good news the customer wants to hear. The rest of your letter will be much more appreciated and convincing. In Fig. 6.18 Michael Trigg is told that he will receive a new reel; in Fig. 6.19 Kathryn Brumfield is informed that she will not be charged for parts or service.

3. Tell customers exactly what happened.   They deserve an explanation for the inconvenience they suffered. Note how the explanations in Figs. 6.18 and 6.19 give only the essential details; they do not bother the reader with side issues or petty remarks about who was to blame. Assure customers that the mishap is not typical of your company's operations. While your comments should not shift the blame, they should center on the unusual reason

Fig. 6.18   An adjustment letter saying "yes."

SMITH SPORTS EQUIPMENT
P.O. Box 287
Tulsa, Oklahoma 74109

September 21, 1981

Mr. Michael Trigg
17 Westwood
Magnolia, MA 02171

Dear Mr. Trigg:

Thank you for alerting us to the problems you had with one of our model
191 spincast reels. I am sorry for the inconvenience the reel has caused
you. A new Smith reel is on its way to you.

We have examined your reel and found the problem. It seems that a
retaining pin on the button spring was improperly installed by one of
our new soldering machines on the assembly line. We have thoroughly
inspected, repaired, and cleaned this soldering machine to eliminate
the problem. Our company has been making quality reels since 1935. We
hope that your new Smith reel brings you years of pleasure and many good
catches, especially next year at the Gloucester Fishing Tournament.

We appreciate your business and look forward to serving you again.

Sincerely yours,

SMITH SPORTS EQUIPMENT

Ralph Montoya

Ralph Montoya
Manager, Customer Relations Department

Fig. 6.19   An adjustment letter saying "yes."

BRUNELLI MOTORS
Route 3A
Giddings, Kansas 62034

October 6, 1981

Ms. Kathryn Brumfield
34 East Main
Giddings, KS 62034

Dear Ms. Brumfield:

We appreciate your notifying us about the problem you have experienced
regarding warranty coverage on your new 1981 Phantom Hawk GT. The bills
sent to you were incorrect, and I have already canceled them. Please
accept my apologies. You should not have been charged for a new shroud or
for repairs to the damaged fan and hose, since all these parts, and labor
on them, are covered by warranty.

The problem was the result of an error in the way charges were listed.
Our firm has just begun using a new system of billing to give customers
better service, and the mechanic apparently punched the wrong code
number on your account. I have instructed the mechanics to double-check
their code numbers before submitting them to the Billing Department.

We value you as a customer of Brunelli Motors. When you are ready for
another Phantom, I hope that you will once again come to our dealership.

Sincerely yours,

BRUNELLI MOTORS

a. Y. O'Donnel

A. Y. O'Donnel
Service Manager

or circumstance for the difficulty. Avoid promising, however, that the problem will never recur. Such an admission is not only unnecessary, but also beyond your control.

4. End on a friendly, and positive, note.   Do not remind the customers of the trouble they have gone through. Leave them with a good feeling about your company. Say that you are looking forward to seeing them again, that you will gladly work with them on any future orders, or that you can always be reached for questions.

Adjustment Letters that Tell the Customer "No"

Writing to tell customers "no" is obviously more difficult than agreeing with them. You are faced with the sensitive task of conveying bad news, while at the same time convincing the reader that your position is fair, logical, and consistent. You should not accuse or argue. Avoid remarks such as the following that blame, scold, or remind customers of a wrongdoing and hence may cost you their business:

- You obviously did not read the instruction manual.
- Our records show that you purchased the set after the policy went into effect.
- The company policy plainly states that such refunds are unallowable.
- You were negligent in running the machine.
- You claim that our typewriter was poorly constructed.
- You were careless in applying the proper measures.
- Your error, not our merchandise, is to blame.
- You must be mistaken about the merchandise.
- As any intelligent person could tell, the switch had to be on "off."

The following five suggestions will help you say "no" diplomatically. Practical applications of these suggestions can be found in Figs. 6.20 and 6.21. Contrast the rejection of Michael Trigg's complaint in Fig. 6.20 with the favorable response to it in Fig. 6.18.

1. Thank customers for writing.   Make a friendly start by putting them in a good frame of mind. The letter writers in Figs. 6.20 and 6.21 say that they are thankful that the customers brought the matter to their attention. Never begin with a refusal. You need time to calm and convince customers. Telling them "no" in the first sentence or two will negatively color their reactions to the rest of the letter. Also, never begin letters with "I was surprised to learn that you found our product defective (or our service inefficient)" or "We cannot understand how such a problem occurred. We have been in business for years, and nothing like this has ever happened." Such openings put customers on the defense.

Fig. 6.20   An adjustment letter saying "no."

SMITH SPORTS EQUIPMENT
P.O. Box 287
Tulsa, Oklahoma 74109

September 21, 1981

Mr. Michael Trigg
17 Westwood
Magnolia, MA 02171

Dear Mr. Trigg:

Thank you for writing to us about the trouble you experienced with our model #191 spincast reel. We were sorry to hear about the difficulties you had with the release button and gears.

We have examined your reel and have found the trouble. It seems that a retaining pin on the button spring was pushed into the side of the reel casing, thereby making the gears inoperable. The retaining pin is a vital yet delicate part of your reel. In order to function properly, it has to be pushed gently. Since the pin was not used in this way, we are not able to refund your purchase price.

We will be pleased, however, to repair your reel for $5.98 and return it to you for hours of fishing pleasure. Please let us know your decision.

I shall look forward to hearing from you.

Sincerely yours,

SMITH SPORTS EQUIPMENT

Ralph Montoya

Ralph Montoya
Manager, Customer Relations

Fig. 6.21   An adjustment letter saying "no."

HEALTH AIR, INC.
4300 Marshall Drive
Salt Lake City, Utah 84113

August 20, 1982

Ms. Denise Southby
Director, Bradley General Hospital
Bradley, IL 60610

Dear Ms. Southby:

Thank you for your letter explaining the problems you have encountered
with our Puritan Bennett MAII type ventilator. We were sorry to learn
that you could not get the high-volume PAO_2 alarm circuit to work.

Our ventilator is a high volume, low frequency machine that is capable
of delivering up to 40 ml of water pressure. The ventilator runs with a
center of gravity attachment that is on the right side of the diode. The
trouble you are having with the high oxygen alarm system is due to an
overload of your piped-in oxygen. Our laboratory inspection of the
ventilator you returned indicates that the high pressure system had
blown a vital adaptor in the machine. Our company cannot be responsible
for any type of overload caused by an oxygen system of which we are
unaware. We cannot, therefore, send you a replacement ventilator free of
charge. Your ventilator is being returned to you.

We would, however, be very glad to send you a new adaptor as soon as we
receive your order. The price of the adaptor is $600, and our factory
representative will be happy to install it for you at no charge. Please
let me know your decision.

We value you as a customer and would welcome the opportunity to assist
you in providing quality health care.

Sincerely yours,

HEALTH AIR, INC.

R. P. Gilford

R. P. Gilford
Customer Service Department

2. State the problem so that customers realize that you understand their complaint. You thereby prove that you are not trying to misrepresent what they have told you.

3. Explain what happened with the product or service before you give customers a decision. Provide a factual explanation to show customers that they are being treated fairly. Convince them of the logic and consistency of your point of view. Rather than focusing on the customer's mishandling of merchandise or failure to observe details of a service contract, state the proper ways of handling a piece of equipment or the terms outlined in an agreement. Instead of writing "By reading the instructions on the side of the paint can, you would have avoided the streaking condition that you claim resulted," tell the customer that "Hi-Gloss Paint requires two applications, four hours apart, for a clear and shiny finish." In this way you remind customers of the right way of applying the paint without pointing an accusing finger at them. Note how the explanations in Figs. 6.20 and 6.21 emphasize the right way of using the product.

4. Give your decision without hedging. Do not say that perhaps some type of restitution could be made later or that further proof would have been helpful. Indecision will infuriate customers who believe that they have already presented a good case. Never apologize for your decision. Avoid using the words "reject," "claim," or "grant." "Reject" is too harsh and impersonal. "Claim" implies your distrust of the customers' complaint and suggests that questionable differences of opinion remain. "Grant" signals that you have it in your power to respond favorably but decline to do so; a grant is the kind of favor a ruler might give a subject. Instead, use words that reconcile.

5. Leave the door open for better and continued business. Wherever possible, help customers solve their problem by offering to send them a new product or part, and quote the full sales price. Note how the second-to-last paragraphs of the letters in Figs. 6.20 and 6.21 do this in a diplomatic way.

Collection Letters

Collection letters are, unfortunately, a part of every business's concern. They require the same tact and fairness as do complaint and adjustment letters. While the majority of your customers will pay their bills promptly, some will not pay precisely on time, and a few others may not pay until they are threatened with legal action or harassment from a collection agency.

Each nonpayment case should be evaluated separately. A nasty collection letter sent after only one month's nonpayment to a customer who is a good credit risk can damage your relationship and send that customer elsewhere. On the other hand, three very cordial, easygoing letters sent over three or four months to a customer who is a poor credit risk may encourage that individual to postpone payment, perhaps indefinitely.

Many businesses send four letters to customers before turning matters over to an attorney or a collection agency. These letters are mailed to poor credit risks at shorter intervals than to good ones. Each letter in the series employs a different technique, ranging from giving compliments and offering flexible credit terms to issuing demands for immediate payment or threats of legal consequences. One small hospital uses the four collection letters illustrated in Figs. 6.22 through 6.25 to encourage ex-patients to pay their bills.

The letter in Fig. 6.22 typifies the function of a first collection letter. It is a friendly reminder that an account is due. The tone of the letter is cordial and sincere—now is not the time to say "pay up or else." A first collection letter should stress how valuable the customer is, as does the first paragraph in Fig. 6.22. Note also that the first paragraph underscores how pleased the hospital is to have provided the care the patient needed. The last sentence of that paragraph unobtrusively introduces the word "finances" in the context of service. The second paragraph, after allowing for possible questions concerning the bill, makes a request for payment. Inducements to make that payment are offered: (1) a flexible payment schedule and (2) an escape from the inconvenience (or embarrassment) of receiving past-due notices. The bottom of the letter conveniently lists payment-schedule options available to the patient.

If after a month to six weeks, a customer still does not make a payment, send a second letter, such as the one illustrated in Fig. 6.23. This letter begins with a gentle reminder that the balance due has not yet been paid. The second paragraph politely inquires if something is wrong, thus admitting the hospital's recognition that not all nonpayments stem from a patient's willful neglect. While this second collection letter understands that there might be some "difficulty," it firmly reminds the patient to pay if there is no financial trouble. The last sentence makes another strong appeal to the patient's community obligation. Note that unlike the first letter, no payment schedule appears at the bottom of the letter, thus giving the patient a chance to explain any delay.

When still more time elapses and no payment is made, creditors send a third letter, an example of which appears in Fig. 6.24. The creditor's tone and tactics have changed. From the cooperative tone of "What's wrong, can we help?" in the second collection letter, the third letter switches to the much more direct "We have waited a long time. Pay, or at least begin to pay, your bill now." The third collection letter, which must be more forceful than the second, announces that serious consequences will result if the creditor does not receive a payment from the customer. The vague threat, "further action," wisely does not commit the hospital to take legal action or to speak to a collection agency, its last resort. The third letter should still give the delinquent customer a way out, and so this one contains some useful, face-saving options listed at the bottom of the letter.

If after receiving these three letters, a customer still does not respond, the creditor sends a fourth letter containing a specific threat that will be car-

Fig. 6.22   A first collection letter.

BALDWIN COUNTY HOSPITAL
P.O. Box 222
Notown, MA 02138

May 15, 1981

Re: Inpatient Services
Date of Hospitalization: April 1-5, 1981
Balance Due: $3725.48

Dear Mr. Peterson:

We are grateful that we were able to serve your health needs during your
recent stay at the Baldwin County Hospital. It is our continuing goal to
provide the best possible hospital care for residents of Baldwin County
and its vicinity. You will readily understand that to do so we must keep
our finances up to date.

Our records show that the above balance remains due on your account.
Unless you have a question concerning the figure, we would appreciate
receiving your prompt payment. If you are unable to pay the full amount
at this time, we will be happy to set up a schedule of partial payments.
Just fill in the appropriate blanks below, and return this letter to us.
That will enable us to avoid billing you on a "Past Due" basis. Thank
you for your cooperation.

Sincerely,

Morris T. Jukes

Morris T. Jukes
Accounts Receivable Department

( ) I will pay $_____ ( ) weekly; ( ) monthly, on my account.

( ) Enclosed is a check for full payment in the amount of $_____

_____

Signature

Fig. 6.23   A second collection letter.

BALDWIN COUNTY HOSPITAL
P.O. Box 222
Notown, MA 02138

June 19, 1981

Re: Inpatient Services
Date of Hospitalization: April 1–5, 1981
Balance Due: $3725.48

Dear Mr. Peterson:

Since we have not received a reply to our letter of May 15, we are writing to remind you of the balance that remains on your account.

If there is some difficulty, drop by and see us today; we will do our best to help. Otherwise, we would appreciate receiving your payment in full by return mail.

Our ability to provide health services to others depends to a great extent upon your cooperation. Please do not let us down.

Sincerely,

Morris T. Jukes

Morris T. Jukes
Accounts Receivable Department

---

ried out. Note, though, how the letter in Fig. 6.25 does not begin with that bad news. Instead, it reminds the patient of all the efforts the hospital has expended to collect its bills. The letter clearly points out that the time for concessions is over. Then it announces what consequences will result if the patient still does not pay. The letter gives proper legal notification that the patient has ten days to respond. The fourth collection letter attempts to frighten the customer into payment and does not have to seek or give any explanations. If the hospital, or any company, failed to carry out its threat to turn delinquent accounts over to a collection agency or attorney, it would quickly get a reputation for having all bark but no bite—a reputation that would make it difficult to collect its debts in the future.

Fig. 6.24   A third collection letter.

BALDWIN COUNTY HOSPITAL
P.O. Box 222
Notown, MA 02138

July 24, 1981

Re: Inpatient Services
Date of Hospitalization: April 1–5, 1981
Balance Due: $3725.48

Dear Mr. Peterson:

We regret that we have received no response from you to our letters of
May 15 and June 19 concerning your outstanding balance.

Because so much time has elapsed, we must now require full payment (or
your signed agreement to make regular installment payments) within the
next ten days.

If we have not heard from you by August 23, it will become necessary for us
to take further action.

Sincerely,

Morris T. Jukes

Morris T. Jukes
Accounts Receivable Department

(   ) I will pay $_____   (   ) weekly; (   ) monthly, on my account.

(   ) Enclosed is a check for full payment in the amount of $_____.

_____
Signature

Fig. 6.25   A fourth and final collection letter.

BALDWIN COUNTY HOSPITAL
P.O. Box 222
Notown, MA 02138

August 27, 1981

Re: Inpatient Services
Date of Hospitalization: April 1-5, 1981
Balance Due: $3725.48

Dear Mr. Peterson:

During the past few months we have written you several times concerning your outstanding balance.

As you may recall, we offered to arrange for installment payments or to help you in any way that we could. Since you have not responded, we must demand your payment in full at this time.

If we do not hear from you within ten (10) days, we will have no alternative but to turn your account over to our collection agency.

Sincerely,

Morris T. Jukes

Morris T. Jukes
Accounts Receivable Department

▶ Exercises

1. Write a memo to your employer saying that you will be out of town two days next week and three the following week for one of the following reasons: (a) to inspect some land your firm is thinking of buying, (b) to investigate some claims, (c) to look at some new office space for a branch your firm is thinking of opening in a city five hundred miles away, (d) to attend a conference sponsored by a professional society, or (e) to pay calls on customers. In your memo, be very specific about dates, places, times, and reasons.

2. Send a memo to your public relations department informing it that you are completing a degree or work for a certificate and indicate how the information could be useful for its publicity campaign.

3. Write a memo to the payroll department notifying it that there is a mistake in your last paycheck. Explain what the error is and give precise figures.

4. You are a manager of a local art museum. Write a memo to the Chamber of Commerce in which you put the following information into proper memo format:

   Old hours: Mon.–Fri. 9–5; closed Sat. except during July and August when you are open 9–12.
   New hours: Mon.–Th. 8:30–4:30; Fri.–Sat. 9–9

   Old rates: $1.00 children over 12; adults $1.50; children under 12 free
   New rates: $1.50 children over 12; adults $2.50; children under 12 free and must be accompanied by an adult.

   Added features: Paintings by Thora Horne, local artist; sculpture from West Indies and pottery from Central America in display area all summer; guided tours available with a party of six or more; lounge areas will offer patrons sandwiches and soft drinks, only during the months of May, June, July, and August

5. Select some change (in policy, schedule, or personnel assignment) you encountered in a job you held in the last two or three years and write an appropriate memo describing that change.

6. Rewrite the following memo subject lines, making them more precise and helpful:

Schedules	Deliveries
Vacations	Refrigerators
New Equipment	Doors
Benefits	IVs
Safety	Radios
Insurance	Policy Changes

7. Order merchandise from a company. Specify the quantity, size, stock number, cost, and also include delivery instructions, the date by which you must receive the merchandise, and the way in which you will pay for it.

8. Imagine that you have answered your supervisor's phone and a customer places a small order and wants you to make sure that your supervisor receives the message. Write an appropriate message for your supervisor, using a phone message form.

9. Write a letter of inquiry to a utility company, a safety or health care agency, or a company in your town, asking for a brochure describing its services to the community. Be specific about your reasons for requesting this information.

10. In which course(s) are you or will you be writing a paper or report? Write to an agency or company that could supply you with helpful information and request its aid. Indicate why you are writing, indicating precisely what information you need, why you need it, and offer to share your paper or report with the company.

11. Rewrite to improve the following sentences appearing in letters of inquiry:
    (a) Do you have any facts on minicomputers that I could use in a term paper?
    (b) I am thinking of coming to Jonesboro Community College sometime soon. I need some information about your programs.
    (c) I would like to have the phone number of any dealer in my town who sells Acme business machines.
    (d) Your public relations department should be able to handle my request quickly.
    (e) Did your company ever hire employees without a high school education? Send me your hiring facts for the last ten years.
    (f) I need some information about housing costs in Chicago.

12. Write a one-page assessment of an ad in a magazine or a TV commercial in which you can identify the four parts of a sales message.

13. Write a sales letter addressed to an appropriate audience on one of the following topics:
    (a) why they should major in the same subject you did
    (b) why they should live in your neighborhood
    (c) why they would be happy taking a vacation where you did last year
    (d) why they should dine at a particular restaurant
    (e) why they should shop at a store you have worked for or will work for
    (f) why they should have their cars repaired at a specific shop
    (g) why they should give their real estate business to a particular agency
    (h) why they would enjoy doing their cooking on a particular stove

14. Find at least two sales letters you or your family have received and evaluate them according to how well they follow the four parts of a sales letter discussed in this chapter.

15. Write a sales letter about the effectiveness of sales letters to an individual who has told you that almost everyone throws them away as soon as they get them.

16. Write a thank-you letter in response to one of the following:
    (a) a gift you have received
    (b) a letter of congratulation sent to you

(c) a letter of recommendation someone wrote for you

(d) some business that was directed to you or your employer

(e) a dinner or other social occasion to which you were invited by a customer or your employer or agency

17. Write a congratulation letter to someone for one of the following:
    (a) being promoted
    (b) winning an award at school
    (c) being named salesperson of the month
    (d) completing a special course or degree
    (e) being elected to public office
    (f) concluding a business deal (selling a product, renegotiating a contract)
    (g) opening a new store or branch
    (h) joining your firm or agency

18. Send a follow-up letter to one of the following individuals:
    (a) a customer who informs you that he will no longer do business with your firm because your prices are too high
    (b) a family of four who stayed at your motel for two weeks last summer
    (c) a church group that used your catering services last month
    (d) a customer who exchanged a dress or coat for the purchase price
    (e) a customer who bought a new car from you one year ago
    (f) a company that bought a year's supply of pens from you nine months ago

19. Write a complaint letter about one of the following:
    (a) an error in your utility or telephone bill
    (b) discourteous service you received on an airplane or bus
    (c) a frozen food product of poor quality
    (d) a shipment that arrives late and damaged
    (e) an insurance payment to you that is fifty dollars less than it should be
    (f) a public service TV station's policy of not showing a particular series
    (g) junk mail that you are receiving

20. Write the complaint letter to which the adjustment letter in Fig. 6.19 (p. 158) responds.

21. Write the complaint letter to which the adjustment letter in Fig. 6.21 (p. 161) responds.

22. Rewrite the following complaint letters to make them more precise and less emotional:

(a) Dear Sir:

I am writing to chew you morons out about the enclosed four shutters for four fans shipped to me recently. These were back-ordered from an original shipment. These shutters are not working properly, and have caused us considerable trouble in the operation of our business.

I would like to have your full comments about these shutters as soon as possible.

Sincerely yours,

(b) Dear Sir:

We recently purchased a machine from your New York store and paid a great deal of money for it. This machine, supposedly the best model in your line, has caused us nothing but trouble each time we used it. Really, can't you do any better with your technology?

We expect you to stand by your products. The warranty you give with them should make you accountable for shoddy workmanship. Let us know at once what you intend to do about our problem. If you cannot or are unwilling to correct the situation, we will take our business elsewhere, and then you will be sorry.

Sincerely yours,

23. Write an adjustment letter saying "no" to the customer who received the "yes" adjustment letter in Fig. 6.19 (p. 158).

24. Rewrite the following ineffective adjustment letter saying "yes":

Dear Mr. Smith:

We are extremely sorry to learn that you found the suit you purchased from us unsatisfactory. The problem obviously stems from the fact that you selected it from the rack marked "Factory Seconds" In all honesty, we have had a lot of problems because of this rack. I guess we should know better than to try to feature inferior merchandise along with the name—brand clothing that we sell. But we originally thought that our customers would accept poorer quality merchandise if it saved them some money. That was our mistake.

Please accept our apologies. If you will bring your "Factory Second" suit to us, we will see what we can do about honoring your request.

Sincerely yours,

25. Rewrite the following poor adjustment letter saying "no":

Dear Customer:

Our company is unwilling to give you a new toaster or to refund your purchase price. After examining the toaster you sent to us, we found that the fault was not ours, as you insist, but yours.

Let me explain. The motor in our toaster is made to take a lot of
punishment. But being dropped on the floor or poked inside with a
knife, as you probably did, exceeds all decent treatment. You
must be careful if you expect your appliances to last. Your
negligence in this case is so bad that the toaster could not be
repaired.

In the future, consider using your appliances according to the
guidelines set down in warranty books. That's why they are
written.

Since you are now in the market for a new toaster, let me suggest
that you purchase our new heavy-duty model, number 67342, called
the Counter-Whiz. I am taking the liberty of sending you some
information about this model. I do hope you at least go to see one
at your local appliance center.

Sincerely,

26. Assume that you work in a student services department at a local college
    and that you have been asked to write collection letters to those graduates
    who are not paying off their student loans on time. Write a series of four
    collection letters to be sent at appropriate times. The first letter is sent
    after the student misses only one payment, the second letter after two
    nonpayments, the third letter after three nonpayments, and the fourth
    letter after four nonpayments.

27. Rewrite the following collection letter twice, the first time making it ap-
    propriate for a first notice and the second time making it suitable for a
    second notice.

    Dear Customer:

    You may recall that you owe us the slight sum of $64.56 for the
    plumbing work we did for you in January. To you such bills may
    appear trivial, but in order to stay in business we have to
    collect from everyone, from the little guy like you to the big
    companies we help.

    Do not be a problem for us. Pay what you owe. If you do not send us
    a check for the above amount in the next few days, we will somehow
    get the money out of you. Whether you pay the easy way by sending
    us a check now or whether we put a hard-nosed collection agency on
    your case is entirely up to you.

    Sincerely yours,

SECTION III

GATHERING AND
SUMMARIZING
INFORMATION

7

Finding and Using Library Materials

A personnel director asked an applicant during a job interview to name the titles of two or three major journals in the applicant's field. When the applicant could not come up with any titles, chances for employment at the company seemed slim. The question was typical, fair, and relevant. The interviewer knew that an applicant's success in the job depends on the quality of information supplied to the employer. Employers expect carefully researched answers; they will not be satisfied with guesses.

Research, or the careful investigation of material found in books, magazines, pamphlets, films, or any other sources (including resource people), is a vital part of every occupation. You might conduct informal research by telephoning someone in the next department for information or thumbing through a company catalog. Or you might engage in formal research by studying reference works in a library or by preparing statistical or analytical surveys. You must be informed about the latest developments in your field, and you must be able to communicate your findings accurately and concisely. Doing research is a practical skill like swimming, running, or typing. Once learned, it is easy to perform. Knowing how to do research in your field offers lifelong benefits.

The information in Chapter 7 can save you from suffering the embarrassment experienced by the job applicant above. Specifically, Chapter 7 discusses major reference works—where to find them and how to use and document them. The appendix to this chapter contains information about specific reference works (indexes, encyclopedias, dictionaries, abstracts, and handbooks) that will be extremely valuable to you in your research.

▶ The Library and Its Sections

You may think of your library as a single building, but that building is divided into many sections. When you walk into a library, probably the first section you see is the circulation desk—in many ways, the business center of the library. You go to the circulation desk to borrow or return books, to pick up materials you may have ordered from another library, or to find out if a book has been checked out. From the circulation desk you can move to any one of the following parts of the library to use materials. (The page numbers after each area refer to the page numbers of this chapter where you will find a description of the particular unit and the materials in it.)

The Card Catalog

The card catalog, your guide to the library, will be located in a prominent place, usually near the entrance. Housed in cabinets with numerous drawers, the card catalog contains three-by-five-inch index cards for each book, film-strip, tape recording, or microfilm your library owns. The card catalog does not contain information about articles in magazines or journals. For information on the contents of individual magazines or journals, you will have to consult your library's periodical holdings list and the periodical indexes discussed later in this chapter.

How Material in the Card Catalog is Alphabetized

There are three ways to find a book in the card catalog. You can look for it under the author's name, under the title, or under the subject it discusses. Some libraries may have separate cabinets for each of these three designations (author, title, subject), while at other libraries, especially small ones, all three designations are included in one cabinet. Information in all three categories is listed alphabetically, either letter by letter or word by word. These ways of alphabetizing entries can make a big difference, as the following examples show:

Letter by letter

fire	firefly
firearm	firetrap
fire drill	fire wall
fire escape	

Word by word

fire	firearm
fire drill	firefly
fire escape	firetrap
fire wall	

The letter-by-letter method is based on the sequence of individual letters regardless of whether an entry contains one word or two. Hence, *firearm* comes before *fire drill*. Under the word-by-word method, each entry is alphabetized according to the letters in the first word, whether that entry is made up of one word or two. *Fire wall* comes ahead of *firearm* and *firefly* because the word *fire* is a part of both of these words and alphabetically precedes them. Find out which method your library uses so you can look up entries more quickly and more accurately. The following alphabetical rules apply to both methods and will help you search for an entry in the card catalog.

1. An author's last name beginning *Mc* is listed as if the *Mc* were spelled *Mac;* so *McDonald* will be listed in the card catalog as if it were *Mac-Donald*. Hyphenated last names are found at the end of the alphabetical letter beginning the first of two hyphenated names. A book by Alan Jones-Davies, for example, would be listed at the end of the J's, not under the D's.
2. Disregard definite and indefinite articles—*the, a,* or *an*—at the beginning of a title. A book with the title *A New Fashion Guide* will be found in the N's.
3. Abbreviations, acronyms (HUD, NATO, VISTA, and other words formed from the first letters of several words), and numbers are alphabetized as if they were spelled out in full. A book entitled *Mr. and Mrs. Average American* will be found in the title section of the card catalog under *Mister; 22 Ways to Better Health* is listed under *Twenty-Two*. A book written by IBM would be listed under *International Business Machines*. And a study put out by the ANA could be found in the author section under the *American Nurses Association*.

Author Card

One way to find a book is to locate the author card in the card catalog. Spell the author's name correctly and record first names or initials accurately. If you know just the last name, and if it is a common one, your search may take a great deal of extra time. An *author card* for a book by Martin Meyerson can be seen in Fig. 7.1. To find Meyerson's book, you would look under the M's until you come to Meyerson and then find Martin. The author card(s) tells you what titles by that author are in your library. Each card will tell you where to find the book, when it was written, who published it, and where. Figure 7.1 is coded to show you what each number, abbreviation, and symbol means.

Fig. 7.1   An author card in the card catalog.

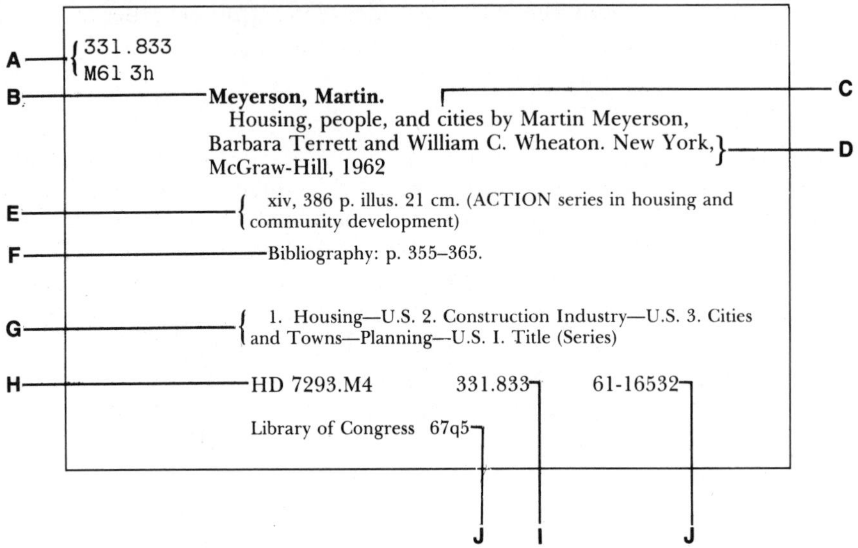

A The *call number* locates the book in the library. In this case the library has filed the book according to the Dewey decimal system.

B The *author's name* is always listed with the last name (surname) first. Sometimes a card also gives the author's date of birth and, if the author is deceased, the date of death. If a book has more than one author or editor, only the author whose name appears first in the book is listed in the upper-left-hand corner of the card.

C The *title* of the book.

D The names of any *coauthors or coeditors and pertinent publication information*—city, publisher, and date of publication.

E A *physical description of the book*—number of pages from the preface (usually numbered in lower-case Roman numerals) through the index, whether the book is illustrated (illus.) and the height (in centimeters) of the book. Also noted is whether the book is part of a special series or is issued under a special imprint (or publishing arrangement).

F This book contains a *bibliography* on pages 355 to 365.

G List of the *other headings in the subject catalog under which the book is listed.*

H The *Library of Congress designation* for this book would be in the A position if the library followed the Library of Congress system of classification rather than the Dewey decimal one. "Library of Congress" means that a copy of the book is in the national library.

I The *Dewey decimal number*.

J *Identification numbers used by librarians.* You need not be concerned with this designation.

Title Card

Figure 7.2 shows a *title card*. It is identical to an author card except that the title of the book is listed twice—once as a heading on top of the card and again as part of the entry itself. It is easy to find this card when you know the first word of the title. Keep in mind that the articles *a, an,* or *the* at the beginning of the title are omitted in alphabetizing. With the Meyerson book you do not have an article for the first word of the title; just search for the book under the H's in the title section of the card catalog.

Subject Card

Figure 7.3 shows the *subject card* for the Meyerson book. Again, the subject card is identical to the author card except that a subject heading—marked with distinctive red or black ink—is located at the top of the card. Many times students start with the subject section of the card catalog, since they do not have titles or authors in mind early in their search. The subject catalog also

Fig. 7.2   A title card in the card catalog.

```
331.833
M613h                  Housing, people and cities.

          Meyerson, Martin.
               Housing, people, and cities by Martin Meyerson,
          Barbara Terrett and William C. Wheaton. New York,
          McGraw-Hill, 1962.

               xiv, 386 p. illus. 21 cm. (ACTION series in housing and
          community development)

               Bibliography: p. 355–365.
                    1. Housing—U.S. 2. Construction Industry—U.S. 3. Cities
          and Towns—Planning—U.S. I. Title (Series)

          HD 7293.M4          331.833          61-16532

          Library of Congress   67q5
```

Fig. 7.3   A subject card in the card catalog.

```
331.833
M613h        CONSTRUCTION INDUSTRY–UNITED STATES

          Meyerson, Martin.
               Housing, people, and cities by Martin Meyerson,
          Barbara Terrett and William C. Wheaton. New York,
          McGraw-Hill, 1962.

               xiv, 386 p. illus. 21 cm. (ACTION series in housing and
          community development

               Bibliography: p. 355–365.


                    1. Housing—U.S. 2. Construction Industry—U.S. 3. Cities
          and Towns—Planning—U.S. I. Title (Series)

          HD 7293.M4          331.833          61-16532

          Library of Congress   67q5
```

lists reference works (abstracts, bibliographies, dictionaries, handbooks, and indexes) that will guide you to specific titles.

The subject section divides a topic into subheadings or groups and alerts readers to other, related topics. Looking under the subject section for "construction," you would first find a cross-reference, or "see also," card, illustrated in Fig. 7.4. This card alerts you to other subject categories (references) you should check for information in addition to the cards gathered under the "construction" heading. Next, you would find the following breakdown of the topic with appropriate books listed for each:

- construction equipment
- construction dictionary
- construction handbook
- construction, housing
- construction, industry

Stopping at the last subheading, "construction, industry," you could find even more subclassifications:

- accounting
- automation
- contracts
- costs
- data processing
- law and legislation
- management
- personnel
- subcontracting
- United States

Meyerson's book would be found under this last subheading, "United States."

Fig. 7.4   A "see also" card in the card catalog.

```
see also

CONSTRUCTION—UNITED STATES
BUILDING
ENGINEERING
```

Subject cards break down topics into subcategories and list appropriate titles under each subcategory or helpfully refer readers to other parts of the subject catalog. They also list on the entry card beneath the title of the book other relevant topics to consult directly. Examine the Meyerson card in Fig. 7.3. Following the bibliographic information, the card lists three other subject areas that will help readers find additional information: (1) housing, (2) construction, and (3) cities and towns.

The Stacks

The majority of space in a library is taken up by the stacks—rows of shelves where the books are stored. Your library may have open or closed stacks. If the stacks are open, you are free to walk along the rows to find the books you need. If they are closed, a member of the library staff will find a book for you after you present a call slip identifying—by author, title, and number—the book you want.

Call Numbers

Regardless of which system your library uses, you will have to know the call number of the book you want. Call numbers or letters are found in the upper left-hand side of the card in the catalog. Your library may use either the Library of Congress (abbreviated LC) or the Dewey decimal system. Table 7.1 shows a section of the LC system and some of the divisions in the Dewey decimal system. The LC system divides all knowledge into twenty-one categories that are differentiated by capital letters of the alphabet. Subdivisions are labeled with a combination of letters and numbers. As its name implies, the Dewey decimal system divides knowledge into ten large categories indicated by numerical groups ranging from 000 to the 900s. Each large division is divided into groups of ten subdivisions. The first number in a Dewey classification indicates the large category of knowledge in which a book is found, and the second and third numbers specify exact areas of that large group.

Meyerson's book, *Housing, People, and Cities,* in the LC system is classified by the letters HD. The letter H indicates that the book falls into the large category marked "social sciences," and D signifies that the book belongs in the subcategory "economics," as opposed to "statistics" (HA) or "sociology" (HM–HX). The Dewey number for Meyerson's book is 331.833—that is, it falls into the 300s, "social sciences," and the 30s of the 300s, the subdivision "economics."

Shelves

Once you know the call number, you should check where the book is shelved if your library has open stacks. Your library may post maps that show the location of books by their call numbers. When you know the approximate location of a book, go to that section of the library and look at the markers posted at the end of each row of stacks. Then walk down the appropriate row

Table 7.1. Headings from call-number sections

Library of Congress	*Dewey Decimal*
Q Science	500 Pure sciences
Q Science (General)	510 Mathematics
QA Mathematics	520 Astronomy and allied
QB Astronomy	sciences
QC Physics	530 Physics
QD Chemistry	540 Chemistry and allied sciences
QE Geology	550 Sciences of earth and other
QH Natural history	worlds
QK Botany	560 Paleontology
QL Zoology	570 Life sciences
QM Human anatomy	580 Botanical sciences
QP Physiology	590 Zoological sciences
QR Microbiology	600 Technology (Applied
	sciences)
R Medicine	610 Medical sciences
R Medicine (General)	620 Engineering and allied
RB Pathology	operations
RK Dentistry	630 Agriculture
RT Nursing	640 Domestic arts and sciences
	650 Managerial services
S Agriculture	660 Chemical and related
S Agriculture (General)	technologies
SB Plant culture	670 Manufactures
SD Forestry	680 Miscellaneous manufactures
SF Animal culture	690 Buildings
SK Hunting	
T Technology	
T Technology (General)	
TA Engineering (General).	
Civil engineering	
(General)	
TJ Mechanical engineering	
and machinery	
TK Electrical engineering.	
Electronics. Nuclear	
engineering	
TP Chemical technology	
TS Manufactures	
TX Home economics	

Library of Congress, Subject Cataloging Division, *LC Classification Outline,* 3rd ed. (Washington, D.C.: U.S. Government Printing Office, 1975); Melvil Dewey, *Decimal Classification and Relative Index The Second Summary,* (1971), p. 450.

Fig. 7.5   Spine of a book with call number.

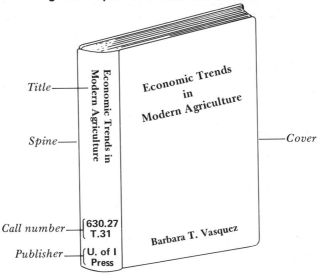

Title —— Economic Trends in Modern Agriculture

Economic Trends
in
Modern Agriculture

Spine ——

—— *Cover*

Call number —— 630.27 T.31

Barbara T. Vasquez

Publisher —— U. of I Press

to find your book. Each book will have its call number on its spine, or where the book is bound, as illustrated in Fig. 7.5. If the book you are looking for is not on the shelf, go to the circulation desk to see if it has been checked out. If so, you can ask the librarian to reserve it for you when it comes back. Perhaps the book can be used only in the library (it is said to be on reserve), in which case, you will have to sign it out from the circulation desk. If the librarian discovers that the book has not been checked out or is not on reserve, it may be misshelved. Check with the library in the next few days to see if it has been found.

▶ Periodical Holdings and Indexes

Your research will not be confined exclusively to books. Some of it will lead you to the wealth of information contained in periodicals. A periodical is a magazine or journal that is published at established, frequent intervals— weekly, bimonthly (or once every two months), quarterly. The word *magazine* refers to periodicals—*Gentleman's Quarterly, Redbook,* or *Time*—that appeal to a diverse audience and that treat popular themes. The word *journal* characterizes technical or scholarly periodicals, such as the *American Journal of Nursing* or the *American Waterworks Journal,* whose audience reads them for professional or scientific information.

Periodicals have certain advantages over books when it comes to your research. Because they take less time to produce than books, periodicals can give you more recent information on a topic. Further, periodicals are not as restricted as books. A book usually discusses one subject from one point of view, but a periodical can contain ten different articles, each covering a separate topic and each offering a different perspective. This is not to imply that you should ignore books and focus solely on magazines or journals. Use both, but be aware of the differences.

To find appropriate articles in magazines and journals, you need to use indexes. An index is a listing by subject, and sometimes also by author, of articles that have appeared within a specified period of time. An index tells you what articles have appeared on your subject, where they were published, who wrote them, and whether they contain any special information, such as bibliographies, illustrations, diagrams and maps, or portraits. You would be lost without indexes. You could never successfully thumb through all the periodicals in the library to determine which ones contain an article you could use. Furthermore, your library might not subscribe to all the journals and magazines that contain articles related to your subject. The indexes let you know what is available beyond your own library's holdings.

The Readers' Guide to Periodical Literature

One of the most useful indexes is the *Readers' Guide to Periodical Literature*, which has been listing information on periodicals since 1900. The *Readers' Guide* indexes information from more than 150 periodicals, mostly popular magazines together with a few scientific journals. The *Guide*'s main purpose is to list periodicals of interest to the general, not technical, reader. Therefore, you will find articles from *Good Housekeeping, Parents' Magazine,* and *Reader's Digest* indexed, but not articles from *Hospitals, Journal of Petroleum Technology,* or *Professional Safety.* For journal articles, you will have to consult the more specialized indexes discussed later in this chapter.

The *Readers' Guide* is published twice a month, except during July and August when only one issue a month is published. Every three months the *Guide* combines issues to form a cumulative index for that period. Every year these three-month indexes are collected and bound into one large yearly index that can weigh as much as a large dictionary. You will find both the single issues of the *Guide* and the large bound ones on tables or shelves in or very close to the reference room.

The *Readers' Guide* allows you to search for an article by topic, subtopic, author's name, and, whenever appropriate, title. At the beginning of every issue you will find two important keys. One key tells you which periodicals were surveyed for that particular issue of the *Readers' Guide.* Along with this information is a list of abbreviations that will be used for those periodicals throughout the issue. For example, *Saturday Review* will be listed as *Sat R, Working Woman* will be found as *Work Wom.,* and *Business Weekly* is abbreviated as *Bus W.* Some periodicals will not be abbreviated in the listings *(Encore, Forbes,* or *People).* The other key lists abbreviations for months, bibliographic facts, and titles. Refer to both these keys as you "decode" the entries in an issue.

Fig. 7.6   An excerpt from the *Readers' Guide*.

```
EXTRASENSORY perception
   Psychic or psychotic? study by Bruce Greyson.
      Hum Behav 8:46 F '79
   Seeing the future; study by John Bisaha. il Hum
      Behav 8:46 F '79
EXTRASENSORY perception in animals
   Do animals have ESP? T. McGinnis. Fam Health
      11:12+ F '79
EXTRATERRESTRIAL life. See Life on other
   planets
EXXON Corporation
   Edict from the sovereign state of Exxon. J.
      O'Hara and I. Urquhart. Macleans 92:25 F 26
      '79
EYE
        See also
   Vision
                Care and hygiene
   Eyes right! C. Ettlinger. il House & Gard 151:
      26+ Mr '79
                Diseases and defects
   Cone inputs to ganglion cells in hereditary
      retinal degeneration. C. M. Cicerone and oth-
      ers. bibl il Science 203:1113-15 Mr 16 '79
   Microsurgery for strokes and visual disorders.
      il Sci News 115:69 F 3 '79
   Wandering eyes; amblyopia study by Merton
      Flom and David Kirchen. il Hum Behav 8:26
      F '79
        See also
   Cataracts (eye defects)

                Movements
   Smooth pursuit eye movements: is perceived
      motion necessary? A. Mack and others. bibl il
      Science 203:1361-3 Mr 30 '79

                Protection
   Eclipse: don't let the sun catch you spying.
      P. Carlyle-Gordge. il Macleans 92:10 Ja 29 '79

                Surgery
   Cataracts: technologic explosion creates debate
      on surgery need. N. S. Jaffe. Sci Digest 85:
      46-8+ F '79
   That dreaded cataract operation can go smoothly
      these days. B. Hitchings. Bus W p 101-2 F 19
      '79
EYE (animals)
        See also
   Vision (animals)
EYE (crustaceans)
   Both photons and fluoride ions excite limulus
      ventral photoreceptors. A. Fein and D. W.
      Corson. bibl il Science 204:77-9 Ap 6 '79
EYE make-up. See Make-up
EYE malformations (animals) See Abnormalities
   (animals)
EYE movements. See Eye—Movements
EYEBROWS
   Shapely brows. il McCalls 106:43-4 F '79
EYEGLASSES
   What's new in eyeglasses. il Glamour 77:180-1 F
      '79
        See also
   Contact lenses
EYES. See Eye
EYESIGHT. See Vision
EYEWITNESSES. See Witnesses
```

Figure 7.6 contains an excerpt from the *Readers' Guide* three-month issue
for February–April 1979. This excerpt, which indexes articles on the eye, will
show you how the *Readers' Guide* is organized and how abbreviations are used.
Like the subject designations in the card catalog, the *Readers' Guide* refers
users to other, related topics in the issue. In this excerpt, the reader is told to

Fig. 7.7 Entries from the *Readers' Guide* for articles by and about one person.

```
FONDA, Jane
   Fonda: I am not more respectable; interview,
      ed by J. Kotkin. il pors New Times 10:58-9
      Mr 20 '78
   Jane Fonda—rebel with many causes; interview,
      ed by M. Ronan. il pors Sr Schol 110:2-4+ Mr
      9 '78
                        about
   Fonda Jane. T. Young. il pors Film Comment
      14:54-7 Mr '78 •
   Jane Fonda: a hard act to follow. D. R. Katz.
      il pors Roll Stone p39-44 Mr 9 '78 •
   Jane Fonda: trying to be everywoman. B. G.
      Harrison. il pors Ladies Home J 95:88+
      Ap '78 •
```

Readers' Guide to Periodical Literature, copyright © 1979, 1980 by The H.W. Wilson Company. Material reproduced by permission of the publisher.

"see also" entries under "vision." The articles on the eye for the three-month period covered by this issue are then divided into appropriate categories—care and hygiene, diseases and defects, and so forth. Note that the entry under "care and hygiene" is translated as follows: C. Ettlinger wrote an article entitled "Eyes right!" that appeared with illustrations (il) in *House and Garden,* vol. 151; the article starts on page 26 and is continued later in the magazine (signified by the + after a page number), and the date of the issue is March 1979. The first article under "diseases and defects" contains a bibliography (bibl) as well as illustrations (il). Moving down to the entry under "eyebrows," note that no author's name is given, only the title, date, and page numbers of the article appearing in *McCalls.* The article was written by a staff member of the magazine and does not carry a by-line.

In addition to listing articles under the subjects they discuss, the *Readers' Guide* indexes articles according to author. Some authors also have articles written about them. In this case the *Readers' Guide* first lists the works by the author and immediately following those articles lists works about the author. Look at Fig. 7.7. The two Jane Fonda interviews (regarded as works by an author) come first, and then come three articles about her. Note that portraits and/or photographs (pors) accompany the article about her.

Specialized Indexes

While the *Readers' Guide* is a good source to consult, remember that the *Guide* is limited to "periodicals of general interest published in the United States." Your research will require you to read professional journals in your field—journals that the *Readers' Guide* does not index. The importance of these professional journals cannot be stressed too heavily. Recall the interviewer's question about the applicant naming journals in his or her area. Professional journals address the specific concerns you face every day on the job. Your knowledge about these studies will make you more valuable to your employer.

Specialized indexes are guides to the literature in particular subject areas—business, farming, foodservice, nursing, public safety, respiratory therapy, and many others. Some indexes cover sixty or more years of work *(Applied Science and Technology Index* or *Index Medicus);* other indexes were established within the past five to ten years *(Criminal Justice Periodical Index* or *Environmental Index).* Refer to the appendix to this chapter for specific information about twelve specialized indexes.

Finding a Periodical in Your Library

Once you find an article in an index, your next job is to locate and read it. First, consult your library's periodical holdings list. A card catalog for periodicals, the holdings list can be a computer printout, a group of index cards in a metal box, or a file (series of folders). The holdings list will tell you to which journals and magazines your library subscribes and how far back the subscription goes. Perhaps your library has a complete backlist of the journal you are looking for or maybe it has issues for only the last three years. Perhaps there is a lapse in the library's holdings for a given periodical; it may have the earlier issues and the latest ones but not some of the issues for the in-between years. If the journal you are looking for is not on your library's periodical holdings list, you will have to go to another library or seek assistance through interlibrary loan.

If the library has the periodical you are looking for, it may be in a number of places, depending on the date of the issue. Recent periodicals are usually shelved alphabetically in a periodicals reading room. If the article you need was written more than a year ago, it may be bound with other issues for that year and gathered together in a hard, permanent cover and shelved like a book. Many libraries shelve bound periodicals alphabetically by title in an area of the library separate from the stacks. Another method of storing back issues is to put them on microfilm, a process of storing information concisely and economically. (Microfilm and microfiche are discussed on pages 194–196.)

▶ Reference Books

The works discussed in this section are kept in the reference room in the library, usually located across from the card catalog. Reference books may not be checked out of the library. More detailed information on specific reference works is given in the appendix to this chapter.

Encyclopedias

The word *encyclopedia* comes from a Greek phrase meaning "general education." Some encyclopedias provide information on an incredibly broad range of subjects. These comprehensive encyclopedias take years to produce and are written by a staff of experts in every major field of knowledge. These experts sign their initials after their work, and you can find out who they are by checking the encyclopedia's preface, where their names are listed after their initials.

The information in an encyclopedia is arranged alphabetically, with some subjects receiving as much as twenty pages of coverage. A general encyclopedia can get you started in your research by explaining some key terms, offering a quick summary, and supplying you with a list of further readings. Another advantage of encyclopedias is the colorful and varied illustrations they offer. Three useful general encyclopedias are *Collier's Encyclopedia, Encyclopaedia Americana*, and *Encyclopaedia Britannica.*

Do not attempt to do all your research using only encyclopedias, however. They have their limitations. For one thing, the information in them is designed for the general reader, not the specialist. For another reason, general encyclopedias, however good, do not contain the most current information on a subject, especially on technical matters. For that kind of up-to-date material, you must consult periodicals. Finally, relying on encyclopedias alone reveals your lack of ability to find and use more specialized and restricted sources.

Certain encyclopedias are limited to special areas of knowledge and will be much more helpful than general encyclopedias. These works include far more background information, technical details and terminology, and references in their bibliographies. Almost every occupation has its own encyclopedia.

Dictionaries

Dictionaries are perhaps the most important reference tool, since they help you to understand the information gathered from other works (books, periodicals, pamphlets) that comprise the bulk of your research. If you do not know the meaning of a term, you will have trouble understanding a discussion in which that term is used. In addition to giving the meaning of words, dictionaries indicate spelling, pronunciation, etymology (word history), and usage. Generally speaking, dictionaries fall into two categories—general English-language dictionaries and more specialized dictionaries used by a specific profession.

English-language dictionaries are either unabridged or abridged. An unabridged dictionary is a large, comprehensive guide to the words of the language. Found in libraries and classrooms, these dictionaries are usually placed on a stand and are extremely heavy. The following unabridged dictionaries are excellent references: *Funk & Wagnalls New Standard Dictionary of the English Language,* the *Oxford English Dictionary,* the *Random House Dictionary of the English Language,* and *Webster's Third New International Dictionary of the English Language.* The *Oxford English Dictionary* is a historical dictionary—that is, it lists the dates (from the first citation) when a word was first used and how it was used and supplies illustrative quotations. Regarded as the greatest dictionary in the language, the *OED* is invaluable.

Abridged dictionaries are much smaller. They can range from a vest or pocket dictionary to a large compilation with photographs and other illustrations. The following abridged dictionaries are useful: the *American Heritage Dictionary,* the *Random House College Dictionary,* and *Webster's New Collegiate Dictionary.*

You will frequently use dictionaries, such as those described in the appendix, that contain the specialized vocabulary of your profession. These specialized, or field, dictionaries not only define the words used in the literature of a profession, but also help to characterize that profession's scope and importance.

Abstracts

An abstract is a type of index. In addition to listing the author's name, title, and publication data, an abstract will give a brief (usually a few sentences) summary of the content and scope of the book, article, or pamphlet. By condensing this information, an abstract can save users hours of time by letting them know if the work is relevant to their topic.

Use abstracts with caution, however, for they are not a substitute for the article or book they summarize. A few sentences highlighting the content of a book or article obviously omit much. When in doubt about what is omitted, read the original work to uncover the details, the rationale, and the dimensions of the whole problem. Never quote from an abstract; always cite material from the original work.

Not every field has an abstracting service, nor is every article or book always abstracted. The abstracts found in the appendix to this chapter should give you a clear idea of the range of fields that do offer this valuable service.

Handbooks, Manuals, and Almanacs

Handbooks, manuals, and almanacs supply you with definitions of terms in your field, statistical facts, explanations of procedures, and authoritative reviews of the kinds of practical and professional problems and solutions you will encounter on the job. In the card catalog these works will be marked *Ref.,* indicating that they are shelved in the reference section of your library.

Numerous reference books are available for each profession. When you look for the reference books in your field, make sure that you use the most up-to-date ones. Information changes rapidly, and outdated works not listing the most recent and improved techniques will not help. Also, consult more than one manual or handbook in your field. Compare individual discussions; different approaches or emphases will help you to research a given procedure more accurately.

▶ Government Documents

The U.S. government, through its numerous, diverse agencies and departments, is engaged vigorously in conducting research and publishing its findings. This published material, collectively referred to as government documents, can be in the form of journal articles, pamphlets, research reports, transcripts of government hearings, speeches, or books. These materials have immense practical value for the research you do in your field. Government reports, for example, will discuss care of the aged, flood insurance, farming techniques, fire precautions, housing costs, outdoor recreation, and urban development.

Three indexes to government documents are especially helpful in guiding you through this vast store of information. While other indexes and guides to government publications do exist, these three are the most useful for the kind of research you will be doing.

1. The *Monthly Catalog of U.S. Government Publications*. Published since 1898 by the GPO (Government Printing Office), this index lists government documents published during that month. The catalog is arranged by agencies that publish or sponsor works (for example, the departments of Agriculture, Commerce, Interior, State, and so forth). There is also a subject, author, and title index at the back of each issue. Each entry provides the author or agency's name, the title, the date, a brief description of the contents of the document (including whether it contains a bibliography, maps, and index), when and where the research was conducted, who sponsored it (including a contract number), the price, and how to order a copy. Figure 7.8 shows you how to interpret a sample entry.

2. The *Index to Government Periodicals*. Published since 1970, this subject and author guide to 170 periodicals published by the federal government is issued quarterly and cumulated annually. The titles of some of these periodicals suggest their research value: *American Rehabilitation, Fire Management Notes, Highway and Urban Mass Transportation, Marine Fisheries Review, Occupational Outlook Quarterly, Pesticides Monitoring Journal,* and *Tree Planters' Notes.* Figure 7.9 shows some entries from this index.

3. The *Index to Publications of the United States Congress*. Published monthly since 1970 by the Congressional Information Service (CIS), this reference work indexes and abstracts House and Senate documents, reports, hearings, investigations, and other publications. It is a particularly valuable guide to legislative investigations and decisions.

States and counties also engage in research and publish their findings. The Library of Congress publishes the *Monthly Checklist of State Publications*, which lists, according to the individual states, such materials as pamphlets,

Fig. 7.8   Sample entry with explanation of codes from the *Monthly Catalog of U.S. Government Publications*.

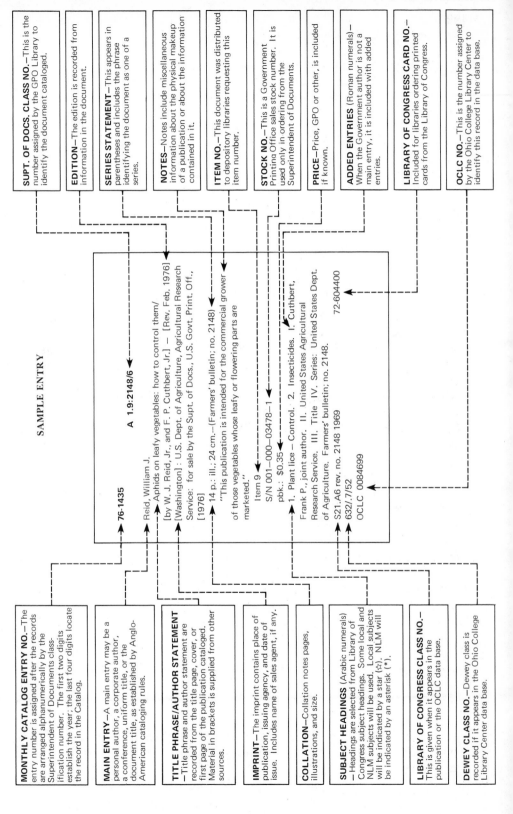

SUPT. OF DOCS. CLASS NO.—This is the number assigned by the GPO Library to identify the document cataloged.

EDITION—The edition is recorded from information in the document.

SERIES STATEMENT—This appears in parentheses and includes the phrase identifying the document as one of a series.

NOTES—Notes include miscellaneous information about the physical makeup of a publication or about the information contained in it.

ITEM NO.—This document was distributed to depository libraries requesting this item number.

STOCK NO.—This is a Government Printing Office sales stock number. It is used only in ordering from the Superintendent of Documents.

PRICE—Price, GPO or other, is included if known.

ADDED ENTRIES (Roman numerals)—When the Government author is not a main entry, it is included with added entries.

LIBRARY OF CONGRESS CARD NO.—Included for libraries ordering printed cards from the Library of Congress.

OCLC NO.—This is the number assigned by the Ohio College Library Center to identify this record in the data base.

SAMPLE ENTRY

76-1435   A 1.9:2148/6

Reid, William J.
  Aphids on leafy vegetables: how to control them/
[by W. J. Reid, Jr., and F. P. Cuthbert, Jr.] – [Rev. Feb. 1976]
[Washington]: U.S. Dept. of Agriculture, Agricultural Research
Service: for sale by the Supt. of Docs., U.S. Govt. Print. Off.,
[1976]
  14 p.: ill.; 24 cm.—(Farmers' bulletin; no. 2148)
  "This publication is intended for the commercial grower
of those vegetables whose leafy or flowering parts are
marketed."
      Item 9
      S/N 001–000–03478–1
      pbk.: $0.35
  1. Plant lice – Control. 2. Insecticides. I. Cuthbert,
Frank P., joint author. II. United States Agricultural
Research Service. III. Title IV. Series: United States Dept.
of Agriculture. Farmers' bulletin; no. 2148.
  S21.A6 rev. no. 2148 1969   72-604400
  632/.7/52
  OCLC 0084699

MONTHLY CATALOG ENTRY NO.—The entry number is assigned after the records are arranged alphanumerically by the Superintendent of Documents classification number. The first two digits establish the year; the last four digits locate the record in the Catalog.

MAIN ENTRY—A main entry may be a personal author, a corporate author, a conference, uniform title, or the document title, as established by Anglo-American cataloging rules.

TITLE PHRASE/AUTHOR STATEMENT—Title phrase and author statement are recorded from the title page, cover, or first page of the publication cataloged. Material in brackets is supplied from other sources.

IMPRINT—The imprint contains place of publication, issuing agency, and date of issue. Includes name of sales agent, if any.

COLLATION—Collation notes pages, illustrations, and size.

SUBJECT HEADINGS (Arabic numerals)—Headings are selected from Library of Congress subject headings. Some local and NLM subjects will be used. Local subjects will be indicated by a star (☆). NLM will be indicated by an asterisk (*).

LIBRARY OF CONGRESS CLASS NO.—This is given when it appears in the publication or the OCLC data base.

DEWEY CLASS NO.—Dewey class is recorded if it appears in the Ohio College Library Center data base.

Fig. 7.9   Some entries from *Index to Government Periodicals*, April–June 1979, p. 96.

FINLAND (cont)

Trade

Finland: continuing revival in economic activity fosters burgeoning demand for U.S. products. Albert Caya, Jr., il Bus Amer 2 9 22-23 Ap 23 79-216

Finland: U.S. sales prospects improve as demand gains strength. Philip Combs, rep, gr Overseas Bus Rep 79-04 13 Mr 79-085

Packaging abroad: packaging and labeling regulations. Cont & Packag 31 24 19-20 Sum-Fall-Wint 78-79-154

FINN, J. J.

1978 annual report, Secretariat. Fed Home Loan Bk Bd J 12 4 70 Mr 79-046

FINN, Joseph T.

Materials requirements for sewer works construction. tab Const Rev 25 1 4-13 Ja 79-152

FINNEY, Lynne D.

1978 annual report, Office of Industry Development. il, tab, gr Fed Home Loan Bk Bd J 12 4 42-49 Mr 79-046

FIR trees

Diseases

Branch mortality of true firs in west-central Oregon associated with dwarf mistletoe and canker fungi. Gregory M. Filip and others. ref, tab, gr Plant Dis Rep 63 3 189-193 Mr 79-087

Pests

Developing a long-range fuel program. John Maupin, il, gr Fire Man Notes 40 1 3-5 Wint 78-79-184

FIRE

Saga of mining's darkest days—the Comstock lode tragedy. il Mine Safe & H 4 1 10-15 F-Mr 79-207

Management

Determining arrival times of fire resources by computer. il, ref, tab Fire Man Notes 39 4 12-13 Fall 78-184

Forest Service and fire administration team up on rural fire problem analysis. R. Michael Bowman, Fire Man Notes 40 1 7 Wint 78-79-184

statistical studies, yearbooks, and histories. At the county level, practical advice and publications are available on a wide range of topics in agriculture, education, foodscience, housing, and water resources.

▶ The Popular Press

The "popular press" includes reading material written in nontechnical language for the general public. Glossy magazines and newspapers comprise the popular press. Many of these magazines are indexed in the *Readers' Guide;* this section will show you how to use newspaper stories and where to find them indexed.

In many ways newspapers provide a valuable source of information relevant to the research you do in school or on the job. News of local events can translate into business for you. Newspapers supply details about forthcoming construction, thus alerting building suppliers, construction workers, realtors, and community service employees of a market for their skills. Newspapers provide information about community projects, financial changes, or recreational facilities that might be equally useful. And newspapers can help you to locate new markets or sites or expand those your company or agency already has.

A thorough guide to the newspapers published in the United States and Canada is the *Ayer Directory of Periodicals.* This work, issued annually, lists the date a paper began publication; its current address, rates, and circulation; and its religious or political preference. The directory also includes a capsule history of the community served by the paper. Unfortunately, it will not refer you to specific stories. For that information you need to consult an index. The best one is the *New York Times Index,* which indexes by subject and author stories that have appeared in its paper since 1851. This index also summarizes stories and reprints the photographs, maps, and other illustrations that accompanied some of the stories. Still another advantage this comprehensive index offers is that you can find the date of an event in it and then check that date in a local paper to see how the second newspaper covered the story. Many libraries have the back issues of the *New York Times* on microfilm.

Another index to consult is the *Newspaper Index,* published since 1972. Although it covers far fewer years than the *New York Times Index,* this work lists the stories published in four newspapers representing four main areas of the country—the East Coast (*Washington Post*), the Midwest (the *Chicago Tribune*), the South (the *New Orleans Times-Picayune*), and the West Coast (the *Los Angeles Times*). You might also consult the *Wall Street Journal,* which publishes its own index.

Every newspaper is indexed. You can find the index to your local newspaper in that section of a newspaper office called "the morgue," where all the back issues of a paper are stored. All you need to use the index is the date of the story you are interested in. Newspapers gladly allow readers access to these back issues and may even help you photocopy a story.

Finally, do not overlook company or neighborhood newspapers. They will often run stories and biographical material that will help you by suggesting markets, indicating possible contacts, and offering valuable statistics.

▶ Audiovisual Materials

Audiovisual materials include sound, still or moving pictures, or both together. Some types of audiovisuals are records, cassettes, tape recordings, photographs, films, and microforms (microfilms, microfiches, and microcards). These materials may be shelved in a separate part of the library that contains the room and proper equipment to use them conveniently and properly. Audiovisual titles are listed in the card catalog and perhaps also in a separate audiovisual catalog. One particular type of audiovisual material, microforms, deserves special attention.

The name *microforms* refers to a number of research tools—microfilm, microfiche, microcards—that all make use of microphotography. Each of these library tools presents a great deal of information reduced from its original size and stored compactly on film or tape. The microform process saves the library space, increases the durability of the documents, and offers libraries a wider range of titles for far less money. Microforms are used frequently in business and industry as well. Hospitals can store patient records much more economically; banks put canceled checks on microforms for safe storage and easy reference; and the government can condense miles of documents for easy and accurate retrieval.

Microfilm

A microfilm is a strip of black-and-white film stored on reels, cartridges, or cassettes on which reduced images are found, such as in Fig. 7.10. These reduced images are microscopic pictures of the pages of books, articles, newspapers, court proceedings, and so forth. The size of these pages has been reduced by microphotography to a fraction of their original size. Believe it or not, "Today, a 1,245-page Bible can be reproduced on a one-inch square piece of microfilm. If the Library of Congress chose, it could store its 270 miles of books and other reference material in six standard filing cabinets" (*Nation's Business,* March 1971, p. 20). A library could save 95 percent of its space if it converted all its holdings to microfilm.

The advantages microfilm offers are many. No library could possibly save all the back issues of a local newspaper, let alone a large, nationally famous paper such as the *New York Times.* Moreover, newspapers tear, fade, and crumble after being used by readers for a few weeks. Using microfilm, a library can store a newspaper's daily issues for a one-month period on one reel, such as any of the reels seen in Fig. 7.10. A special machine called a microfilm reader, similar to the one in Fig. 7.11, must be used. Your library has at least one or two of these machines and possibly more. Your librarian will be pleased to show you how to operate one.

Microfiche

Microfiche (pronounced micro feesh) is a close cousin to microfilm. The microfiche process puts the film of the reduced pages of books, periodicals, catalogs, or any other printed materials on flat, transparent four-by-six-inch cards. Each fiche (or film strip) may hold as many as 90 to 100 pages. Superfiche, an even more compact method of reproduction, can put 300 to 400

Fig. 7.10   Examples of microfilm stored on (a) reels, (b) cartridges, and (c) cassettes

(a)   (b)   (c)

Fig. 7.11   A microfilm reader.

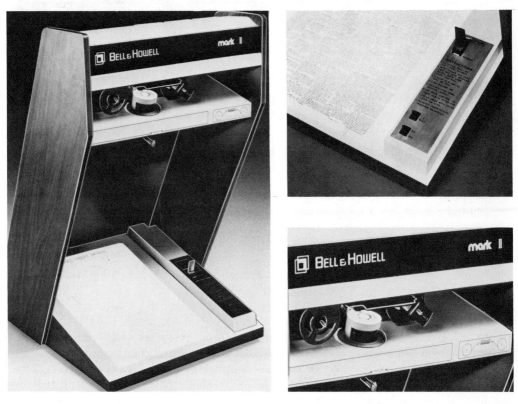

Photos courtesy Micro Photo Division, Bell & Howell Company, Old Mansfield Road, Wooster, OH 44691.

Fig. 7.12   A sample microfiche.

E. Stevens Rice, *Fiche and Reel* (Ann Arbor, MI.: Xerox, n.d.), p. 13. Used by permission.

pages on a single four-by-six-inch card. A common reduction rate is 24:1. Figure 7.12 shows a sample microfiche. More than fifty-five pages of a periodical are placed on this single card. As with microfilm, you need a special machine to see the material condensed onto microfiche. Using a microfiche reader, you slide the four-by-six-inch card onto a tray, push the tray underneath a magnifying lens, and see the material projected and enlarged on a lighted screen. To find the page you want, you simply slide the tray up or down or from right to left.

A *microcard* is identical to a microfiche except that the film is printed on an opaque, not transparent, card.

▶ Note Taking

Note taking is the crucial link between finding sources and writing a report. Never trust your memory to keep all your research facts straight. Taking notes is time well spent. Do not be too quick in getting it done or too eager to begin writing your paper. Careless note taking may cause you to forget page numbers, publishers, dates, or even titles; you might need this information at 2:00 A.M. when the library is closed and your paper is due at 9:00 A.M. Not copying accurately from a source could lead you to omit key words

Fig. 7.13   Note card containing bibliographic information on a source.

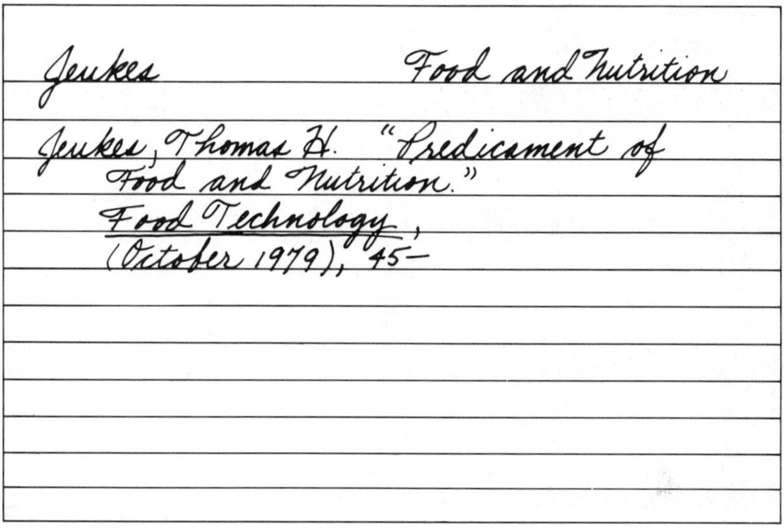

Jenkes   Food and Nutrition

Jenkes, Thomas H. "Predicament of
Food and Nutrition."
Food Technology,
(October 1979), 45–

in a quotation or, even worse, misrepresent or contradict what the author has said. Carelessness could result in crediting one author with another's work.

Basically, you will be taking two kinds of notes. One type will be the sources you read, as in Fig. 7.13. These cards will become your working bibliography. The other type will be reserved for the specific information you take from these sources in the form of direct quotations, paraphrases, or summaries. Figures 7.14 and 7.15 show the kinds of information that can be taken from sources.

How to Take Effective Notes

To take accurate and meaningful notes, follow these practical guidelines:

1. Use three-by-five-inch or four-by-six-inch index cards, and use the same size consistently. Do not be tempted to use slips of paper, looseleaf notebook paper, or notebooks; cards are less likely to get lost, and they will help you to organize, alphabetize, and label material.
2. Write on only one side of the card. It is easier to copy and check information when you list it all on one side.
3. Use a ballpoint pen to write your notes. Felt-tip pens or pencils may smudge. Write legibly; print if necessary.
4. Put only one title (article or book or film) on each card. These cards will later have to be arranged in alphabetical order for your bibliography, and if you forget that three entries are on one card, you could end up retyping your entire bibliography (to put these "missing" entries in), or you could run the risk of leaving them out.

Fig. 7.14   Note card containing a direct quotation.

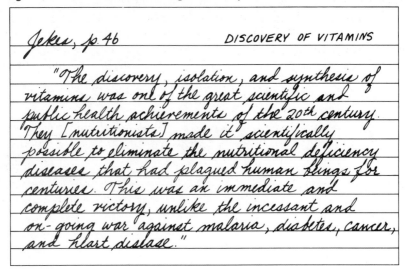

Jekes, p. 46   DISCOVERY OF VITAMINS

"The discovery, isolation, and synthesis of vitamins was one of the great scientific and public health achievements of the 20th century. They [nutritionists] made it scientifically possible to eliminate the nutritional deficiency diseases that had plagued human beings for centuries. This was an immediate and complete victory, unlike the incessant and on-going war against malaria, diabetes, cancer, and heart disease."

Fig. 7.15   Note card containing a paraphrase.

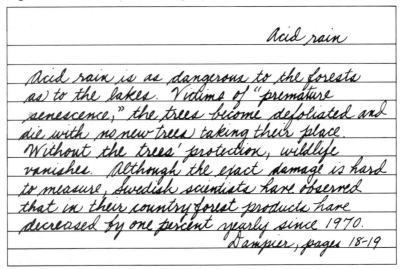

Acid rain

Acid rain is as dangerous to the forests as to the lakes. Victims of "premature senescence," the trees become defoliated and die with no new trees taking their place. Without the trees' protection, wildlife vanishes. Although the exact damage is hard to measure, Swedish scientists have observed that in their country forest products have decreased by one percent yearly since 1970.
                              Dampier, pages 18-19

5. Include full bibliographic information for each source. For books, list author, title, chapter titles, edition, date, city of publication, publisher, and page numbers; for articles, supply author, title, journal, volume number, date, and page numbers.
6. Decode and spell out any periodical index or journal abbreviations. Record periodical entries with their full and accurate bibliographic information. (See the next section of this chapter on documentation.) The abbreviated entries in indexes such as the *Readers' Guide* or the *Applied*

Science and Technology Index are not in acceptable format for footnotes or bibliographic entries in your paper or report.

7. Write down the call numbers of the book or periodical in the upper left-hand corner of the card so you will know where to find the source again if you need it. If you are using more than one library, also indicate at which library you found the source.

8. Write a code word or phrase in the upper right-hand corner to identify the topic treated by the source or the information written on the card from that source. Using code words such as "characteristics," "function of," "history of," or "location" written on your cards will help you to organize when you write your paper.

Following these rules, you should find your note taking is easier to complete. Using note cards will help you verify your sources and record information from them.

To Quote or Not to Quote

Before recording information from sources, ask yourself these three questions: (1) How much should I take down? (2) How often should I copy the author's words verbatim to use direct quotations? (3) When should I paraphrase or summarize? A safe rule to follow is: Do not be a human copying machine. If you write down too many of the author's own words, you will simply be transferring the author's words from the book or article to your paper. You show that you read the work but have not evaluated its findings. Do not use direct quotations simply as a filler.

Direct quotations should be used sparingly and saved for when they count most. When an author has summarized a great deal of significant information concisely into a few well-chosen sentences, you may want to quote this summary verbatim. Or if a writer has clarified a difficult concept exceedingly well, you may want to include this clarification exactly as it is listed. And certainly the author's chief statement or thesis may deserve to be quoted directly. Figure 7.14 contains such an important statement. Just be careful that you do not quote verbatim all of the evidence leading to that conclusion. The conclusion may be pointedly expressed in two or three sentences; the evidence could cover many pages. If you are worried about exactly how much to quote verbatim, keep in mind that no more than 10 or 15 percent of your paper should be made up of direct quotations. Remember that when you quote someone directly, you are telling your readers that these words are the most important part of the author's work as far as you are concerned. Be a selective filter, not a large funnel.

There will be times when a sentence or passage is particularly useful, but you may not want to quote it in its entirety. You may want to delete some words that are not really necessary for your purpose. These omissions are indicated by using ellipsis dots, three spaced dots within the sentence to indicate where the words are omitted (four spaced dots if the omitted words end the sentence). Here are some examples.

	Omitted words within a sentence
Full Quotation:	"Diet and nutrition, which have been studied by researchers, significantly affect oral health."
Quotation with Ellipsis:	"Diet and nutrition . . . significantly affect oral health."
	Omitted words at the end of a sentence
Full Quotation:	"Decisions on how to operate the company should be based on the most accurate and relevant information available from both within the company and from the specific community that establishment serves."
Quotation with Ellipsis:	"Decisions on how to operate the company should be based on the most accurate and relevant information available. . . ."

At times you may have to insert your own information within a quotation. This addition, called an *interpolation,* is made by enclosing your clarifying identification or remark within brackets inside the quotation. For example, "It [the new transportation network] has been thoroughly tested and approved." In other words, anything within brackets is not part of the quotation.

Most of your note taking will not be devoted to writing down direct quotations. It will be concerned with writing paraphrases. A paraphrase is a restatement of the author's ideas point by point in your own words. Even though you are using your own words to translate or restate, you still must footnote the paraphrase because you are using the author's facts and interpretations. You do not use quotation marks, though. When you include a paraphrase in your paper, you should be careful to do three things:

1. Be faithful to the author's meaning. Do not alter facts or introduce new ideas.
2. Follow the order in which the author presents the information.
3. Use paraphrases in your report selectively. You do not want your work to be merely a restatement of another's ideas.

Figure 7.15 shows a note card containing a paraphrase of the following quotation:

> While the effects of acid rain are felt first in lakes, which act as natural collection points, some scientists fear there may be extensive damage to forests as well. In the process described by one researcher as "premature senescence," trees exposed to acid sprays lose their leaves, wilt and finally die. New trees may not grow to replace them. Deprived of natural cover, wildlife may flee or die. The extent of the damage to forest lands is extremely difficult to determine, but scientists find the trend worrisome. In Sweden, for example, one estimate calculates that the yield in forest products decreased by about one percent each year during the 1970's.[1]

---

[1] Bill Dampier, "Now Even the Rain Is Dangerous," *International Wildlife,* 10 (March–April 1980), 18–19.

Paraphrased material can be introduced with an appropriate identifying phrase, such as "According to Dampier's study," "To paraphrase Dampier," or "As Dampier observes."

▶ Documentation of Sources

To document means to furnish readers with information about the materials (books, articles, pamphlets, films, interviews) used for the factual support of your statements. This is what you do when you transfer the information listed on your note cards to footnotes, bibliographies, or reference lists. Documentation serves three functions:

1. Documentation verifies that you have found, read, and incorporated current literature and sources into your paper or report.
2. Documentation gives proper credit to these sources. Citing works by name is not a simple act of courtesy; it is an ethical requirement and, because so much of this material is protected by copyright, a point of law. By documenting your sources, you will avoid plagiarism—that is, stealing someone else's ideas and listing them as your own. If you are found guilty of plagiarism, you could be expelled from school or fired from your job.
3. Documentation tells readers exactly where they can find a specific book or article if they want to read it themselves.

Numerous formats exist for documenting sources in footnotes, bibliographies, and reference lists. Many professions publish their own style sheet or book to provide such instruction (for example, the *Publication Manual of the American Psychological Association*, the Council of Biology Editors' *CBE Style Manual*, the *American Institute of Physics Handbook*) or recommend that writers follow the format used in a specific journal. Every professional group, however, would advise writers *against* using the formats and abbreviations found in periodical indexes such as the *Readers' Guide* or the *Applied Science and Technology Index*. The way information is listed in these sources is not offered as a model in documentation. Before you write a paper or submit a report, ask instructors or employers about preferred format.

It would be impossible here, and pointless to try, to include examples of every way a footnote or reference can be written. Basically, two kinds of documentation exist. One kind uses footnotes and bibliographies. The most common and widely respected model for this type of documentation is the *MLA Handbook* (New York: Modern Language Association of America, 1977). The following sections on preparing footnotes and a bibliography will use the format recommended by the *MLA Handbook*. The second kind of documentation uses the author-date and reference list system, a method common in the sciences and applied sciences. Although no single model exists for this kind of documentation, the section on scientific documentation below discusses the general principles by which sources are listed according to this method.

Footnotes

A footnote can appear in one of two places in your paper or report. It can be placed at the bottom, or foot, of the page where it is cited; or, footnotes can be collected and placed on a separate sheet at the end of your paper or report. In this case, they are no longer called footnotes, but simply notes.[2] It is far more common to collect all your notes and put them on a separate page. Figure 7.16 shows a page of notes. Each note is indented five spaces, and if it is longer than one line, the second line of the note returns to the original margin. You single-space within notes, but double-space between notes.

In the text of your paper you indicate where a footnote belongs by inserting a slightly raised Arabic number in the place to which the source refers. You do this by simply moving the typewriter roller up a quarter of an inch or so. The order in which footnotes are cited in your paper should correspond to the order in which they are listed on your notes page. When readers see [1], they expect to find the information in footnote 1 on the notes page to refer them to the reference cited in the text. Number your notes consecutively; do not begin with a [1] on each new page. When you insert a footnote number, put it after the direct quotation and after the period. Here is a right and a wrong way to do it:

Correct: Alan Johnson claimed that "the cost of doing business in the new mall is twice what it was when the store was located downtown."[1]

Incorrect: Alan Johnson claimed that "the cost of doing business in the new mall is twice what it was when the store was located downtown[1]."

Avoid placing any footnote numbers in the middle of a sentence:

Incorrect: The basic causes of employee unhappiness were poor pay[1], bad fringe benefits[2], and no provisions for overtime.[3]

And don't group footnote numbers together like this:

Incorrect: The basic causes of employee unhappiness were poor pay, bad fringe benefits, and no provisions for overtime.[1,2,3]

Combine all these sources (titles) into one footnote placed at the end of the sentence so readers are not distracted by one footnote piled on another. Too many footnotes can also overwhelm readers. Furthermore, if every sentence or paragraph ends with a footnote, readers will certainly wonder what, if any, ideas or plans are original in the paper.

What Must Be Footnoted?

This question often frustrates the report writer. Become familiar with the guidelines on page 204 and apply them whenever you are asked to prepare a report:

---

[2] In this chapter, notes and footnotes are used interchangeably.

Fig. 7.16   A sample notes page.

NOTES

[1]David T. Stanley, <u>Prisoners Among Us: The Problem of Parole</u> (Washington, D.C.: Brookings Institute, 1976), p. 189.

[2]Ben Meeker, "The Federal Probation System: The Second 25 Years," <u>Federal Probation</u>, 39 (June 1975), 17.

[3]Vincent O'Leary and Kathleen Hanrahan, "The Impact of <u>Morrissey</u> and <u>Gagnon</u> on Parole Proceedings." <u>Journal of Criminal Law and Criminology</u>, 69 (Summer 1978), 165.

[4]Stanley, p. 34.

[5]Interview with Mike Strasky, Chief of Police, Mayfield, June 23, 1979.

[6]"Crime Is Increasing," Editorial, <u>Mayfield Messenger</u>, July 5, 1979, p. 5.

[7]National Council on Crime and Delinquency, Research Center West, <u>Characteristics of the Parole Population, 1977</u> (San Francisco, 1979), p. 13.

[8]Anne M. Heinz and others, "Sentencing by Parole Board: An Evaluation," <u>Journal of Criminal Law and Criminology</u>, 67 (March 1976), 20.

[9]Kevin Krajick, "Are Guidelines a New Kind of Unfairness?" <u>Corrections Magazine</u>, 4 (September 1978), 47.

[10]Kevin Krajick, "Growing Old in Prison," <u>Corrections Magazine</u>, 5 (March 1979), 35.

[11]Krajick, "Guidelines," p. 48.

[12]Krajick, "Growing Old," p. 35.

[13]Krajick, "Growing Old," p. 35.

[14]Krajick, "Guidelines," p. 46.

[15]Heinz and others, pp. 2–3.

[16]"Prisons and Penology," <u>Encyclopaedia Britannica</u>, 1976.

[17]Howard R. Sacks and Charles H. Logan, <u>Does Parole Make a Difference</u>? (Storrs: University of Connecticut School of Law Press, 1979), pp. 33–37. For a different perspective, see Stanley, pp. 101–109; and Krajick, "Guidelines," pp. 47–48.

[18]United States Parole Commission, <u>Procedures Manual</u> (Washington, D.C.: United States Parole Commission, 1978), Appendix 13.

1. Footnote any direct quotations (even a single phrase or word if the context warrants) or any paraphrases. Of course, you do not have to footnote obvious facts, such as normal body temperature, the chemical composition of a type of food or insecticide, well-known dates (the 1969 moon landing), formulas or quotations (from the Bible, Shakespeare, or folklore).
2. Footnote any additional information (collateral readings, other relevant research) you want the reader to know about. These kinds of footnotes are known as "see also" notes because you want the reader to look at these other works, too.
3. Footnote any qualifications or explanations that you do not discuss in your text. For example, you might use explanatory footnotes to tell readers that a certain term is used in a restricted or particular way in your paper. The footnote on p. 202 is such an explanatory footnote.

Footnote Format

When you footnote a source for the first time, you must include the following information and in this order:

Book	*Article or magazine*
author(s)	author(s)
editor(s)	title of article (put in quotation marks)
title (underscored)	
edition (if second or subsequent)	journal (underscored)
place of publication	volume number (in Arabic numerals)
publisher's name	
date of publication	date
page number(s)	page number(s)

- *Book with one author*

    [1]Bram Cavin, <u>How to Run a Successful Florist and Plant Store</u> (New York: David McKay, 1977), p. 45.

Note how a comma follows the author's name, but no comma is placed before the parentheses containing the publisher's city, name, or date.

- *Book with two authors*

    [2]William S. Howell and Ernest G. Bormann, <u>Presentational Speaking for Business and the Professions</u> (New York: Harper & Row, 1971), pp. 73–74.

Both authors' names are listed in the order they appear on the title page; do not worry about alphabetical order.

● *Book with more than three authors*

    [3]K. G. Andreoli and others, <u>Comprehensive Cardiac Care: A Text for Nurses, Physicians, and Other Health Practitioners</u> (St. Louis: C. V. Mosby, 1978), p. 361.

When there are more than three authors, list only the first author's name, and add "and others" without a comma before this phrase. When a book has a subtitle, list it. The title and subtitle are separated by a colon, as in footnote example 3 above.

● *Corporate author*

    [4]National Institute for the Foodservice Industry, <u>Applied Foodservice Sanitation</u> (Lexington, Mass.: D.C. Heath, 1978), p. 74.

A corporate author refers to an organization, society, association, institute, or governmental agency that publishes a work under its own name. In the example above, the Institute (often cited as NIFI) wrote the book. Notice how the state is given after the city. This further identification tells readers that the book was published in Lexington, Massachusetts, as opposed to Lexington, Kentucky, or Lexington, Virginia. The name of the state is not used after well-known cities such as Boston, Chicago, or San Francisco.

● *Second or subsequent edition*

    [5]C. Rollin Neswonger and Philip E. Fess, <u>Accounting Principles</u>, 11th ed. (Cincinnati: South–Western, 1973), p. 212.

The particular edition number is included between the title and the publication data.

● *An edited collection of essays*

    [6]Sharon Van Sell Davidson, ed., <u>PSRO:Utilization and Audit in Patient Care</u> (Saint Louis: C. V. Mosby, 1976), p. 126.

The abbreviation "ed." for *editor* follows the editor's name.

● *An essay included within a collection*

    [7]Diane Baker, "Nursing Service Philosophy," in <u>PSRO: Utilization and Audit in Patient Care</u>, ed. Sharon Van Sell Davidson (Saint Louis: C. V. Mosby, 1976), p. 137.

The name of the author of the article in this collection comes first, then the title of the article followed by the word "in," the title of the collection, and then the editor's name.

- *An article in a journal*

> [8]Gail DuMontelle, "Real Estate Records Storage and Retention," Real Estate Today, 12 (1979), 26.

Note how a footnote to a journal article differs from that to a book. The title is in quotation marks, not underscored; there is no place of publication listed for a journal, the number after the title refers to the volume, and the abbreviation "p." or "pp." is not used to indicate the page number(s).

- *A signed magazine article*

> [9]B. Agnew, "Consumerists Try to Regain Clout," Business Weekly, May 29, 1978, p. 107.

Unlike the more scholarly journals, popular and frequently issued magazines are listed by date and not volume number. Also, the abbreviation "p." or "pp." is used.

- *An unsigned magazine article*

> [10]"When Dream Homes Turn into Nightmares," U.S. News & World Report, December 11, 1978, p. 43.

Many magazine articles do not carry an author's name (or by-line) because they are written by one of the staff members of the magazine. In this case begin with the title.

- *An article in a newspaper*

> [11]Joel Sleed, "Credit Card Users Run into Surcharges on Vacations Abroad," Times-Picayune, March 23, 1980, Sec. 3, p. 15, cols. 1-2.

An accurate footnote to a newspaper article will identify the section, page, and column(s) for the reader.

- *An article in an encyclopedia*

> [12]"Farming." Encyclopedia Americana, 1977.

Because it is a multivolume, alphabetical work, only the particular edition or year of an encyclopedia has to be cited. If you cite the name of an author of an encyclopedia article, begin your footnote with his or her first name, then the last name.

- *A pamphlet*

> [13]Roberta T. Boone, Ghetto Children and Their Diets (Washington, D.C.: U.S. Children's Bureau, 1968), p. 7.

- *A film*

> [14]Understanding Emphysema (Jamaica, New York: Eye Gate Media, 1978), order number TP835.

Underscore the title of a film and include the distributor and order number.

- *Radio or television program*

> [15]Sixty Minutes, CBS, March 23, 1980.

- *A published interview*

> [16]"Interview with Frank Jameson," Findlay Magazine, August 15, 1973, p. 2.

- *An unpublished interview*

> [17]Telephone interview with Professor Barbara Jensen, Physics Dept., Berry College, May 15, 1979.

Indicate how the interview was conducted, with whom (including the person's title), and the date.

- *A questionnaire*

> [18]These percentages were based on a response by twenty-five secretaries to a questionnaire distributed between October 15 and October 30, 1979 in the Seager Building.

Documenting Subsequent References

You may refer to the same title more than once in your paper or report. Full publication information does not have to be repeated each time you cite the

Finding and Using Library Materials

same source. For second and subsequent references to the same source, be guided by brevity and clarity. Students were once taught to use elaborate Latin abbreviations: *op. cit.* for a work that was already cited; *ibid.* when the work was cited two or more times in a row; or *loc. cit.* for the same page numbers of the work cited in a previous note. These abbreviations are not used very often now. Instead, use a form of shortened reference as long as the reader clearly knows what source you are citing. The easiest way to refer to a source in a later footnote is to list the author's name followed by the appropriate page number, always introduced by the abbreviation "p." or "pp."

[1]P. Johnson, "Be the Doctor in the House," Encore, November 27, 1978, p. 18.

[2]E. G. Graves, "Health Care: A Privilege, or a Right?" Black Enterprise, April 8, 1978, p. 8.

[3]Johnson, p. 18.

[4]Graves, p. 8.

If you cite the same work two or three times in a row, use the same kind of shortened form even if the page numbers change:

[5]Johnson, p. 18.

[6]Johnson, p. 19.

[7]Johnson, p. 18.

[8]Johnson, p. 18.

When using two works by the same author, you will have to add more than the author's name and page number(s) to identify the author's particular work for the reader. Use the author's name, a shortened title, and the page number(s):

[1]Edwin W. Patterson, Risk and Insurance Management, 2d. ed. (Washington, D.C.: Small Business Administration, 1970), pp. 23–25.

[2]Edwin W. Patterson, Essentials of Insurance Law, 2d. ed. (New York: McGraw-Hill, 1957), p. 102.

[3]Patterson, Risk, p. 32.

[4]Patterson, Essentials, p. 107.

⁵Patterson, <u>Essentials</u>, p. 94.

⁶Patterson, <u>Risk</u>, p. 32.

Bibliographies

A bibliography is an alphabetical list by author of all the sources you consulted. If a work cited in your bibliography is unsigned, begin with the first word of the title, but disregard the articles *a, an,* or *the.* Include works you actually cited as well as studies you may not have mentioned, but which, because of their relevance to your topic, you want the readers to know about. Do not construe this advice as an invitation to inflate your bibliography to make your paper or report look more impressive. A short report of five or six pages with a bibliography of thirty entries might look suspicious. Include only materials that directly add something new and useful to the topic. Hence, you would not want to list the titles of three textbooks all on the same subject. Include the bibliography at the very end of your project; it is an appropriate collection of materials for the reader's convenience and future (or extended) research.

Figure 7.17 contains a sample bibliography for a report on environmental problems and park planning. Even a quick glance at this sample bibliography reveals major differences in the way you list an entry in a bibliography and in a footnote. These differences, again following the *MLA Handbook,* can be summarized as follows:

1. The same work may be listed many times in footnotes. In a bibliography, list it only once.
2. Unlike a footnote, the second line, not the first, of a bibliographic entry is indented.
3. In a bibliography invert the author's name. The last name comes first, followed by a comma, and then the first name.
4. Put a period after the author's inverted name. Coauthors' names are not inverted. Examine the Sternloff and Warren entry in Fig. 7.17.
5. Books listed in a bibliography, unlike a footnote entry, do not have the place of publication, the publisher's name, or the date enclosed in parentheses. Also, specific page numbers are not listed for a book cited in the bibliography; the entire book is cited.
6. For an article in the bibliography, list inclusive page numbers, since the entire article is cited.
7. When citing two or more works by the same author, do not retype the author's name. Instead, type a line using the underscore key in place of the name in second and subsequent entries. Look at the entries for Raymond F. Dasmann in Fig. 7.17.

Fig. 7.17   A sample bibliography.

BIBLIOGRAPHY

Andrews, Ralph. "Planning is Basic to Recreational Philosophy."
    Editorial. Recreation, (February 1965), 59.

Brown, William Edward. Islands of Hope: Parks and Recreation in
    Environmental Crisis. Washington, D.C.: National Recreation and
    Park Association, 1971.

Dasmann, Raymond F. The Destruction of California. New York: Collier
    Books, 1966.

_____. A Different Kind of Country. New York: Macmillan, 1968.

Dattner, Richard. "Parks for the Year 2000." American City and County.
    92 (November 1977), 39–44.

"The Environment and Our Parks." Evansville Gazette, March 31, 1980,
    p. 11, col. 1.

"Guidelines for Reducing Damage in Parks and Recreation Facilities."
    Public Works, 109 (December 1978), 58–60.

Kraus, Richard. "Recreation and Parks Under Fire." Parks & Recreation,
    8 (January 1973), 24–27.

Linde, R. "Planning for Recreational Traffic." Traffic Engineer, 43
    (July 1973), 24–25; 52–54.

Marston, Lance. "Land Use Dilemma." Water Spectrum, 10 (Spring 1978),
    1–9.

Mead, M. "Crisis of Self: America's Secret War." Remarks at the 1973
    Congress for Recreation and Parks. Parks & Recreation, 9 (March
    1974), 24–28.

"Parks." Encyclopedia of Urban Planning. New York: McGraw–Hill, 1974

"Playgrounds for a Price: Private Parks." Time, January 15, 1979.
    p. 47.

"Public Parks Are Our National Heritage." Public Service Commercial.
    Channel 17, Madison, Wisconsin, January 20, 1980.

Randolph, Nancy. Park Commissioner, Rock County, Wisconsin. Interview
    about public parks in Rock County. Janesville, Wisconsin, February
    10, 1980.

Sternloff, Robert E., and Roger Warren. Park Recreation Maintenance
    Management. Boston: Holbrook Press, 1977.

Zeldin, Marvin. "Congress Creates but Doesn't Appropriate, and the
    Public is Left With Only Paper Parks." Audubon, 75 (March 1973),
    113–116.

▶ Documentation in Scientific and Technical Writing

The MLA method of documentation just described is not used in scientific or technical writing. It is employed primarily in the humanities. Other methods of citing and documenting sources do not use footnotes or bibliographies. In place of these forms of recording sources many professions use the author-date method of documentation or the ordered references method. Both methods rely on parenthetical documentation; that is, rather than using footnotes with raised Arabic numerals, the particular information about the source is placed directly in the text within parentheses. A brief overview of these two methods will show how this is done.

The Author-Date Method

With this method the writer does not use footnotes or note numbers at all. Instead, information about a reference or quotation is placed in the text of the paper or report. For example:

> The theory that new housing becomes increasingly expensive as buyers move farther north has been recently advanced (Jones, 1978, p. 13).

The reader sees that Jones advanced this theory in 1978 and specifically on p. 13. If Jones's name were mentioned in the text, "Jones advances the theory that new housing . . . ," only (1978, p. 13) would be listed. To find Jones's work, readers turn to an alphabetical list of references at the end of the paper, report, or article where, under Jones, they find a bibliographic entry for the work. Unlike a bibliography, such as the one in Fig. 7.17, only works actually cited in a paper are listed in the reference list. If two works by Jones were cited, the references for both of them are given. If they were done in the same year, they are differentiated in the text *and* in the list of references by a lower-case letter "a" and "b." For example:

> Housing is increasingly more expensive on the north side than on the south (Jones, 1978a, p. 22).

> A recent study has established a demographic pattern for small cities in the Midwest (Jones, 1978b, p. 73).

In the accompanying list of references, the two works by Jones might be listed as follows:

> Jones, T. 1978a. The cost of housing on Lincoln's northside. Urban Studies, 72:10–24.

> Jones, T. 1978b. Demographic density in three Midwestern small cities University of Missouri Press, Columbia.

According to this method of documentation in the reference list, only the first word of the title (even if it is *a, an,* or *the*) and proper nouns are capitalized. Titles are neither underscored (books, journals) nor put into quotation marks (articles). The volume number of a journal is often underscored or italicized and followed by a colon to separate it from the page numbers that are listed immediately thereafter. It is important to remember that this system uses no keyed number (footnote) approach, as in the MLA format.

The Ordered References Method

Like the author-date method, the ordered references method uses parenthetical documentation, but uses numbers rather than authors' names to identify a source. The references in a paper are numbered in the order in which they appear. For example,

```
Three new products help reduce bacterial infection in restaurant
kitchens (7:47).
```

The "7" indicates that this is the seventh source found in the reference list; "47" refers to the page number of that source. Sources, therefore, are not listed in alphabetical order, as they are in the author-date method. Each time a source is mentioned, the same number is used. If your first cited source is listed again near the middle or end of your paper, or if it is cited three times in a row, it is still listed parenthetically as (1:   ). The page numbers after the colon may or may not change.

▶ Appendix: Reference Works

After the title of each of the following reference works is a brief annotation indicating, sometimes with a direct quotation taken from the particular work, its audience, organization, and coverage. The dates in parentheses after indexes and abstracts refer to the year in which they began publication.

Indexes

Applied Science and Technology Index (1913). This work surveys 250 magazines and journals from a wide variety of fields (construction, earth science, forestry, industrial graphics, microbiology, optical technology, telecommunications, and transportation are just a few); appears monthly (except for August) and is organized by subject headings with subheadings frequently used. From 1913 to 1958 it was entitled the *Industrial Arts Index.*

Biological and Agricultural Index (1945). This index is published monthly with quarterly and yearly cumulative issues. Formerly called *Agricultural Index,* this work indexes about 200 periodicals in such fields as agricultural economics, animal husbandry, ecology, foodscience, forestry, horticulture, marine biology, nutrition, soil science, and veterinary medicine. Organization is by subject headings; it also contains a separate section on book reviews.

Business Periodicals Index (1958). Published monthly, this index surveys a wide range of business journals in such areas as accounting, business communications, office machines, personnel, and real estate. It includes articles under both subjects and titles.

Criminal Justice Periodical Index (1975). Published yearly, this index contains both an author and subject list. It is a guide to articles in more than 100 journals in the fields of law enforcement, corrections, paralegal, security, and traffic enforcement.

Cumulative Index to Nursing & Allied Health Literature (1955). Published bimonthly, this index surveys over 250 journals and magazines in the nursing and allied health fields. Nurses, respiratory and physical therapists, social workers, radiologic and medical technicians will find a convenient guide to literature in their fields. A two-part index—one a subject guide to periodicals and the other an alphabetical index of these subjects—makes it easier to use the first part.

Education Index (1929). This index is published every month except July and August. It lists periodicals that deal with all aspects of education from driver training to adult and continuing education.

Environmental Index (1971). Published annually, this index "offers *keyword direct access* to more than 55,000 citations appearing in 2,000 of the world's most significant environmental publications. To provide a comprehensive and accurate environmental perspective, the index compiles and cross-references environmental material from major scientific, technical, professional, trade and general periodicals, government documents, proceedings, research reports, newspapers, books and speeches."

Hospital Literature Index (1945). Published quarterly, this "is a subject-author index of literature about the administration, planning, financing of medical care facilities and about administrative aspects of medical, paramedical, and prepayment fields." It is arranged by subject headings. While it does not survey nursing literature, it does cover administrative and educational issues in allied health fields (dietetics, dental hygiene x-ray technology, medical technology, physical and respiratory therapy).

Index to Legal Periodicals (1926). This index is published monthly, except September, and contains a subject and author index to more than 350 law journals published worldwide. "Case notes or discussions of recent cases are listed by the names of the case discussed at the end of the subheading 'Cases.' " It also includes a book review index.

Index Medicus (1879). Published monthly by the National Library of Medicine in Washington, D.C., this index surveys 2,500 journals in medicine and ancillary fields (e.g., medical technology, medical records, respiratory therapy, etc.) published worldwide. It contains subject and author sections and translates titles of articles written in a foreign language. This index is invaluable for students in the health sciences.

Index of Supermarket Articles (1935). Published by the Supermarket Institute in Chicago, this index surveys articles on supermarkets and food suppliers published in such journals as *Chain Store Age, Grocery Editions, Progressive Grocer, Supermarket Merchandising,* and *Supermarket Manager.*

Social Sciences Index and Humanities Index (1907). Known as the *International Index* from 1907 to 1965 and the *Social Sciences and Humanities Index* from 1965 to 1974, these two works now list articles in many of the social sciences (e.g., sociology, political science) and the humanities.

Encyclopedias

The Arnold Encyclopedia of Real Estate, edited by Alvin Arnold and Jack Kusnet. Boston: Warren, Gorham & Lamont, 1978. 1 volume. A topical "Entry Finder" at the back "classifies selected entries into twelve major subjects."

Encyclopedia of Accounting Forms and Reports. 3 vols. Englewood Cliffs, New Jersey: Prentice-Hall, 1964. This work provides a survey of reports used in accounting practice (vol. 1), accounting systems (vol. 2), and specific industries (vol. 3).

Encyclopedia of Animal Care, edited by Geoffrey P. West. 12th ed. Baltimore: Williams and Wilkins, 1977. 1 vol.; 265 illustrations. This work gives information on "the diseases, breeding, and health of domesticated animals and is intended for farmers, public health officials, and breeders who do not need a veterinary reference work or who need more detail than a popular magazine provides."

Encyclopedia of Careers and Vocational Guidance, edited by William E. Hopke. Rev. ed. Chicago: Ferguson, 1972. 2 vols. It contains numerous pictures, drawings, tables, and graphs about employment opportunities; a glossary of terms is also included.

Enclyclopedia of Computer Science, edited by Anthony Ralston. New York: Petrocelli / Charter, 1976. 1 vol. This work has a helpful list of titles on related subjects at the beginning of each section. It also has appendixes on abbreviations, acronyms, mathematical notations, and numerical tables.

Encyclopedia of Food Technology and Food Service Series. Westport, Connecticut: Avi Publishing. Vol. 1 *The Encyclopedia of Food Engineering*, edited by C. W. Hall, A. W. Farrall, and A. L. Rippen, 1971. Vol 2 *The Encyclopedia of Food Technology*, edited by Arnold H. Johnson and Martin S. Peterson, 1974. Vol. 3 *The Encyclopedia of Food Science*, edited by Arnold H. Johnson and Martin S. Peterson.

The Encyclopedia of Management, edited by Carl Heyel. New York: Van Nostrand Reinhold, 1973. 1 vol. This work is a guide to 25 core management subjects; it also gives cross-references within each subject.

Encyclopedia of Marine Resources, edited by Frank E. Firth. New York: Van Nostrand Reinhold, 1969. 1 vol. Information on the "most significant aspects of the ocean's resources" will be of interest to biologists, food technologists, fishery management specialists, and others.

Encyclopedia of Materials Handling, edited by Douglas Woodley. New York: Pergamon, 1964. 2 vols. It contains valuable chapters on machines (conveyors, elevators, cranes, hoists, trucks, etc.), unitization, and loading and transportation.

Encyclopedia of Modern Architecture. New York: Harry N. Abrams, 1964. 1 vol. This work contains an introduction on the history of architecture and divisions by countries and types of architecture; it also includes entries on individual architects.

Encyclopedia and Dictionary of Medicine, Nursing, and Allied Health, edited by Benjamin F. Miller and Claire Brackman. Philadelphia: W. B. Saunders, 1978. 1 vol. Using information from *Dorland's Illustrated Medical Dictionary*, this work contains 139 illustrations and 12 appendixes.

Encyclopedia of Photography, edited by Willard D. Morgan. New York: Greystone, 1977. 19 vols. Each volume contains its own table of contents. Beautifully illustrated, it includes information on historical, scientific, aesthetic, and technical subjects.

Encyclopedia of Practical Photography, edited by Eastman Kodak Company. Garden City, N.Y.: Amphoto, 1979. 14 vols. In this work the "emphasis . . . is on practical advice and instruction in using light, film, and chemicals to get the most of your equipment. Here you will find the how-to information necessary for actual production of photographic images."

Encyclopedia of Textiles, edited by the editors of *American Fabrics Magazine*. Englewood Cliffs, New Jersey: Prentice-Hall, 1972. 1 vol. This is a "reference guide for every person concerned with the producing and marketing of fibers and fabrics, and for the professions of designing and advertising which service the textile industry." A lavishly illustrated work, this encyclopedia contains information on the history, production, and manufacturing of natural and manmade fibers, colors and dyes, and textile printing.

Encyclopedia of Urban Planning, edited by Arnold Whittick. New York: McGraw-Hill, 1974. 1 vol. A preface describes and defines urban planning. Numerous pictures, maps, and drawings and a bibliography at the end of each section are included in this encyclopedia, which provides information on international projects, urban renewal, legislation, and other topics.

McGraw-Hill Encyclopedia of Energy, edited by Daniel N. Lapedes. New York: McGraw-Hill, 1981. 1 vol. This encyclopedia is divided into two sections—"Energy Perspectives" and "Energy Technology." The *Encyclopedia* "with its more than 300 articles written by specialists is designed to aid the student, librarian, scientist, engineer, teacher, and lay reader with any information on any aspect of energy from the economic and political to the environmental and technological."

McGraw-Hill Encyclopedia of Environmental Science, edited by Daniel N. Lapedes. New York: McGraw-Hill, 1974. 1 vol. This work contains 300 alphabetically arranged articles, most of which include a bibliography. There is also an analytical index.

McGraw-Hill Encyclopedia of Food, Agriculture & Nutrition, edited by Daniel N. Lapedes. New York: McGraw-Hill, 1977. 1 vol. Following five feature articles are 400 alphabetically arranged articles on subjects dealing with "the cultivation, harvesting, and processing of food crops; food manufacturing; and health and nutrition—from the economic and political to the technological."

McGraw-Hill Encyclopedia of Science and Technology, Daniel N. Lapedes, Editor in Chief. New York: McGraw-Hill, 1977. 15 vols; vol. 15 is an index. Extremely wide-ranging, this is the most comprehensive encyclopedia you can consult for scientific and technological subjects.

Goodheart-Wilcox Automotive Encyclopedia, edited by W. K. Toboldt and Larry Johnson. South Holland, Illinois: Goodheart-Wilcox, 1981. 1 vol. Detailed guide to auto repair and maintenance.

The New Encyclopedia of Furniture, edited by Joseph Aronson. New York: Crown, 1967. 1 vol. This work contains numerous drawings and designs of period pieces. A bibliography and a glossary of designers and craftsmen is found at the end of the work.

Wyman's Gardening Encyclopedia, edited by Donald Wyman. New York: Macmillan, 1977. 1 vol. This encyclopedia contains a table of contents to such horticultural topics as plants, trees, lawns, pesticides, fungicides, and insecticides that are discussed in detail in this helpful work.

Dictionaries

Dictionary of Architecture and Construction, edited by C. M. Harris. New York: McGraw-Hill, 1975. This dictionary provides definitions of terms "encountered in the everyday practice of architecture and construction and in their associated fields." It emphasizes terms from the building trades and includes information on "building products and materials, and related terms dealing with their design, appearance, performance, installation, and testing"; it also covers construction equipment.

Dictionary of Business and Finance, edited by Donald T. Clark and Bert A. Gottfried. New York: Crowell, 1957. It contains master and specific entries and covers such subjects as "accounting, advertising, banking, commodities, credit, export, finance, government, imports, insurance, investments, labor law, merchandising, personnel, purchasing, retailing, real estate, selling, shopping, statistics, the stock market, traffic, warehousing, work measurement."

Dictionary of Nutrition and Food Technology, edited by Arnold E. Bender. New York: Chemical Publishing Company, 1976. This dictionary is for students in agriculture, commerce, foodscience, dietetics, home economics, sociology, and medicine. "The purpose of this dictionary is to assist the specialist from one field to understand the technical terms used by the variety of specialists in the food fields."

Dictionary of Practical Law, edited by Charles F. Hemphill, Jr., and Phyllis D. Hemphill, Englewood Cliffs, New Jersey: Prentice-Hall, 1979. "This dictionary was prepared for the needs of law students, paralegal courses, legal secretaries, and students in the administration of justice, corrections, and rehabilitation. It was also written for the needs of working police officers, and for those who simply want a definition of legal terms in everyday language."

Duncan's Dictionary for Nurses, edited by Helen A. Duncan. New York: Springer, 1971. This dictionary "defines many terms relevant to the nursing field but not found in medical dictionaries"; it also includes those medical terms that the nurse uses.

Fairchild's Dictionary of Textiles, edited by Isabel B. Wingate. 5th ed. New York: Fairchild, 1979. It includes "terms, often of several words used or once used in the textile industry, to identify the thousands of fiber-based products employed for either the consumer or industrial purposes, along with the fibers and production processes and major equipment." It is useful to "people in all branches of the industry: manufacturing, sales, producers, designers."

Funk & Wagnalls Dictionary of Data Processing Terms, edited by Harold A. Rodgers. New York: Funk & Wagnall, 1970. This work "attempts to cover the terms used in reference to hardware, programming, software, logic, and Boolean algebra, and also the terms used in ancillary fields, such as data communications."

McGraw-Hill Dictionary of Scientific and Technical Terms, edited by Daniel N. Lapedes. New York: McGraw-Hill, 1974. It includes terms used by professionals in agriculture, ecology, data processing, food engineering, graphic arts, medicine, microbiology, navigation, oceanography, ordinance, petrology, and veterinary medicine; it supplies "also known as" terms and emphasizes definitions rather than pronounciation.

Paramedical Dictionary, edited by Jacob Edward Schmidt, M.D. Springfield, Illinois: Charles C. Thomas, 1969. This is a "practical dictionary for the semi-medical and ancillary professions" such as "physical therapists, medical laboratory technicians, masseurs, medical secretaries, occupational therapists, public health officers, social workers, dietitians, optometrists, court stenographers, speech therapists, x-ray technologists, dental assistants, and others"; it is "ideally suited" for paramedics because it meets their needs the way a highly detailed medical dictionary may not.

Private Secretary's Encyclopedia Dictionary, edited by Mary A. DeVries. 2nd ed. Englewood Cliffs, New Jersey: Prentice-Hall, 1970. This work contains information on all aspects of secretarial practice in "non-technical, readily understandable language and is arranged into large categories (office procedures and practices, written communication, business law and organization, accounting and finance, and real estate and insurance) that are further divided." Definitions of terms appear under appropriate categories.

Stedman's Medical Dictionary. Baltimore, Maryland: Williams and Wilkins, 1976. This is a highly technical work that contains terms from all medical specialties. Heavily illustrated, it provides information on pronunciations, etymologies, and word groups.

Abstracts

Abstracts for Social Workers (1965). Published quarterly by the National Association of Social Workers, this abstract contains a subject and author index. Topics are divided into six categories, of which "Fields of Service" is the largest.

Abstracts on Criminology and Penology (formerly *Excerpts Criminologica*) (1961). This is "an international abstracting service covering the etiology of crime and juvenile delinquency, and control and treatment of offenders, criminal procedure, and the administration of justice."

Air Pollution Abstracts (1970–1976). Compiled by the Air Pollution Technical Information Center of the Environmental Protection Agency, this work contains a subject and author index and surveys periodicals, books, hearings, investigations, and other legislative actions.

Applied Ecology Abstracts (1974–). Compiled monthly by Information Retrieval Limited, this abstract reviews 5,000 journals for appropriate articles. Subject categories include terrestial and aquatic resources, control, agrochemicals, grasslands, wetlands, and pollution and pollutants.

Biological Abstracts (1926–). This work surveys more than 5,000 journals in every biological field; it also lists new books.

Criminal Justice Abstracts (1968–). This work is issued quarterly by the National Council on Crime and Delinquency; it contains an author and subject index.

Metals Abstracts (1968–). Known as *Metallurgical Abstracts* (1934–1967). This abstract covers more than 1,000 journals.

Nursing Research. Beginning with the 1960 volume, each issue of this journal has carried "Abstracts of Reports of Studies in Nursing"; the Spring 1959 issue contained "Abstracts of Studies in Public Health Nursing, 1924–1957."

Oceanic Abstracts (1964–). This work surveys information on oceans (pollution, food source, oil exploration, geology) found in periodicals, books, and reports from government and private agencies. It was known as *Oceanic Journal* (1964–1967) and *Oceanic Citation Journal* (1968–1971).

Psychological Abstracts (1927–). This abstract appears in two bound volumes a year and offers "nonevaluative summaries of the world's literature in psychology and related disciplines"; it includes a subject and author index. Some of the topics are nervous disorders, motor performance, sex differences, and sleep disorders.

Sociological Abstracts (1952–). Issued five times a year, this work divides literature into 31 categories (e.g., poverty, violence, women's studies). Issues are bound every three months; it contains a subject and author index.

Solar Energy Update (1978–). Published monthly by the Technical Information Center of the Department of Energy (Oak Ridge, Tennessee), this work provides abstracting and indexing coverage of current scientific and technical reports, journal articles, conference papers and proceedings, books, patents, theses, and monographs.

Handbooks, Manuals, and Almanacs

These works provide practical advice and professional information that will be of value to you in courses and in the work you do for your employer. The following list will give you some examples of handbooks, manuals, and almanacs available in different fields.

Building Construction Handbook, edited by Frederick S. Merritt. New York: McGraw-Hill, 1975.

Chilton's Automobile Repair Manual. Philadelphia, Chilton. Issued annually.

The Complete Secretary's Handbook, 4th ed., Lillian Doris and Besse M. Miller. Englewood Cliffs, New Jersey: Prentice-Hall, 1977.

CRC Handbook of Marine Science, edited by F. G. Walton Smith. Cleveland: CRC Press, 1974. 2 vols.

Fire Protection Handbook, 14th ed., edited by Gordon P. McKinnon and Keith Tower. Boston: National Fire Protection Association, 1976.

The Good Housekeeping Woman's Almanac, edited by Barbara McDowell and Hana Umlauf. New York: Newspaper Enterprise Association, 1977.

The Nurse's Almanac, edited by Howard S. Rowland. Germantown, Maryland: Aspen Systems Corporation, 1978.

U.S. Government Manual. Washington, D.C.: Government Printing Office. Issued annually.

► Exercises

1. Find out if your library gives patrons a map or description of its holdings. If it does, bring a copy of the map or description to class. If the

library does not offer such a map or description, draw one of your own indicating the location of the circulation desk, the card catalog, the reference room, the stacks, the periodicals room or section, government documents, and audiovisuals.

2. In the subject section of the card catalog find a topic that is subdivided in the way this chapter showed you books on construction are listed. After you do this, divide these subdivisions even further until you have a restricted topic for a research report. Bring your list of subdivided topics to class.

3. Find any book in the library and write a brief description of the steps you took to locate that book—from your search in the card catalog to your actually checking the book out of the library. Refer to your map in question 1.

4. Using the materials discussed in this chapter, locate the following works in your major. If your library does not have them, select titles that are most closely related to your major and explain how they would be useful to you.
   (a) an index to periodicals
   (b) titles of three important journals or magazines
   (c) an abstract of an article appearing in one of these journals
   (d) a term in a specialized dictionary
   (e) a description or illustration in a specialized encyclopedia
   (f) a film or tape recording
   (g) two government documents
   (h) a story in the *New York Times* or one of the newspapers covered by the *Newspaper Index* which, in the last year, discussed a topic of interest to students in your major

5. Prepare a bibliography of fifteen periodical articles for the restricted topic you listed in question 2. At least five of these articles should come from periodicals not listed in the *Readers' Guide*.

6. Ask a professor in your major what he or she regards as the most widely respected periodical in your field that your library subscribes to. Find a copy of this periodical and explain with examples its method of documentation. How does it differ from the MLA method?

7. Put the following pieces of bibliographic information in proper footnote form according to the MLA method of documentation:
   (a) New York, Hawthorn Publishing Company, John Anderson, 1978, pages 95–97, second edition, *A New Way to Process Film.*
   (b) *American Journal of Nursing*, Mary Sue Barton, September 1970, pages 45–46, "How to Treat Patients Transferred from ICU."
   (c) *The FCC Procedures and Manual Book*, the Federal Communication Commission, the Government Printing Office, price $8.50, available after June 1976, page 32, Washington, D.C.

(d) *Southern Living*, Margaret Holmes Franklin, page 45, May 1975, "News and Reactions from Baltimore County."

(e) an interview with your local police chief that took place in the college auditorium after he delivered a talk on crime prevention on Wednesday, April 2, 1980.

(f) today's editorial in your local newspaper.

(g) Pyramid Films, Inc., *Pulse of Life*, 1976, Santa Monica, California, order number 342br.

(h) *Essays on Food Sanitation*, John Smith, editor, Framingham, Massachusetts, 3rd edition, pages 345–356, Mary Grossart (author), Albion Publishing Company, "Selection of Effective Chemical Agents."

(i) *Time*, "Inflation Eats Up the Pie," page 34, December 1979.

8. Put the footnotes you compiled in question 7 into the format that one of the major periodicals (listed in 4b) uses.

9. Choose a term that is frequently used in your profession—a technical, scientific, or occupational word or phrase. Then look up its meaning in a (a) specialized dictionary or encyclopedia and (b) general dictionary or encyclopedia. You might also check the *Oxford English Dictionary*. Write a brief report (one or two paragraphs) on how these definitions differ— that is, what's left out in the general dictionary and why?

10. Write a paraphrase of one of the following paragraphs:

(a) Deep-fat frying is a mainstay of any successful fast-food operation and is one of the most commonly used procedures for the preparation and production of foods in the world. During the deep-frying process, oxidation and hydrolysis take place in the shortening and eventually change its functional, sensory, and nutritional quality. Current fat tests available to food operation managers for determining when used shortening should be discarded typically require identification of a change in some physical attribute of the shortening, such as color, smoke, foam development, etc. However, by the time these changes become evident, a considerable amount of degradation has usually already taken place.[3]

(b) Ponds excavated in areas of flat terrain usually require prepared spillways. If surface runoff must enter an excavated pond through a channel or ditch, rather than through a broad shallow drainageway, the overfall from the ditch bottom to the bottom of the pond can create a serious erosion problem unless the ditch is protected. Scouring can take place in the side slope of the pond and for a considerable distance upstream in the ditch. The resulting sediment tends to reduce the depth and capacity of the pond. Protect by placing one or more lengths of rigid pipe in the ditch and extend them over the side slope of the excavation. The extended portion of the pipe or pipes may be either cantilevered or supported with timbers. The diameter of the

---

[3] Vincent J. Graziano, "Portable Instrument Rapidly Measures Quality of Frying Fat in Food Service Operations," *Food Technology*, 33 (September 1979), 50. Copyright © by Institute of Food Technologists. Reprinted by permission.

pipe or pipes depends on the peak rate of runoff that can be expected from a 10-year frequency storm. If you need more than one pipe inlet, the combined capacity should equal or exceed the estimated peak rate of runoff.[4]

(c) The transient nature of the foster child, whether he is in his natural family or after coming into care, is a problem for the nurse who tries to provide adequate health care. Large segments of the child's past may not be known to her. A medical history may be entirely absent or extremely spotty. There may be no record of early childhood shots, serious accidents, illnesses, hospitalizations, allergies, or food dislikes. The child himself is often a very poor source of information. For example, when he talks about his parents, one is unsure whether he means his natural parents, some past foster parents, or the fantasized parents he wished he had.[5]

---

[4] U.S. Department of Agriculture, Soil Conservation Service. *Ponds for Water Supply and Recreation* (Washington, D.C.: U.S. Department of Agriculture Handbook No. 387, 1971), p. 48.

[5] Robert L. Geiser and Sister M. Norberta Malinowski, "Realities of Foster Child Care," *American Journal of Nursing*, 78 (March 1978), 431. Copyright by the American Journal of Nursing Company. Reprinted by permission.

8

Summarizing Material

A summary is a brief restatement of the main points in a book, report, article, meeting, or convention. A summary saves readers hours of time, because they do not have to study the original or attend a conference. A concise summary can reduce a report or article by 85 to 95 percent or capture the essential points of a three-day convention in a one-page memo. Moreover, a summary will tell readers if they should even be concerned about the original; it may be irrelevant for their purposes. The fact that important points appear in a summary automatically shows how significant they are to the writer of that summary.

Invaluable tools, summaries can be found all around you. Television and radio stations regularly air two-minute news broadcasts—sometimes called "newsbreaks"—to summarize in a few sentences the major stories covered in more detail on the evening news. Popular news magazines such as *Time, Newsweek,* or *U.S. News & World Report* have a large readership because of their ability to condense seven days of news into short, readable articles highlighting key personalities, events, and issues.

Newspapers also employ summaries for their readers' convenience. Daily newspapers such as the *Wall Street Journal* or weekly papers such as *Barron's: A Business and Financial Weekly* or the *National Law Journal* print brief summaries on the first page of news stories that are discussed in detail later in the paper. Some newspapers simply print a column entitled "News Summary" on the first or second page of an issue to condense major news stories. *Facts on File's News Digest* comprehensively summarizes world news every two weeks. Figure 8.1 illustrates a summary that appeared in *Facts on File* of federal action on loans to farmers. Note how a few paragraphs capture and emphasize the most significant data that may have taken weeks and numerous reports or stories to record. The *Reader's Digest,* one of the most widely read publications

Fig. 8.1 A summary of federal loans to farmers.

Fed Increases Loans to Farmers. The Federal Reserve Board April 17 acted to increase loans to small businesses and farmers by allowing as much as $3 billion in additional borrowing to small banks.

The Fed said it would make that money available to small banks and banks with heavy seasonal needs, such as those in farming areas, at the discount rate of 13%.

Fed officials said that would mean loans could be offered at 15% to 17% interest, substantially below current market rates.

The interest rates would be set by the individual banks.

A Fed spokesman said that only banks with less than $100 million in deposits and those that had lent a large percentage of their deposits would be eligible for the program.

Farmers in the Midwest and South had in many cases been unable to obtain credit for crop planting because of banks' shortages of funds or had been unwilling to pay interest rates ranging higher than 23%. Small business owners were also faced with higher than expected interest rates in trying to maintain inventory or in expanding their businesses. ☐

Facts On File (April 8, 1980), p. 286. Reprinted with permission. © Facts On File, Inc./1980.

in America, is devoted largely to condensing articles, stories, and even books while still preserving the essential message, flavor, and wording of the original.

On the job, writing summaries will be one of your regular and important responsibilities. Each profession has its own special needs for summaries. Chapter 12 discusses a variety of reports—progress, sales, periodic, trip, test, and incident—whose effectiveness depends on a faithful summary of events. You may be asked to summarize a business trip lasting one week in one or two pages for your company or agency. A busy manager may ask you to read and condense a ninety-page report so that she will have a knowledgeable overview of its contents. Or your job may require you to keep supervisors informed of congressional action. To do this, you may want to consult a handy reference work such as the *Congressional Quarterly Almanac* that succinctly summarizes Congress's deliberations and decisions and supplies readers with just enough facts to understand what has happened and why. To cite another example of using summaries on the job, acute-care nurses must write a one- or two-page discharge summary for patients who are being referred to another agency (home health, nursing home, rehabilitation center). These nurses must read the patient's record carefully and summarize what has happened to the patient since admission to the hospital. They must note any surgeries, treatments, diagnoses, and prognoses and indicate necessary follow-up treatments (medication, office visits, out-patient care, radiotherapy).

▶ Contents of a Summary

The chief problem in writing a summary is deciding what to include and what to omit. A summary, after all, is a much abbreviated version of the original; it is a streamlined review of *only* the most significant points. You will not help your readers save time by simply rephrasing large sections of the original and calling the new version a summary. All you will have succeeded in doing is to supply readers with another report, not a summary. You need to make your summary lean and useful by briefly telling readers about the main points—the purpose, scope, conclusions, and recommendations. A summary should concisely answer the readers' two most important questions: (1) What findings does the report or meeting offer? and (2) How do these findings apply to my business, research, or job?

How long should a summary be? While it is hard to set down precise limits about length, effective summaries are generally between 5 and 15 percent of the length of the original. The complexity of the material being summarized and your audience's exact needs can help you to determine an appropriate length. To help you know what is most important for your summary, the following suggestions outline what to include and what to omit.

What to Include in a Summary

The following points tell you what to include in a summary:

1. *Purpose.* A summary should indicate why an article or report is being written or a convention held or a meeting convened. (Often a report is written or a meeting is called to solve a problem or to explore new areas of interest.) Your summary should give the reader some kind of brief introduction (even one sentence will do) indicating the main purpose of the report or conference.
2. *Essential specifics.* Include information on the names, costs, codes, places, or dates essential to understanding the original. To summarize a public law, for example, you need to include the law number, the date it was signed into law, and the name(s) of litigants.
3. *Conclusions or results.* Emphasize what was the final vote, the result of the tests, the proposed solution to the problem.
4. *Recommendations or implications.* Readers will be concerned especially with important recommendations—what they are, when they can be carried out, why they are necessary.

What to Omit in a Summary

The following points tell you what to omit in a summary:

1. *Opinion.* Avoid injecting opinions—your own, the author's, or speaker's. You do not help readers grasp main points by saying that the report was too long or that it missed the main point, or that a salesperson from Detroit monopolized the meetings, or that the author in a digression took the Land Commission to task for failing to act properly. A later section of this chapter will deal with evaluative summaries (pp. 238–240).
2. *New data.* Stick to the original article, report, book, or meeting. Avoid introducing comparisons with other works or conferences, because readers will expect a digest of only the material being summarized.
3. *Irrelevant specifics.* Do not include any biographical details about the author of an article. Although many journals contain a section entitled "notes on contributors," this information plays no role in the reader's understanding of your summary.
4. *Examples.* Examples, illustrations, explanations, and descriptions are unnecessary in a summary. Readers must know outcomes, results, recommendations—not the events leading up to those results.
5. *Background.* Material in introductions to articles, reports, and conferences can often be excluded from a summary. These "lead-ins" prepare a reader of the report for a discussion of the subject by presenting background information, anecdotes, and facts that will be of little interest to readers who want a summary to give them the bare essentials.
6. *Reference data.* Exclude information in footnotes, bibliographies, appendixes, tables, or graphs. Again, all such information supports rather than expresses conclusions and recommendations.
7. *Jargon.* Technical definitions or jargon in the original may confuse rather than clarify the essential information the general reader is seeking.

▶ Preparing a Summary

To write an effective summary, you will have to read the material very carefully, making sure that you understand it thoroughly. Then you will have to identify the major points and exclude everything else. Finally, you will have to put the essence of the material into your own words. This process demands an organized plan. Use the following steps in preparing your summary:

1. Read the material once in its entirety to get an overall impression of what it is about.   Become familiar with large issues, such as the purpose and organization of the work, and the audience for whom it was written. Look for obvious signals or techniques—headings, subheadings, words in italics or boldface type, notes in the margin—that will later help you to classify main ideas and summarize the work. Also see if the author has included any minisummaries within the article or report or if there is a concluding summary after an article or a chapter of a book.

2. Reread the material. Read it twice or more often if necessary. To locate all and only the main points, underline them in the work; or, if the work is a book or an article in a journal that belongs to the library, take notes on a separate sheet of paper. (You may find it easier to photocopy articles so that you can underline.) To spot the main points, pay attention to the key words introducing them. Such words often fall into the following categories:

(a) *Words that enumerate:* first, second, third; initially, subsequently, finally; next; another; "The procedure was used in three circumstances."

(b) *Words that express causation:* accordingly, as a result, because, consequently, subsequently, therefore, thus

(c) *Words that express contrasts and comparisons:* although, by the same token, despite, different from, faster, furthermore, however, in contrast, in comparison, in addition, less than, likewise, more than, more readily, not only . . . but also, on the other hand, the same is true for . . . , similar, unlike

(d) *Words that signal essentials:* basically, best, central, crucial, foremost, fundamental, indispensable in general, important, leading, major, obviously, principal, significant

Also pay special attention to the first and last sentences of each paragraph. Often the first sentence of a paragraph contains the topic sentence, and the last sentence summarizes the paragraph or provides some type of transition to the next paragraph. And be alert for words signaling information you do not want to include in your summary, such as the following:

(a) *Words announcing opinion or inconclusive findings:* from my personal experience, I feel, I admit, in my opinion, might possibly show, perhaps, personally, may sometimes result in, has little idea about, questionable, presumably, subject to change, open to interpretation

(b) *Words pointing out examples or explanations:* as noted in, as shown by, circumstances include, explained by, for example, for instance, illustrated by, in terms of, learned through, represented by, such as, specifically in, stated in

3. Collect your underlined material or notes and organize the information into a rough-draft summary. Do not be concerned about how your sentences read at this stage. Use the language of the original, together with any necessary connective words or phrases of your own. You will probably have more material here than will appear in the final version. Do not worry; you are engaged in a process of elimination. Your purpose at this stage is to extract the principal ideas from the examples, explanations, and opinions surrounding them.

4. Read through your rough draft and delete whatever information you can. See how many of your underlined points can be condensed, combined, or eliminated. You may find that you have repeated a point. Check your draft against the original for accuracy and importance. Make sure that you are faithful to the original by preserving its emphases and sequence.

5. Now put the edited version into your own words. Again, make sure that your reworded summary has eliminated nonessential words. Connect your sentences with conjunctive adverbs (*also, although, because, consequently, however, nevertheless, since*) to show relationships between ideas in the original. Compare this final version of your summary with the original material to double-check your facts.

6. Do not include remarks that indicate that you are writing a summary. Such remarks might be: "This is a summary of a report given in Dallas last month"; "The author of this article states that water pollution is a major problem in Baytown"; "On page 13 of the article three examples, not discussed here, are found."

7. Identify the source you have just summarized. Do this by including pertinent bibliographic information in the title of your summary or in a footnote.

Figure 8.2, a 1,500-word article entitled "Counting on the Census," appeared in the *Journal of American Insurance* and hence would be of primary interest to insurers. Assume that you are asked to write a summary of this article for your boss, a busy insurance executive. By following the steps outlined previously, you would first read the article carefully two or three times and then underscore the most important points, signaled by key words. Note what has been underscored in the article. Also study the comments in the margins; these explain why certain information is to be included or excluded from the summary.

Fig. 8.2   An original article with important points underscored for use in a summary.

Counting on the Census

Delete introductory material, here used to provide a background

Probably no other people but Americans have such an obsession with constantly counting and cataloguing themselves. With help from computers, we've now got more information about ourselves than ever

Journal of American Insurance (Winter 1979/80), pp. 13–15. Reprinted by permission.

Delete details of lesser importance

Important conclusion

Include significant point

Delete explanations and examples

Important finding

Delete explanation and following quotation

before: an awe-inspiring amount of information, highly sophisticated and often very specific in nature.

With so much data-mania around, it's no wonder that the most well-known survey, that just-completed, once-a-decade population count conducted by the Census Bureau, is generating more interest than ever. Aside from the controversies—questions about its accuracy and debate over the problem of illegal aliens—Americans are paying attention to the 1980 Census because not only will it confirm our own notions of what we, as a nation have become, but also because there's a lot of cold hard cash riding on the results

This massive survey will document, on both a large and local scale, the far-reaching social changes of the 1970's. It will chronicle what has happened to each of us over the past ten years: if, like other Americans, we've moved often, and ever south and westward; if we've had smaller families, and bought larger homes. The population count will lend a certain sense of continuity, or historical perspective to these changes, measuring them against nearly 200 years of American demographic history. The fact that the twentieth census will find a majority of one and two person households (they numbered nearly half in 1970 and have been on the rise ever since) is all the more remarkable in light of the 1790 count, in which half of all those fledgling American households consisted of six or more people, and only a tenth had one or two persons living alone.

Results from the headcount will add depth and specificity to what we already know, filling in the outlines of our broadbrush figures.

Include "important" information

Delete statistics

Significant conclusion

Key words signaling important application

Delete facts indicating former use

Include financial use

Key phrase pointing to important application

Combine types of programs

Delete examples

"Surveys may tell you what's happened," says Roger Herriot of the Census Bureau, "the census tells you to whom and where."

The <u>final tally</u> will <u>reveal</u> both small group and small area data—<u>important, useful information</u> that is <u>available nowhere else</u>. A <u>housewife's</u> decision to <u>return to work</u> is <u>significant</u> as part of a <u>national trend</u> (since 1978, half of all American women age 16 and older—42 million of them—were in the labor force); yet it's even <u>more meaningful</u> when also placed <u>in</u> the <u>context</u> of how many other women of the same age, living in the same state, town, or even neighborhood, are also working.

<u>On the more pragmatic side</u>, the census appeals to our more avid interests, as we are urged to stand up and be counted to get our fair share—of political representation, and federal money. The constitutionally-mandated count is no longer just a means of changing the boundaries of congressional districts to reflect population shifts; since 1970, it <u>also</u> has been used to <u>determine</u> where and how more than <u>$50 billion in public welfare and federal revenue-sharing money will be spent. Of special interest</u> to insurers are <u>federal programs</u> on <u>vocational rehabilitation, highway safety, law enforcement assistance, energy research and development, and alcohol and drug abuse,</u> which are among the more than 100 programs using census statistics to guide the allocation of funds to states and local communities. Funding for the Cooperative Extension Service, for example, hinges upon a state's rural and farm population; while spending for the Headstart program relies on the number of children of poverty-level families in a particular community.

Key words "also much" introducing important idea

There is <u>also much</u> that the insurance industry, the <u>property/casualty side of the business</u> included, can <u>cull</u> from the reams of data generated by <u>the census.</u> The count will be industry's first opportunity for a look at the demographic trends of the next decade, trends which will play a <u>major role in shaping business</u> in the years just ahead.

Include reason why census is so important to insurers

This glimpse into the future will allow insurers, known for their sophisticated application of data, to <u>evaluate</u>—and <u>anticipate</u>—these <u>changes</u> on a local level, where business is actually conducted.

Include relevant change affecting insurers; delete statistics

<u>One change</u> in store for this country is that, in the 1980's, the <u>elderly as a group</u> will be <u>getting larger.</u> Between 1950 and 1978, that part of our population age 65 and older doubled in size, and it is expected to increase even further in the coming years. <u>This means</u> a growing need for <u>more resources</u> to meet the <u>financial and medical requirements of the elderly</u>—<u>two areas where the insurance industry will play a vital role</u>.

Include these "two areas" significantly highlighted by key words "vital role"

Another important point, but delete the statistics

<u>Also</u> getting its first few gray hairs will be the "baby boom" generation, whose members now fall into <u>the 25 to 34 age group.</u> The <u>fastest-growing segment of the population,</u> its ranks swelled by 35 percent between 1970 and 1978, according to census figures. Members of this group, who have dominated the social changes of the past 20 years, will again set the pace in the next decade. They'll enter their prime years in terms of earning and buying power, pumping up <u>demand</u> for both durable goods and housing, as well as <u>property insurance</u> to cover their investments.

Emphasize insurance needs

Include main point here

<u>Indeed, property/casualty insurers</u> will be able to <u>glean</u> some <u>valuable information from the ques-</u>

"Although" points to subordinate idea; delete it and examples

Major observation

Delete examples of types of questions

Restatement of main point

Delete explanation

Delete example

tions asked on this year's census. Although only two relate directly to property insurance (one asks homeowners the annual premium for fire and hazard insurance on their property; another inquires whether the regular monthly mortgage payment includes these payments or not), <u>more than half of all the questions are concerned with housing.</u> Some are general, requesting information on owning or renting, the number of rooms in living quarters, and the type of building; while others are quite specific; asking how you heat your home, which fuel you use for cooking, house and water heating, and how much you pay each month for electricity, water, gas, oil or coal (interestingly, census tests have shown that people tend to overestimate their utility costs).

Compiling housing data has been a census assignment since 1850, yet the <u>emphasis</u> placed <u>on the topic on this year's questionnaire is unprecedented</u>. This is due, in part, to the growing number of requests the Census Bureau has received about housing in general, and shelter costs in particular, according to Census housing expert Bill Downs, who says that federal agencies, as well as state and local governments are among the big users of this type of information.

A 1976 bureau survey found, for example, that the average owner of a mortgaged home was paying 18 percent of his annual income in that year for the mortgage, real estate taxes, property insurance, utilities, fuel, and trash collection. <u>How much that figure will change in 1980</u>, in light of soaring fuel costs, and other factors such as the 45 percent jump in the average price of a new, one-family home, <u>should</u>

Include main point relevant to insurers	be of wide interest to property insurers, among others.
Of less significance, but still include	Also of interest but of somewhat more limited use, will be both the number and size of America's homes. Analysts predict that the 1980 count will find that the number of housing units in this country
Delete statistics	has increased 20 percent since the last census was taken in 1970: twice the rate of the population growth. Along with an increase in the number of households (at a rate three times as fast as that of the rise in population between the years 1970 and 1978 alone), these
Include main points	figures reflect a continuing decline in the average size of households.
Delete statistics following this point	At the same time people are choosing to live with fewer other people, they are also living in larger houses. Between 1970 and 1976, the number of five-room housing units (homes, mobile homes and trailers, apartments, and condominiums) rose from 16.9 to 19.2 million; while homes with seven or more rooms grew in number from 11.9 to 15.9 million.
	Unless a change is imminent, this trend, which reflects to a degree the self-indulgent and free-spending life-style cultivated by many during the 1970's, has dire implications for our energy needs in the future. Fewer people in bigger living areas means energy inefficiency, wasting the energy and
Delete opinion and qualification	resources needed to construct and heat these homes—a loss that increased conservation can only partly remedy.
Parallel point	Equally ominous in view of the energy crunch, and of interest to
Key phrase for audience	automobile insurers, is the fact that
Include essential point	the 1980 census should show no let-up in America's dependence on the car as a means of transportation. In 1975, of the 73 million

Delete statistics

households in the U.S., nearly 63 million had at least one automobile, according to census bureau figures. Further, owning a home seems to go hand-in-hand with owning a car: nearly all homeowners have at least one car, while renters are considerably less likely to purchase a vehicle. Moreover, the number of two-car households more than doubled between 1960 and 1975, and is expected to have jumped even higher in the years since.

Key word indicating another conclusion

Delete clarifying statistics

Key word emphasizing results

The final report, however, may shed light on one transportation alternative. Questions on the number of one-ton trucks and vans, and on whether people who use cars, trucks, or vans to get to work ride with other people (and if so, how many) will give transportation planners as well as auto insurers some insight into the extent of car and van pooling. This information is the first step in learning how to encourage more people to try this energy-efficient way for commuting.

Key reference to audience's use of information

Not essential point

Of course, insurance companies use many sources of information other than the once-a-decade census to keep themselves abreast of important demographic changes. Yet insurers, like many other businesses, still count on the census and the more than 300,000 pages of resulting statistics to tell them where we've been, and where we as a nation are going.

Brief restatement of article thesis

Delete information in tables—used only for support

	1970	1980	% Change
Population of the U.S.	207,976,452	222,000,000 (est.)	9%
No. of Housing Units in the U.S.	69,000,000	86,000,000 (est.)	23%
No. of Households in the U.S.	64,000,000	79,000,000 (est.)	26%

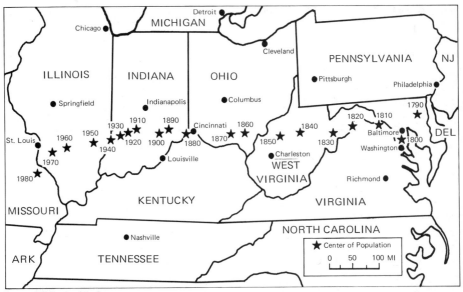

Source: U.S. Bureau of the Census

Westward Ho!

If the United States were a gigantic table, and everybody stood up right now where they lived, where would the table balance? This may seem like a question of demographic trivia, but in 1980 it will take on historical importance as the nation's center of population moves, for the first time, west of the Mississippi River.

Delete data explaining map—not essential to article

After the first census in 1790, the center of population was just east of Baltimore. It has moved slowly westward ever since, reflecting the general migration of the population. After the 1970 census, it was just south of Mascoutah, Illinois, about 30 miles east of the Mississippi. After the 1980 headcount, the center of population will move across the river and slightly to the south, reflecting the recent population shift to sunbelt states.

After you have identified the main points, extract them from the article and, still using the language of the article, join them into a coherent rough-draft summary as in Fig. 8.3. The necessary connective words added to the language of the original article are underscored. This rough draft then has to be shortened and rewritten in your own words to produce the compact final version of your summary as in Fig. 8.4. Only 153 words long, this summary is 12 percent of the length of the original article and records only major conclusions relevant to the audience for the article.

To further understand the effectiveness of the summary in Fig. 8.4, review the wordy and misleading summary of the same article in Fig. 8.5. The

Fig. 8.3   A rough-draft summary of Fig. 8.2.

Aside from the controversies about its accuracy, Americans are
paying attention to the 1980 Census because there's a lot of cold,
hard cash riding on the results. This massive survey will document
far reaching social changes. The twentieth census will find a
majority of one- and two-person households, all the more remarkable
in light of the 1790 count. The final tally will reveal important
useful information available nowhere else. A housewife's decision to
return to work is significant as part of a national trend, <u>and</u> even
more meaningful in context. On the more pragmatic side, the census
count is no longer just a means of changing boundaries <u>but</u> it also
affects where $50 billion in public welfare and federal revenue-
sharing will be spent. Of special interest to insurers are federal
programs on vocational rehabilitation, highway safety, law
enforcement assistance, and energy research. There is also much the
property/casualty side of the business can gain from the census,
<u>which will</u> play a major role in business—evaluating and anticipating
changes. One change is that the elderly population will be
increasing. This means more resources—financial and medical—in two
areas where the insurance industry will play a vital role. Also, the
25 to 34 age group, which is the fastest growing part of the
population, will demand property insurance. Indeed, property/
casualty insurers will glean valuable information from the questions
asked on the census, more than half of all the questions are
concerned with housing. <u>This</u> is an emphasis on the topic of this
year's questionnaire <u>that</u> is unprecedented. How much <u>costs for
houses</u> will change should be of wide interest to property insurers
among others. Also of interest but of somewhat more limited use, the
number and size of American houses <u>have</u> increased. Along with an
increase in the number of households, <u>there is</u> a continuing decline
in the average size of households. At the same time people are
choosing to live with fewer other people, they are also living in
larger houses. This trend has dire implications for our energy needs
in the future. Fewer people in bigger living areas mean energy
inefficiency. Equally ominous and of interest to automobile insurers
the 1980 census should show no letup in America's dependence on the
car as a means of transportation. Further, owning a home seems to go
hand in hand with owning a car; renters are less likely to purchase a
vehicle. The final report, however, may shed light on one
transportation alternative. Questions on the number of trucks and
vans and on whether people who use cars, trucks, or vans to go to work
will ride with other people will give transportation planners as well
as auto insurers some insights into the extent of car and van
pooling. This information will be the first step in learning how to
encourage this energy-efficient way for commuting. Insurance
companies use many sources of information, yet insurers still count
on the census.

Fig. 8.4   A final summary of Fig. 8.2.

A lot of money rides on the results of the 1980 Census. Information on
where we live, our household size, and women in the work force
affects the funding of federal programs. Because many of these
programs concern public safety, health, and energy, they are of
crucial importance to insurers. Census figures will also help
insurers evaluate the needs of future policy holders. A larger
elderly population will require more medical and financial
assistance; the fast-growing adult population (ages 25-34) will need
more property insurance. Since a majority of census questions deal
with housing, property/casualty insurers will learn more about
increasingly expensive home ownership. The census will also tell
insurers that Americans will waste energy by occupying larger homes
with fewer people per household. Moreover, homeowners (as opposed to
renters) will buy more cars for transportation. However, information
on vehicle pooling may give auto insurers encouraging news about
energy conservation.

Fig. 8.5   A poor summary of Fig. 8.2.

Nonessential introductory material	Americans like to keep track of themselves with very advanced computers. People wonder, though, about the
Possible flaw in census not important to article's thesis	accuracy of the census as a counting tool since it sometimes includes information about illegal aliens. But the census, a part of America's demographic history since 1790, does
Delete historical background and official's name	serve many important functions, says Roger Herriot of the Census Bureau in Washington, D.C. The census tells us that half of all American women over the
Minor point in article given major attention; new information and opinion also added	age of 16 work full time. Also, the census establishes our congressional districts, and this is very important for our representatives, especially if they find themselves in a new district because of changes in the population. The census also helps allocate federal
Examples not necessary; do not call attention to summary	funds for such programs as the Cooperative Extension Service and Headstart, which are important programs to list in this summary. Furthermore, the census
Omit opinion	helps predict future insurance

	business, always a laudable goal. Old
Ambiguous statement; misses main point that elderly group is increasing	people and the young, too, will increase our population. But as far as property insurance is concerned, only two
	questions appear on this topic on the
Distorts article, which deals with value of census for insurers	census which is almost exclusively concerned with what home fuels, mort-
	gages, and building materials we have.
	Bill Downs says the government needs
Statistics not related to insurers	this kind of information. It is no wonder since 1976 people paid 18 percent of their income for housing and will
How is all this relevant to insurers?	pay 45 percent in 1980. Extravagant Americans want big houses, big cars, and will waste energy using them. Americans
Distorts article, which emphasizes usefulness of census for insurers; this statement makes census sound unimportant for insurers and overemphasizes a minor point in conclusion of article	should use car pools. But the insurance companies, as the last crucial para- graph of the article states, will not be at too bad a disadvantage since they can rely on other sources of information than what is provided in the census.

latter not only is too long, but also dwells on minor details at the expense of major points. It includes unnecessary examples, statistics, and names; it even adds new information while ignoring crucial points about the function of the census to insurers. But even more serious, this summary distorts the meaning and thwarts the intention of the original article. The reader concludes that the article says the census is not very valuable for insurers—just the opposite of the point the article makes. The way to avoid such mistakes is by not overemphasizing minor points, by making sure that all parts of your summary agree with the original, and by not letting your own opinions cloud issues that the author of the article stresses.

▶ Evaluative Summaries

To write an evaluative summary, follow all the guidelines previously discussed in this chapter except one. The one major exception is that an evaluative summary includes your *opinion* of the material.

Your instructors and employers will often ask you to summarize and assess what you have read. In school you may have to write a book report or compile a critical, annotated bibliography commenting on the usefulness of the material you found in those sources. On the job your employer may ask you to condense a report and in your summary judge the merits of that report, paying special attention to whether the report's recommendations should be followed, modified, or ignored. Your company or agency may also ask you to write short evaluative summaries of certain proposals or applications it has received or perhaps of conferences you might have attended.

An evaluative summary is usually short—not more than 5 to 10 percent of the length of the original. Your evaluations should blend in with your summary of the material. Rather than save all your assessments until the end of your summary, place them directly next to the summary of the points to which they apply so that your reader sees them in context. Keep in mind that your evaluations will be considered recommendations. You may also want to include an especially helpful quotation from the original to emphasize the kind of recommendation you are making. In evaluating the material, include information on both the content and style of the original. Here are some questions on content and style that you should answer for readers of your evaluative summary.

Evaluating the Content

1. *How carefully is the subject researched?* Is the material accurate and up to date, or are important details missing? Where could the reader find the missing information? If the material is inaccurate, will the whole work be affected or just a part of it? Exactly what has the author left out?
2. *Is the writer or speaker objective?* Are conclusions supported by evidence? Is the writer or speaker following a particular theory, program, or school of thought? Is this fact made clear in the source? Has the author or speaker emphasized one point at the expense of others?
3. *Does the work achieve the goal?* Is the topic too large to be adequately discussed in a single talk, article, or book? Do the recommendations make sense? Is the work sketchy? Are there digressions, tangents, or irrelevant materials?
4. *Is the material relevant to the audience for whom you are writing your evaluative summary?* How would that audience use it? Is the entire work relevant or just part of it? Why? Would every member of your profession profit from reading the work or only certain specialists? Would this work be useful for all members of your agency or only those working in certain areas? Why? What specific answers in the work would help to solve a problem you or others have encountered on the job?

Evaluating the Style

1. *Is the material readable?* Is it well written and easy to follow? Are there helpful headings, careful summaries, and appropriate examples?
2. *What kind of vocabulary does the writer or speaker use?* Are there many technical terms? Is the language precise or vague? Would your audience have to skip certain sections that are too complicated?
3. *What visuals are included?* Charts? Graphs? Photographs? Are they used effectively? Are there too many or too few of these visuals?

Fig. 8.6 An evaluative summary of an article.

R. Alec Mackenzie and Billie Sorensen, "It's About Time . . ." The
Secretary, 40 (January 1980), 12–13.

This practical article acquaints secretaries with ways to decrease
interruptions that rob them and their bosses of time. Instead of
practicing an open–door policy, managers could save time by
observing a "quite hour" to curtail drop–in visitors and calls
Secretaries could help their bosses during this time by controlling
drop–in visitors and handling minor details. Many valuable
suggestions are given on how secretaries can further save their
bosses' time by arranging and limiting meetings. Because
secretaries' desks are located in busy areas, partitions could
control some of their interruptions. But the authors wisely point out
that managers forced to use the same arrangement lose privacy and
flexibility. Partitions are unsuitable for conferences, encourage
socializing, and are uneconomical. This readable and profitable
article suggests techniques that will help all office personnel to
save one of the manager's most valuable assets—his or her time.

Figures 8.6, 8.7, and 8.8 contain evaluative summaries. Note how the
writer's assessments are woven into the condensed version of the original.
Figure 8.6 contains a student's opinions of an article summarized for a class
in office management procedures. Figure 8.7 shows an evaluative summary
in memo format written by an employee who has just returned from an out-
of-town seminar. Another kind of evaluative summary—a book review—is
shown in Fig. 8.8. Many journals print book reviews to inform their professional audiences about the most recent studies in their field. Reviews condense and assess books, reports, government studies, tape cassettes, films, and
other materials. The short review in Fig. 8.8 comments briefly on style, provides clarifying information, and explains how the book is developed.

▶ Minutes

Minutes of a meeting are a special type of summary you may be asked to
write. If you are appointed secretary at an office meeting or for a committee
or organization to which you belong, you will be required to submit to members of that group an official record of the actions taken. That record, known
as the minutes of a meeting, is distributed usually within twenty-four or forty-
eight hours after the meeting has adjourned. Copies of the minutes will be
on file as a matter of record and may be used as evidence in a court of law
about actions taken by a group or problems raised in front of that group.
Minutes also help individuals recall what happened at a previous meeting and
assist them to prepare for a forthcoming one.

Fig. 8.7   An evaluative summary of a seminar.

SABINE COUNTY HOSPITAL
Sabine, TX 77231

TO: Marge Geberheart, R.N.   SUBJECT: Evaluation of Physical
       Director of Nurses   Assessment Seminar
FROM: Paul Danders, R.N.   DATE: September 10, 1981

This practical and worthwhile seminar was conducted by Doris Gandy,
R.N., and Rick Vargas, R.N., both on the staff of Houston Presbyterian
Hospital. The one-day seminar was divided into three units: (1)
Techniques of Health Assessment, (2) Assessment of the Chest Cavity, and
(3) Assessment of the Abdomen.

Techniques of Health Assessment:

Four procedures used in physical assessment—inspection,
percussion, palpation, auscultation—were carefully defined and
demonstrated. Also stressed was the proper use of the stethoscope and
ways of conducting a patient history. We were asked to take a history
from the person next to us. Return demonstrations were used throughout
the seminar and meant we did not have to wait until we returned to work to
practice our skills.

Assessment of the Chest Cavity:

After an external inspection of the chest, we turned to a discussion
of the proper placement of the hands for palpation and the significance
of various breath sounds. Using stethoscopes, our instructors helped us
identify areas of the lung. We also listened to heart sounds and
identified valve movements. The film we saw on examining the heart and
lungs was ineffective, since it included too much information for us to
grasp all at once.

Assessment of the Abdomen:

The instructors warned that the order of examination of the abdomen
differs from that for the chest cavity. Auscultation, not percussion,
follows inspection so that bowel sounds are not activated, thus calling
into question the results of a physical assessment. The instructors then
clearly discussed the location of the organs in the abdominal quadrants,
how to palpate these organs, and how to detect bowel sounds.

Conclusion:

I would strongly recommend this kind of seminar for nurses whose
expanding role in the health care system will include more detailed
physical assessments. Although the seminar covered a wealth of
information, the instructors admitted that they only discussed the
basics. In the future, however, it would be better to offer a separate
seminar on the chest cavity and another on the abdomen instead of
combining these two areas.

Fig. 8.8 A book review.

Forty Years of Murder: An Autobiography. *By Keith Simpson. Charles Scribner's Sons, 597 Fifth Ave., New York, NY 10017. 1979. 319pp. Cloth/$12.95.*

This is a fascinating, readable narrative of cases handled by one of the world's leading pathologists during his forty years as a medico-legal examiner for the British Home Office. In language largely devoid of technical terminology, the author presents a series of murder cases investigated throughout his career and relates how, working backward by piecing together scant bits of evidence, he reaches a logical conclusion on how a victim met a grim death and identifies the perpetrator. The clues he works with for the most part are bits of flesh, tissue, and bone; soiled or tattered pieces of clothing; or, as in one case, gallstones which were not destroyed by sulphuric acid in which the victim's body was immersed. The cases range from young women whose battered bodies were found in desolate places to a prince of Siam who was assassinated in bed. The author includes some interesting bouts in court with defense attorneys who attempted to discredit his forensic testimony and how he successfully refuted such challenges.

Reproduced from *The Police Chief* magazine, March 1980, with permission of the International Association of Chiefs of Police.

The way in which a meeting is conducted may be governed by highly formal parliamentary procedures known as *Robert's Rules of Order.* Usually, though, business and community meetings are less formal. Still, certain matters of protocol generally are observed at meetings. For example, a chairperson (or convener) usually brings a list of topics to be discussed; this list is known as the *agenda.* Participants then make *motions* (proposals) about these and other topics and then approve, modify, or vote against them. "I move that we accept the Acme Corporation's bid on the two new heating units"; "I would like to change the wording of the original motion to read 'All employees on the night shift will receive a $0.75 per hour differential.' " Each motion is then *seconded* (endorsed) by another member of the group. A member who cannot attend may send a *proxy* (substitute) to vote. A motion may be *carried* (passed), defeated, withdrawn, or *tabled* (postponed).

To be effective, minutes should be short. Obviously, you cannot repeat what everyone has said. Readers will be more interested in what participants did than in what they said or how they felt about it. Emphasize the decisions made or the conclusions reached. For example, do not mention any motions (or discussions of them) that have been withdrawn. Nor should you spend a great deal of time on discussions of other motions. Save your readers' time by condensing, in your own words, lengthy discussions and debates (pro and con) as well as reports presented at meetings. Concentrate on the major facts surrounding motions that are voted on. List each motion exactly as it is worded in its *final* form and spell accurately and consistently the names of those proposing and seconding the motion (not T. Richey in one place and Terry Richey or Office Manager Richey in others). Finally, record precisely the vote for each motion (carried 11 to 2).

Do not inject your opinions into the minutes. Watch for any words that interpret (positively or negatively) rather than impartially record. "The motion was offered just in time"; "Each motion was relevant to the topic"; and "The motion was poorly stated" violate the rules of impartiality. When you cite individuals by name, do not qualify their actions, saying that "Mr. Sanders pushed the point for the third time" or that "Mrs. Hicks customarily offered the right solutions." And resist any urge to summarize the usefulness of a discussion or the meeting itself: "The proceedings cleared up a lot of doubts the subcommittee had expressed"; "The meeting was productively short and simple"; or "Little was accomplished today."

The essential points to include in your minutes are as follows:

1. The name of the company, agency, group, committee, or organization holding the meeting.
2. The subject of the meeting—regular monthly meeting, special sales meeting, rules committee meeting.
3. The date, time, and place of the meeting.
4. The names of those present and those absent (if your list does not exceed twenty or twenty-five individuals).
5. The time the meeting actually begins once a *quorum* (sufficient number of members present) arrives.
6. The approval or amendment of the minutes of the previous meeting, or that their reading is waived by a majority of those present.
7. Any old business—further discussion and votes on motions tabled at previous meetings.
8. Any reports (merely submitted or read) from standing committees (permanent) or *ad hoc* committees (created for a special purpose).
9. The new business of the meeting—motions proposed, seconded, and voted on. Indicate briefly the discussion preceding the motion and then the names of those making and seconding the motion. Indicate how the vote is taken—by secret ballot, a show of hands, by voice—and its results, including the number of abstentions (decisions not to vote on a motion), if any.
10. The business to be continued at the next meeting—reports to be made, motions to be voted on. If studies or other tasks are to be performed in the meantime, specify who is to do them, how, and why.
11. The time the next meeting is to be held—date and hour—and where it is to be held.
12. The time the meeting is officially concluded.
13. Your signature as the recording secretary verifying the accuracy of the minutes.
14. The signature of the chairperson, president, or convener.

Figure 8.9 shows the minutes of a meeting incorporating each of these fourteen parts. Not every meeting, of course, will require all of them. Observe the use of subheadings and the numbering of business issues for the readers' convenience.

Fig. 8.9   Minutes of a meeting.

THE CITY OF HAMPTON
Minutes of the Hampton City Council Open Meeting
February 2, 1982

PRESENT: Thomas Baldanza, Grace Corlee (President), Virginia Downey,
Victor Johnson, Roberta Koos, Kent Leviche (Secretary), Ralph
Nowicki, Barbara Poe, Willard Ralston, Daniel Sullivan,
Morgan Tachiashi, Janeen Vanessa, Wanda Wagner, and Carlos
Zandrillia

ABSENT: Millard Holmes, Wendy O'Gorman

The meeting was held in Room 102 of City Hall and began at 7:04 P.M. with
Grace Corlee presiding. The minutes of the previous meeting (January 4,
1982) were approved as read.

OLD BUSINESS:

The Council returned to a discussion of a motion tabled at the last
meeting concerning holding open meetings twice a month rather than once
a month. The motion, which was made by Barbara Poe and seconded by
Willard Ralston, was voted on and defeated 9 to 5.

REPORTS:

Two reports were given.

Victor Johnson noted that the Downtown Beautification Committee had
been in touch with both the State Office of Historical Landmarks and the
U.S. Department of Housing and Urban Development about their help
(financial and architectural planning) to Hampton in restoring the
Brandon Building. Johnson said he expected to hear from both departments
before next month's meeting.

Giving a report on the Zoning Committee, Wanda Wagner observed that
fourteen requests for changes had been submitted in January. The Zoning
Board has already approved ten of them including rezoning South Evans
Street from residential to medical.

NEW BUSINESS:

1. The problems with the downtown parking meters were discussed.
   Besides difficulties with maintaining them, local merchants have
   complained that the meters are bad for business. Roberta Koos claimed
   that removing them would decrease city revenue and increase parking
   violations. But Morgan Tachiashi saw greater losses to the city from

Fig. 8.9 (continued)

Minutes   2   February 2, 1982

decreased business in the downtown section because of the meters. He therefore moved, and Virginia Downey seconded, that the parking meters should be removed from the downtown section of the city. The motion carried 10 to 4 by secret ballot. Grace Corlee said she would forward an official order to Police Chief Dunn for the removal of the meters effective March 15, 1982.

2. Mrs. Cal Ricks, President of the Park Ridge Citizens Group, appeared before the Council requesting that automatic traffic lights be installed at the intersection of Brown and Crawford Avenues. After listening to her comments about the dangers to pupils at the Epstein School from speeding cars and the increased flow of traffic from the Granger Furniture Plant, the Council voted unanimously to install automatic signals at the intersection of Brown and Crawford Avenues.

3. Congratulations were extended to Carlos Zandrillia for being honored as an Outstanding Citizen by the Hampton Chamber of Commerce.

4. A committee to study ways to increase tourism to Hampton was formed. The committee members appointed were Janeen Vanessa (chairperson), Ralph Nowicki, and Victor Johnson. President Corlee speaking for the Council requested that the committee especially study the use of Lake Hughes in tourism advertisements and asked for a preliminary report in two months.

5. Thomas Baldanza moved, and Virginia Downey seconded, a motion to set aside $2500.00 from the Recreation Department budget for the improvement of equipment at Alice V. Davis Park. The motion carried by a vote of 12 to 1, with 1 abstention.

There being no further business, the meeting was adjourned at 9:37. The next open meeting of the Hampton City Council was set for March 6 at 7:00 P.M. in Room 102 of City Hall.

don't necessarily need respectfully

Respectfully submitted,

Kent Leviche

Kent Leviche, Secretary

Minutes Approved

Grace Corlee

Grace Corlee, President

▶ Abstracts

The Differences Between a Summary and an Abstract

The terms "summary" and "abstract" are often used interchangeably, resulting in some confusion. This is because there are two distinct types of abstracts—*descriptive abstracts* and *informative abstracts*. The informative abstract is another name for a summary; the descriptive abstract is not. Why? An informative abstract (or summary) gives readers conclusions and indicates the outcomes, results, or causes. Look at the summary in Fig. 8.4. It explains why the census is important for insurers—the census helps insurers provide better coverage to specific groups.

A descriptive abstract is short, usually only two or three sentences; it does not go into detail or give conclusions. Hence it is not a summary. A descriptive abstract provides table-of-contents information—what topics a work discusses, but not how or why they are discussed. Here is a descriptive abstract of the article summarized in Fig. 8.4 (p. 237):

> The census will provide information about changes in America's housing preferences, transportation, and energy needs. This data will be valuable to insurers.

Figure 8.10 contains a group of descriptive abstracts about books of interest to professionals in public welfare. In a few words each abstract tells

Fig. 8.10   Descriptive abstracts of books.

Adult Illiteracy in the United States: A Report to the Ford Foundation
By Carman St. John Hunter and David Harman. New York: McGraw Hill, 1979. 206 pp. $10.95.
   Defines the scope of illiteracy in the U.S.—a problem of major proportions that prevents many disadvantaged poor from being able to deal positively with the demands made by society—and calls for a long-range national strategy to eradicate the problem.

The Adoption of Black Children: Counteracting Institutional Discrimination
By Dawn Day. Lexington, Mass.: D.C. Heath, 1979. 156 pp. $15.95.
   Looks at how the adoption system works and suggests realistic ways of raising the adoption rate of black children.

Community Mental Health in the Social Work Curriculum
By Allen Rubin. New York: Council on Social Work Education, 1979. 84 pp. $4.
   Describes the place of community mental health in our nationwide service delivery system, evaluates suitability of the MSW level curriculum in the U.S., and offers examples of curriculum innovations.

Public Welfare, 32 (Spring 1980). 49. Reprinted with permission of the American Public Welfare Association.

what kinds of information the books contain, but does not reveal the solutions, plans, views, or recommendations that the authors of these books advance.

Where Abstracts are Found

Abstracts can be found in one of the following three places:

1. At the beginning of an article, report, or conference proceedings; on a separate page; or on the title page of the report.
2. On the table-of-contents page of a magazine, briefly highlighting the features of the individual articles in that issue, or at the beginning of the chapter in a book or in advertisements.
3. In reference works devoted exclusively to publishing collections of abstracts of recent and relevant works in a particular field (e.g., *Abstracts of Hospital Management Studies, Science Abstracts, Sociological Abstracts*). See Chapter 7 (p. 189) for a discussion of the usefulness and limitations of abstracts.

▶ Exercises

1. Summarize a chapter of a textbook you are now using for a course in your major field. Provide an accurate bibliographic reference for this chapter (author of the textbook, title of the book, title of the chapter, place of publication, publisher's name, date of publication, and page numbers of the chapter).

2. Summarize a lecture you heard recently. Limit your summary to one page.

3. Listen to a television network evening newscast and also to a later news update on the same station. Select one major story covered on the evening news and indicate which details from it were omitted in the news update.

4. Bring an article from the *Reader's Digest* to class and the original material it condensed, usually an article in a journal or magazine published six months to a year earlier. In a paragraph or two indicate what the *Digest* article omits from the original. Also point out how the condensed version is written so that the omitted material is not missed and does not interfere with the reader's understanding of the main points of the article.

5. Assume that you are applying for a job and that the personnel manager asks you to summarize your qualifications for the job in two or three paragraphs. Write those paragraphs and indicate how your background and interests are suited for the specific job, which you should mention by title at the outset of your first paragraph.

6. The following summary of a speech given at an energy congress contains a number of key words to signal major divisions and emphases in that speech. Find those key words and phrases and discuss their effectiveness.

Today's lamps produce 100 times as much light and operate for thousands of hours longer than Edison's original carbon filament lamp did in 1879, General Electric executive Robert T. Dorsey told government, commerce and industry leaders at a meeting of the World Energy Engineering Congress in Atlanta.

Two new areas of technology are being used to increase the light output produced by incandescent filaments, said Mr. Dorsey, manager of lighting technology development at GE's Lighting Business Group, Cleveland.

One deals with the optical design of the bulb, such as the 75-watt elliptical reflector lamp which delivers as much light as a standard 150-watt reflector bulb in a variety of downlight fixtures.

A second area of technological improvement for incandescent lamps is the development of coatings for spherical bulbs which transmit light but reflect infrared back to the filament, Mr. Dorsey said. This allows the filament to be operated at a more efficient temperature and with fewer watts. Laboratory models have been designed which increase the filament efficiency by as much as 20%, the GE executive said.

The most significant development in the fluorescent lamp field, Mr. Dorsey reported, is the combining of a high efficiency 35-watt fluorescent lamp with a new ballast which incorporates several technological advances. Among these is a formed coil wire which conducts heat away from the inner part of the core, and improved circuitry which provides a better wave shape to the lamp. This new ballast/lamp combination cuts energy use 15 to 20%.

In the area of lighting technology, Mr. Dorsey cited the advances made in task and ambient lighting but cautioned about potential drawbacks. One obstacle, he warned, is the problem of acoustical privacy. Another is that most of the direct lighting built into furniture today has the wrong light distribution and creates serious ceiling reflections. Daylight and indirect illumination are being evaluated for ambient lighting, said Mr. Dorsey, but both have glare, efficiency and maintenance problems. Ceiling-mounted fixtures, he maintained, are preferable both in terms of economics and energy.

Great strides are also being made in computer technology and lighting design with the advent of personal computers, Mr. Dorsey noted. Computers are being widely used to design nonuniform lighting layouts, calculate equivalent sphere illumination and predict visual comfort probability for a space. Numerous computer programs also are available for lighting cost analysis to determine payback and return on investment for one lighting system compared with another, and for maintenance programs to calculate the point at which lamps should be replaced and fixtures cleaned, he said.

Control technology was still another area cited by Mr. Dorsey that can mean significant energy and cost savings for management. Most of today's control systems, he believes, need to operate large numbers of lighting fixtures if they are to be economical. The next generation in light control technology, however, will be "smart" fixtures which will know their address and how to obey commands from a central computer or microprocessor, Mr. Dorsey predicted. This means building intelligence into the fixtures in the form of a signal decoder or as a component.

Concluding, the internationally known lighting engineer outlined the important role thermal technology plays in bringing lighting heat under control.

"One should never recommend additional light to provide additional heat for a building since this represents neither a cost-effective nor an energy-efficient option," Mr. Dorsey said. "However, when brought under control, it can have a significant positive impact on a building's heating cycle and a relatively small impact on cooling cycle."[1]

7. Write a summary of one of the following articles:
   (a) "Microwaves," in Chapter 1, p. 15.
   (b) "Intensive Care for Your Typewriter," below.
   (c) "Preventive Maintenance," p. 251.

8. Write a descriptive abstract of one of the articles you selected in exercise 7.

Intensive care for your typewriter

by W. Tim Meiers

Are you guilty of carelessness with your typewriter? Carelessness can result in a typewriter that doesn't operate properly and in needless repair calls.

Although typewriters with mistake-correcting capability are becoming increasingly widespread, most secretaries must still cope with hand corrections by (1) erasing, (2) using strike-over correction paper, or (3) using paint-over correction fluid. Surprisingly, these methods for correcting errors can lead to service calls.

How many times, for example, have you been told to move the carriage to one side or the other when erasing and to brush the erasings away from the machine? How often do you follow that suggestion? There's actually a practical, valid reason for such advice. Erasings that fall into the segment can cause slow-striking type bars. The slow-striking type bars will usually be those bars located near the center of the segment where most of the erasings will fall.

Strike-over paper also presents a similar debris problem but less can be done about it; the carriage has to be positioned wherever the strike-over is to be made. When you insert and withdraw strike-over paper, however, patience is indeed a virtue. The coating on the correction paper scrapes off on the cardholders, the type bar guide, and the ribbon vibrator. Like erasings, the scraped off coating can fall into the segment, causing slow-striking type bars.

If patience is advisable when you use correction paper, it's definitely a necessity when you use correction fluid. When mistakes on a page you are typing are "painted over" and the paper is rolled back into typing position *before* the correction fluid has dried, some of the fluid probably will come off onto the feed rolls. Over a period of time, as the feed rolls become coated with correction fluid, they become slick and paper

---

[1] *The Office* (March 1980), 211–212. Reprinted with permission.
W. Tim Meiers, "Intensive Care for your Typewriter," *Today's Secretary* (November 1980), 31. Reprinted with permission of Today's Secretary, Gregg Division, McGraw-Hill Book Company, copyright November 1980.

slippage begins to occur. Such slippage is especially noticeable when you are typing near the bottom of a page because the paper is being held by only the front feed rolls.

How frequently do you wave various liquids above your typewriter? As you might guess, liquids spilled into a typewriter can result in expensive service calls. Simply put, soft drinks and sweetened coffee, when spilled, are absolute demons. They act like glue all over your typewriter. Some of the troubles that spilled liquids can cause include slow-striking bars (segment glued), sluggish keys (keyboard glued), and utter mechanical chaos (internal mechanical components glued).

You can also avoid service calls by not using your typewriter as a work bench. While seated at a typewriter, it is not unusual to clip, un-paper clip, hand staple, or unstaple stacks of papers. A common tendency is to perform these tasks near or above the typewriter. A paper clip or staple dropped into a machine can dislocate the springs, lodge under the keyboard, and bind moving parts.

When dealing with paper clips and staples, make an effort to work away from your typewriter. Certainly it takes only a second to use a paper clip or remove a staple, but equally true, it takes only a second to drop one.

Inevitably, certain office situations will require that your typewriter be unplugged and moved. It also seems inevitable that after a typewriter has been moved, it won't operate correctly. But if you are aware of a few simple trouble areas when moving a typewriter (or supervising one being moved), you can prevent more needless service calls.

Most typists know that typewriter keys cannot be depressed when the machine switch is off. This is because connected with the on-off switch of most typewriters is a device called a line lock, which "locks" the keyboard when the switch is off but "unlocks" the keyboard when the switch is on.

What frequently happens when a typewriter is unplugged and moved is that the on-off switch accidentally gets turned on. Remember that on many typewriters the keys *can* be depressed when the typewriter is turned on *even if* the machine is unplugged. The keys that get depressed when a typewriter is being moved are usually the ones near the edge of the keyboard, such as the carriage return, tabulator, shift, and space. Thus when the machine is plugged in again, it jams.

When moving a typewriter, be conscientious of the on-off switch and make certain that it stays off. When carrying a typewriter, keep your thumbs away from the keyboard.

Although this may seem ludicrous, another cause of service calls is a typewriter that is not plugged in. Believe me, it happens. It happens mostly when a typewriter has been unplugged but not moved. Custodians, construction workers, or even fellow office workers might unplug your typewriter for whatever reason and forget to plug it back in. Sure enough, it can be a perplexing situation when your typewriter won't even turn on.

A service call that necessitates merely plugging in a machine can be both embarrassing to you and expensive to a business. Depending on service contracts, a business can be billed—and probably will be billed—for such a service call. Check the plug if your typewriter won't turn on. One final hint is to try a different outlet if your typewriter is plugged in but still won't turn on. Electric outlets can go bad.

Despite all of your efforts to avoid service calls, repairs will occasionally be needed. But even then, you can help if you will learn the names of the different parts of your typewriter as explained in the owner's manual. That way you can be more specific when describing a typewriter malfunction to a repair person. You'll make this person's work easier and have your typewriter back into use sooner.

Preventive maintenance

The mention of maintenance in connection with concrete often brings a puzzled look to people's faces. Everyone knows steel must be painted to prevent rusting and wood must be treated to postpone rotting. But concrete?

It is an eloquent endorsement of our favorite construction material that preventive maintenance of concrete is a little known subject. Concrete frequently performs well even when left strictly on its own. However, there are applications where a little periodic maintenance will greatly extend the useful life of concrete.

Sweeping-Washing

A look at the list of agents that attack concrete, which appears in this issue, will help users and specifiers evaluate the suitability of the type of concrete floor being proposed for a job. Being the rugged performer that it is, concrete will take in stride the many materials it comes in intimate contact with. A concrete floor can co-exist with some of the materials that attack concrete very slightly or slowly if proper housekeeping procedures are followed. If these detrimental materials are regularly removed from the floor to minimize contact time, the floor will often last a considerable period of time.

Dairies should be especially vigilant in terms of floor washing, and not just for reasons of cleanliness. Milk spilled on a concrete floor will not attack the floor immediately, but it is likely to sour soon and form lactic acid. If not washed away before it soaks into the surface, the potential for deterioration exists.

If a plant floor is subject to spillage of fine materials that could act as abrasives, a rigid schedule of washing, sweeping or both is warranted. The same is true for spillage of fluids that are slippery or flammable.

Protective coatings are available to prevent or minimize chemical attack. These must be carefully selected and they frequently require periodic reapplication. It is suggested that a detailed schedule of this type of maintenance be initiated and followed without deviation.

When designing a floor to be subjected to occasional chemical spillage, consideration should be given to achieving a highly reflective, hard-troweled surface. For high-traffic areas, a heavy-duty, off-white floor can be achieved by use of a dry shake when the floor is being finished. The light color encourages good housekeeping practices—not to mention lower energy costs because of reduced lighting requirements—and the dense surface resists infiltration of spilled materials. In addition, the high concentration of the sound, well-graded natural or metallic aggregates (components of the dry shake) at the surface of the floor renders it much more durable under heavy traffic. If traffic is not heavy, ceramic-faced bricks set in a durable mortar on a concrete base can be a means of preventing chemical attack.

Joint Maintenance

Joints are vitally needed components of a concrete structure but they also are potentially its Achilles' heel. Most joints (excluding some structural ones) are incorporated

"Preventive Maintenance," *Concrete Construction* (January 1981), 9, 11–12. Reprinted by permission from *Concrete Construction* Magazine, World of Concrete Center, 426 South Westgate, Addison, Illinois 60101

into plans for the purpose of accommodating movement. Each provides a controlled plane of weakness to channel cracking into a straight-line configuration that can be maintained much more easily than random cracks. The joint might be used any place where drying shrinkage, differential settlement or other change could set up horizontal or vertical stress greater than the tensile or shear strength of the concrete. Whether joints are formed or sawed, their function remains the same.

To the layman, a concrete building can frequently represent one of the most monumental—and static—man-made edifices. In reality, however, concrete is continually moving, growing and shrinking in response to changes in temperature and load. Thus, when a crack forms, a joint has merely begun to perform its function. It must retain its ability to accommodate movement if it is to be successful; if it locks—becomes immobile—the concrete is likely to adjust to repeated stress by cracking.

Unfilled joints, especially in floors, are likely to become clogged with dirt, aggregate particles and other materials that eventually cause them to lose their ability to move. To prevent this, maintenance crews must be especially vigilant to keep the joints clear of such debris.

A more practical approach to joint maintenance in industrial buildings and warehouses is to fill them with sealants that resist infiltration of foreign matter and accommodate movement for long periods of time. Joints in vertical surfaces and most outdoor applications are best sealed with elastomeric sealants. These should not be applied to the full depth of the joint, but to a depth that is less than the joint width. The bottom of the joint is first filled with a nonbonding backing material to support the sealant while it cures.

Interior floor movement due to temperature is likely to become very little, and after the floor has undergone most of its drying shrinkage the joint seldom undergoes much further opening and closing. For this reason floor joints are usually sealed with less deformable sealants, particularly where they are called on to support the loads of wheeled traffic. Joints should be regularly inspected to ensure that they are functioning as required.

Prevent Scaling

Many areas are subject to snow and ice that impede or threaten the safety of both foot and vehicular traffic. Plowing can take care of the snow but there remains the danger of ice. The virtually universal response to that problem is to broadcast a deicer over the surface of the flatwork. Good air-entrained concrete that has gained sufficient strength will stand up well to appropriate deicers. But if the concrete has inadequate air content, too high a water-cement ratio, too little strength, or has been improperly finished, scaling is probably on the horizon.

Care should be taken to see that new driveways and sidewalks are made with concrete containing sound aggregates and sufficiently high compressive strength (4000 psi[1]* at age 28 days), and that it is correctly placed, finished and cured. After the concrete has been thoroughly cured, the flatwork should have a chance to dry for 28 days before the onset of the freeze-thaw cycles of winter. If possible, deicers should

---

* Superscript numbers refer to metric equivalents listed with this article.

not be used on concrete less than one year old—certainly not used the first winter on concrete placed late that summer or fall. (It should be borne in mind that deicers can be dropped onto slabs from the undersides of cars and trucks.)

Applications of linseed oil can help prevent deicer scaling on concrete surfaces, especially in newly placed flatwork. The linseed oil forms a coating of low permeability that retards the infiltration of salt solutions into the concrete. Sealers that form completely impermeable barriers should not be used because they can cause the concrete to become saturated and thus more vulnerable to damage from freezing and thawing. Two coats of the linseed oil should be applied to clean, dry slabs before the weather becomes cold. Prepare a solution of one part boiled linseed oil to one part kerosene or mineral spirits (by volume). Apply it uniformly over the slabs at the rate (recommended by American Concrete Institute Committee 302) of 40 to 50 square yards per gallon[2] for the first coat and 67 square yards per gallon[3] for the second coat, allowing the surface to dry thoroughly between applications. (The National Ready Mixed Concrete Association recommends application at the rate of 25 square yards per gallon.[4]) Because linseed oil darkens the surface of concrete, it should be applied as uniformly as possible. A broom may be used for small areas; a tanker with a spray bar is effective for large slabs. Linseed oil treatment should be reapplied every two to four years, depending on exposure and condition of the concrete.

The type of deicer used is critical; the user should ascertain what kind is used for his sidewalks and driveways. Even some commercially prepared deicers have been found to be chemicals that are highly destructive to concrete surfaces. No ammonium or sulfate salt should ever be used on concrete. They react chemically with concrete and they seriously and rapidly erode or disrupt the surface of even the best concrete. Sodium chloride (halite), calcium chloride, urea, and most of the commercial deicing compounds are effective and do not chemically attack good concrete. (Sodium chloride can damage surrounding vegetation.)

Dusting Floors

A concrete floor that is correctly designed for the service expected and is properly installed will not dust. However, some companies do inherit a floor that dusts and are not able to replace or resurface it. Under some conditions it is possible to reduce the amount of dusting through proper maintenance procedures.

First, the cause of dusting must be determined. If it is dusting because aggregates at the floor surface are being cracked and pulverized by traffic, the only alternatives are to resurface the concrete or reduce the traffic. Some types of curing compounds produce fine dust under traffic but this is usually a short-lived phenomenon.

If dusting of the floor is the result of inadequate curing, carbonation of the surface caused by using unvented heaters while curing, or other poor practices that inhibit proper cement hydration, a temporary alleviation can be obtained with a commercial liquid treatment containing magnesium fluosilicate, zinc fluosilicate or sodium silicate (the first two are generally the most effective). These react to form hard crystals that can reduce the amount of dusting experienced in light- or possibly medium-duty floors. They must be reapplied periodically, the frequency of reapplication depending on the severity of dusting and the amount of traffic. Concentration of the active ingredient varies with the brand used so it is necessary to follow the manufacturer's application instructions.

This article has been concerned primarily with maintenance that deals with such practical matters as scaling and dusting and has not attempted to deal with such architectural matters as sandblasting or steam cleaning to remove dirt or stains. However, whether the concern is practical or aesthetic, concrete is the construction material most likely to perform best for the longest time with the least amount of maintenance.

Metric equivalents

(1) 28 megapascals

(2) 9 to 11 square meters per liter

(3) 15 square meters per liter

(4) 5.5 square meters per liter

9

Preparing a Questionnaire and Reporting the Results

A questionnaire asks carefully selected respondents to supply answers to a list of questions. Properly designed, questionnaires can be valuable reference tools that measure the changing winds of opinion, help forecast trends, and record a wide range of statistical data. Opinion sampling can be a very elaborate operation requiring expertise in psychology, statistics, and computer science. Some questionnaires, therefore, are costly, sophisticated measuring devices prepared by firms that specialize in gathering information. Other questionnaires, including the ones described in this chapter, are shorter, less formal ones for use on the job or in school. Chapter 9 shows you how to design this type of questionnaire, distribute it, and summarize the results.

▶ The Usefulness of Questionnaires

Questionnaires are useful to all parts of a society that wants to be informed about itself; they play a particularly practical role in schools, business and industry, and government. As a student, you may have completed a questionnaire recently asking you to evaluate a course or a program. You can find questionnaires on campus about extracurricular activities, the hours a pool or tennis court is open, the quality of food at a cafeteria. These questionnaires seek to measure student opinion to improve campus life—academic and social. In addition to answering a questionnaire, you may at some point in your college career have to design one to gather information for a report or paper.

Questionnaires in business can increase a company's or agency's sales and profits by determining the consumer's needs. A customer's likes and dislikes readily translate into buying power. To determine what consumers say they want, a store can distribute a questionnaire asking for specific comments on store hours, a particular line or brand of merchandise, credit policies, effectiveness of salesclerks, services after the sale, and the like. A brief questionnaire left in hotel guest rooms is found in Fig. 9.1. By analyzing the answers to the short questions, the hotel will know better where to advertise, what to stress in those advertisements, and what to correct or expand in its dining room and recreational facilities.

The government is actively engaged in gathering facts and opinions from its citizens. Every ten years a long questionnaire from the Bureau of the Census asks detailed questions about occupation, income, health, language, and household size. The answers to this lengthy questionnaire help determine how many representatives are sent to Congress and how much of the tax dollar returns to the communities. At the local level, elected officials or civic leaders may distribute questionnaires asking whether a street should be converted into a four-lane highway, a residential area rezoned for shopping facilities, or a new water treatment plant constructed.

Mail Questionnaires versus Personal Interview Questionnaires

There are some important practical differences between gathering information by mailing a questionnaire or by conducting an interview. Mail question-

Fig. 9.1   A short questionnaire.

We hope that you enjoyed your stay at the Happiness Hotel. In order to make your return visit even more pleasurable, would you please take a few minutes to fill out this questionnaire. Thank you. We hope to see you again—soon.

1. How did you find out about the Happiness Hotel?
   ☐ friends   ☐ travel agent   ☐ magazine ads   ☐ billboard

2. What condition was your room in when you checked in?
   ☐ spotless   ☐ satisfactory   ☐ unsatisfactory

3. How would you describe your maid service?
   ☐ excellent   ☐ good   ☐ fair   ☐ poor

4. How was the food in our dining room?
   ☐ superior   ☐ good   ☐ satisfactory   ☐ needs improvement (please specify)

5. Please rank in order of preference the recreational facilities you used often at Happiness Hotel.
   ☐ pool   ☐ tennis courts   ☐ golf course   ☐ horseback riding

Name_____   Room number_____
(optional)

naires have the following advantages over interviews:

1. Mail questionnaires can save time and money. A questionnaire put in the mail will reach individuals whether they live in your town or across the country. Contrast this method of collecting information with interviews, which require appointments, travel, and time.
2. Mail questionnaires can be completed in the privacy of the home or office by respondents who will not be embarrassed by an interviewer's eye-to-eye questions about age, income, grievances, or preferences. A questionnaire can assure respondents of anonymity and give them more time to answer. Interviews require immediate responses.
3. Properly worded, mail questionnaires can elicit honest, unthreatened responses. An interviewer, on the other hand, can unintentionally sway a respondent by gesture, tone of voice, or facial expression.

Mail questionnaires do have some drawbacks. The response rate can be very low, because people may think that filling out the questionnaire is a waste of time. Even if they do fill it out, you never know when respondents plan to return the questionnaire. Generally, though, a mail questionnaire is a much more useful method of gathering information than is the interview. You can reach more people in less time with less expense. Reserve interviews for times when you have a very small number of people to reach (not more than ten or fifteen) and when those individuals are authorities in the field, rather than a cross section of a given population.

A Questionnaire's Two Audiences

You have two primary audiences to keep in mind when you prepare a questionnaire: (1) the respondents who will fill out your questionnaire and (2) the individuals who will read your report based on the questionnaire responses. You may later share the results (or, occasionally, even the report itself) with respondents, but they are not the primary audience for whom you write your report. Respondents usually do not make decisions on how to translate opinions into action. The questionnaire links both groups. For example, students, employees, patients, or customers complete a questionnaire to give facts, express opinions, or emphasize the need for change. Using their responses, you write a report for an employer or elected official who can decide what changes, if any, need to be made.

How carefully you poll your questionnaire audience will determine how successful you are with your report audience. You will not meet the needs of either group if your questionnaire contains gaps. Questionnaires that are vague or confusing will produce a report containing these same weaknesses. Your questions must be clear, concise, and relevant. Respondents will then have a better opportunity to voice their opinions. Because your report readers will not have the time to read every questionnaire, they will depend on you to summarize the results accurately, arrange them into neat categories, and provide pertinent recommendations.

Chapter 9 emphasizes the needs of both audiences. It first discusses choosing a restricted topic, writing effective questions, and preparing a successful, attractive questionnaire. It then outlines how to select respondents, distribute the questionnaire, and tabulate the results. How to meet report readers' specific expectations comprises a second part of the chapter and includes guidelines on how to condense information, record numbers properly, incorporate direct quotations, and make recommendations.

▶ Choosing a Restricted Topic

Before constructing your questionnaire, you must settle on a restricted topic. The key to finding such a topic is remembering that successful questionnaires solicit answers to help solve a particular problem or initiate a specific change. Responses to precise questionnaires can help you to formulate a knowledgeable recommendation to share with your employer or teacher. The more precise your topic, the more accurate your recommendation will be. A school, business, or agency would soon go bankrupt if it were concerned only with the vague or the general. The topic of your questionnaire should lead to specific action.

If you decided to write a questionnaire on working conditions in your place of employment, you might have found a practical subject but not a precise one. What, specifically, are you interested in learning? You certainly could not write a report on every aspect of your working conditions. There is too much involved. You would spread yourself, your recommendations, and your respondents' answers too thin if you tried to tackle this vast subject. Begin by asking yourself what is included in the topic. Can it be broken into smaller, more easily handled parts? What smaller, more precise topics can you find in the large issue "working conditions"? Here are some:

supervisors	eating facilities
coworkers' responsibilities	lighting
schedules	safety measures
grievance committees	temperatures
union involvement	profit sharing
fringe benefits	machinery
salaries	coffee/rest breaks
parking	promotions

Choose a restricted topic from these subjects and build your questionnaire around it. You will be able to more easily determine respondents' opinions when you ask them about fringe benefits or safety measures than when you ask a series of general questions. The results from your questionnaire, consequently, will be more precise, easier to organize, and more understandable and useful to readers.

Another example of how a large topic can be scaled down into more practical ones might be helpful. Perhaps you want to question respondents about television. That is a roomy topic, so you will have to narrow the range. For example, are you interested in the different kinds of television stations?

Public Broadcasting System
the three major networks, ABC, CBS, NBC
Christian Broadcasting Network
independent stations, English language
independent stations, foreign language
cable television networks

Each of these station types is also a very broad subject. You will have to ask yourself exactly what you want the respondents to say about one aspect of television. Again, make a list of suitable topics.

editorials	personalities
children's programs	news broadcasts
schedules	community service messages
advertising rates	sporting events
reception in your area	contemporary issues programs

By developing a questionnaire on one of these much more limited subjects, you will achieve useful results.

▶ Writing the Questions

Relevant Questions

Once you have a topic, ask this question: "Exactly what kinds of information about this topic am I looking for?" Determine the types of information you need and then include only relevant questions. Since many of the questionnaires you will have to write are brief (ten to twenty questions), make every question count. However interesting a side issue may be, keep it off your questionnaire. Why ask respondents to write more than is necessary? And why risk distracting them with irrelevant issues?

To illustrate the process of selecting only relevant questions, let's assume that you work for Speedee Tax Consultants and that your manager wants you to write a questionnaire to determine whether first-time customers approve of what Speedee is doing. You are to ask them questions about your service, the time and money they invested, and their suggestions for improving your service. Anything else is unnecessary. The questions on the left side below would be relevant for your questionnaire; those on the right would not.

Relevant questions	*Irrelevant questions*
Did anyone help you fill out your return last year?	Were you good in high school mathematics?
Did you earn any income outside this state?	Do you consider yourself a blue- or white-collar worker?
Did you have to file a state form this year?	Do you find the state or federal form more confusing?

How did you hear about Speedee?	Have you ever been audited by the IRS?
Did you make an appointment to speak to a Speedee consultant?	Should the IRS extend the filing deadline to June 1?
Was there ample parking room?	What make of car do you drive?
How long did you have to wait if you did not have an appointment?	Did you think the Speedee office was tastefully decorated?
Was the Speedee consultant courteous?	Do you know how much training our employees receive?
Were the consultant's explanations clear or were they given in terms you did not understand?	What kind of calculator did the Speedee consultant use?
On the federal return, were you told whether the short or long form was better for you?	Are there too many tax loopholes for the rich to escape paying their fair share?
Which form (long or short) did you file?	Are you currently employed?
Did the consultant show you how you could lawfully reduce the amount you owed? Increase your refund?	What will you do with your refund, if you receive one?
Were the costs for Speedee's services clearly explained?	Will you have to live on a tighter budget next year?
Did you find those costs fair?	Do you know the name of the owner of Speedee's or how many people we helped last year?
Would you come to Speedee next year?	Would you write your representative in Congress if you had to pay back more than five hundred dollars?

The relevant questions stick to the issue of most concern to the Speedee Service—transforming first-time customers into repeat business. The irrelevant questions stray from the issues of service and costs.

Two Basic Types of Questions

In preparing a questionnaire you can write two kinds of questions: open-ended (or essay) questions and closed questions. The following sections define each type of question, provide examples, and point out their benefits and drawbacks.

Open-Ended Questions

An open-ended, or essay, question asks respondents to formulate their answers without being given any options, thus allowing much freedom of expression. It encourages respondents to elaborate. Open-ended questions use verbs that elicit amplified responses—*appraise, comment on, compare, de-*

scribe, discuss, estimate, evaluate, explain, judge. Here are some sample open-ended questions:

Describe the changes you would make in the registration process at Mesa College.

Explain which part of your job is the hardest to perform and why.

Why did you attend Monmouth College?

Judge the effectiveness of a family health practice where a registered nurse screens patients and decides which ones see a doctor.

Comment on how you would correct abuses in the food stamp program here in Taylorsville.

Open-ended questions are useful for a variety of purposes. They provide a practical means of soliciting information on subjects that would otherwise require options too numerous (or impossible) to list one by one. For example, the question above on why students attend a particular college might bring back ten or twelve different and valid answers, some of which might never have occurred to you. Open-ended questions may also be helpful in gathering information on sensitive professional issues. Furthermore, respondents will reveal how knowledgeable they are, thus allowing you to gauge the value of their opinions.

Open-ended questions can be of value to you even before you write the final version of your questionnaire. You can send a few open-ended questions to a small sample of your respondents who, in their answers, can suggest the kinds of topics and options to include on the final questionnaire. And on the final copy of your questionnaire the last question can be an open-ended one asking respondents to comment in detail on any topic covered in the questionnaire or on any topic you may have overlooked.

Finally, open-ended questions are valuable for lengthy studies searching for in-depth responses. If you have much time and relatively few (under fifteen or twenty) respondents, a questionnaire composed mainly of open-ended questions can be rewarding.

But open-ended questions can also pose problems for you and your respondents. This kind of question requires a great deal of effort from respondents, who will have to organize, compose, and write their answers. If your question is not direct and sufficiently focused, you could easily get many irrelevant answers from respondents. Moreover, valuable answers might be mixed with these irrelevant comments. Finally, responses to open-ended questions are challenging to summarize, especially when large groups are surveyed, and these responses must be properly coded. (A later section of this chapter, pp. 275–277, discusses one way to code, record, and tabulate responses.)

Closed Questions

Closed questions offer respondents a limited number of choices to mark or write in. Because closed questions are easier to code and tabulate, they are used more often than open-ended questions. Closed questions fall into the four categories shown on the next two pages.

1. Questions that offer only two choices. These are sometimes called dichotomous questions, because they present the respondent with a dichotomy, or a division of the subject into two mutually exclusive parts. The respondent's choice is limited to one of these two parts. Use this type of question only when the topic can be reasonably understood and explained in either/or terms.

(a) Yes/no questions

Should women be drafted? yes_____ no_____

Is there a history of breast cancer in your family? yes_____ no_____

Have you already taken Banking 117—Principles of Banking Operations? yes_____ no_____

(b) True/false questions

People who smoke in public places should be fined. true_____ false_____

Licensed Practical Nurses should, after special training, be allowed to start IV's. true_____ false_____

Lanse Street must be changed into a one-way street. true_____ false_____

(c) Two specific objects or types identified

Which kind of radio station do you prefer? AM_____ FM_____

Where would you rather shop? downtown___ the mall___

What kind of stove does your apartment have? gas_____ electric___

2. Multiple-choice questions. These questions usually offer respondents three to five answers from which to choose. One of those answers can include a category marked "other," asking respondents to list "option not given," "do not know," or "undecided."

What type of domesticated animal would you choose for a pet?
dog_____ cat_____ bird_____ fish_____ other (please specify)_____

Which kind of music do you like to listen to most often?
rock 'n' roll_____ country/western_____ jazz_____ classical_____ blues_____

Which agent called on you last month?
Ms. Kelly_____ Mr. Tumbrel_____ Ms. Baldwin_____ Mr. Lopez_____
No one called_____

How many times a day do you use the Fast Copier?
1_____ 2_____ 3_____ 4_____ more than 4 (please specify)_____

3. Ranking questions. With these questions a respondent is asked to assess the relative significance of a series of options and to assign each a value, often by labeling them 1, 2, 3, 4.

Indicate your order of preference for the kind of nursing you would like to do after graduation:
acute care_____ industrial_____ home health_____ school_____

Please rank the following reasons in order of importance as to why you decided to do your banking at First National.
Superteller_____ Saturday hours_____ Totalpak checking_____ Location____
Investment accounts_____

Rank the following types of cuisine in terms of their appeal to you.
Chinese_____ Mexican_____ Italian_____ French_____ German_____

4. Short-answer questions. These questions require respondents to fill in the blank or write a brief sentence.

Give your date of birth (day, month, year):_____

How long have you lived at your current address?_____

Give the names of any community groups to which you belong:_____

_____

What was your chief reason for accepting a job at Peterson's?_____

_____

Which types of power tools do you use most often in your job?_____

_____

Where does your spouse work?_____

Reliable and Valid Questions

Writing questions that work requires much thought and testing. Questions must be reliable *and* valid. A reliable question has the same meaning each time it is asked. It stands the test of time and is precisely and objectively worded so that respondents do not answer it one way on Monday and another way on Wednesday, depending on their mood. Reliable questions are not tricky or filled with loaded words; they are firm and constant. Valid questions do the job the writer intended—that is, they elicit the desired information. An invalid question contains ambiguous, vague words, thus calling into doubt any response made to it. Valid questions are worded so that respondents can understand exactly what the questioner wants to find out. To write reliable and valid questions, follow these suggestions:

1. Phrase your questions precisely. Specify exact quantities, times, or money. The questions below are vague:

Is there enough free swim time at the pool? yes____ no____

If you were offered a good salary, would you work inside a nuclear power plant? yes____ no____

Is industry responsible for pollution? all____ some____ none____

Words like *enough, good, industry,* and *pollution* are vague. Someone trying out for the swim team will interpret "enough" to mean far more hours than does the respondent who goes to the pool two times a week for relaxation. A "good" salary is equally imprecise. The final question does not identify the industry (plastics, textile, oil refinery, paint, rubber), the type of responsibility (through dumping waste into water, into the air, burying contaminants), and the kind of pollution (air, water, food, soil) involved. To correct vague questions, use exact words, as the following revised examples show:

How many hours of free swim time should
there be at the pool each day?   1____   2____   3____   4____

Would you work inside a nuclear power plant
for $25,000 a year?   yes____   no____

Has All-Fix, Inc., dumped any oil in the marsh
near your home within the last six weeks?   yes____   no____

2. Ask manageable questions.   Broad questions, such as the following, ask respondents to write ten pages just to begin answering them.

What do you think of our government?

What is your view of the economy?

What insurance will a homeowner need?

Like a vague question, a broad question offers the respondent no direction. The words *government, the economy,* and *insurance* cover a multitude of issues. Wide open, general questions like these really list the whole subject of the questionnaire rather than having each question cover one restricted part of the topic. That one large question needs to be cut into many smaller, more manageable queries. For example, by "government" does the writer mean federal, state, county, or local? And which governmental function, agency, or service (or lack of service) is involved? "The economy" also covers a lot of territory—should the respondent comment on the rate of inflation last month, current interest rates for new home loans, the percentage of unemployment in one city or in one profession, the national trade deficit, or what? When you ask about insurance for a homeowner, do you expect your respondents to discuss all kinds of insurance—life (term and whole life), medical, personal property, and even burial? A request for such an extensive amount of information in a single essay answer would overwhelm even an actuary (an expert in computing statistics on insurance risks and premiums). Replace a broad question with a more manageable one, such as the following examples show:

Do you agree with Governor Thompson's plan to lend
money to the Chicago Board of Education?   yes____   no____

Should the United States government lend money to Acme
Businesses in 1983?   yes____   no____

What percentage of your monthly house payment goes for
mortgage insurance?   _____%

3. Write questions that let respondents decide for themselves. Avoid using loaded words, such as those in the following questions:

> Should we continue to waste taxpayers' money on the construction of the George Street Bridge?
>
> Do you believe we have elected too many weirdos to city council?
>
> Isn't it useless to keep making agriculture majors submit daily reports?
>
> Should the government start the draft to make sure we have quality and quantity in America's armed services?

You reveal an emotional bias and thereby prejudice respondents with words like *waste, weirdos, useless,* or *quality and quantity.* The last example is particularly unfair because it suggests that those who answer "no" are against a strong America. Keep the language of your questions impartial, as in these revised examples:

> Would you vote for continuing work on the George Street Bridge?   yes_____ no_____
>
> Do you believe your neighborhood is adequately represented on the city council?   yes_____ no_____
>
> Do you want agriculture majors to submit daily reports?   yes_____ no_____
>
> Do you believe that there should be a draft?   yes_____ no_____

A question like the following one demands a "yes" response:

> Residents of Lake Wells need better sewerage facilities, don't they?

Rephrase the question to eliminate bias:

> Do Lake Wells' residents need more sewerage facilities?   yes_____ no_____

4. Your questions should not insult or indict the respondent. No matter how a question such as "Have you stopped beating your spouse?" is answered, it accuses the respondent of the deed. The following two questions are worded improperly:

> Are you still getting speeding tickets?
>
> Have you missed many payments lately?

Do not assume that respondents have ever received speeding tickets or missed payments. Instead, ask if they ever did get a ticket or miss a payment.

> Did you ever receive a ticket for speeding?   yes_____ no_____
>
> Have you ever missed a payment?   yes_____ no_____

If the answer is yes, you can ask the number of tickets or missed payments in a following question.

5. Do not write a question that requires the respondent to do your research. Courtesy requires that you not ask them to go to any more trouble than it takes to fill out the questionnaire. Avoid questions such as the following:

> Ask your immediate superior to supply you with the number of models sold last month and please list that number.

> After checking your files and last year's order book, indicate the differences between this year's engine specifications and last year's.

You are imposing on respondents when you require them to speak to other people or when you make them search their records to answer your question. If you want information from a supervisor, send that individual a separate questionnaire. If you want to know about last year's records, consult them yourself.

6. Limit your questions to recent events. Do not ask respondents to search their memories to recall opinions they held years ago or to discuss details of an event they may not now clearly remember. The following questions are inappropriate:

> Was your apartment building constructed with energy conservation in mind?

> What was your exact gas mileage for city driving when you purchased your brand-new Cougar in 1979?

> What kinds of meals did you eat on your vacation two years ago?

7. Write questions in language appropriate for your audience. A questionnaire directed to specialists may well include a few technical terms. If respondents are not familiar with your jargon, avoid it. Patients asked about hospital service would have difficulty understanding this question:

> Did you receive p.r.n. meds stat?   yes＿＿   no＿＿

Reworded as follows, the question is easier to answer:

> Were you given medications when you
> needed them?   yes＿＿   no＿＿

Avoid pretentious vocabulary as well:

> Did the policy of merit raises exacerbate the crew's feelings?

Translated into understandable terms, this question reads:

> Did the policy of merit raises anger the
> crew?   yes＿＿   no＿＿

8. Each question should cover only one item. Do not confront respondents with a question that may demand an unnecessary, misleading, or contradictory choice. For example, "Do you prefer the Beatles or the Rolling Stones?" asks respondents to choose between the two. But respondents may like both groups and could not register their preference as the question is worded. Make two separate questions to be sure of obtaining a reliable response. The following question is also poor, because it assumes that respondents will automatically agree with both adjectives:

Are the new models more streamlined
and economical than last year's?   yes____   no____

Some may think that the new models are more streamlined but less economical than last year's, while others think just the reverse. Again, ask two separate questions, and do not use more than one adjective per question.

Overloading a question with a series of short interrogative words (*why? how? where? when? what?*) at its close should also be avoided. For example:

Approximately how many times have you visited Baltimore in the last year?
Why? When? For how long? How did you travel?

9. Do not ask the same question twice. A question writer may think that there is a fine, subtle difference between two questions, but respondents may be unable to detect any difference. Check one question against another. Make sure, for example, that a question 2 does not duplicate a question 7.

(2) What is your favorite television program?
(7) Which program do you like to watch most on television?

(2) State your opinion about when placebos should be used.
(7) What are the values of placebos?

The writer of the first set of redundant questions failed to see that a favorite program means the one you like to watch. In the second pair the writer wrongly saw a difference between the use of placebos and their value. If they are prescribed for specific patients or used in different kinds of tests, these uses automatically characterize the placebo's value.

10. In multiple choice questions supply respondents with clearly differentiated options. The following question confusingly presents overlapping choices:

What kind of car do you think gets the best mileage in the city?
(a) a compact
(b) a subcompact
(c) a foreign-made car
(d) an American car
(e) a diesel

These choices are not distinct. A compact or subcompact may also be either a foreign or an American car. The same is true of the diesel. Confronted with these options, respondents are asked two or three questions at the same time. Any answer they would give will be invalid and incomplete. Turn such a question into three separate questions:

(1) Do you think that a compact or a subcompact gets better mileage in the
     city?   compact____   subcompact____

(2) Name any American-made car that equals or surpasses the best import in city mileage_____

(3) Would a diesel or a gasoline engine be more economical in city driving?   diesel_____   gasoline_____

11. Include all necessary options in multiple-choice questions and those that ask respondents to rank items.   Omissions are especially dangerous when respondents are forced to choose between two extremes and are not given enough options for qualified agreement or disagreement. For some types of questions, give respondents the option of saying that they have no opinion or that they see no change. Here are some ineffective questions because they have limited (omitted) options:

Do you believe in the death
penalty for all cases?   yes_____   no_____

How do you feel about the new
uniforms we are required to
wear?   I like them_____   I do not like them_____

When is the busiest time at
your factory?   morning_____   afternoon_____

Respondents might believe in or oppose the death penalty, but only in certain circumstances; they may approve of one part of a uniform code and not another; and workers may find a night shift the busiest or want to say that the workload varies from one week to another. As these questions are worded, valid responses are impossible. Make the first question, for example, valid by including differentiated options, as follows:

never _____ murder   of   a   police   officer _____ any   murder _____ other _____ undecided _____

▶ Writing Effective Instructions

A clear and brief set of instructions should appear at the very top of the first page of your questionnaire. To emphasize instructions, you might want to use boldface type or capital letters for certain points. In addition to showing respondents how to fill in their answers, instructions can summarize the topic the questionnaire surveys. A clear set of instructions will emphasize how easy a questionnaire is to answer and will increase your chances of having respondents complete the questionnaire.

Specifically, what should you tell respondents in your instructions? Indicate the kinds of questions they will be answering—multiple-choice, ranking, fill-in-the-blank, essay. Clearly specify how respondents are to indicate their choices—are they to put a check (√), an X, circle a response, or underscore their answers? Look at the questionnaire in Fig. 9.2 for an example of helpful, explicit instructions. It is also important to be consistent in the kinds of questions you use and the method respondents are to employ to answer

Fig. 9.2   A portion of a questionnaire with explicit instructions.

National Restaurant Association
1976 Travel Study

Name _____   Code _____

City _____

Directions: Listed below are a number of statements, some of which deal with eating out and restaurants and some of which deal with general life-style factors. For each statement listed, we would like to know whether you personally agree or disagree with the statement.

After each statement, there are five numbers from one to five. The higher the number, the more you tend to disagree with the statement. The lower the number, the more you tend to agree with the statement. The numbers 1-5 can be described as follows:

1. I strongly agree with the statement.
2. I generally agree with the statement.
3. I neither agree nor disagree.
4. I generally disagree with the statement.
5. I strongly disagree with the statement.

For each statement, please circle the number that best describes your feelings about that statement.

(After you complete the questionnaire, please place this form into the attached stamped, self-addressed envelope and mail.)

Statement	Strongly Agree				Strongly Disagree
1 I prefer to order a la carte rather than order a dinner.	1	2	3	4	5
2 I prefer a service charge be automatically added to my bill rather than having to tip.	1	2	3	4	5
3 I like to try new and different menu items.	1	2	3	4	5
4 I prefer a self-service salad bar to being served a salad at the table.	1	2	3	4	5
5 I usually tip a fixed percentage of the bill regardless of the service I get.	1	2	3	4	5
6 Atmosphere is just as important as the quality of the food in selecting a restaurant.	1	2	3	4	5
7 I love to eat.	1	2	3	4	5
8 I usually look for the lowest possible prices when I shop.	1	2	3	4	5
9 Information I get about a product from a friend is usually better than what I get from advertising.	1	2	3	4	5
10 I have annual physical check-ups.	1	2	3	4	5
11 If a new restaurant opened in town, I would probably be among the first to try it out.	1	2	3	4	5
12 My days tend to follow a definite routine, such as eating meals at a regular time, etc.	1	2	3	4	5
13 I exercise regularly.	1	2	3	4	5
14 I enjoy most of my business trips.	1	2	3	4	5
15 Sometimes I like to do things on the "spur of the moment."	1	2	3	4	5
16 I would like to take a trip around the world.	1	2	3	4	5
17 Most people are in too much of a rush.	1	2	3	4	5
18 I like fast-food restaurants.	1	2	3	4	5
19 When I must choose between the two, I usually dress for fashion, not for comfort.	1	2	3	4	5
20 I often wish for the good old days.	1	2	3	4	5
21 I like to be considered a leader.	1	2	3	4	5
22 A party wouldn't be a party without liquor.	1	2	3	4	5
23 I would rather spend a quiet evening at home than go to a party.	1	2	3	4	5
24 I like to pay cash for everything I buy.	1	2	3	4	5
25 I love the fresh air and out-of-doors.	1	2	3	4	5
26 I follow at least one sport very closely.	1	2	3	4	5
27 I enjoy a cocktail before dinner.	1	2	3	4	5
28 I often check prices, even for small items.	1	2	3	4	5
29 I eat more than I should.	1	2	3	4	5
30 No matter how fast our income goes up, we never seem to have enough.	1	2	3	4	5
31 I often seek out the advice of my friends regarding which brands to buy.	1	2	3	4	5
32 I like to try new and different things.	1	2	3	4	5
33 I feel uneasy when things aren't neat and organized.	1	2	3	4	5
34 I just can't relax when eating out.	1	2	3	4	5
35 I prefer to use a credit card rather than cash when eating out.	1	2	3	4	5
36 Business takes me away from home more often than I'd like.	1	2	3	4	5
37 I am an impulsive individual.	1	2	3	4	5
38 I'd like to spend a year in some foreign country.	1	2	3	4	5

The Restaurant Habits of the Business Traveler, prepared by Edward J. Mayo for National Restaurant Association Consumer Attitudes Survey Series, June 1976. Reprinted with permission of the National Restaurant Association.

them. For example, do not force respondents to jump from a group of multiple-choice questions to a set of ranking ones and then back to multiple-
choice. Do not have respondents circle some answers and check others. As
was noted earlier, many questionnaires composed of one type of closed question do conclude with an open-ended question for further comments. However, this shift in question type is commonly used and therefore is not disturbing to respondents.

Indicate whether respondents are to sign their names or remain anonymous. If their signatures are optional, say so. Tell respondents the date by
which you would like them to return the questionnaire and include a postage-
paid envelope. Give your name, address, and telephone number and offer
any assistance. Even though this information may duplicate what you have
written in a cover letter (discussed on p. 275 of this chapter), give it anyway.
It is safer to repeat the information than to risk having the respondent not
know when and where to return the questionnaire.

Make your instructions as clear as possible. Respondents will be annoyed
if they are frequently interrupted by new instructions. If you use a term or
concept that must be defined or explained, do it in the question itself. For
example:

Is there any encumbrance (lien, mortgage, judgment, or
easement) on your property?   yes_____ no_____

A question may require some kind of clarification for a respondent to answer
it properly:

Which session is best for you to attend?
(each session lasts 3 hours)

▶ Presenting an Attractive Questionnaire

The visual impression your questionnaire makes may determine whether
or not respondents complete it. If your questionnaire looks sloppy and is difficult to read and follow, respondents will not bother with it. Therefore, strive
to make your questionnaire neat, clear, and easy to read and answer. A questionnaire printed on a faded mimeo sheet or on a copying machine that
leaves smudges will not invite quick replies, if any. Consider having the questionnaire copied on attractive paper by a printer. Proofread meticulously.
Also make sure that your questionnaire contains a title, a place for the respondent's name, if desired, and instructions. To review the material discussed so far in this chapter, examine Fig. 9.3, a questionnaire distributed by
Auburn University. It is a fine example of a carefully worded, clearly arranged questionnaire. Note that because travelers complete this questionnaire
while resting at an Alabama hospitality center, the questionnaire does not
contain instructions on where and when it should be returned.

Fig. 9.3   A carefully worded, clearly arranged questionnaire.

AUBURN UNIVERSITY TRAVEL SURVEY
In Cooperation With
Alabama Bureau of Publicity and Information

Dear Traveler: Thank you for traveling in Alabama. We would like to make Alabama a more enjoyable travel destination or vacation state.   Please help us by completing this form **if you have not already done so on this trip.** There is no need to sign your name.

1 Season of travel: 1 □ Dec.-Feb.   2 □ Mar-May   3 □ June-Aug   4 □ Sep.-Nov.

2 Home: City _____ State/Country _____

3 Major point *away from home* you are now traveling to/returning from:

6 City/Place _____ State _____

8 Principal mode of travel: 1 □ Highway   2 □ Air   3 □ Bus   4 □ Rail

Number and age of persons in party:

Males	Females
9 _____ Under 14	15 _____ Under 14
10 _____ 14-17	16 _____ 14-17
11 _____ 18-29	17 _____ 18-29
12 _____ 30-49	18 _____ 30-49
13 _____ 50-64	19 _____ 50-64
14 _____ 65 or over	20 _____ 65 or over

Activities engaged in while in **Alabama only**—check as many as apply:

21 □ Passing thru only
22 □ Passing thru, but engaging in the
following activities checked
23 □ Visiting friends/relatives
24 □ Visiting historical sites/places
25 □ Beaches/swimming
26 □ Commercial attractions (gardens,
amusement parks/centers, etc.)

27 □ Business
28 □ Golfing
29 □ Camping
30 □ Boating/fishing
31 □ Watching sports
32 □ Personal affairs
33 □ Attending show or event
34 □ Attending convention/meeting

35 _____ How many days spent in Alabama on this trip?

37 _____ How many nights spent in Alabama on this trip?

39 _____ How many days spent on entire trip?

Nights in **Alabama** were (or will be) at:
41 □ Home of friend or relative
42 □ Motel
43 □ Hotel
44 □ Rented house/apartment

45 □ Cabin/cottage
46 □ Tent
47 □ Recreational Vehicle
48 □ Travel Trailer

While in **Alabama only**, how much will your party spend on this trip for:

49 _____ Lodging

52 _____ Food and beverages

55 _____ Auto expenses (gas, oil, etc.)

58 _____ Entertainment/sightseeing

61 _____ Recreation/sports

64 _____ Other purchases

67 Annual family income (for statistical purposes only):
1 □   Under $5,000
2 □ $5,000-10,000
3 □ $10,000-15,000

4 □ $15,000-20,000
5 □ $20,000-25,000
6 □ $25,000-30,000

7 □ $30,000-40,000
8 □ $40,000-50,000
9 □ $50,000 or over

We welcome your comments. Please write them on the back side.

THANK YOU FOR YOUR HELP

James W. Adams, "Travel in Alabama, 1980," December 31, 1980, p. 56. Reprinted by permission from Dr. James W. Adams, Associate Professor of Transportation, Department of Marketing and Transportation, Auburn University.

▶ Selecting Respondents

Once you have restricted your topic and have determined who will read the results of your questionnaire and why, you will have a better idea about the kinds of individuals you need to question. To receive useful answers, you have to exercise great care in selecting your respondents; you cannot do it haphazardly. Finding appropriate respondents for extremely technical questionnaires involves sophisticated sampling strategies far beyond the scope of this book. Texts on statistics and audience surveys will contain detailed instructions explaining the specialized methods used by pollsters like George Gallup or Lou Harris; such pollsters can survey small sections of the population and predict outcomes with less than a 2 percent margin of error. Although not offering this kind of statistical information on sampling techniques, the following discussion does suggest guidelines you can follow when selecting respondents.

To how many people must you send a questionnaire in order to have reliable results? The answer depends on your statistics. If you are interested in finding out how radiologic technicians in a particular hospital feel about rotating shifts, then your respondents would be all the radiologic technicians in that one hospital. Similarly, if you want to determine whether your sorority chapter should have a barbeque or dance at the end of the spring term, you would question every member of your chapter. But your respondents may not always belong to such a limited and easily accessible group. Many times you will have to consider a larger audience, whose members could not all be reached and questioned individually. You might want to find out how customers at a certain store feel about a warehouse branch of that store that would sell merchandise at a reduced rate. Certainly you could not question everyone who shops at this store. Or you might be interested in surveying how a certain profession (dairy farmers, dietitians, medical secretaries) would react to a piece of impending legislation. Being unable to question everyone in a particular profession, you would use some form of sampling.

Systematic Random Sampling

The most respectable, and valid, way of finding respondents is to follow the *systematic random sampling* technique. Much marketing research is done this way. According to this technique, you choose your target audience or population (all the nurses in your hometown, all students attending your college, all holders of credit cards from a department store), and from this large target population you obtain a cross section by selecting names at random from the group. For example, from a college directory listing the names of all students enrolled at your school you can choose by random selection every tenth name or, for a smaller margin of error, every fifth name. Thus all respondents (all students listed in the school directory) have an equal chance of being selected for your sample. This equal chance is the heart of the random sampling technique. Figure 9.6 (to be discussed in detail later in this chapter) contains a report on student opinion of a campus newspaper. The editors of the paper could not question the entire student body, so they sent a questionnaire to every sixth name in the directory and had a 66.66 percent response rate.

Citing another example, let's say that you wanted to find out the customers' preferences for shopping hours at your store. You could stand outside the store and ask everyone who happens to walk by. However, you could be talking to people who are visitors to your town and who never have or never will shop at the store, or you could select residents of the town who just stopped to avoid the rain and who never have purchased a thing at the store. To obtain a cross section of those who in fact are customers of the store, you must select as your target population those who are on record as having purchased goods from the store. Perhaps their names are on record as credit card holders. You could then go through the store's list of credit card holders and by random selection pick out names of individuals to whom you will send your questionnaire.

Another way to get a statistically valid sample is to randomly pick names out of the residential listings of your town's telephone book. This selection technique would be a good one if you wanted to find out how a relatively small (under 30,000 people) town or suburb felt about a bond proposal or welfare services.

Stratified Random Sampling

Another valid sampling technique is known as *stratified random sampling*. This approach is used when you have a number of different groups or subgroups to question; it means that you survey each group proportionately. For example, you want to find out how carefully prepared students thought they were after they graduated from your school's criminal justice program. You would have to question not only the students, but also the attorneys and law enforcement officials with whom the students worked. In order to get a cross section of these three groups, you would have to question each group according to the same percentage, for example, 20 percent. If there were a hundred students, you would have to send your questionnaire to twenty of them; if there were forty law enforcement officials, you would have to question eight; and if there were twenty attorneys, you would have to include four in the sample.

Quota Sampling

Still another type of sampling technique is known as *quota sampling*. Use this technique with great care, for it can lead you astray. Here you choose an audience almost as one would select a quota. You might question the first twenty-five males and first twenty-five females you meet. Such a sampling might be helpful if, for example, it consisted of customers in a store who all saw a dishwasher and you wanted to get their opinions of that dishwasher. The population is chosen arbitrarily and not selected as carefully as it would be with random sampling, but such a group can help answer your questions, since everyone has seen the product. The problem with quota sampling is that it can lead to a distorted sample in many circumstances. If you wanted to poll student opinion about a campus radio station and all you did was ask for the opinion of ten of your friends who you knew did not like the station, your sample would be biased. These ten friends are a homogeneous (presorted) group that may not truly represent the view of the student body. To get a valid sample, you would have to obtain a larger sample to ensure coverage of a variety of ideas and opinions.

▶ Distributing a Questionnaire

Before submitting your questionnaire to respondents, have someone evaluate it. Ask a student in your major, a teacher, or a coworker to read your questionnaire and tell you whether any of your questions are vague, misleading, or irrelevant. Have that individual pay particular attention to the options you list for multiple-choice questions; make sure that the options are reasonable and sufficient. Preliminary screening may take a few days, but in the long run you will save much time and energy. If you send out a questionnaire flawed by poorly worded or irrelevant questions, the answers you receive will be of dubious value. You will have to redo the questionnaire, or you may find yourself busy explaining the questions verbally to respondents who call you for help.

Once you are sure that the questionnaire is right, deliver or mail it to your respondents. Whenever feasible, give it to respondents in person; this gesture will create goodwill and will increase your chances of receiving a completed questionnaire back from these individuals. Make sure your questionnaire reaches respondents at times convenient for them, not just for you. Do not give questionnaires to respondents when other commitments prevent their answering you. For example, students preparing for final or state board examinations will not postpone their studies to fill out your questionnaire. Some large companies close for two weeks in the summer and give all employees and supervisors a vacation. Sending a questionnaire to anyone just before or during shutdown would be pointless. Asking for completed questionnaires around the Christmas holidays is equally ill-advised. If you are aware that respondents will be on vacation, busy, or out of town on business, send your questionnaire at another time.

If you mail your questionnaire, send it by first-class mail and include a stamped, self-addressed envelope. Respondents are far more likely to answer when you make it as easy as possible for them. Make certain that the respondents' names and addresses are correct. People will not be inclined to respond if you spell their names incorrectly or if you address them with a Mr. when they are a Ms. or vice versa. Some given names (Pat, Leslie, Terry) apply to both men and women. If you are uncertain, omit the courtesy title and write "Dear Pat Hayes" or "Dear Terry Bronti."

When you mail the questionnaire, enclose a cover letter and consider the following procedures:

1. Introduce yourself and tell why you are writing.
2. Explain why you are sending the questionnaire.
3. Emphasize how important the respondent's answers are.
4. Tell what benefits the respondent can gain by answering—the most important function of the letter.
5. Discuss the kind of questionnaire you have devised.
6. Ask that the questionnaire be returned by a specified time.
7. Perhaps promise a gift for returning the questionnaire.
8. Thank the respondent and promise to inform him or her of the major outcomes.

Depending on your topic and the kind of questionnaire you have constructed, you may also want to assure respondents that their answers will remain confidential. Or you might want to promise them anonymity. Not being required to sign their names, respondents will have no concern that anyone, including you, knows what they have answered. Figure 9.4 (p. 276) illustrates a sample cover letter sent with a questionnaire.

▶ Tabulating Responses

A new phase of your research begins with the return of your questionnaire. You will have to count the completed questionnaires and keep a record of their specific responses. Tallying is an important link between the questionnaire and the report; a mistake here can distort (or defeat) all your other efforts.

Responses can be tallied in numerous ways. If the number of your respondents is large and your employer has a computer to tabulate their answers, you should consult with someone in the computer department before you start to count or categorize responses. A computer consultant can suggest different ways of coding options to your questionnaire to make sure the computer will assess them properly. Responses may be translated into numerical (or alphabetical) symbols to represent various responses. For example, to program responses for a question 1, which calls for a yes or no answer, you may be told that yes = 1 and no = 2, and one of these numbers will be put into row 1 or column 1 representing question 1. A "yes" response to question 1, therefore, may be coded as 1-1; a "no" response would be fed into the computer as 1-2. A "no response" might be a 1-3.

If you are using a small number of respondents for a school project, civic group, or if you lack access to a computer, you will have to tabulate by hand. Your record keeping will be relatively easy if you follow a consistent and orderly system for listing and categorizing information. One good method is to buy a large yellow legal-size note pad and use a separate tally sheet for each question on your questionnaire. Write the question and its number at the top

Fig. 9.4   A cover letter sent with a questionnaire.

CASSON'S DEPARTMENT STORES
1800 South Paulina
Topeka, Kansas 66620

June 3, 1981

Mr. Howard Anderson
73 Crestway Park Drive
Topeka, Kansas 66621

Dear Mr. Anderson:

Thank you for purchasing your new Clearvision television set from
Casson's. Your opinions about our store and its service policies are
important to us.

For this reason, I am writing to ask you to complete the enclosed
questionnaire. It should not take more than ten minutes of your time,
and your answers will enable us to provide you with even better service
for your set. You will find twelve multiple-choice questions; you will
have an opportunity to elaborate on any of your answers, if you wish.

The questionnaire is easy to return. Just put it in the enclosed
postage-paid envelope and drop it in the mail. It would help us to have
the questionnaire back by June 27. If you have any questions, please
give me a call at 783-3423, extension 41.

Once again, thanks for shopping at Casson's. We will let you know how the
results of the questionnaire will improve our service to you.

Sincerely yours,

Susan Shapiro

Susan Shapiro
Customer Services

Encl. Questionnaire

---

of the sheet; directly beneath the question, list horizontally the options (the
range of choices) that the question offers. For dichotomous questions you will
have two columns; for multiple-choice, as many columns as there are choices.
For closed questions, be sure to include the category "no response" in a separate column. If respondents give two contradictory answers to one question,
indicate "no response" in your tally. You have no means of knowing which
answer was intended.

With separate tally sheets for every question, you will be ready to tabulate responses. When a questionnaire comes in, assign it a code number. The first questionnaire to be returned could be labeled 01, the second 02, the third 03, and so forth. List the identifying numbers (and the names of respondents, if requested, after the numbers) vertically on the left-hand side of each tally sheet. Then, as you check each questionnaire in, you can record a respondent's answer to an individual question in the correct column on the appropriate tally sheet. Figure 9.5 (p. 278) illustrates a sample master tally sheet for question 1.

The use of separate tally sheets for each question offers these advantages:

1. You are better able to tabulate, organize, and summarize responses for each question, since all answers to that question are on one sheet.
2. You can more easily check responses against individual questionnaires, since each response is coded by identification and question number.
3. You have the flexibility of comparing responses to various questions by simply pulling tally sheets for these questions and laying the sheets side by side.
4. You have a record of the number of questionnaires returned by any specific date.
5. You can conveniently keep a running tally and will not have to wait until all your questionnaires are in to begin counting.

Coding and tabulating open-ended questions may present problems. You will have to make option columns as you go along, but still impose some type of manageable limits on these options. When you read essay answers, use a highlighter pen to mark the exact comment that most relevantly answers the question. That comment may be buried in a thicket of useless remarks; the highlighter pen will make it stand out. A different color highlighter pen can be used to identify statements you foresee quoting directly in your report, thus making them easier to find later.

▶ Writing Effective Reports

After tabulating the responses, you will have to write a report on your findings. The report should accomplish three functions: (1) summarize the range of responses, (2) draw conclusions, and (3) make recommendations. The report may be brief—a one-page memo or a two-page letter will suffice. At first you may wonder if such a memo or letter is long enough, considering the time and effort you have devoted to the project. But the chief function of the report is to consolidate responses and comment on them. The report should give readers the big picture, of which individual questionnaires are only a part. Providing generalizations based on individual responses, the report does not duplicate every response you have obtained or identify every individual who made a response. If so, the results would not have to be tabulated and summarized. You could simply give the completed questionnaires to readers.

Fig. 9.5   A tally sheet.

		YES	NO	
	Question 1: Have you ever served in the Armed Forces ?			
		YES	NO	
01	John Malone		X	
02	Bill Brownly	X		
03	Kathy Rivers	X		
04	Ruth Tapes		X	
05	Henry Stuart		X	
06	Tim Gordon	X		
07	Shirley McManus		X	
08	Debbie Buzak	X		
09	Donald Shatz		X	
10	Willa Jackson		X	
11	Bruce Page	X		
12	Mary Holka		X	
13	Frances Watts		X	
14	Richard Saperstein	X		
15	Terry Myers		X	
16	Roberta Zimmerman		X	
17	Paula Huppard		X	
18	Chris Sholds	X		
19	John Tzarki	X		
20	Billy Lamar	X		
21	Lucy Bennini		X	
22	Marge Appleby	X		
TOTALS		10	12	

Writing a report means being selective. Selectivity is not a problem with responses to closed questions. Unless a respondent provides two choices for a dichotomous or multiple-choice question, you will simply tabulate his or her response with all the others you receive. Open-ended questions are more challenging to summarize. Respondents will include more than you can use; while some of their information may be extremely interesting, it may also be irrelevant. Remember, the report is not a catchall for every comment written in response to an open-ended question. Your report should reflect only those answers that will help readers reach a decision. Figure 9.6 contains a sample report and the questionnaire on which it is based. Study this report to see how information is selected and condensed. You might want to refer to this report throughout the following discussion.

Fig. 9.6   A report and the questionnaire on which it is based.

TO: Professor Marion Andretti
           Faculty Adviser, the Campus Informer
FROM: Debrah H. Hinkel, Bob Banks, Joe Moore, Alice Frantione
SUBJECT: Student Opinion of the Campus Informer
DATE: September 24, 1982

Since a number of us have recently joined the staff of the Informer, we wanted to assess student opinion of the campus newspaper in order to guide our future editorial decisions. To obtain a clearer sense of students' needs, we distributed the enclosed questionnaire to a random sample of 300 students out of 1,800 students at Detroit Community College during the week of September 1–7.

Two hundred students replied, giving us a fair cross section. Respondents came from every major in occupational education, with a slight majority (42 percent) representing three areas—nursing, automotive mechanics, and retail merchandising. Since many of our respondents (53 percent) have spent at least two semesters at DCC, they are familiar with the campus.

For the most part, these respondents are loyal readers of the Informer. Fifty–four percent read each issue of the paper, while 31 percent said they look at the paper at least once a week. Only 7 percent admitted that they rarely read the Informer. Of most interest to our readers are articles on campus events and sporting activities, the two areas ranked first and second by 76 percent of the students. Sixty–nine percent of the students noted that the ads were the third most significant reason for reading the paper. News of academic programs and school clubs ranked fourth and fifth in student interest, according to 71 percent of the respondents.

Most students (68 percent) think the <u>Informer</u> should continue to be published twice a week, although a small percentage of these students (21 percent, or 27 students) want to see the <u>Informer</u> come out on Monday and Friday rather than on Tuesday and Friday. There was little support for a daily paper (20 percent) and even less for a weekly or bimonthly one (12 percent). (Students probably think there is not enough news for a daily paper, and that news would be too old if it appeared a week or two weeks late.)

The <u>Informer</u> did not receive very high marks on its appearance. Forty-six percent of the students thought the layout was only average, while 23 percent of the students believed that the size of our type is too small, that the blue color of our paper is too dark, and the placement of articles is inconsistent. Gladys Potter, a sophomore welding major, offered this representative comment: "It's hard to follow a story when it is continued on one or two other pages, because the subsequent headlines aren't always clear." A related complaint deals with our photographs. Although 27 percent of the students thought we use enough, 42 percent would like to see us use more. "Stories are more enjoyable when an accompanying picture clarifies or highlights the action," stated a business student who has been at DCC for three semesters. Students were much more satisfied with the way articles are written. Seventy-two percent thought that the language was easy to understand.

There was also a consensus about retaining our "Faculty Profile" feature. Eighty-two percent of the students like to know about the faculty. As one graphic arts major put it: "I find it interesting to learn about a teacher's hobbies, family, and professional accomplishments."

RECOMMENDATIONS:

Based upon the responses to our questionnaire, and especially to the last question on proposed major changes in the paper, we offer the following recommendations:

1. Increase the point size of type and change the color of our paper from blue to white or cream for easier reading.

2. Try to use more photographs, especially in our coverage of sports events.

3. Expand our ads section and group together different types of ads—jobs, items for sale, housing, entertainment——and supply a heading for each group.

4. Run our "Faculty Profile" in each issue, rather than printing it only once or twice a month.

Please take a few minutes to fill out the following questionnaire about the Campus Informer, our student newspaper. We on the newspaper staff are eager to know what you think about the paper so that we can make sure that it serves your needs. Please return your questionnaire to Debrah H. Hinkel, the editor, at Scott Hall 107 by Tuesday, September 14. If you have any questions, drop by the newspaper office in Scott Hall or call 264-3450 between noon and six p.m. Your viewpoints are important. Thanks. Please feel free to sign or not sign your name.

Name_____

1. How many semesters have you attended Detroit Community College?
   ___ 1
   ___ 2
   ___ 3
   ___ 4
   ___ more than 4

2. What is your major?_____

3. How often do you read the Informer?
   ___ twice a week, or every time it comes out
   ___ once a week
   ___ once every two weeks
   ___ I rarely look at it

4. Rank your reason for reading the Informer (first=1, second=2, etc.)
   ___ find out about sports events
   ___ learn more about academic programs
   ___ look at the ads
   ___ follow campus events
   ___ learn more about campus clubs

5. How often would you like to see the Informer published?
   ___ daily
   ___ twice a week (as it is now)
   ___ once a week
   ___ once every two weeks

6. How would you evaluate the Informer's layout (its physical appearance)?
   ___ outstanding
   ___ very good
   ___ average
   ___ poor

```
 7. Is the Informer written in clearly understood language?
    ___ yes
    ___ no

 8. What do you think of the number of pictures used in the Informer?
    ___ not enough
    ___ just right
    ___ too many

 9. Should the Informer continue to run its "Faculty Profile"
    feature?
    ___ run as is (once or twice a month)
    ___ run more often (every issue)
    ___ run less often (once every two months)
    ___ delete it

10. What one major change would you like to make in the Informer?
```

Rules for Writing Numbers

Your report will rely heavily on numbers, especially percentages. Spell out the word *percent* in a report; do not use a symbol (%). When listing responses in terms of percentages, express the specific percentage in numbers, not words:

> *Incorrect:* Because of inflation, fifty-eight percent of the workers will not buy a new car this year.
>
> *Correct:* Because of inflation, 58 percent of the workers will not buy a new car this year.

Remember one exception to listing percentages as figures. If a percentage begins a sentence, write the percentage *as a word:*

> *Incorrect:* 55 percent of the sales force thought that the new lights were easy on their eyes.
>
> *Correct:* Fifty-five percent of the sales force thought that the new lights were easy on their eyes.

You can also list a percentage parenthetically:

> *Correct:* A majority of students (75 percent) prefer the quarter to the semester system.

The word *percentage* should not be used for *percent. Percentage* is used without numbers to indicate a range or a size:

> *Incorrect:* A large percent of the residents favored the new health care policies.
>
> *Incorrect:* A thirty-five percentage of the residents favored the new health care policies.
>
> *Correct:* A large percentage of the residents favored the new health care policies.

Explaining What the Numbers Mean

Numbers in your report will make it effective and impressive. However, beware of letting figures speak for themselves. Your report is not a statistical table. Organize and assess the numbers you include by telling readers what those numbers mean, why they are important, and how they characterize various opinions. Numbers are most meaningful when they are placed in a context readers will understand and welcome. Avoid writing a wooden opening that provides no background information:

> *Poor:* A fifteen-question questionnaire was distributed to forty students at Coe Community College between the dates of February 15 and February 28, 1980.

Provide a brief explanation of the reasons why you constructed and distributed the questionnaire. Supply information that will help readers connect your topic to the need you saw to question people about it. The lifeless opening just cited could be transformed for the reader's benefit into this kind of introduction:

> *Good:* For the last two semesters, students at Coe Community College have complained about the textbook rental service. In order to determine what types of changes students wanted, I constructed a questionnaire and sent it to forty students from seven different majors.

In discussing responses to specific questions, use numbers selectively. Prepare readers for the numbers you cite. Do not overwhelm readers with a series of unorganized and uninterpreted figures. If you simply list every response to every question, you will confuse readers. It is your job to impose some order by briefly and simply summarizing the responses.

> *Poor:* Question 2 asked respondents: "How long have you lived in the Hillcrest subdivision?" Twenty-seven percent said they lived in Hillcrest for more than five years; 17 percent indicated they were residents there for at least three years; 34 percent said they lived in Hillcrest for more than one year; and 22 percent said they lived in Hillcrest for less than one year.

> *Good:* A clear majority of the respondents (78 percent) have lived in the Hillcrest subdivision for more than one year.

Here is another example in which unorganized responses are thrown at the reader:

> *Poor:* For question 3 ("How would you evaluate the service you received after the sale?"), respondents answered as follows: 35 percent said it was all right but a little slow; 25 percent thought it was not adequate; and 40 percent said they had no complaints.

To eliminate confusion, divide the responses into two manageable groups. Readers will profit from a conclusion such as the following:

> *Good:* Customers were generally satisfied with the service after the sale; only 25 percent answered that it was inadequate.

The revision above shows the writer's desire to present only essential facts. For example, in reporting responses to yes/no questions, there is no need to give percentages for both the yes answers and the no answers: 75 percent liked the new office hours; 25 percent did not. When you write that 75 percent liked the new office hours, you do not have to tell the reader that 25 percent did not. Of course, if a number of respondents left the question blank, you will have to state that fact.

Using Direct Quotations

In addition to recording percentages, you may want to include a few direct quotations for emphasis. A direct quotation, if it is carefully worded, can serve three useful functions: (1) it can precisely capture the views of an entire group, (2) it might contain a colorful or apt expression that can enliven your report, and (3) it can lend support to your recommendation, especially if it comes from a recognized authority. Because of their summary power, direct quotations will make your report more compact, relevant, and credible.

Choose direct quotations carefully and use them sparingly. Figure 9.6, for example, contains only three quotations. To avoid bias, try not to use the same person for each quotation you cite; your report will appear prejudiced if you do not give equal time to both sides. If you are distributing a questionnaire on grading procedures at your college, you might ask whether students prefer one comprehensive final examination to a number of tests. By recording only the following quotation, you would present an unfair picture of students as being lazy:

> Students in favor of a single comprehensive final examination liked the freedom from daily preparation and weekly quizzes. As a sophomore majoring in environmental resources noted, "You're playing Russian roulette, but it's worth it for the extra time you have during the semester."

By adding the following observation, you will be giving a more balanced view:

> Those opposed to a single, comprehensive examination, however, worried that they could have a bad day or not know what the instructor was looking for. A junior plant science major summarized much of this group's thinking when she wrote, "I want to have more than one chance to make a good grade."

Before using a direct quotation, always obtain permission. If given, put the exact words of the person you are quoting in double quotation marks. And, whenever possible, identify the respondent by name, status, position, or major.

Writing a Recommendation

A recommendation should show readers how to transform respondents' answers into action. You can recommend that readers perform certain actions (often by a set time), refrain from performing actions, or choose between alternatives.

Make your recommendations specific and clear-cut. Readers will not benefit from general or indecisive comments. Since profits, customer satisfaction, and improved service may depend on your recommendations, be precise. If you hedge, you betray both respondents and readers. To say that you are not sure what should be done reveals shortcomings. The following recommendations leave no doubt concerning a definite course of action:

> Based on the respondents' answers, I recommend that we do three things:
>
> - Expand the employee parking lot to include space for one hundred more cars by August 1, 1984.
> - Install gates around the parking lot.
> - Station a security guard on Norris Street between shifts to direct traffic.

Keep your recommendation section short. A single concluding paragraph should be enough. You might want to list recommendations as separate items, each preceded by a raised period, or bullet, as the example above shows, or by numbers, as in Fig. 9.6. Or you may want to give your recommendations without itemizing them, as in Fig. 9.7. Do not repeat unnecessary percentages and comments you have already listed in your report. Focus instead on the way readers can accomplish what respondents do or do not want. Usually your recommendation will be easy to formulate. It will entail implementing what the majority of respondents want done. Your hardest job will be finding a practical solution to the problem as the respondents define it. It would be foolish to express the reverse of what respondents want without hard facts to back up your opposition. By so doing, you invalidate your questionnaire and discredit yourself. Your recommendation should help readers; they are looking for facts to support the right decision.

In some instances, however, you will find that opinions on a crucial issue are almost equally divided. With no majority opinion to guide you (and your readers), your recommendation will take on added significance. Make a recommendation, but admit that opinion is divided. Mary Snyder in Fig. 9.7 endorses the city of Madison as the convention site but includes a necessary

Fig. 9.7   A report, the questionnaire on which it is based, and a cover letter.

```
TO:      Gerald Morgan, President, Northern Chapter WREA
FROM:    Mary Snyder  MS
SUBJECT: Report on Convention Preference Questionnaire
DATE:    6 February 1981


     Four weeks ago, when the state office asked us to poll our chapter
members about their preferences for this year's convention, I
volunteered to prepare, distribute, and summarize the results of a
questionnaire. Judging from the responses to that questionnaire (a copy
of which is attached), distributed over the last three weeks, next
year's convention will be well attended and productive. One hundred of
our 136 members returned the questionnaire: 22 secretaries/recep-
```

tionists, 57 salespersons, 12 brokers, and 9 builders. Eighty-five percent of these individuals attended last year's convention in Green Bay.

Opinion is sharply divided between Madison (38 percent) and Milwaukee (35 percent) for the site of the convention. Respondents were more in agreement when it came to the length of the convention; 69 percent want it to last 2½ days during the week, not the weekend. Pat Laskey, a salesperson from Door County, added later in his questionnaire that "if the convention were any shorter, we could not get our business completed; if it were any longer we would be away from the office too long." Many members want to get back home the third day.

To get to the convention, 64 percent of our members will come by car. Actually, the number of cars will be less, since twenty respondents expressed an interest in forming a carpool when asked for further suggestions in question 13. Sixty-one percent of our members will bring spouses with them. This preference plus the fact that some of our members will be sharing rooms accounts for the large request for single rooms with double beds (41 percent) and twin beds (33 percent).

An impressive majority (88 percent) wants the annual presidential address scheduled for the banquet. This may be one of the few times our chapter members see each other at meals. Sixty-seven percent disliked the idea of having meals included in the price of the convention. A representative comment comes from Marsha Jabolowicz, a receptionist from Rhinelander, "I want to be able to go to different places suited to my schedule; I do not want to be tied to a rigid itinerary." If they miss each other at meals, members may likely see each other at night spots. Forty percent prefer going to a nightclub for convention entertainment; and 32 percent voted for dancing ("a swinging disco") to be included.

Our members will represent our chapter in force on state committees. Eight-two percent have agreed to serve on a committee; the committee on marketing captured the attention of 59 members.

RECOMMENDATIONS:

On the basis of these responses, I think we should tell the state office that our members prefer a 2½-day convention in Madison, although Milwaukee is a strong alternate location. We will need a large block of double occupancy rooms; and meals should not be part of the convention package, but dancing or a nightclub should. Further, our members want the presidential address delivered at the banquet.

Our members' preferences are clear in most instances. In forwarding their responses to the state office, I would recommend that we try to charter a bus for those individuals (36 percent) who did want group transportation provided.

A Questionnaire on
Preferences for the 1981 Convention of
the Wisconsin Real Estate Association

Dear Members of the Northern Chapter of the WREA:

Please complete the following questionnaire so that our state office will be better able to plan for this year's convention. Your comments will help make this year's gathering even more productive than last year's.

Thank you for returning your questionnaire to me by 30 January. A stamped self-addressed envelope is included. If you have any questions, please write or call me.

Sincerely yours,

Mary Snyder

Mary Snyder
Mary's Realty
724 Kane Avenue
Superior, WI 54880
882-5030

Name_____

Business address_____

Business telephone_____

Home address_____

Home telephone_____

1. What kind of membership do you hold in the WREA?
   ___ secretary/receptionist
   ___ salesperson
   ___ broker
   ___ builder

2. Did you attend last year's WREA convention in Green Bay?
   ___ yes
   ___ no

3. Where would you like the 1981 WREA convention to be held?
   ___ Milwaukee
   ___ Madison
   ___ Eau Claire
   ___ La Crosse
   ___ other (please specify)_____

4. How long would you like the convention to last?
   ___ 1 day
   ___ 1½ days
   ___ 2 days
   ___ 2½ days
   ___ 3 days

5. When would like the convention to be held?
   ___ during the week
   ___ on the weekend

6. How would you like to travel to the convention?
   ___ by car
   ___ by bus
   ___ fly
   ___ have group transportation provided

7. Will your spouse accompany you?
   ___ yes
   ___ no

8. What kinds of accommodation will you need?
   ___ single room (one bed)
   ___ single room (two twin beds)
   ___ single room (two double beds)
   ___ two rooms

9. When should the presidential address be given?
   ___ at a breakfast meeting
   ___ at a luncheon meeting
   ___ at a banquet
   ___ alone–at a separate meeting

10. Would you prefer to see meals included in the cost of the convention fees?
    ___ yes
    ___ no

11. What type of entertainment do you think the WREA should provide at the convention?
    ___ dancing
    ___ theater
    ___ night club
    ___ other (please specify)

```
12. Which state committees would you be willing to serve on?
    ___ finance
    ___ marketing
    ___ appraisal
    ___ planning
    ___ I do not want to serve on a committee

13. Please add any further comments about any of the previous questions
    or any other relevant topic you think the WREA should consider.
```

warning. There may be times, too, when a majority opinion still calls for qualification. In recommending that a chartered bus be ordered, Ms. Snyder in Fig. 9.7 at once acknowledges the majority's wishes, but still allows for the most flexible interpretation of the responses. No one loses by the recommendation that she submitted.

▶ Exercises

1. Write a memo to an employer—previous or current—about a specific problem that needs investigation. Indicate why a questionnaire would be the best means of gathering information and stress how the results would lead to increased sales, better service, or greater productivity. In your memo specify whom you will question, how you will get their names and addresses, and the timetable you will follow in constructing the questionnaire, distributing it, making a tally, and writing the report.

2. Select some area of interest to a civic organization, club, fraternity or sorority, union, or church group to which you belong. In a letter to the president of this organization, explain how a questionnaire on this specific area would help the group—in membership, long-range planning, meetings, dues, etc. Volunteer to construct a questionnaire and to distribute it to members of the organization.

3. Write an appropriate closed question (dichotomous, multiple-choice, ranking, or fill-in-the-blank) for each one of the following topics. Where necessary, supply appropriate options.
   (a) marital status
   (b) health
   (c) income
   (d) religion
   (e) credit rating
   (f) expectation for promotion

(g) vacation preferences
(h) a household product
(i) college tuition
(j) local liquor laws
(k) medical costs
(l) security on campus
(m) airplanes vs. buses for travel
(n) writing a résumé
(o) reduced rates for senior citizens
(p) garbage pickup
(q) a local television station
(r) telephone service

4. The following closed questions (and some of their options) are incorrectly worded. Rewrite the questions and the options to eliminate vague terms, loaded words, jargon, overlapping responses, double adjectives, an insufficient range of responses, and the other kinds of errors discussed in this chapter.

(a) Should our city risk legalizing gambling?   yes___   no___

(b) Are people upset with the new leash
laws?   yes___   no___

(c) I find everything I need at one store.   true___   false___

(d) What kind of classes do you like?
___ morning
___ afternoon
___ evening
___ fifty-minute
___ seventy-minute

(e) Do you regularly read a newspaper or current events magazine?   yes___
no___

(f) Would you characterize yourself as being carpophagous?   yes___ no___

(g) Do you agree that teaching sex education in our schools has lead to more teenage pregnancies, abortions, and loose morals in our already too permissive society?   agree___ disagree___

(h) Are you married or divorced?   yes___ no___

(i) What kind of beverage do you like?
___ coffee
___ tea
___ milk
___ soft drinks
___ carbonated drinks

(j) Do you vote in all elections as a patriotic citizen?   yes___ no___

(k) Have you purchased any articles of clothing recently?   yes___ no___

(l) Into which group would you place yourself?
___ full-time employee
___ part-time employee

___ work weekends only
___ work nights

(m) Don't you think our government has spent too much money on relocating refugees?   yes___ no___

(n) Did you see the recession coming four years ago?   yes___ no___

(o) Give the name of the person who, in your opinion, cheats most on the time card:_____

(p) How often do you ride your bicycle?
___ not very often
___ a few times
___ several times
___ as much as I can

(q) Rank the following in their order of importance to you:
___ fringe benefits
___ health insurance policy
___ two-weeks paid vacation
___ company car

(r) Is your education meaningful to you now?   yes___ no___

(s) Where do you live?
___ with my parents
___ in a trailer court
___ in a duplex
___ by myself
___ in an apartment building

(t) All housing loans should be guaranteed by the federal government, shouldn't they?   yes___ no___

(u) Do you like to swim and to fish?   yes___ no___

(v) Did the RPT come in the morning or the afternoon?   A.M.___ P.M.___

(w) Do you understand enough mathematics to be able to complete this simple form by yourself?   yes___ no___

(x) Haven't students at Northeast College been forced to wait too long for an official transcript of their work to be sent out?   yes___ no___

(y) What is your opinion of the economics textbook you have used this term?
___ It is excellent; I have really understood difficult concepts.
___ It is great; I like the way information is clearly listed.
___ It is horrible; I think it is confusing.
___ It is very bad; I never was given enough examples.

(z) Would you ever consider associating yourself with a union?   yes___ no___

5. Rewrite the following open-ended questions to make them more precise and answerable.

   (a) What kinds of experiences have you had in the hospital?
   (b) What improvements in city services are necessary in the future?
   (c) Describe your philosophy of life.
   (d) What kinds of entertainment do you like?
   (e) Compare and contrast the kinds of housing opportunities in your town.

    (f) What appeals to you about your chosen career?
    (g) Comment on any changes you have seen in the last year.
    (h) Describe in detail all the lectures you have attended this term.
    (i) What kinds of investments should a family make today?
    (j) Comment on the state of the environment.
    (k) Tell me all you know about horse husbandry.
    (l) Should transportation be increased?
    (m) Does the government impose too many regulations on citizens?
    (n) What are some problems in higher education today?
    (o) What agencies are most successful today?
    (p) Evaluate the significance of dairy farming on the national economy.
    (q) Discuss food management.
    (r) What are your career opportunities?
    (s) What kinds of information are important to you in your work?

6. The following questionnaire contains unclear instructions, an inconsistent format, poorly worded and irrelevant questions, and inappropriate options. Rewrite the instructions and the questionnaire.

> Hi, how are you today? We think that it would be a good idea for everyone to participate soon in a coffee fund. Complete the enclosed questionnaire soon and return it to me. You will have to circle some of the responses, check others, and write in still some others. Answer all the questions you feel confident about. If you check "I do not drink coffee" for any of the responses, use a pen or pencil; this will help flag your answer. If you do not check this as a response, use a blue or black pen. When you see questions asking for opinions you would rather not give, answer them anyway.

    (1) Do you like working here?   yes___ it's all right___ no___

    (2) How long have you worked in this office?   0–1 month___ 3–12 months___
        1–3 years___ 4–8 years___ more than 8 years but less than 12 years___
        more than 12 years___

    (3) What is your current salary?_____ Is it fair?_____

    (4) Do you have a cup of coffee before work?   yes___ I do not drink coffee___
        sometimes___ no___ it varies___

    (5) When do you drink most of your coffee?   AM___ PM___ nights___

    (6) Where do you get your coffee while at work?
        ___ I bring a Thermos bottle from home.
        ___ I purchase it before coming to work.
        ___ I stop off at a restaurant and have it.
        ___ I borrow some.
        ___ I do not drink coffee.

    (7) How much coffee do you drink at work?
        ___0–2 cups a day ___1–2 cups ___3–5 cups ___more than 5 cups a
        day ___I do not drink coffee ___I seldom drink coffee at work

    (8) How do you like your coffee? Circle one of the following:
    (a) black   (c) freshly perked
    (b) black with sugar   (d) decaffeinated

(e) cream   (h) freeze-dried

(f) milk   (i) decaffeinated freeze-dried

(g) dry roasted   (j) mellow roast blend

(9) Would you like to have a coffee fund in our office?
  (a) Yes, right now.
  (b) Yes, not right now.

  If you circled (b), answer one of the following:
  __within the next month
  __within the next six months
  __within the next year
  (c) No, but I would not oppose a coffee fund.
  (d) No, I think it is a bad idea.

(10) Do you think a coffee fund would be a good idea?   yes__ no__

(11) Would a coffee fund bring people together?   yes__ no__ I do not know right now__

(12) Should we let people buy coffee by the single cup? If so, how much should we charge per cup?
  __ we should charge .05¢ a cup
  __ twenty cents a cup
  __ thirty-five cents
  __ whatever they want to contribute

(13) Should we allow people outside our office to participate in the coffee fund? yes__ no__ on a limited basis__

(14) How much should we charge people outside the office for a cup of coffee?
  __ ten cents   __ thirty cents
  __ fifteen cents   __ thirty-five cents
  __ twenty cents   __ the same as we pay
  __ twenty-five cents __ twenty to thirty cents a cup
  __ I do not want them to buy our coffee

(15) Who should prepare the coffee and collect for it?
  __ Let's hire a caterer.
  __ Everyone in the coffee fund should take a turn.
  __ We should appoint two people.
  __ We should draw lots.
  __ Each of us should share the responsibility by drawing lots.

(16) Please add any other comments. You might want to again state whether you are in favor of the fund, how much coffee you drink, and whether the office manager should provide the funds or the time to prepare the coffee.

7. Construct a questionnaire for the topic you selected in either question 1 or question 2 above. Distribute it, and then, after tabulating the responses, prepare a report about your findings for your employer or the president of the organization to which you belong. Also supply your employer or president with a blank copy of the questionnaire and a sample cover letter you may have sent out with your questionnaire.

10

Designing Visuals

Experts estimate that as much as 80 percent of our learning comes through the visual sense. Words, of course, form a large part of our visual information. In conjunction with words, visual aids (hereafter shortened to "visuals") convey a giant share of the facts we receive. Visuals are especially useful on the job because they help readers to see what you are discussing. Chapter 10 surveys the kinds of visuals you will encounter most frequently and shows you how to read, construct, and use them.

The kinds of visuals we will deal with can be divided into two categories—tables and figures. A table lists information in parallel columns or rows for easy comparison of data. Anything that is not a table is considered a figure, including graphs, circle charts, bar charts, pictographs, organizational charts, flow charts, maps, photographs, and drawings. Before looking at the various kinds of visuals, you may find it helpful to know more about the benefits they offer and the caution you must exercise in using them.

▶ The Usefulness of Visuals

What can visuals do to improve your written work? Here are four reasons why you should use them. Each of the four points is graphically reinforced in Fig. 10.1.

1. Visuals arouse immediate interest. Their size, shape, color, and arrangement are dramatic. They also offer readers eye relief from looking at sentences and paragraphs. Note how eye-catching (in both number and shape) the symbols are for the world's ten most populous countries repre-

Fig. 10.1   A visual showing the ten most populous countries in 1975.

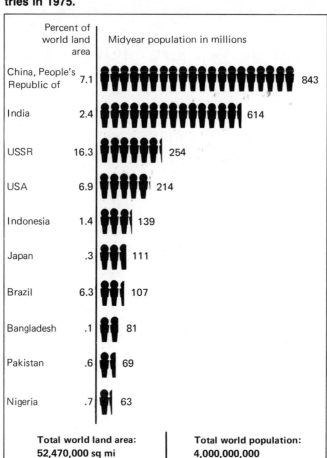

U.S. Department of the Census, *Pocket Data Book, USA 1976* (Washington, D.C : Government Printing Office, 1976), p. 4.

sented in Fig. 10.1. A visual captures readers' attention by setting important information apart.

2. Visuals simplify concepts.   Because many readers are visually oriented, graphics unlock doors of meaning. A visual shows ideas in action when a verbal description may be less forceful or even baffling. The vastness of a country's population and how that population compares with other nations' is much easier to grasp and to remember because of the picture symbols in Fig. 10.1. Simply saying that China has more people than India or the Soviet Union does is not as effective in words as it is in pictures. Other kinds of visuals also make learning easier. For example, a visual could show the interior parts of a machine or enlarge one element of a piece of equipment to clarify its function. Readers would therefore feel more confident about operating the machine or performing a procedure.

3. Visuals condense a large quantity of information into a relatively small space. Figure 10.1 collects twenty different pieces of information about ten countries—their populations and the amount of land they occupy—and records the data in far less space than it would take to describe these facts in words. How many times would a writer have to repeat the words *population, land area, percent, more, less, greater, lower, in comparison,* or *in contrast*? A visual states a fact once without having to repeat it. And even if the writer transcribed all the facts in Fig. 10.1 into words, readers would not be able to understand the percentages as easily as they can because of the rows of symbols.

4. Visuals emphasize relationships. Through the use of arrangement and form, visuals quickly show contrasts, similarities, growth rates, downward and upward movements, spirals, fluctuations in price and time, and the influence of one item on another. Figure 10.1 shows not only how countries compare in population, but also how population compares with land area. India, for example, has about two and one-half times more people than the Soviet Union does, but occupies about one-eighth the space. Other kinds of visuals (pie and bar charts) show the relationship of parts to the whole. And the curve of a graph can indicate the time sequence of various events, such as average annual snowfall.

▶ Choosing Effective Visuals

You will have to select visuals very cautiously. The following suggestions may help you to answer two important questions: (1) When should I use a visual? and (2) How many of them will I need?

1. Use visuals only when they are strictly relevant for your purpose. They should not be included simply as decoration for impressing readers. A short report on fire drills does not need a picture of a fire station to enhance it; a list of instructions on how to write a company order does not require a picture of an individual writing at a table.
2. Use visuals in conjunction with, not as a substitute for, written work. Visuals do not take the place of words. A set of illustrations or a group of tables alone will not satisfy readers looking for evaluations of the details those visuals present.
3. Make sure that visuals do not interfere with your message. Too many visuals (some of them duplicating information in your text) will distract readers. If something is self-explanatory, do not include a visual. Avoid visuals that include many more details than you discuss or, worse yet, that present contradictory information.

4. Consider carefully how helpful a specific visual will be for readers. Elaborate computer-sketched graphs are unnecessarily complex for a community group interested in a clear representation of the rise in food prices over a three-month period. Generally, the less technical your audience, the more helpful a visual is. Determine whether your audience is picture-oriented or word-oriented.

5. Never include a visual of poor quality. Each visual should be clear and easy to read. Do not assume that readers will have magnifying glasses on their desks or that they will not mind a messy drawing or a faded blueprint.

6. When you construct your own visual, do a model or sample first; do not attempt to make a perfect visual on the first try.

▶ Writing About Visuals

Never include a visual without mentioning it in your paper or report. Readers must be told clearly where the visual is located and why it is there. The following guidelines on identifying, inserting, introducing, and interpreting visuals will help you use them more efficiently.

1. Identifying visuals.   Each visual must have a number and/or title that indicates the subject and the way in which it is discussed. An unidentified visual is meaningless.

> Figure 1: Paul Jordan's Work Schedule, January 15–23.
> Figure 3: The Proper Way of Applying a Modified T-Bandage to the Perineum.
> Figure 5: Income Estimation Figures for Weekdale Shopping Center.

If you use a visual that is not your own work, you must identify your source (a specific newspaper, magazine, textbook, federal agency, or individual). If your paper or report is intended for publication, you are required by law to obtain permission to reproduce copyrighted material from the copyright holder.

2. Inserting visuals in the text.   Place visuals as close as possible to the discussion of them. Do not introduce a visual before a discussion of it, for readers will naturally wonder why it is there at all. But do place illustrations at the beginning of a lengthy discussion. Do not force readers to go through an elaborate discussion and then present a visual that would have simplified that discussion. Be sure to tell readers where the visual is found—"directly below," "on the opposite page," "to the right," "at the bottom of the next page." If the visual is small enough, insert it directly in the text (rather than on a separate page).

3. Introducing visuals.   Refer to the visual by its number and, if necessary, mention the title as well. In introducing the visual, though, do not just insert a reference to it; relate the visual to the context of your discussion.

Here are three ways of writing a lead-in sentence for visuals:

> *Poor:* Our store saw a dramatic rise in the shipment of electric ranges over the five-year period as opposed to the less impressive increase in washing machines. (See Figure 3.)

This sentence does not tie the visual represented in Figure 3 into the sentence where it belongs. The visual just trails insignificantly behind.

> *Improved:* As Figure 3 shows, our store saw a dramatic rise in the shipment of electric ranges over the five-year period as opposed to the less impressive increase in washing machines.

Mentioning the visual in Figure 3 at the beginning is distracting. Readers will want to stop and look at the visual immediately.

> *Best:* Our store's dramatic rise in the shipment of electric ranges over the five-year period, as opposed to the less impressive increase in washing machines, is shown in Figure 3.

This sentence is the best of the three because the figure reference and the explanation are in the same sentence, but the reference is not a distraction.

4. Interpreting visuals. In addition to mentioning a visual by number and title, it may also be necessary to tell readers why it is there and what specifically to look for. Of course, you should not spend time repeating information that is obvious from looking at the visual. But there will be occasions when you will want to (or have to) interpret the visual for an audience. A director of an alumni association, eager to sell alumni life insurance, used the following table and then supplied a "sales" conclusion for it:

> Consider this table based upon the U.S. Department of Labor Consumer Price Index for the past ten years. The value of insurance-benefit dollars decreases right along with dollars used in everyday expenses.

Average annual inflation rates

Year	Inflation Rate	Relative Dollar Value
1969	5.4	$1.00
1970	5.9	.95
1971	4.3	.89
1972	3.3	.85
1973	6.2	.82
1974	10.9	.77
1975	9.1	.69
1976	5.8	.63
1977	6.5	.60
1978	7.7	.55
1979	11.3	.51
1980	12.2	.45

If you haven't looked at your life insurance coverage recently, you may be surprised. Benefit levels thought sufficient just a few years ago may be inadequate for current and future needs. For example, a $10,000 benefit from 1969 would have to be increased to $22,222 in 1980 to provide the same level of protection.

Sometimes the figures in a visual tell an incomplete or misleading story and you will need to interpret them in context. In a study on the benefits of vanpooling, one writer supplied the following visual:

Travel time (in minutes): Automobile versus vanpool

Private Automobile	*Vanpool*
25	32.5
30	39.0
35	45.5
40	52.0
45	58.5
50	65.0
55	71.5
60	78.0

Source: U.S. Department of Transportation, *Increased Transportation Efficiency Through Ridesharing: The Brokerage Approach*, Washington, D.C., January, 1977, DOT-OS-40096, p. 45.

The writer also called attention to what the visual did not say:

Although it is estimated that the travel time in a vanpool may be as much as 30% longer than in a private automobile (to allow for pickups), the total trip time for the vanpool user can be about the same as with a private automobile because vanpools eliminate the need to search for parking spaces and walk to the employment site entrance.[2]

▶ Tables

Tables, or parallel columns or rows of information, often present statistical data that have been compiled over several weeks or months. The figures are then organized and arranged into categories to show changes in time, dis-

---

[1] Example used courtesy Department of Alumni Relations, Northwestern University, Evanston, Illinois.

[2] James A. Devine, "Vanpooling: A New Economic Tool," *AIDC Journal*, 15 (Oct. 1980), 13. Reprinted by permission.

tance, cost, employment, or some other quantifiable variable. The visuals on pp. 299 and 300 are tables.

But the tabular form can present more than numerical information. Lists of words can also be put into tables. Tables in textbooks summarize material for easy recall—causes of wars, symptoms of diseases, provisions of a law. Various forms of business organizations are compared in Table 10.1 (p. 302). Observe how the table easily summarizes much information and arranges it in quickly identifiable categories.

To construct a table properly, you must know how to type and label it. Refer to Table 10.2 (p. 303) as you read the following instructions.

Typing a Table

First determine the size of the table. If it is small (two or three columns) and you include it within the text, make sure that the table is centered on the page and that you use margins. Leave at least one inch of white space above and below the table. If the table has a title, place it at the top (figure titles may go underneath the visual), and triple space before and after the table. You might first want to draw a border and then very neatly with a straightedge (ruler) put in the columns. Then you will have the right spaces and slots in which to insert your numbers or words. Leave enough space between columns so that the table will not look crowded or be difficult to decipher.

If the table is large (running to five or six columns), use a separate sheet of paper. Again, depending on the size of the table, type the rows at the top of the page or turn the piece of paper broadside and then type the table that way. If possible, use the same margins as with the text of your paper. Make sure that the reader can easily understand the numbers and letters of your table.

Labeling a Table

Provide headings for both the column and subcolumns; in Table 10.2 the column is entitled "Years attending," and the subcolumns are the years (1965, 1970, 1975, 1980) about which the table gives data. Also provide a title for the *stub*—the first vertical column on the left-hand side. The stub heading is "Period of service" in Table 10.2. The stub lists the items (the wars and conflicts in which the Lincoln-area veterans participated) that are broken down under the subheadings. To separate the stub title and column/subcolumn headings from the body of the table, draw a rule across the table as in Table 10.2.

Label the categories appropriately and consistently. If some form of measurement is consistently involved, include the unit of measurement as part of the column heading—weight (in pounds), distance (in miles), time (per hour), quantity (per dozen). The unit of measurement should not be repeated for each entry in a column. Also, units should be consistent; do not

Table 10.1 Comparison of forms of business organization

	Single proprietorship	Partnership	Corporation
Ease of organization	Easiest	Moderately difficult	Most difficult
Capital generally available for operation	Least	Intermediate	Most (best able to raise capital)
Responsibility	Centered in one person	Spread among partners	Policy set by directors; president supervises day-to-day operation
Incentive to succeed	Centered in one person	Spread among partners	Spread among many people
Flexibility	Greatest	Intermediate	Least
Ability to perform varied functions (production or purchasing, accounting, selling, etc.)	Dependent on one individual's versatility	Dependent on capabilities of two or more individuals	Best able to employ individuals with different capabilities
Possibility of conflict among those in control	None	Most prone to conflict, especially if partners have equal interest in business	Chain of command reduces internal conflict; wide ownership minimizes disagreement
Taxation	No corporate income tax	No corporate income tax	Corporate income tax
Distribution of profits or losses	All to proprietor	Distributed to partners in accordance with terms of partnership agreement	Profits retained or given to stockholders as dividends; losses reduce price of stock
Liability for debts in event of failure	Unlimited	Unlimited, but spread among partners	Limited to each stockholder's investment
Length of life	Limited by one individual's life span (or until he goes out of business)	Limited (partnership is reorganized upon death or withdrawal of any partner)	Unlimited (with ownership of shares readily transferable)

Source: Reprinted by permission of the publisher from *Introductory Economics*, 4th ed., by Sanford D. Gordon and George G. Dawson (Lexington, Mass.: D. C. Heath and Company, 1980), p. 75.

Table number

Subcolumn heading

Column heading

Table 10.2   Veterans attending Lincoln-area VFW Posts[a]

Period of service	*Years attending*			
	1965	*1970*	*1975*	*1980*
World War I	85	59	55	22
World War II	1415	1330	1309	1100
Korean Conflict	239	240	230	205
Vietnam[b]	62	389	423	585

Source: Lincoln VFW Association ◄——— Origin of data
[a]Does not include Bayside, Morton, or Westover. ⎱ Footnotes
[b]August 1964–May 1975   ⎰

Stub

jump from miles to meters, pounds to ounces.

Wrong:	*Weight*	*Height*
	120 lbs	165 cm
	132 lbs	5′ 9″
	122 lbs	5′ 7″
	58.5 kg	172 cm

Correct:	*Weight* *(in kilograms)*	*Height* *(in centimeters)*
	54.0	165
	55.2	176
	54.9	166
	58.5	172

If something in the table needs to be explained or qualified, put in a foot-note (often signaled by a small raised letter: [a] or [b]) in the table where the in-formation is to be further identified or qualified. The letter will then refer readers to an explanation directly below the table. In Table 10.2 the [a] after the title points to the qualification that three communities are not considered in the Lincoln area when data for the table were gathered. The [b] after the Vietnam entry in the stub clarifies the official dates for that conflict.

▶ Figures

As mentioned at the beginning of this chapter, any visual that is not a table is classified as a figure. We will now look at nine types of useful figures, starting with graphs.

Graphs

Graphs transform numbers into pictures. They take statistical data presented in tables and put them into rising and falling lines, steep or gentle curves. They vividly portray changes, fluctuations, trends, increases and decreases in profits, building permits, employment, energy, temperatures, or any other numbers that change frequently. The way the lines rise and fall in the graph depicts the kinds of changes that are taking place and sometimes helps readers forecast trends. The resulting pictures are more dramatic than tables and are easier to read and interpret. Many issues of the *Wall Street Journal*, for example, contain a graph on the first page for the benefit of busy readers who want a great deal of financial information summarized quickly.

Basically, a graph consists of two lines—a vertical axis and a horizontal axis—that intersect to form a right angle as in Fig. 10.2. The space between the two lines contains the picture made by the graph (in Fig. 10.2 the amount of snowfall in Springfield between Nov. 1979 and April 1980). The vertical line represents the dependent variable; the horizontal line, the independent variable. The dependent variable is influenced most directly by the independent variable, which is almost always expressed in terms of time or distance. Hence, in Fig. 10.2 the given month affects the amount of snow Springfield received. The vertical axis is read from bottom to top; the horizontal axis is read from left to right. When the dependent variable occurs at a particular time on the independent variable (horizontal line), the place where the two

Fig. 10.2   A graph is made by plotting data on the vertical and horizontal axes.

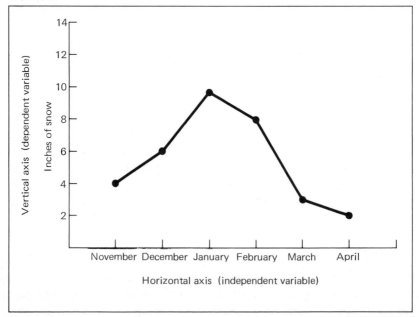

points intersect is marked, or plotted, on the graph. After the points are plotted, a line is drawn to connect them; the resulting curve gives a picture of which months had the greatest snow and which the least and what the overall pattern of snowfall was in Springfield.

The way in which scales are set up is crucial to the success of a graph. Many graphs may not have ranges indicated by equally spaced lines, (tick marks):

But on most of the graphs you construct, use tick lines as a scale to show values, distances, or time as in Fig. 10.2. The topic will dictate the intervals to use. The time scale (independent variable) can be calculated in minutes, hours, days, or years.

A temperature-pulse-respiration graph is illustrated in Fig. 10.3. The day is divided into six 4-hour periods, and seven days are represented on one sheet. The temperature axis is divided into degrees (with .2° differences), and a heavy black line shows the normal line, making it easier to spot dangerous elevations. The pulse measurements are registered in two-beat differences (each dot represents two beats within the larger grouping of tens). And the respirations are also measured in twos, each dot there representing every time a patient takes two breaths. Note that the temperature and pulse scales have *a suppressed zero line*; they begin with 95° and thirty beats, not with zero. It would be impossible to have lower numbers for pulse and temperature and expect a patient to live. But the respiration scale begins with zero because it has a lower range (0–60). If these recordings were expressed in tabular form, they would be hard to follow because they would deprive the reader of a curve depicting much information quickly and impressively.

The graphs in Figs. 10.2 and 10.3 contain only one line per category. But a graph can have multiple lines to show how a number of dependent variables (conditions, products) compare with each other. The relative popularity of beef and veal, pork, and lamb and mutton in the daily diet of Americans can be seen in the graph in Fig. 10.4. The graph contains a separate line for each of these three meat groups. At a glance readers can see how the three meat groups compare and also how many pounds of each group were consumed annually. Note how every group is clearly differentiated from the others by means of dots, dashes, or an unbroken line. Color, if available, can also help distinguish lines. Also, note how each line is clearly labeled so that the label does not cover up other lines or their points of intersection. If the lines do run close together, a *legend*, or explanatory note, underneath or above the graph identifies individual lines. Never put the legend within the graph; readers may confuse legend information for the data depicted in the graph. Although some graphs may contain as many as five or six lines, it is better to limit multiple-line graphs to two or three lines (or dependent variables) so that readers can interpret the graph more easily.

Fig. 10.3   A temperature-pulse-respiration graph showing the breakdown within ranges.

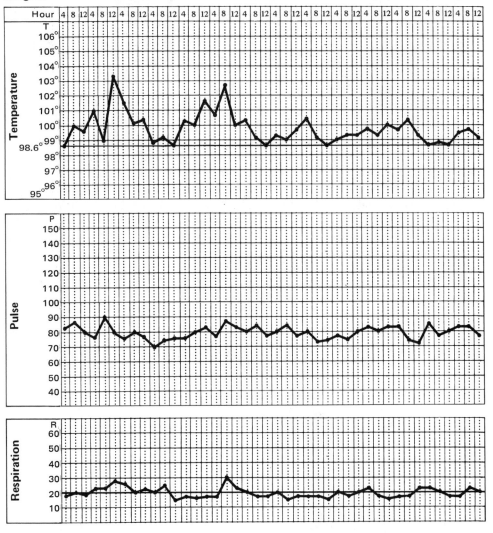

Keep in mind the following guidelines when you construct a graph:

1. Inform readers what your scale is: how many dots, boxes, or spaces equal what amounts or times. You may want to use graph paper that has hatch marks or carefully divided lines.
2. Keep the scale consistent and realistic. If you start with hours, do not switch to days or vice versa. If you are recording annual rates or accounts, do not skip a year or two in the hope that you will save time or be more concise. Do not jump from 1972, 1973, 1974 to 1976, 1977, 1978. Put in all the years you are surveying.

Fig. 10.4   A graph with three dependent variables showing meat consumption per person.

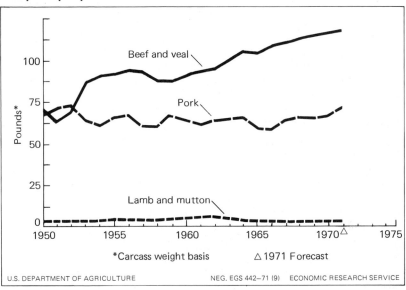

U.S. DEPARTMENT OF AGRICULTURE   NEG. EGS 442–71 (9)   ECONOMIC RESEARCH SERVICE

U.S. Department of Agriculture, *The 1971 Handbook of Agricultural Charts*, Agricultural Handbook, no. 423, p. 72.

3. For some graphs there is no need to begin with a zero, as was seen in Fig. 10.3. For others, you may not have to include numbers beyond seven or eight.
4. Do not draw a line or plot a curve that goes outside the limits of the graph and extends beyond the margin of the page.

Circle Charts

Circle charts are also known as pie charts, a name that descriptively points to their construction and interpretation. The full circle, or pie, represents the whole amount (100 percent)—an entire industry, profession, or population group. The full circle can stand for the entire budget of a company or family, or it can represent just a single dollar of that budget and show how it is broken down for various expenses. Each slice of the pie, then, stands for a part of the whole. A circle chart effectively allows readers to see two things at once—the relationship of the parts to one another and the relationship of the parts to the whole. Figure 10.5 shows an example of a circle chart.

The circle chart is one of the most easily understood illustrations. For that reason, it is popular in government documents (the Bureau of the Census relies heavily on it), financial reports to investors, and advertising. Although many circle charts are based on tables, tables can be very complex and

Fig. 10.5 A circle chart showing the proposed Midtown city budget for 1982.

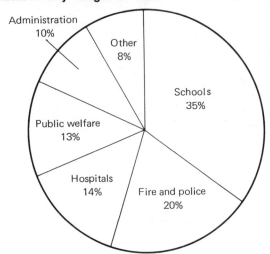

dry and are also more detailed than circle charts. The circle gives percentage totals: the table shows how those percentage groups are broken down.

To construct a successful pie chart, you will need a compass to make your circle and a protractor to measure sections of it. The mathematical principle underlying the construction of the circle chart is simple. A circle contains 360°. Translated into percentages, $100\% = 360°$, $10\% = 36°$, and $1\% = 3.6°$. To determine how much space you need for each of your slices, or wedges, calculate the percentage of the whole it expresses and then multiply that number by 3.6. For example, if you are drawing a circle chart to represent a family's budget, the percentage/degree breakdown might be as follows:

Housing	25%	90.0°
Food	22%	79.2°
Energy	20%	72.0°
Clothes	13%	46.8°
Health care	12%	43.2°
Miscellaneous	8%	28.8°

The following five rules will help you to construct a circle chart:

1. Do not divide a circle, or pie, into too few or too many slices. If you have only three wedges, consider using another type of visual to display them (a bar chart, for example, which will be discussed later). If you have more than seven or eight wedges, you will divide the pie too narrowly, and the overcrowding will destroy the dramatic effect of the illustration. All the individual slices of the pie must total 100 percent.
2. Put the largest slice of the pie first, at the 12:00 o'clock position, and then move clockwise with proportionately smaller slices. Beginning with the biggest slice, you call attention to its importance. (The one exception is

that the "other" category [see rule 3 below] is often placed last, as in the left-hand circle in Fig. 10.5, even though it is larger than one or more of the previously labeled slices.)

3. Avoid listing a number of small slices separately. Rather than individually listing slices of small percentages (2 percent, 3 percent, 4 percent), combine these small pieces into one slice labeled "Other," "Miscellaneous," or "Related Items."

4. Label each slice of the pie. If the slice is large enough, write the identifying term or quantity inside, but make sure that it is easy to read. Do not put in a label upside down or slide it in vertically. All labels should be horizontal for easy reading. If the individual slice of the pie is small, do not try to squeeze in a label. Draw a line to the outside of the pie nearest the slice and write the appropriate label there, as in Fig. 10.5.

5. You can shade or color each slice of the pie to further separate the parts. If you do, be careful not to obscure labels and percentages; also make certain that adjacent slices can be distinguished readily from each other.

Bar Charts

A bar chart shows a series of vertical or horizontal bars to indicate comparisons of statistical data. Vertical bars are used to show increases in quantities (students using a library) in Fig. 10.6. Horizontal bars depict increases in distance (the number of feet the shotput is thrown by a women's track and field

Fig. 10.6   A vertical bar chart showing the number of students using the Adams Memorial Library.

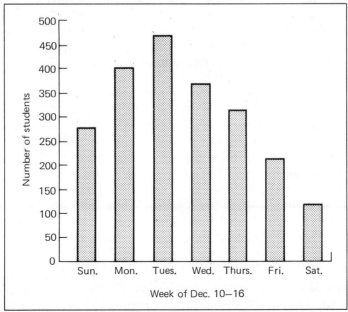

Fig. 10.7   A horizontal bar chart showing length of shotput throws by a women's track and field team.

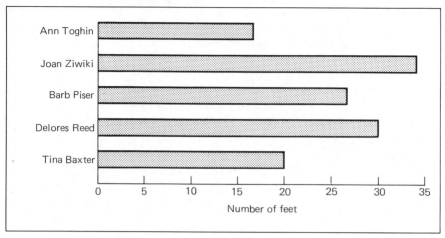

team) in Fig. 10.7. Bar charts make a dramatic visual impression on the audience. They are valuable tools in sales meetings to demonstrate how well (or poorly) a product, a service, the company, or a salesperson has done. You often see bar charts at an office recording the financial goals for the United Way or other charitable drives.

Bar charts are less exact than tables, as Figs. 10.6 and 10.7 show. Note that the number of students using the library or the number of feet the shotput is thrown are not expressed in precise figures, as they would be in a table, but are approximated by the length of the bar. Do not assume, however, that the bar chart is inaccurate; many bar charts are based on tables. What you lose in precision with a bar chart, you gain in visual flair. Another advantage of a bar chart over a line graph is that a bar chart is easier to make. Finally, a bar chart is much more fluid and dynamic than a circle. The circle is static; the bar chart (like the graph) presents a moving view.

When should you use a bar chart rather than a table or graph? Your audience will help you decide. If you are asked to present statistics on costs for the company accountant, use a table. There the reader demands a precise listing; an accountant does not judge a visual by its eye appeal. However, if you are presenting the same information to a group of stockholders or to a diverse group of employees, a bar chart may be more relevant; such readers are interested in seeing the statistics in action. They are more concerned with the effects of change than with underlying causes and precise statistical details. Since it is limited to a few columns, however, a bar chart cannot convey as much information as a table or graph.

Types of Bar Charts

One of the most common types of bar charts is the one shown in Fig. 10.6. Each undivided bar represents one day of the week, and the height of the

Fig. 10.8   A multiple-bar chart showing world cotton exports.

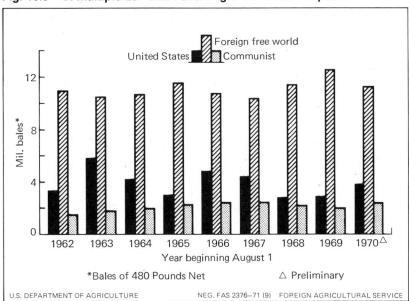

U.S. Department of Agriculture, *The 1971 Handbook of Agricultural Charts,* Agricultural Handbook, no. 423, p. 119.

bar corresponds to the number of students using the library on that day. To read the chart effectively, you simply note where the top of the bar is in relation to the vertical scale on the left. The chart compares one type of data (the number of students using the library) over a period of time (one week in the school year).

Another type of chart—a multiple-bar chart—is represented in Fig. 10.8. Three differently shaded bars are used for each year to represent the amount of cotton exported by three areas of the world. A legend at the top of the chart explains what each bar stands for. This chart measures the same item (cotton exported) over a period of time (nine years) by different countries. Consider how wasteful it would be to provide three separate charts for each of the three areas of the world. It would also be more difficult for readers to compare the exports among the three regions, since the exports would have to be collected separately and then brought together for comparison of the results. A word of caution is in order about multiple-bar charts: Never use more than four bars in a group for any one year. Otherwise, your chart will become crowded and difficult to read.

Still another kind of bar chart is the segmented, or crosshatched (divided), bar, used to show differences within a given category for each comparison. The differences are the components, percentages, or subgroups that make up the whole. A single segmented bar representing the per capita cost for hospital care in 1977 is seen in Fig. 10.9. The entire bar totals $297, the payment for which came from four sources (direct payments, private health

Fig. 10.9 A segmented-bar chart showing per capita hospital care spending by funding source for fiscal year 1977.

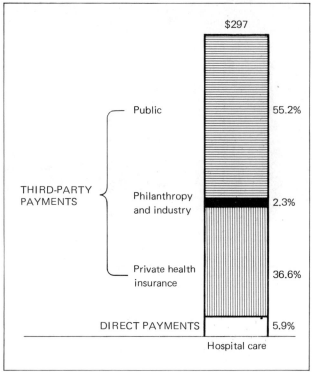

Robert M. Gibson and Charles R. Fisher, "National Health Expenditures 1977," *Social Security Bulletin,* 41 (July 1978), 10.

insurance, philanthropy and industry, and the public). Each of these sources is represented by a different type of shading on the one column. Combined, the multiple sources account for all hospitalization payments.

Making a Bar Chart

To construct a useful bar chart, follow these instructions:

1. Make all the bars the same width; vary only the height (or length) to show differences.
2. Select an appropriate scale, and inform the readers about proportions. Be realistic. Do not construct a bar chart in which columns go off the page or are so small that readers cannot easily note differences. Look at the scale in Fig. 10.6, where each division of the vertical column represents fifty students. Keep such divisions consistent; do not make one ten students and another twenty. Also, begin with zero so that the reader can

correctly chart fluctuations. Use appropriate proportions on the horizontal scale as well.

3. Identify and use distinctive markings and shading on divided bars. Supply a clarifying legend for readers or otherwise indicate the meaning of different portions of a single crosshatched bar, as in Figure 10.9. But do not introduce unnecessary marks or decorations.

Pictographs

Similar to a bar chart, a pictograph uses pictures instead of bars to represent differences in statistical data, as in Fig. 10.1. The pictures or symbols appropriately represent the item(s) being compared. Sometimes the number of pictures indicates change, as in Fig. 10.10, where the cartoon figures show Social Security recipients and workers. A pictograph can also show quantities by increasing the size of the picture or symbol for each year, as in Fig. 10.11, rather than increasing the number of symbols.

If you use a pictograph, it is usually better to increase the number of symbols rather than their size. (Sizes are often difficult to construct accurately and hard for the reader to interpret.) Whatever type of pictograph you use, though, always indicate the precise quantities involved by placing numbers after the pictures so that the reader knows exactly how much the pictures represent.

Fig. 10.10   A pictograph indicating change in the relationship between Social Security recipients and workers.

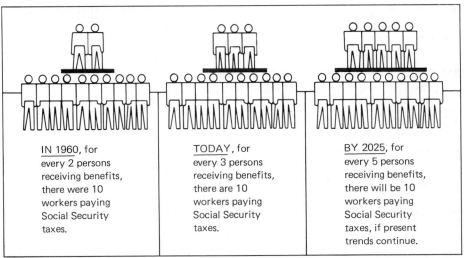

IN 1960, for every 2 persons receiving benefits, there were 10 workers paying Social Security taxes.

TODAY, for every 3 persons receiving benefits, there are 10 workers paying Social Security taxes.

BY 2025, for every 5 persons receiving benefits, there will be 10 workers paying Social Security taxes, if present trends continue.

Reprinted from *U.S. News & World Report*, Jan. 12, 1981, p. 65. Copyright 1981 U.S. News & World Report, Inc.

Fig. 10.11   A pictograph indicating increases in U.S. peanut production.

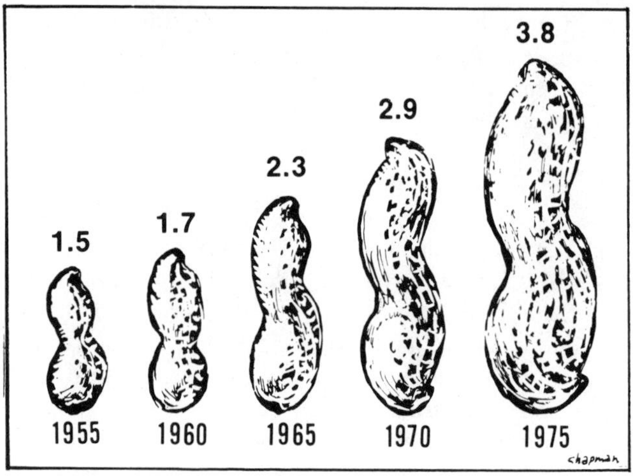

Congressional Quarterly Weekly Report, 34 (Sept. 11, 1976), p. 2483. Reprinted by permission.

Organizational Charts

Unlike the types of charts discussed so far, the organizational chart does not contain statistical data; nor does it record movements in space or time. Rather, it pictures the chain of command in a company or agency, with the lines of authority stretching down from the chief executive, manager, or administrator to assistant manager, department heads, or supervisors to the work force of employees. The organizational chart also shows the various offices, departments, and units out of which the company or agency is constituted and through which orders and information flow. Organizational charts help to inform employees and customers about the composition of the company and also help to coordinate employee efforts in routing information to appropriate departments.

An organizational chart shows relationships by connecting rectangles (boxes), circles, or lines to each other, starting at the top with the chief executive and moving down to lower-level employees. (Sometimes the name of the individual holding the office is listed in addition to the title of the office.) Examine the organizational charts in Fig. 10.12 and 10.13. Positions of equal authority are on parallel lines, and all jobs under the supervision of one individual are joined by bracketing lines. See, for example, the three services directly under the supervision of the Director of Agriculture Economics in Fig. 10.12. Individuals who serve in advisory capacities or who are directly responsible to a higher administrator are listed with broken or dotted lines, as depicted in the unit clerk positions in Fig. 10.13.

Fig. 10.12 An organizational chart showing the major offices that comprise the U.S. Department of Agriculture.

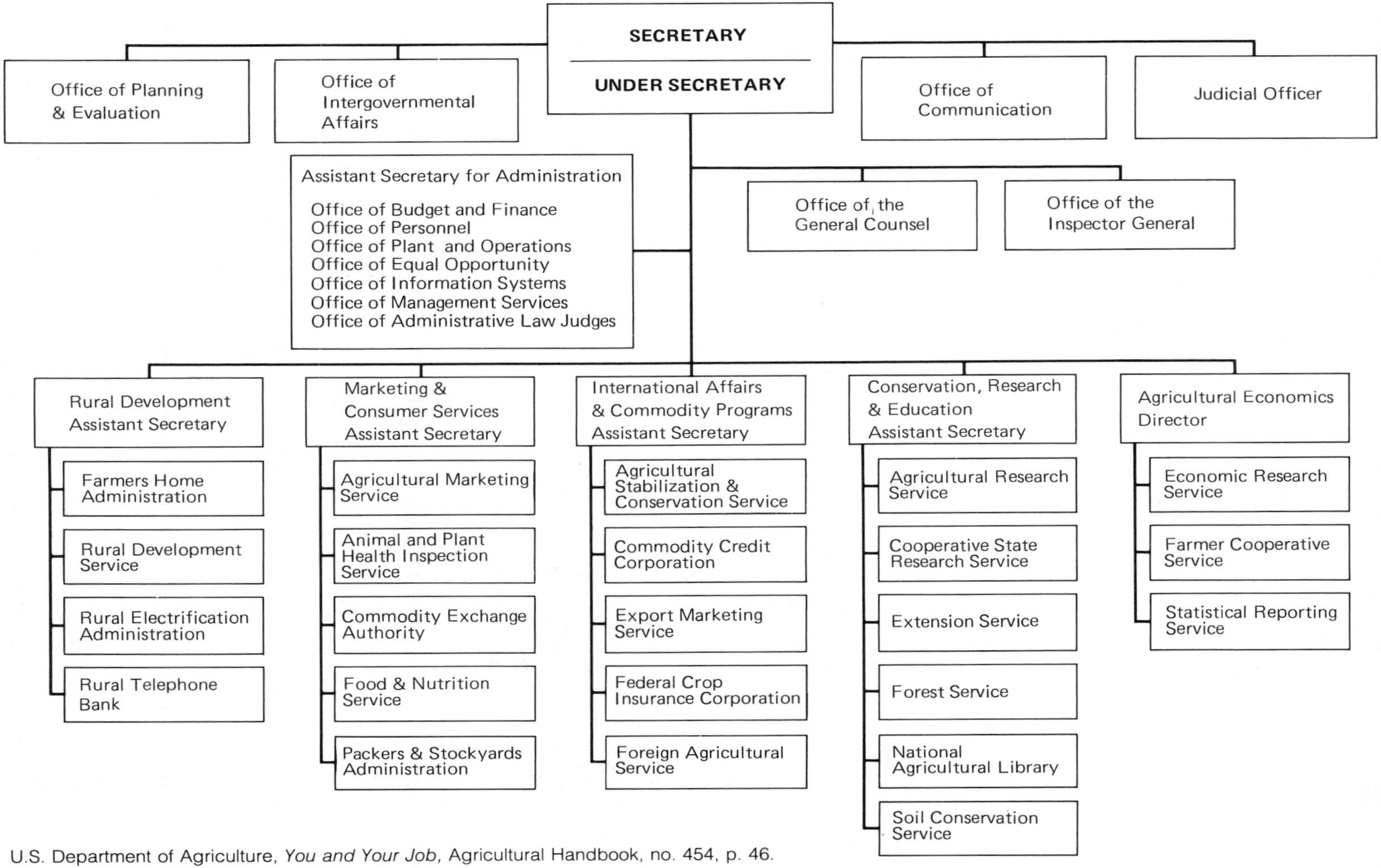

U.S. Department of Agriculture, *You and Your Job*, Agricultural Handbook, no. 454, p. 46.

Fig. 10.13   An organizational chart showing critical care nursing services at Union General Hospital.

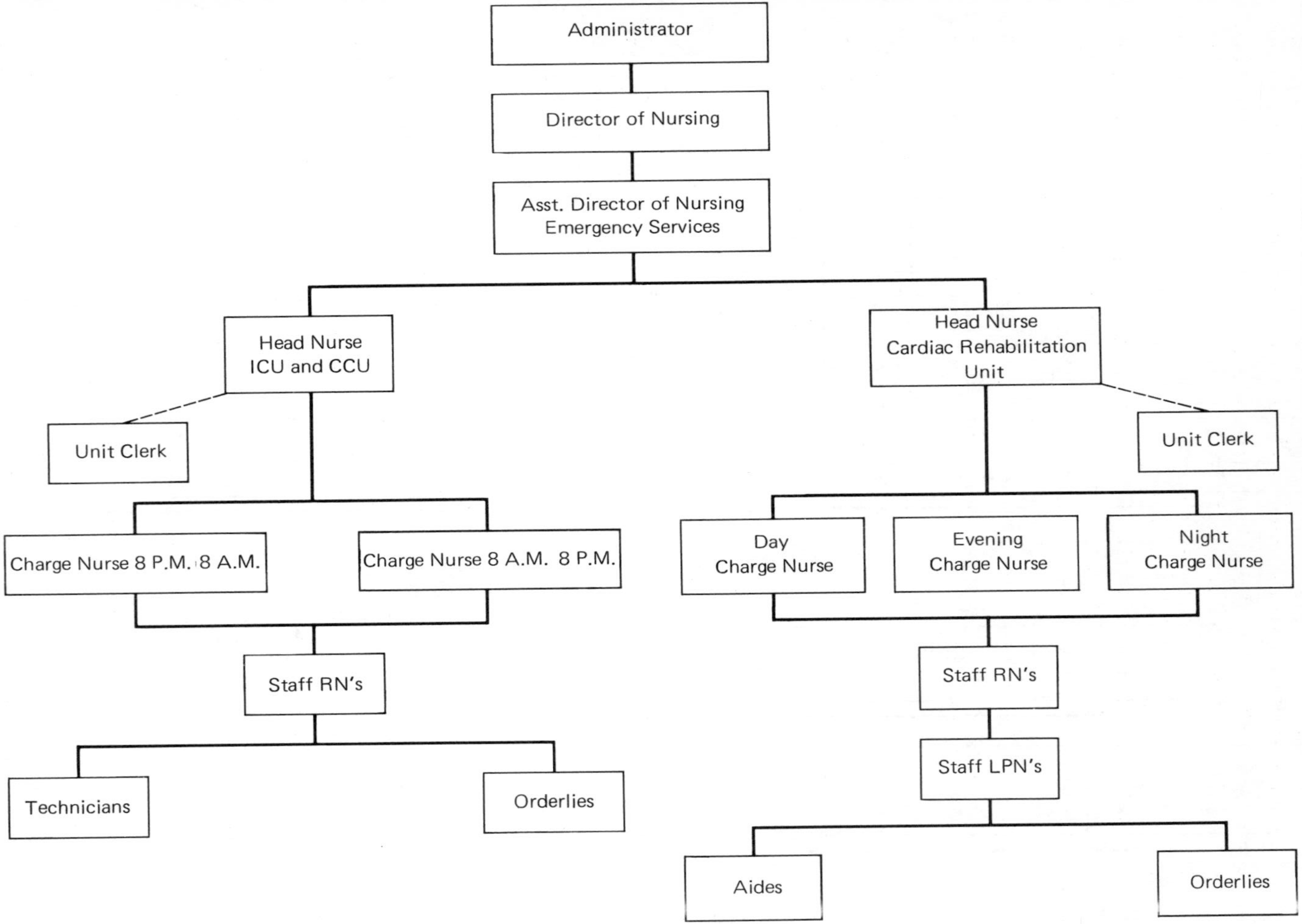

When you draw an organizational chart, first determine how much of the company or agency you want to picture. All the major offices that comprise the U.S. Department of Agriculture (USDA) are depicted in Fig. 10.12. Note that the organizational chart does not list specific staff and line positions, but instead concentrates on the various offices that comprise the USDA. On the other hand, just one branch of nursing services at a large metropolitan hospital—the division of critical care nursing—is presented in Fig. 10.13. Note that the intensive and cardiac care units work two shifts a day (8 A.M. to 8 P.M.; 8 P.M. to 8 A.M.), while the cardiac rehabilitation unit works three shifts in a twenty-four-hour period.

After selecting the extent to which you want to visualize the organization, draw appropriate circles or boxes to represent units. The shapes should be large enough to contain the titles of the offices they represent. Make sure you label each shape; otherwise, the reader will not know which unit is being depicted. If you are representing just a portion of your organization, you must say so in your text.

Flow Charts

Like the organizational chart, a flow chart does not present statistical information. But as its name implies, a flow chart does show movement. It displays the stages in which something is manufactured, accomplished, or produced from beginning to end. Flow charts can also be used to plan the day's or week's activities or, for accounting purposes, to show how income data go into a balance sheet.

A flow chart tells a story with arrows, boxes, and sometimes pictures. Boxes are connected by arrows to visualize the stages of a process. The presence and direction of the arrows tell the reader the order and movement of events involved in the process. Flow charts often proceed from left to right and back again, as in Fig. 10.14. Or, they can also be constructed to read from top to bottom, as in Fig. 10.15. Computer programming instructions

Fig. 10.14   A flow chart showing steps to be taken before graduation.

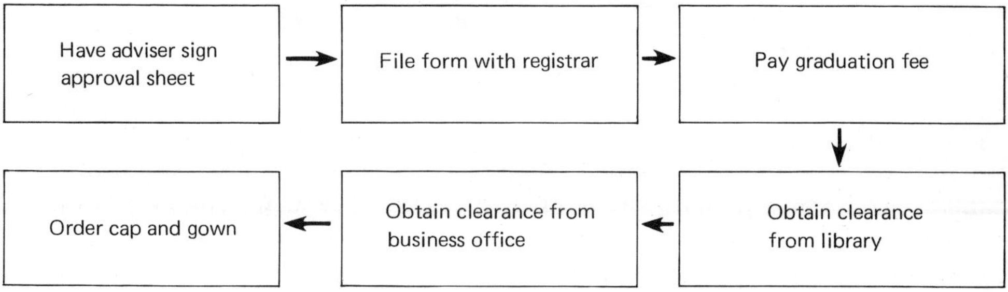

Fig. 10.15   A flow chart showing the 1978 Corporation Return, Form 1120, Simplified.

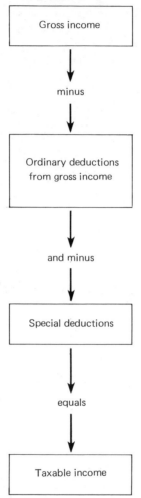

frequently are written in this way. The more complex flow chart in Fig. 10.16 depicts stages in the operation of a nuclear power plant; readers are asked to follow arrows in several directions. The jagged lines show the contents of the cooling coil and reactor. The cooling water enters from and returns to sources (a pond or pool, the ocean) not shown at the right-hand side of the chart.

In Fig. 10.17, which depicts the route of a check, the arrows proceed in a counterclockwise direction. In this example, the flow chart is a "closed" system. The cycle is completed when Mrs. Jones's canceled check returns to her.

Fig. 10.16   A complex flow chart showing the operation of a nuclear power plant.

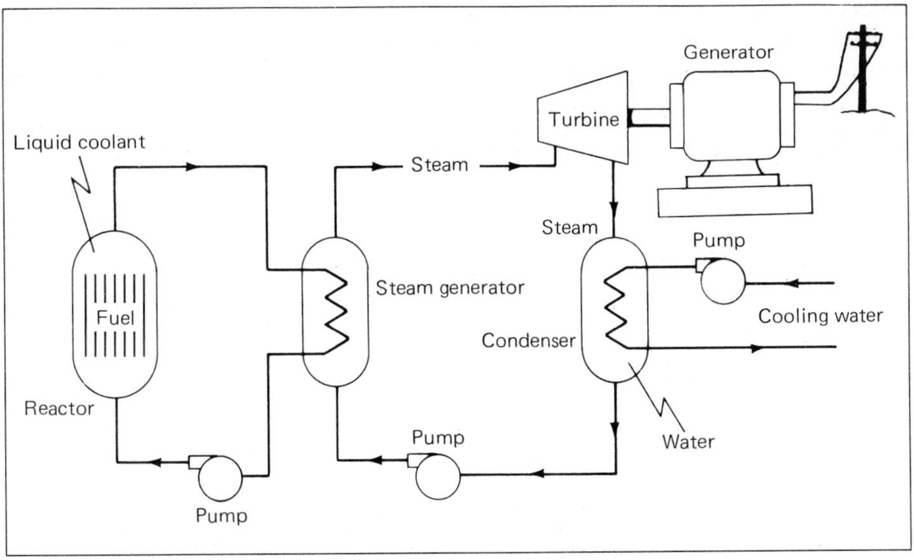

Reprinted by permission of the publisher from *An Environmental Approach to Physical Science*, by Jerry D. Wilson (Lexington, Mass.: D.C. Heath and Company, 1974), p. 363.

Fig. 10.17   A flow chart with a "closed" system showing the route of a check.

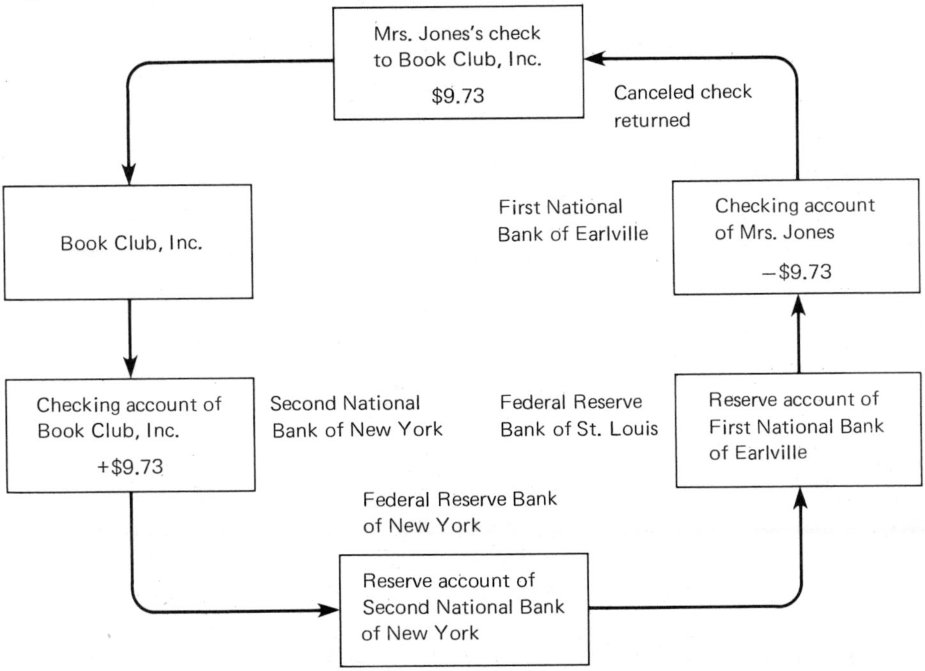

Reprinted by permission of the publisher from *Introductory Economics*, 4th ed., by Sanford D. Gordon and George G. Dawson (Lexington, Mass.: D.C. Heath and Company, 1980), p. 309.

A flow chart should clarify, not complicate, a process. Do not omit any important stages, but at the same time do not introduce unnecessary or unduly detailed information. Do show at least three or four stages, however. As with the organizational chart, use shapes that are large enough so that labels can be read quickly and easily. Mark every step with words or numbers. Arrows should be straight, and the various stages should appear in the correct sequence.

Maps

The maps you use on the job may range from highly sophisticated and detailed geographic tools to simple, hand-drawn sketches. You may use a small-scale map that shows large areas (a continent, a state, a county) in rough outline without great detail, such as the map in Fig. 10.18. Or you may need a large-scale map that displays a good deal of social, economic, or physical data (such as population density, location of retail businesses, hills, expressways, or rivers). That kind of detail is given in the map used by the Smithville Water

Fig. 10.18   A small-scale map showing location of world's record water depth for petroleum exploration.

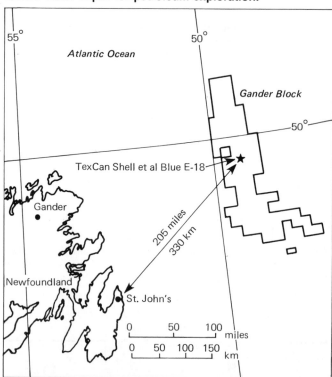

World Oil (December 1979), p. 87. Reprinted by permission.

**Fig. 10.19   A large-scale map showing location of Smith-
ville Water Department's filter plants and pumping stations.**

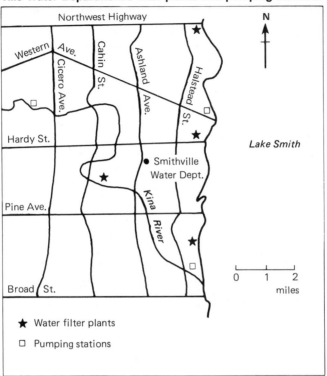

Department in Fig. 10.19. Look at the campus map included in your college
catalog. How much detail does it supply and of what kind?

Your job requirements will dictate how detailed your map should be. Architects and builders need extremely detailed blueprints showing the location
of pipes, heating ducts, and easement lines. An urban planner involved in
developing a new community or an employee submitting site plans for a company's new location will require less detailed maps. Between these two extremes, the individual working for a government agency investigating fire or
flood damage to a neighborhood may require a map that indicates individual
houses without presenting detailed features of those dwellings. On other occasions, a simple map showing customers how to get to a business or campers
how to find different types of campsites in a state park will suffice.

You may have to construct your own map or find one in a published
source (a government document, an atlas, or a publication of an auto club).
If you photocopy the map from your source, remember that you will not be
able to reproduce colors or fine shading. When preparing a map to include
in a report, follow these steps:

1. Put your map on the same size paper as the rest of the report. You may
   be able to purchase a blank map that contains only the shape of the area

so that you can fill in the details. Or you may want to trace from a copy of a map the boundaries of the area onto a sheet of paper.

2. Provide a distance scale that identifies the proportion of inches to miles or inches to feet ($1'' = 10$ miles).

3. Use dots, lines, colors, symbols (Δ, $\times$, $\circ$, $\square$) or shading to indicate features. Markings should be clear and distinct.

4. If necessary, include a legend providing a key to dotted lines, colors, shadings, or symbols. A legend is the key to your map. Note the legend for water filter plants and pumping stations in Fig. 10.19.

5. Eliminate any features (rivers, elevations, county seats) that do not directly depict the subject you are discussing. For example, a map showing the crops grown in two adjacent counties need not show all the roads and highways in those counties. But if you are recording the location of a restaurant in a small city, major access roads must be listed. A map showing the presence of strip mining needs to indicate elevation, but a map depicting population or religious affiliation need not include topographical (physical) detail. Reservoirs, lakes, and highways are essential in a map locating fire-damaged zones, details easily omitted in a map depicting strip mines.

6. Indicate direction by including an arrow and then citing the direction to which it points, for example N $\uparrow$.

Photographs

Correctly prepared, photographs are an extremely helpful addition to job-related writing. The photograph's chief virtues are realism and clarity. To a reader unfamiliar with an object or a landscape, a photograph may provide a much more convincing view than a simple drawing. Photographs of "before and after" scenes are especially effective.

The company you work for may have a photography or art department to assist you with your picture taking and preparation. A photograph can be touched up by enlarging crucial sections, deleting unnecessary parts (called *cropping*), or inserting white arrows on a black-and-white glossy to draw a reader's attention to relevant details.

If photographic cosmetics are unavailable, however, you will have to use special care when you take a picture. The most important point to remember is that what you see and what the camera records might be two different sights. Before you take a picture, decide how much foreground and background information you need. Include only the details that are *necessary and relevant* for your purpose. Inexperienced photographers need to remember the following four points:

1. Keep the camera *in focus*, and make sure that the lighting is proper.

2. Select the *correct angle*. Choose a vantage point that will enable you to record essential information as graphically as possible.

3. Give the *right amount of detail*. Pictures that include too much clutter compete for the reader's attention and detract from the subject. A realtor

wanting to show that a house has an attractive front does not need to include sidewalks or streets. At the other extreme, do not cut out a necessary part of a landscape or object. Avoid putting people in a photograph when their presence is not required to show the relative size or operation of an object.

4. Take the picture from the *right distance*. The farther back you stand, the wider your angle will be, and the more the camera will capture with less detail. If you need a shot of a three-story office building, your picture may show only one or two stories if you are standing too close to the building when you photograph it. Standing too far away from an object, however, means that the photograph will reduce the object's importance and record unnecessary details.

To get a graphic sense of the effects of taking a picture the right or the wrong way, study the photographs in Figs. 10.20, 10.21, 10.22, and 10.23. A clear and useful picture of a hydraulic truck (often called a "cherry picker") used to cut branches can be seen in Fig. 10.20. The photographer rightly placed the truck in the foreground, but included enough background information to indicate the truck's function. The worker in the gondola helps to

Fig. 10.20 A good photograph—truck in foreground, enough background information, and worker to show size and function of truck.

Fig. 10.21 A poor photograph—taken from the wrong angle so that everything merges and becomes confusing.

Photograph by David Longmire.

Photograph by David Longmire.

Fig. 10.22   A poor photograph—focus is on worker, but there is nothing else to identify person or work going on.

Fig. 10.23   A poor photograph—focus is on work going on, but there is nothing to indicate that worker is operating from a hydraulic truck.

Photograph by David Longmire.

Photograph by David Longmire.

show the size of the parts of the truck and also enables the reader to visualize the truck in operation.

In Fig. 10.21 everything merges because the shot was taken from the wrong angle. The reader has no sense of the parts of the truck, their size, or their function. Another kind of error can be seen in Fig. 10.22. Here the photographer was more interested in the person than in a piece of equipment. But looking at this picture, the reader has no idea where the worker came from or what he is doing up there. Finally, the reader looking at Fig. 10.23 has a view of work going on, but no idea of the truck from which the worker is performing the job.

Drawings

A drawing serves many functions. For example, it can show where an object is located, how a tool or machine is put together, or what signals are given or steps taken in a particular situation. A drawing can explain the appearance of an object to individuals who may never have seen it. A drawing is also helpful to individuals who may have seen the object, but do not have it in front of them as they read your work. By studying your drawing and following your discussion, readers will be better able to operate, adjust, repair, or order parts for equipment.

Unless you can call on the services of an expert professional photographer, you will find that drawings have two advantages over the ordinary photograph:

1. The artist can include as much or as little detail as necessary in a drawing. A pen or pencil will put down only as much as the user wants it to. The eye of the camera is not usually so selective; it tends to record everything in its path, including details that may be irrelevant for your purpose.
2. A drawing can show interior as well as exterior views, a feature that is particularly useful when the reader must understand what is going on under the case, housing, or hood.

You do not have to be a Rembrandt to create drawings. A steady hand and a careful eye are the only skills necessary. Often the only tools you will need are a straightedge (a ruler), a compass, a protractor, and crayons or colored pens. A drawing can be simple, such as the one in Fig. 10.24, showing

Fig. 10.24 A drawing showing where to place smoke detectors in a house.

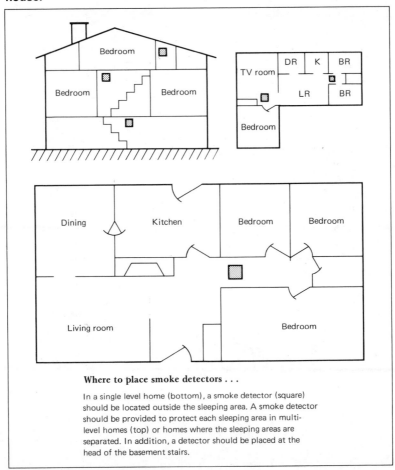

Where to place smoke detectors . . .

In a single level home (bottom), a smoke detector (square) should be located outside the sleeping area. A smoke detector should be provided to protect each sleeping area in multi-level homes (top) or homes where the sleeping areas are separated. In addition, a detector should be placed at the head of the basement stairs.

Southern Building (Dec. 1978–Jan. 1979), p. 10. Reprinted by permission.

Fig. 10.25   A drawing using stick figures to show correct landing and take-off signals.

U.S. Department of Transportation, *Flight Training Handbook*, AC 61-21A, p. 54.

Fig. 10.26   A cutaway drawing showing construction of sanitary sewers with a steel trenching box.

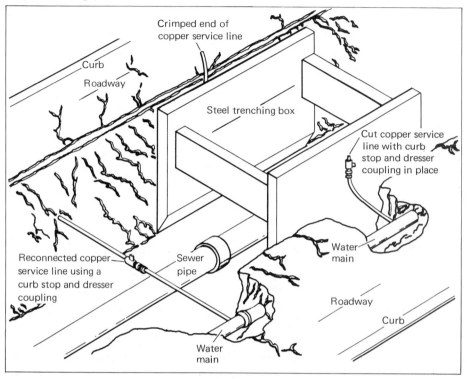

Crimped end of
copper service line

Curb

Roadway

Steel trenching box

Cut copper service
line with curb
stop and dresser
coupling in place

Reconnected copper
service line using a
curb stop and dresser
coupling

Sewer
pipe

Water
main

Roadway

Curb

Water
main

August A. Guerrera, "Grounding of Electric Circuits to Water Services: One Utility's Experience." Reprinted from *Journal of the American Water Works Association,* 72 (Feb. 1980), 86 by permission. Copyright 1980, the American Water Works Association.

readers exactly where to place smoke detectors in a house. A photograph could not give such an uncluttered picture. Stick figures may also be a useful part of a drawing, as in Fig. 10.25, which shows correct landing and take-off signals for pilots.

A more detailed drawing can reveal the interior of an object. Such sketches are called *cutaway drawings* because they show internal parts concealed from view. The underground pipes and service lines in a sanitary sewer are shown in Fig. 10.26. The earth banking left in the foreground of the sketch shows where these pipes are buried.

Another kind of sketch is known as an *exploded drawing*. The drawing blows the entire object up and apart to show how the individual parts, each kept in order, are arranged. An exploded drawing of a chair is seen in Fig. 10.27. The owner can better see how the chair is assembled and can more easily determine how to repair it.

Fig. 10.27 An exploded drawing of a chair.

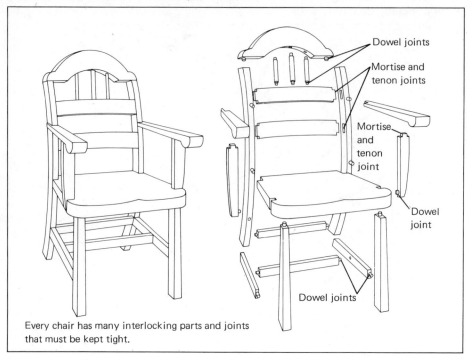

Dowel joints

Mortise and tenon joints

Mortise and tenon joint

Dowel joint

Dowel joints

Every chair has many interlocking parts and joints that must be kept tight.

From Reader's Digest *Fix-It Yourself Manual,* p. 67. Courtesy of Reader's Digest Association, Inc.

When you construct your own drawings, follow these rules:

1. Whenever necessary, indicate which view of the object you are presenting (e.g., aerial, frontal, lateral, reverse, exterior, or interior).
2. Keep the parts of the drawing proportionate unless you are purposely enlarging one section. Then provide readers with a scale.
3. Do not include any extra details. Even the addition of a line or two might distort the reader's view. A sketch serves a practical purpose, not an aesthetic one. Do not add decorations to make a drawing look fancy.

▶ Glossary

By way of review, the following is a glossary of terms used in this chapter:

Bar chart: A visual using vertical or horizontal bars to measure different data in space and time; bars can also be segmented to show multiple percentages within one bar. Bar charts are used to show a variety of facts for easy comparison.

Captions: titles or headings for visuals.

Circle chart: a visual shaped in a circle, or pie, whose slices represent the parts of the whole. Circle charts portray budgets, expenditures, shares, and time allotments.

Cropping: the process of eliminating unnecessary, unwanted details of a photograph by reproducing only the desired portion.

Crosshatching: the process of marking parts of a visual with parallel lines that cross each other obliquely; used to differentiate one bar or slice of a circle chart from another.

Cutaway drawing: a sketch in which the exterior covering of an object has been removed to show an interior view.

Dependent variable: the element (cost, employment, energy) plotted along the vertical axis of a line graph and most directly influenced by the independent variable.

Exploded drawing: a sketch of an entire object that has been blown up and apart to show the relationship of parts to one another.

Figures: any visuals that are not tables—charts, drawings, graphs, pictographs, photographs, maps.

Flow chart: a sketch revealing the stages in an activity or process.

Graph: a picture that represents the relationship of an independent variable to one or more dependent variables; produces a line or curve to show their movement in time or space. Graphs are used to depict figures that change often—temperatures, rainfall, prices, employment, productions, and so forth.

Independent variable: the element, plotted along the horizontal axis of a graph, which most directly and importantly affects the dependent variable; most often, the independent variable is time or distance.

Large-scale map: a map that shows a great deal of detail, whether physical (elevations, rivers), economic (income levels), or social (population, religious affiliation).

Legend: the explanation, or key, indicating what different colors, shadings, or symbols represent in a visual.

Organizational chart: a visual showing the structure of an organization from the chief executive to the work force of employees. An organizational chart reveals the chain of command with areas of authority and responsibility.

Pictograph: a visual showing differences in statistical data by means of pictures varying in size, number, or color.

Pie chart: see **Circle chart**.

Small-scale map: a map that depicts large areas without detail (a town, with no streets or subdivisions represented or a state with no cities shown).

Stub: the first column on the left-hand side of a table; contains line captions, listing those units to be discussed in the columns.

Suppressed zero: a graph beginning with a larger number, when it would be impossible or impractical to start plotting at zero.

Table: a visual in which statistical data or verbal descriptions are arranged in rows or columns.

Tick marks: equally spaced marks drawn on the vertical or horizontal scale of a graph to show units of measurement; see **Crosshatching.**

▶ Exercises

1. Record the highest temperature reached in your town for the next five days. Then collect the highest temperature reached in three of the following cities—Boston, Chicago, Dallas, Denver, Los Angeles, Miami, New Orleans, New York, Philadelphia, Phoenix, San Francisco, Seattle—over the same five days. (You can get this information from a newspaper.) Prepare a table showing the differences for the five-day period.

2. Go to a supermarket and get the prices of four different brands of the same product (hair spray, aspirin, a soft drink, a box of cereal). Put your findings in the form of a table.

3. The Foreign Agricultural Service of the USDA supplied the following statistics on the world production of oranges (including tangerines) in thousands of metric tons for the following countries during the years 1969–1972: Brazil, 2,005, 2,132, 2,760, and 2,872; Israel, 909, 1,076, 1,148, 1,221; Italy, 1,669, 1,599, 1,766, 1,604; Japan, 2,424, 2,994, 2,885, 4,070; Mexico, 937, 1,405, 1,114, 1,270; Spain, 2,135, 2,005, 2,179, 2,642; and the United States, 7,658, 7,875, 7,889, 9,245. Prepare a table with this information and then write a paragraph in which you introduce the table and draw conclusions from it.

4. Keep a record for one week of the number of miles you drive each day. Then prepare a line graph depicting this information.

5. The price of gasoline in one city was as follows:

	1979	*1980*
January	59.9	99.9
February	62.9	109.9
March	67.9	119.9
April	68.9	123.9
May	73.9	128.9

Make a multiple-line graph showing a comparison of gasoline prices for the two years. Distinguish the two different lines.

6. Prepare a circle chart showing the breakdown of your budget for one week or one month.

7. According to the U.S. Bureau of the Census, in 1972 the distribution of all companies classified in each enterprise industry was as follows: min-

erals, 0.4%; selected services, 33.3%; retail trade, 36.7%; wholesale trade, 6.5%; manufacturing, 5.3%; and construction, 17.8%. Make a circle chart to represent this distribution.

8. Construct a segmented-bar chart to represent the kinds and numbers of courses you took in a two-semester period or during your last year in high school.

9. Prepare a bar chart for the different brands of one of the products in exercise 2. Write a paragraph introducing this illustration.

10. Find a pictograph in a textbook or magazine and make a bar graph from the information contained in it. Then write a paragraph introducing the bar graph and drawing conclusions from it.

11. Make an organizational chart for a business or agency you worked for recently. Include part-time and full-time employees, but indicate employees' status with different kinds of shapes or lines. Then write a brief letter to your employer, explaining why such an organizational chart should be distributed to all employees.

12. Prepare a flow chart for one of the following activities:
    (a) setting a table in a restaurant
    (b) jumping a "dead" battery
    (c) giving an injection
    (d) crocheting an afghan
    (e) painting a set of louvered doors
    (f) making an arrest
    (g) training a dog
    (h) making homemade wine
    (i) putting out an electrical fire
    (j) any job you do

13. Make a map representing at least two blocks of your neighborhood. Include with appropriate symbols any stores, police or fire stations, churches, parks, or schools. Supply a legend for your readers.

14. Draw a map for a visitor who wants to know how to get from your college library to the downtown area of your city. Supply a distance scale.

15. Draw an interior view of a piece of equipment you use in your major; then identify the relevant parts.

16. Find a photograph that contains some irrelevant clutter. Write a letter to the photography department of a company for which you presumably work that wants to use the photograph. Tell the department what to delete and why.

17. Make a simple line drawing of only the relevant portions of the photograph in exercise 16. Explain in two paragraphs why the drawing is better than the photograph.

SECTION IV

INSTRUCTIONS AND REPORTS

11

Writing Clear Instructions

Clear instructions are essential if work is to get done in business and industry. This chapter contains suggestions on how to prepare, organize, write, and arrange instructions.

▶ The Importance of Instructions

Instructions tell, and frequently show, how to do something. They indicate how to perform a procedure (draw blood); operate a machine (run a forklift); assemble, maintain, or repair a piece of equipment (a photocopier); or locate an object (coils in a circuit). Readers use instructions for reasons of safety, efficiency, convenience, and economy. Product labels in a medicine chest, for example, inform users when and why to take the medications and how much to take. Owners' manuals instruct buyers on how to avoid the inconvenience of a product breakdown by keeping the product in good working order. Magazines such as *Popular Mechanics, Popular Photography,* and how-to books offer consumers money-saving instructions on topics ranging from repairing their homes to training guard dogs. You might want to read some of these how-to publications to see how they identify and meet the needs of their audiences.

As part of your job, you may be asked to write instructions for your fellow workers as well as for the customers who use your company's services or products. Your employer stands to gain or lose much from the kinds of instructions you write. Imagine how costly it would be if employees had to stop their work because they could not understand a set of instructions. Also, your employer may lose money if the instructions to customers are unclear. Clearly written instructions can save your company service calls. Even more important, careful instructions can help to prevent damage claims or even lawsuits. Poorly written instructions may result in injury to the person trying to follow them.

▶ The Variety of Instructions

Instructions vary in length, complexity, and format. Some instructions are one word long—*stop, lift, push, erase.* Others are a few sentences long: "Use a warm, damp cloth before glue dries. Be sure to close after using. Store in an upright position." These short instructions are appropriate for the numerous, relatively nontechnical chores performed every day. For more elaborate procedures, however, detailed instructions as long as from a page to an entire book are necessary. When your firm purchases a new computer or a piece of earth-moving equipment, it will receive an instruction pamphlet or book containing many steps, cautionary statements, and diagrams. Many businesses prepare their own training manuals containing instructions for 200 or 300 different procedures. Hospitals, for example, supply each unit with a manual giving information on how to do everything from charting temperatures to giving intravenous infusions.

Instructions can be given in paragraphs or in lists, and you will have to determine which format is most appropriate for the kinds of instructions you write. Figures 11.1 and 11.2 show two sets of instructions written in paragraph format. In Fig. 11.1 hospital employees are told how to prepare and administer a sitz bath; in Fig. 11.2 park rangers are told how to repair a halyard, or tackle, used to raise a flag or move a pulley.

The instructions shown in Figs. 11.3 and 11.4 are printed in list form. In Fig. 11.3 typists will find directions on how to change a ribbon on an IBM Selectric typewriter; the directions in Fig. 11.4 give details on how to assemble an outdoor grill.

Either a straight narrative account or a list can be used if your employer asks you to put instructions in a memo or letter. The following example shows an instructional memo that uses a list:

```
TO:     All Laundry Room Staff  DATE:     January 30, 1982

FROM:   Candy Dwyer            SUBJECT:  Fire evacuation
        Safety Engineer                  procedures

In the event of a fire in the laundry, follow these instructions:

   1. Turn in an alarm. Dial extension 311.
   2. Shut off all machinery.
   3. Turn off all projector fans.
   4. Vacate area.
   5. Close interior doors.
```

Fig. 11.1   Instructions on how to prepare and administer a sitz bath.

First, adjust water temperature dial to 105–110°F. Then turn on the faucet and fill sitz tub with enough water to cover the patient's hips. Before assisting patient into the tub, place bath towel in the bottom of the tub. Allow the patient to sit in the tub for 15–20 minutes. At the end of this time, help patient out of the tub. Then dry the patient thoroughly.

Fig. 11.2   Instructions on how to repair a halyard.

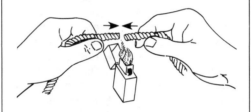

Easy Temporary Join for Synthetic Ropes

If you are faced with the problem of reeving a new halyard on a flagpole or mast, or through a block or pulley in an inaccessible location, the solution can be easy if both old and new lines are made of nylon or polyester (Dacron, Terylene, etc.). Simply join the ends of the old and new lines temporarily by melting end fibers together in a small flame (a little heat goes a long way). Rotate the two lines slowly as the fibers melt. Withdraw them from the flame before a ball of molten material forms, and if the stuff ignites, blow out the flame at once. Hold the joint together until it is cool and firm.

R. I. Standish, *Parks*, 51 (April–June 1980), p. 21.

Fig. 11.3   Instructions on how to change the ribbon on an IBM Selectric typewriter.

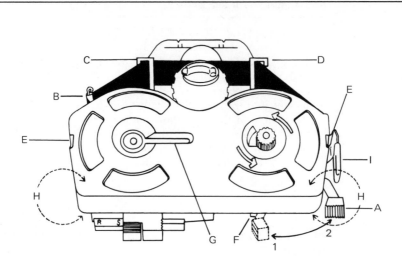

To Remove a Ribbon

- Center the Carrier and turn the motor OFF.
- Lift the cover.
- Keep the Paper Bail against the Platen.
- Move the Ribbon Load Lever A* to the load position 1 until it snaps against the Stop F.
- Using both hands, hold the Ribbon Cartridge at the front corners H and lift straight up.

* The Ribbon Load Lever on the IBM Correcting "Selectric" Typewriter cannot be moved if the Tape Load Lever I is in the load position.

To Install a New Ribbon

- Be sure the Ribbon Load Lever A is in the load position 1.
- Put the ribbon leader (uninked portion) over the *outside* of the Guidepost B and Ribbon Guides C and D. *Failure to do so will cause ribbon breakage.*
- Position the Ribbon Cartridge so that it fits between the Spring Clips E. Firmly push down both ends of the Cartridge.
- Thread the leader through Ribbon Guides C and D.
- Turn the Knob on the Cartridge in the direction of the arrow until the leader disappears inside the cartridge.
- Move the Ribbon Load Lever A to the type position 2.
- Close the cover.

Note: The name and reorder number of each ribbon appear on the underside of the Ribbon Cartridge.

Fig. 11.4   Instructions on how to assemble an outdoor grill.

ASSEMBLY INSTRUCTIONS

The instructions shown below are for the basic grill with tubular legs. If you have a pedestal grill, or a grill with accessories, check the separate instruction sheet for details not shown here.

NOTE: Make sure you locate all the parts before discarding any of the packaging material.

TOOLS REQUIRED ... A standard straight blade screwdriver is the only tool you need to assemble your new Meco grill. If you have a pedestal grill, you will need a 7-16 wrench or a small adjustable wrench.

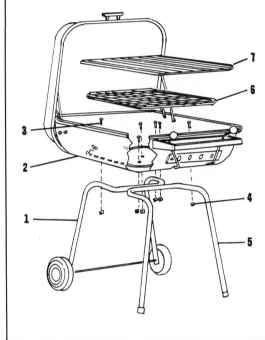

1. Before you start, take time to read through this manual. Inside you will find many helpful hints that will help you get the full potential of enjoyment and service from your new Meco grill.

2. Lay out all the parts.

3. Assemble roller leg (1) to bottom rear of bowl (2) with 1¼" long bolts (3) and nuts (4).

4. Assemble fixed leg (5) to bottom front of bowl (2) with 1¼" long bolts (3) and nuts (4).

5. Place fire grate—ash dump (6) in bottom of bowl (2) between adjusting levers.

6. Place cooking grid (7) on top of adjusting levers. Make sure top grid wires run from front to back of grill.

Mecco Assembly Instructions and Owners Manual, Metals Engineering Corp., P.O. Box 3005, Greenville, TN 37743. Reprinted by permission.

▶ Before Writing Instructions

Regardless of their format (paragraphs or lists), instructions have to be clear, complete, and easy to follow. Readers probably will not be able to ask you questions; they will have to rely on your written instructions. Your goal in writing those instructions is to get readers to perform the same steps you followed and, most important, to obtain the same results you did. Writing instructions is like teaching. You have to understand the material yourself and know the best way of presenting it.

Review the procedure or the construction of the equipment you are describing. Make sure that you know the rationale (reason) for doing something, the various sections or parts of the equipment, and the results of the operation. Next, actually perform the procedure (assembling, repairing, maintaining, ordering, dissecting). If possible, go through a number of trial runs.

Also, before you begin writing the instructions, try to determine your readers' level of experience and education. A set of instructions accompanying a chemistry set would be much different in terminology, abbreviations, and detail from a set of instructions a professor gives a class in organic chemistry:

> *General*   Place 8 drops of vinegar in a test tube and add a piece of limestone
> *Audience:*   about the size of a pea.
>
> *Specialized*
> *Audience:*   Place 8 gtts of CH_3COOH in a test tube and add 1 mg of CO_3.

Do not assume that your readers have done the procedure or have operated the equipment as many times as you have. (If they had, there would be no need for your instructions.) The readers may never have seen the particular machine or have performed the specific procedure. Keep the following piece of advice always in mind: No writer of instructions ever disappointed readers by making directions too clear or too easy to follow. Use language and symbols that will be readily understood. If someone is puzzled by your directions, you defeat the reasons for writing them.

► Selecting the Right Words and Visuals

To write instructions that readers can understand and turn into action, follow these guidelines:

1. Use verbs in the imperative mood. Imperatives are commands that have deleted the pronoun "you." Almost all the sentences in Figs. 11.1, 11.2, and 11.3 contain imperatives: "adjust water temperature" for "you adjust water temperature"; "fill the sitz tub with enough water" for "you fill the sitz tub with enough water"; "lift the front of the cover" for "you lift the front of the cover." Deleting the "you" is not discourteous, as it certainly would be in a letter or a report. Instructions are best expressed as commands to show that the writer speaks with authority. Instructions say "These steps work, so do it exactly this way." Imperatives also get the reader to do something specific without hesitation. Do not water down your directions with statements such as "Please see if you can remove the outside panel"; "Try to allow the mixture to cool for five minutes"; or "If at all possible, adjust the thermostat to 78°."

Wishy-washy statements may lead the reader to believe that there are some choices involved, when in fact there are none. For this reason, avoid *might, could, should:* "you might want to ignite the fire next" does not have the force of "ignite the fire next." Instead, choose action verbs *(apply, close, cut, dissect, drain, drop, insert, push, rub, shut off, turn, wipe).*

2. Write clear, short sentences. Since readability is especially important in instructions, keep sentences short, under twenty words and preferably under fifteen. Note that the sentences in Figs. 11.1, 11.2, 11.3, and 11.4 are, for the most part, under fourteen words. Avoid the passive voice. In place of "The air blower is to be used last," write "Use the air blower last." Also avoid addressing the reader as "one" or "the user": "The user should apply the air blower last" or "One must use the air blower last" are, again, best listed as "Use the air blower last." You can keep your sentences clear by avoiding ambiguity. Do not write a direction that sends the reader a message opposite from what you intend. A direction such as "Before using the soldering iron on metal, clean it with Freon" may mislead the inexperienced welder to put Freon on the iron rather than on the metal that is to be cleaned. Similarly, "Perform venipuncture with the arm in a downward position" does not clearly specify whose arm is to be in that position; appropriately revised, the instruction reads "Put the patient's arm in a downward position."

3. Use precise terms for measurements, distances, and times. Indefinite, vague directions leave users wondering if they are doing the right thing. The following imprecise directions are better expressed through the revisions listed in parentheses: "Turn the distributor cap a little." (How much is "a little?" "Turn the distributor cap three-quarters of an inch."); "Pack the contents in a bag." (What bag? "Pack the contents in a one-eighth-inch barrel bag."); "Let the contents stand for a while." (How long? "Let the contents stand for ten minutes.").

4. Use connective words as signposts to specify the exact order in which something is to be done (especially when your instructions are written in paragraphs). Words such as *first, then, before* in Fig. 11.1 help readers stay on course, telling them how and why the various procedures are connected to produce the desired results.

5. Label each step with a bullet as in Fig. 11.3, **a number** (Fig. 11.4), **or a dagger** (†) (when you present your instructions in a list). Plenty of white space between each step, too, distinctly separates steps for the reader. If circumstances permit the use of color, employ it sparingly to set off important elements of your instructions.

6. Whenever feasible, use visuals to make your instructions easier to understand and follow. The illustration in Fig. 11.2 reinforces the process of joining the two parts of the halyard by fire; the diagram in Fig. 11.3 labels the typewriter parts that users must understand if they are to insert a new ribbon. Another frequently used visual in instructions is the exploded drawing, such as that in Fig. 10.27, to help owners see how the various components of the chair fit together for easy repair. The types of visuals you can use will, of course, depend on the procedure or equipment you are describing. A simple line drawing such as that illustrated in Fig. 11.5 not only makes the order of the steps clear, but also helps to eliminate any confusion readers may have about the two kinds of postage to use when returning their product with a complaint letter. Note in Fig. 11.6 how line drawings and symbols (triangle, square, circle) graphically portray the proper use of fire extinguishers. Place visuals next to the steps to which they refer, not on another page or at the bottom of the page. To gain the most from visuals, readers must be able to see the illustrations or diagrams immediately before and after reading the directions that they clarify. Assign each visual a number (Figure 1, Figure 2), and in your directions tell readers where those visuals can be found ("to the

Fig. 11.5   Instructions on how to mail an appliance.

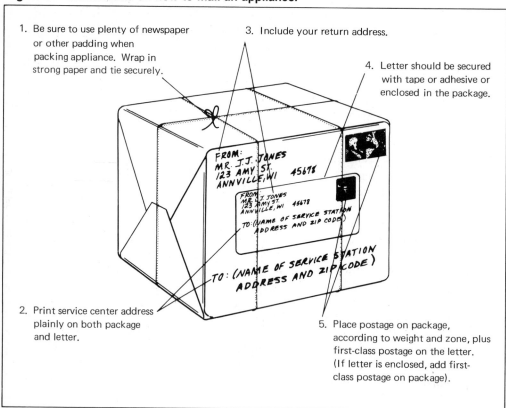

1. Be sure to use plenty of newspaper or other padding when packing appliance. Wrap in strong paper and tie securely.

2. Print service center address plainly on both package and letter.

3. Include your return address.

4. Letter should be secured with tape or adhesive or enclosed in the package.

5. Place postage on package, according to weight and zone, plus first-class postage on the letter. (If letter is enclosed, add first-class postage on package).

Fig. 11.6   Instructions on the proper use of fire extinguishers.

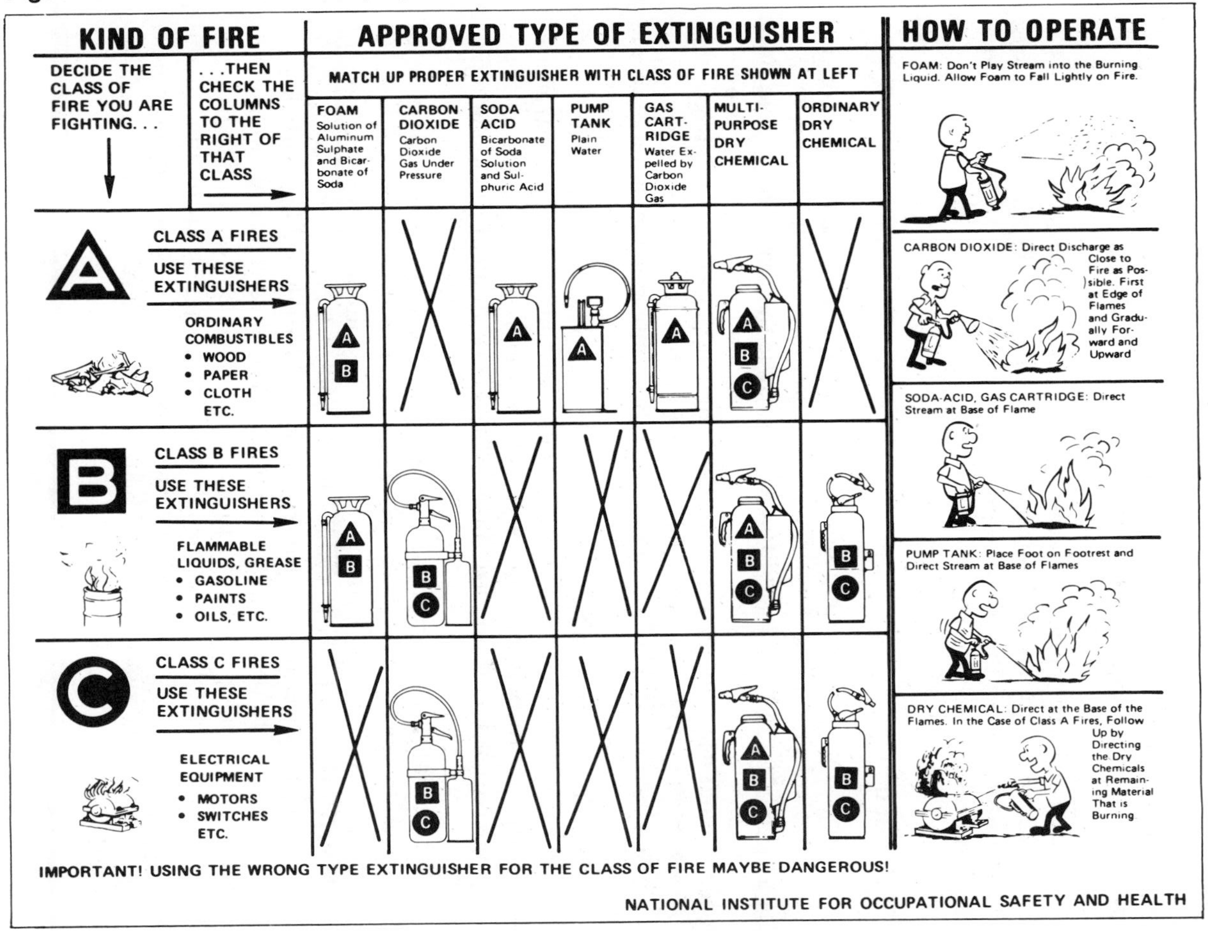

KIND OF FIRE	APPROVED TYPE OF EXTINGUISHER							HOW TO OPERATE
DECIDE THE CLASS OF FIRE YOU ARE FIGHTING... / ...THEN CHECK THE COLUMNS TO THE RIGHT OF THAT CLASS	MATCH UP PROPER EXTINGUISHER WITH CLASS OF FIRE SHOWN AT LEFT							
	FOAM — Solution of Aluminum Sulphate and Bicarbonate of Soda	CARBON DIOXIDE — Carbon Dioxide Gas Under Pressure	SODA ACID — Bicarbonate of Soda Solution and Sulphuric Acid	PUMP TANK — Plain Water	GAS CARTRIDGE — Water Expelled by Carbon Dioxide Gas	MULTI-PURPOSE DRY CHEMICAL	ORDINARY DRY CHEMICAL	
CLASS A FIRES — USE THESE EXTINGUISHERS — ORDINARY COMBUSTIBLES • WOOD • PAPER • CLOTH ETC.	A B	X	A	A	A	A B C	X	FOAM: Don't Play Stream into the Burning Liquid. Allow Foam to Fall Lightly on Fire.
CLASS B FIRES — USE THESE EXTINGUISHERS — FLAMMABLE LIQUIDS, GREASE • GASOLINE • PAINTS • OILS, ETC.	A B	B C	X	X	X	A B C	B C	CARBON DIOXIDE: Direct Discharge as Close to Fire as Possible. First at Edge of Flames and Gradually Forward and Upward
CLASS C FIRES — USE THESE EXTINGUISHERS — ELECTRICAL EQUIPMENT • MOTORS • SWITCHES ETC.	X	B C	X	X	X	A B C	B C	SODA ACID, GAS CARTRIDGE: Direct Stream at Base of Flame

PUMP TANK: Place Foot on Footrest and Direct Stream at Base of Flames

DRY CHEMICAL: Direct at the Base of the Flames. In the Case of Class A Fires, Follow Up by Directing the Dry Chemicals at Remaining Material That is Burning

IMPORTANT! USING THE WRONG TYPE EXTINGUISHER FOR THE CLASS OF FIRE MAYBE DANGEROUS!

NATIONAL INSTITUTE FOR OCCUPATIONAL SAFETY AND HEALTH

National Institute for Occupational Safety and Health.

left of these instructions"; "see the sketch at the right"). Wherever necessary, label parts of the visual material. Make sure the visual looks like the object the user is trying to assemble, maintain, or repair. Furthermore, inform readers if a part of an object is missing or reduced in size in your visual.

▶ The Three Parts of Instructions

Except for very short instructions, such as those illustrated in Figs. 11.1, 11.2, 11.3, and 11.4, a set of instructions generally contains three main parts: (1) an introduction, (2) a list of equipment and materials, and (3) the actual steps to perform the process.

The Introduction

Whether you need an introduction depends on the particular process or machine you are describing. Short instructions require no introduction or only a brief one- or two-sentence introduction such as the one in Fig. 11.4. More complex instructions require lengthier introductions. For instance, a ninety-page manual may contain a two- or three-page introduction. An introduction should be proportional to the kinds of instructions to be given. Instructions on how to sand a floor will not need a one-page introduction on how friction works.

The function of an introduction is to provide readers with enough *necessary* background information to understand why and how your instructions work. An introduction must make readers feel more comfortable and better prepared. Accordingly, an introduction can do one or all of the following:

1. State why the instructions were written or indicate the function of the particular process or machine. Here is an introduction from a safety procedure describing the protective lockout of equipment: "The purpose of this procedure is to provide a uniform method of locking out machinery or equipment. This will prevent the possibility of setting moving parts in motion, energizing electrical lines, or opening valves while repair, set-up and adjustment, or cleaning work is in progress." Instructions on how to write an appraisal of a piece of property might list these purposes: (1) to estimate the value of the property, (2) to indicate which owner's interest is being appraised if the property is jointly owned, (3) to provide a legal description of the property.

2. Indicate how a particular machine or procedure works. Explain the scientific or management principles by which a device or procedure operates. A brief discussion of the "theory of operation" will help readers understand why something works the way your instructions say it should. The introduction to instructions on how to run a machine begins by stressing the function of the machine: "These instructions will teach you how to operate an autoclave. The autoclave is used to sterilize surgical instruments through live additive-free steam." Laboratory experiments usually begin with a discussion of reasons why a particular effect will occur or how something develops under certain circumstances. Such discussion sometimes describes a scientific law or principle. For example, the following paragraph introduces an experiment on osmosis, the process by which fluids flow from one cell to another.

> The distribution of water among the various fluid compartments of the body is determined in part by the solute [dissolved substance] content of these fluids. Since most solutes penetrate cell membranes relatively slowly, water, because of its abundance and permeability, plays an important role in establishing osmotic equilibrium between cells and their environment. When placed in a solution whose water concentration is different from that in its own protoplasm, a cell either gains or loses water. The process of direct migration of solvents through membranes is called osmosis. This experiment will demonstrate the movement of water across a membrane because of differences in solute concentration across the two sides.[1]

3. State why such instructions are significant. Directions to students in the health sciences on performing an experiment on surface tension contain this sentence in the introduction: "Surface tension plays an important role in many phenomena, including inflation and deflation of lung alveoli in respiration." Many instructions in training manuals contain introductions that stress the educational benefits to the user: "These instructions will serve as a valuable training tool for the beginning draftsman, showing him or her the proper ways of preparing detailed drawings that will be useful in woodwork manufacturing today."

4. Establish how long it should take the user to complete all steps of the instructions. If the users know how long a procedure should take, they will be in a better position to judge whether they are doing it correctly—if they are waiting too long or not long enough between steps or if they are going too slowly or too quickly: "It should take about three and one-half hours from the time you start laying the floor tiles until the time they dry well enough to walk on."

5. Inform the user about any special circumstances to which the instructions apply. Some instructions precede others or are used only on special occasions. Readers must be informed about those changes or emergency situations. A supervisor of a large chemical plant sent employees the memo contained in Fig. 11.7 to describe operating procedures to be followed during

---

[1] Byron A. Schottelius, John D. Thomson, and Dorothy D. Schottelius, *Physiology: Laboratory Manual*, 4th ed. (St. Louis: C. V. Mosby, 1978), p. 11. Reprinted by permission.

Fig. 11.7   An example of special circumstances to which the instructions apply.

To: All Shift Supervisors
    All Firefighters

From: Robert A. Ferguson

Subject: Operating Procedures During Energy Shortages

Date: October 10, 1982.

<u>BOILER ROOM OPERATION</u>

The following policy has been formulated to aid in maintaining required pressures during periods of low wood flow and severe natural gas curtailment.

All boilers are equipped with lances to burn residue or #6 fuel oil as auxiliary fuels. When wood is short, #6 oil should be burned in #2 and #3 boilers at highest possible rate consistent with smoke standards. To do this, take these steps:

1. Put #6 oil on #3 boiler lances.

2. Shut down overfire air.

3. Shut down forced draft.

4. Turn off vibrators.

5. Keep grates covered with ashes or wood until ash cover exists.

This will result in an output of 25,000 to 35,000 lbs./hr. steam from #3 boiler and will force wood on down to #4 boiler.

If required, the same procedure can be repeated on #2 boiler.

Fig. 11.8 Instructions that describe a safety procedure.

HERCULES

HATTIESBURG PLANT
SAFETY PROCEDURE #7
WELDING AND HOT WORK PERMIT PROCEDURE

1.0 Permits Required

All work in hazardous areas involving the use of equipment or tools
which may produce heat or sparks shall require a HOT WORK PERMIT. The
following are examples of jobs requiring HOT WORK PERMITS: Welding,
burning, soldering, babbitting, sand blasting, chipping, grinding,
drilling, and the use of portable pumps or tools powered by internal
combustion engines or non-explosion proof motors, Remington stud
driver.

2.0 Hazardous Area Defined

All areas of the plant are defined as hazardous areas except the
following, which are defined as non-hazardous: Shop Area (including
the Boiler Shop, Tractor and Auto Shop, Machine Shop, Pump Shop,
Pipe Shop, Welding Shop, and Salvage Yard), Mill Room, Shredder
House, Power House Boiler Room and Engine Room, Office and Office
Annex, the five Smoke Houses, and smoking lounge in the Laboratory,
Area Maintenance Shops.

Used by permission of Hercules Incorporated.

energy shortages. Note the brief introduction emphasizing the special circumstances. A safety procedure introduction in Fig. 11.8 informs users when they
have to obtain a hot work permit, by first defining the term and then supplying examples of the jobs requiring that permit.

Not every introduction to a set of instructions will contain facts on all the
categories of information listed above. Some instructions will not require that
much detail. You will have to judge how much background information your
specific instructions call for.

List of Equipment and Materials *apply*

Immediately after the introduction, you should inform readers of all equipment or materials they will need. This list should be complete and clear. Do not wait until the readers are actually performing one of the steps in the instructions to tell them that a certain type of drill or a specific kind of chemical is required. They will have to stop what they are doing to find this equipment or material; moreover, the procedure may fail or present hazards if users do not have the right equipment at the specified time.

Do not expect your readers to know exactly what size, model, or quantity you have in mind. Tell them precisely. For example, if a Phillips screwdriver is necessary to complete one step, specify this type of screwdriver under the heading *Equipment and Materials;* do not just list "screwdriver." Here are some additional examples of unclear references to equipment and materials, with more helpful alternatives listed in parentheses after them: solution (0.7% NaCl solution); maps (four aerial reconnaissance maps); pencils (two engineering pencils); electrodes (four short platinum wire electrodes); file (cheese-grater file); sand (10-lb bag of sand); needle (butterfly needle); water (10 gallons untreated sea water).

If you are concerned that readers will not understand why certain equipment or materials are used, give the explanation in parentheses after the item. For example, listing alcohol and cotton as materials needed to take a blood pressure might confuse readers not familiar with the uses of these materials. A clarifying comment after the materials such as "used to clean stethoscope headphones" would help. The following example, "Instructions for Absentee Voters," contains such helpful comments:

> This absentee ballot package has been sent to you at your request. It contains the following items:
>
> 1. Sample paper ballot (for information only).
> 2. Official ballot (this is a punch card).
> 3. Punching tool.
> 4. Envelope with attached declaration.
> 5. Preaddressed return envelope.

Voters will know that the punch card is their official ballot and that it does not look like the sample ballot because of the parenthetical information in number 2. The point is reinforced later in the directions by this statement:

> IMPORTANT
> Punch only with tool provided—never with a pencil or pen.
> Your vote is recorded by punching this ballot card—not by marking the paper ballot.
> Do not return the sample paper ballot.

Some equipment and material sections may also warn readers about limitations and dangers in using specific materials. The makers of a small appliance give these instructions on cleaning the "No-stick finish" on their Wok:

> Always use a nylon pad such as Dobie or Scotch-Brite Cookware Scrub'n Sponge. A dishcloth may give No-stick finish a clean look, but it will not remove tiny food particles which settle into the finish. If not removed, they will burn when the Wok is reheated, causing stains and reducing the non-stick qualities of the finish. Do not use a metal pad or abrasive cleaning powder.[2]

An even more detailed list of materials used to clean and smooth wood surfaces follows.

REFINISHING

Preparing the Surface

Before attempting to refinish a wood item, be sure the surface is smooth and free from dirt, dust, and grease.

Materials. The following materials are suitable for cleaning and smoothing wood surfaces:

Abrasives.

■ *Sandpaper.* Sandpaper is not made of sand as the name suggests. It is made of various kinds of abrasive material applied to paper or cloth backing and made in sheet, drum, belt, and other forms. Sandpaper is made in various grades ranging from No. 4/0 to No. 1. No. 4/0 is used when an extra fine finish is required; No. 2/0 for a fine finish; No. 1/2 for rubbing down undercoats of paint and varnish in preparation for final finish; and No. 1 to No. 3 for sanding down old coats of paint that are in too bad a condition to be repainted.

■ *Sanding Disks.* Sanding disks are flat, circular pieces of sandpaper of various types, sizes, and coarseness for use on a power sander. These disks can also be used either on a disk or rotary hand sander.

■ *Commercial Steel Wool.* Steel wool is a fluffy or wool-like mass of steel turnings. It is made in grades No. 00, 0, 1, and 3, ranging from extra fine to coarse. It is a mild abrasive for rubbing down and smoothing wood and is well suited for removal of light rust from metal prior to repainting.

Cloth, Sponges, and Waste.

■ *Jute Burlap.* Jute burlap is a coarse, heavy, loose-woven material. It is used for all general purpose cleaning.

---

[2]Reprinted by permission of The West Bend Company.

■ *Osnaburg Cotton Cloth.* Osnaburg cloth is a coarse, heavy cloth used as a substitute for jute burlap and serves the same purposes.

■ *Cotton Wiping Cloth.* This cloth is relatively free from lint. It is used as a substitute for cotton waste, especially when lint deposits are undesirable, and as a substitute for sponges when washing wood and metalwork. It can be used to apply strong soap, lye, soda ash, or other solutions which will deteriorate sponges quickly.

■ *Cellulose Sponge.* This is a man-made (synthetic) material. It *cannot* be used with solutions containing soda ash, trisodium phosphate, or caustic soda (lye) because they will break down the fibers and ruin the sponge.

■ *Natural Sponge.* This is a natural material that has great liquid absorption capacity and becomes soft when wet without losing its original toughness. It is used with mild cleaning solutions. Solutions of soda ash, trisodium phosphate, and caustic soda affect the natural sponge the same as the synthetic sponge.[3]

Instruction Steps

The heart of your directions will consist of clearly distinguished steps that readers must follow to achieve the desired results. To make sure that you help your readers understand your steps, observe the following rules:

1. Put the steps in their correct order. If a step is out of order or is missing, the entire set of instructions can be wrong or, worse yet, dangerous. Double-check your steps before you write them down. Each step should be numbered to indicate its correct place in the sequence of events you are describing. Never put an asterisk (*) before or after a step to make the reader look somewhere else for information. If the information is important, put it in your instructions; if it is not, delete it.

2. Group closely related activities into one step. Sometimes closely related actions are grouped together into one step to help the reader coordinate activities and to emphasize their being done at the same time, in the same place, or with the same equipment. Study the following instructions listing the receptionist duties for a ward clerk in a hospital.

(1) Greet patients warmly and make them feel welcome. Never fall into the trap of groaning and saying "not another one." Remember the patient probably did not want to come to the hospital in the first place.

(2) Check the identity bracelet against the summary sheet and addressograph plate. If the bracelet is not on the patient's wrist, place it there immediately. Set about correcting any errors you may find in any of this information at once.

---

[3] U.S. Army Manual FM 43-4, *Repair of Wood Items*

(3) If asked, escort the patient to his room. Explain the signal light, answer any questions, and introduce the patient to his roommate, if any.
(4) Notify the head nurse and/or the nurse assigned to that room of the patient's arrival.
(5) Notify the admitting physician by phone of the patient's arrival and location. If the patient lacks admission orders, mention this to the physician's secretary at this time.[4]

Note how step 3 contains all the duties the ward clerk performs, once patients are taken to their rooms. It is easier to consolidate all the activities that take place in the room—explaining machinery, answering questions, making introductions—than to list each as a separate step. But be careful that you do not overwork a single step. To combine steps 4 and 5 above would be wrong, and impossible, for those two distinct steps require the ward clerk to speak to someone in person and to make a phone call. These two actions are two separate stages in a process. But do not divide an action into two steps if it has to be done in one. For example, instructions showing how to light a furnace would not list as two steps actions that must be performed simultaneously.

Incorrect: Step 1: Depress the lighting valve.
           Step 2: Hold a match to the pilot light.

Correct: Step 1: Depress the lighting valve while holding a match to the pilot light.

3. Give the reader hints on how best to accomplish the procedure. Obviously, you cannot do this for every step, but if there is a chance that the reader might run into difficulties or may not anticipate a certain reaction, by all means provide assistance. For example, telling readers that a certain aroma or color is to be expected in an experiment will reassure them that they are on the right track. Particular techniques on how to operate or service equipment are also helpful: "If there is blood on the transducer diaphragm, dip the transducer in a blood solvent, such as hydrogen peroxide, Hemosol, etc." If readers have a choice of materials or procedures in a given step, you might want to list those that would give the best performance: "Several thin coats will give a better finish than one heavy one."

4. State if one step directly influences (or jeopardizes) the outcome of another. Since all steps in a set of instructions are interrelated, you could not (and should not) have to tell readers how every step affects another. But stating specific relationships is particularly helpful when dangerous or highly intricate operations are involved. You will save the reader time, and you will stress the need for care. Forewarned is forearmed. For example:

Step 2: Tighten fan belt. Failure to tighten the fan belt will cause it to loosen and come off when the lever is turned in step 5 below.

---

[4] Myra S. Willson, *A Textbook for Ward Clerks and Unit Secretaries* (St. Louis: C.V. Mosby, 1979), p. 70. Reprinted by permission.

Do not wait until step 5 to tell readers that you hope they did a good job in tightening the fan belt. That information comes after the fact.

5. Insert warning, caution, and note statements only where absolutely necessary. A warning statement tells readers that a step, if not prepared for or performed properly, can endanger their safety:

> WARNING: UNPLUG AIR CONDITIONING UNIT BEFORE CLEANING.

> WARNING: DO NOT TOUCH EXPOSED WIRE.

A caution statement tells readers to take certain precautions—wear protective clothing, check an instrument panel carefully, submit forms in triplicate, use special care in running a machine, measure weights or dosages exactly.

> CAUTION
> MAKE SURE BRAKE SHOES WON'T RUB TIRE AND THAT SHOES MATE WELL WITH RIM WHEN BRAKES ARE APPLIED.

Because of the extremely important information they impart, warning and caution statements should be graphically set apart from the rest of the instructions. There should be no chance that readers will overlook them. Put these statements in capital letters, in boldface type, in boxes, in different colors (red is especially effective), or in any or all of the above. Warning and caution statements should not be used just because you want to emphasize a point. Putting too many of these signals in your instructions will decrease the dramatic impact they should have on readers. Use them sparingly—only when absolutely necessary.

A note statement simply adds some clarifying comments:

Note: All models in XY series have a hex nut in the upper right, not left, corner.

The following instructions on how to paint a garage floor contain steps that offer hints on how best to do the job, comment on how one step affects another, and issue warning, caution, and note signals. Not all instructions require this amount of detail. Use such comments and signals only when the procedure you are describing calls for them and when they will help your readers.

HOW TO PAINT A GARAGE FLOOR

Cleaning the Floor

(1) Remove anything sitting on the floor.

(2) Scrape areas where there is old chipped paint with metal scraper. For hard-to-reach places such as corners or underneath pipes, use a 3-inch wire brush. New paint will not stick to the floor if old paint is not first removed.

(3) Sweep the floor first with a broom; then to make sure that all particles of dust and dirt are removed, use a vacuum sweeper.

(4) Open all windows for proper ventilation. Fumes from cleaning solution used in step 5 should not be inhaled.

> CAUTION: USE PROTECTIVE EYEWEAR AND RUBBER GLOVES FOR NEXT STEP.

---

(5) Mop the entire floor with a solution composed of the following ingredients:
⅓ box of Floorex
1 quart of bleach
10 quarts of water
1 cup powdered detergent

> WARNING: DO NOT USE DETERGENTS CONTAINING AMMONIA. AMMONIA ADDED TO THESE INGREDIENTS WILL CAUSE AN EXPLOSION.

Note: Do not worry if the mixture does not appear soapy; it does not need suds to work.

(6) For any stubborn grease spots that remain, sprinkle enough dry Floorex powder to cover them entirely. Scrub these spots with a 5-inch wire brush.

(7) Rinse the entire floor thoroughly with water to remove cleanser. Allow floor to dry before painting (30 min).

Painting the Floor:

(8) Mix the paint with a stirrer ten or fifteen times until the color is even. Pour the paint into the paint tray.
Note: If the paint has not already been shaken by machine before being opened, shake the can for about three minutes, open, and stir the contents for about five to ten minutes or until the paint is mixed.

(9) With the 3-inch paint brush, paint around the baseboard. Come out at least two to three inches so that roller used in the next step will not touch the wall.

(10) Paint the rest of the floor with a roller attached to an extension handle. A roller handles much more easily than a brush and distributes the paint more

smoothly. Move the roller in the same direction each time. Overlap each row painted by one-half inch so as to leave no spaces between rows of paint.

(11) Allow two hours to dry. The floor will be ready to walk on.

> CAUTION: DO NOT DRIVE VEHICLES ONTO FLOOR FOR TWENTY-FOUR HOURS. TIRES WILL PICK UP NEW PAINT.

▶ Exercises

1. Bring to class two examples of short directions that require no introductions or lists of materials and equipment. Indicate why these instructions are effective by commenting on how precise, direct, and useful they are. Look for these two examples on labels, carton panels, or backs of envelopes.

2. Find at least one example of a long set of instructions that contains an introduction; list of materials and equipment; and warning, caution, and/ or note statements. Bring this example to class and be prepared to show how the various steps in this set of instructions follow the principles outlined on pages 349–352 in this chapter.

3. Find a set of instructions that does not contain any visuals, but which you think should have some graphic materials to make it clearer. Design those visuals yourself and indicate where they should appear in the instructions.

4. Write a set of instructions on one of the following topics. Identify your audience. Include an appropriate introduction, list of equipment and materials, and whatever visuals you think will help your readers. Also, insert warning, caution, and note statements wherever they are necessary.
   (a) inserting a nasogastric tube
   (b) changing a cash register tape
   (c) changing a flat tire
   (d) hemming a skirt
   (e) building a campfire
   (f) running a stencil
   (g) planting a tree
   (h) flossing a patient's teeth after cleaning
   (i) finding and plugging a leak in a tire
   (j) taking reservations at a hotel/motel
   (k) cleaning a vinyl roof of a car
   (l) pruning hedges
   (m) shaving a patient for surgery
   (n) jumping a dead car battery
   (o) using the Heimlich maneuver to help a choking individual

(p) dressing a store window to display merchandise

(q) reading a blueprint

(r) taking a blood pressure

(s) filling out an income tax return

(t) removing a stain from an article of clothing

(u) installing a wind turbine on a roof

(v) fingerprinting a suspect

(w) cooking a roast

(x) arranging a footlocker for inspection

6. The following set of instructions is confusing, vague, and out of order. Rewrite these instructions to make them clear, easy to follow, and correct. Make sure that each step follows the guidelines outlined in this chapter.

Reupholstering a Piece of Furniture

(1) Although it might be difficult to match the worn material with the new material, you might as well try.

(2) If you cannot, remove the old material.

(3) Take out the padding.

(4) Take out all of the tacks before removing the old covering. You might want to save the old covering.

(5) Measure the new material with the old, if you are able to.

(6) Check the frame, springs, webbing, and padding.

(7) Put the new material over the old.

(8) Check to see if it matches.

(9) You must have the same size as before.

(10) Look at the padding inside. If it is lumpy, smooth it out.

(11) You will need to tack all the sides down. Space your tacks a good distance apart.

(12) When you spot wrinkles, remove the tacks.

(13) Caution: in step 11 directly above, do not drive your tacks all the way through. Leave some room.

(14) Work from the center to the edge in step 11 above.

(15) Put the new material over the old furniture.

P.S. Use strong cords whenever there are tacks. Put the cords under the nails so that they hold.

12

Short Reports

Business and industry cannot function without written reports. A report may be defined as a collection of data on any topic—money, travel, time, personnel, equipment, management—that an organization must keep track of in its day-to-day operations. Reports tell whether schedules are being met, costs contained, sales projections surpassed, clients and patients efficiently served. Reports also are likely to be required if unexpected problems occur. Your readers will be people you work for or with—supervisors, customers, clients, colleagues in your office or in another section of your firm. You may write an occasional report in response to a specific question, or you may be required to write a daily or weekly report on routine activities about which your readers expect detailed information. Many organizations—clinics, mass transportation systems, schools—must submit regularly scheduled reports in order to maintain their funding by state or federal agencies.

To give you a sense of some of the topics that you may be required to write about, here is a list of various reports that are found in business and industry:

appraisal report	medicine / treatment error report
audit report	operations report
construction report	periodic report
design report	production report
evaluation report	progress report
experiment report	project completion report
incident report	recommendations report
inventory report	research report
investigative report	sales report
laboratory report	status report
library report	test report
manager's report	trip report

Discussing each of these reports is too large a task for one chapter. Instead, Chapter 12 will concentrate on six of the most common types of reports you are likely to encounter in your professional work:

1. periodic reports
2. sales reports
3. progress reports
4. trip reports
5. test reports
6. incident reports

The first five reports can be called *routine reports* because they give information about planned, ongoing, or recurring events. *Incident reports,* on the other hand, describe events that writers did not foresee or plan for—accidents, breakdowns, delivery delays, or work stoppages. All six, however, may be termed "short" reports. That is, they are brief and deal with current happenings rather than with long-range forecasts. Brief reports focus on the "trees," not the "forest."

▶ How to Write Short Reports

The most important point to keep in mind is that reports are written for readers who need information so that they can get a job accomplished. Never think of the reports you write as a series of short notes jotted down for *your* convenience. Under each of the following categories you will find guidelines applicable to writing *any* short report you encounter. More specific information pertinent to particular types of reports is given within a discussion of those reports later in this chapter.

1. Length. Reports are *brief*—one paragraph to two or three pages. They get right to the point and do not waste a busy reader's time. Some reports ask for nothing but numbers—for example, the glucose level on a blood test. A progress report, however, calls for written evaluations.

2. Format. Reports are written in memo or letter format or on specially prepared forms distributed by an employer. When you are writing to individuals outside your business or agency, you will generally use a letter format. The memo format is used when communicating with individuals within your company. Prepared forms can be used for both types of readers—those you work with as well as those outside your company.

3. Content. The emphasis is on facts: costs, eyewitness accounts, observations, statistics, test measurements. Impressions and guesswork are outlawed. Readers want a straightforward account of current events. Past activities may sometimes be mentioned, but only to clarify the present and to help readers follow current details. Always specify the exact period of time the report covers and indicate A.M. or P.M. Just listing "Thursday" is not enough. Give the date. To record time in compact and specific terms, employers may use a twenty-four-hour clock: 1:00 A.M. is 0100 hours; 1:00 P.M. is 1300 hours. An event occurring on February 19, 1981, at 2:30 P.M. is 81/2/19/1430—year, month, day, time (hours/minutes). Give precise locations as well. "Highway 30" is not as helpful as "Highway 30, three miles southeast of the Morton exit." Call a machine by its precise technical name. Never use "thing," "gizmo," or "contraption" to refer to parts or tools. Refer to individuals by their proper names, not nicknames (Buddy, Lindy, Red, Sis, Shorty).

   4. Organization.   Begin with a statement of purpose. Tell readers why you are writing the report and then provide a clear description of the events or the process. Listing events in chronological order is probably the easiest way to organize information. Or you might use helpful headings that divide information into easily understood categories. Here is an outline to follow when you are not required to submit a specially prepared form:

   1. Purpose—why does the reader have to be informed of events?
   2. Time—when did it happen?
   3. Location—where did it happen?
   4. Procedure—how was it done?
   5. Results—what was the outcome?
   6. Recommendations—what should the reader do with the results?

   Note that the placement of recommendations in a short report may vary. Some employers may prefer to see recommendations at the beginning of the report, as in Fig. 12.8. Sometimes this section may be omitted. Some reports simply require a summary of what actions were taken. Other reports, though, require the writer to tell readers what actions to take. Keep in mind that your suggestions should be practical and results-oriented. Review the discussion of recommendations at the end of Chapter 9 on the questionnaire, p. 284, to help you formulate helpful, action-oriented suggestions.

▶ Periodic Reports

   Periodic reports, as their name signifies, provide readers with information at regularly scheduled intervals—daily, weekly, bimonthly, monthly, quarterly. They help a company or agency keep track of the quantity and quality of the services it provides and the amount and types of work done by employees. Information in periodic reports helps managers and other supervisory personnel make schedules, order materials, assign personnel, budget funds, and, generally speaking, determine community or corporate needs.

   You may already be familiar with some kinds of periodic reports. For example, if you have ever punched a timecard and turned it in at the end of the week, you were filing a periodic report. Or, if you have ever taken inventory in a stockroom, you were preparing a periodic report.

Periodic reports are used for numerous jobs. Delivery services require drivers to keep a daily record documenting the number of packages delivered, the time, and the location. A log, another kind of periodic report, is shown in Fig. 12.1. At the end of a tour of duty, for example, law enforcement officers submit a daily activity log showing hours worked and actions taken. Employees at television and radio stations may have to keep weekly reports of calls received by the station to aid management in determining the types of programming to offer. Many realtors provide brokers with a weekly report of the number and type of listings taken, shown, or sold.

Periodic reports follow no set format. Most often, though, employers supply routine forms on which to list information. These forms, such as the one illustrated in Fig. 12.1, are relatively easy to complete. They ask for numbers, dates, codes, and expenses; occasionally a few clarifying or descriptive comments have to be added. Clearly distinguished categories on routine forms help organize information.

Fig. 12.1 A log, a type of periodic report.

Reprinted courtesy of the Denver Police Department.

Other kinds of periodic reports may require more writing. You may be responsible for compiling a report based on individual periodic reports. Figure 12.2, a report submitted to a police captain, summarizes, organizes, and interprets the data collected over a three-month period from individual activity logs similar to the one in Fig. 12.1. Such a report answers the reader's questions about the frequency and types of crimes committed and the work of the police force in the community. Because of this report, Captain Alice Martin will be better able to plan future protection for the community and to recommend changes in police services.

▶ Sales Reports

Sales reports provide businesses with a necessary record of accounts, purchases, and profits over a specified period of time. They are important at var-

Fig. 12.1   (continued)

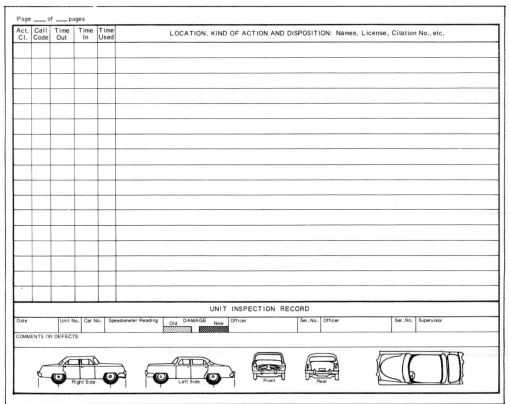

Fig. 12.2   A quarterly periodic report.

GREENFIELD POLICE DEPARTMENT
Greenfield, Texas 77003

TO: Captain Alice Martin

FROM: Sergeant Daniel Huxley *D.H*

SUBJECT: Crime rate for the first quarter of 1980

DATE: April 12, 1980

From January 1 to March 31, 1,276 crimes were committed in Greenfield, representing a 20 percent increase over the 1,021 crimes recorded during the previous quarter.

The following report discusses the specific types of crimes organized into three categories: felonies, traffic, and misdemeanors.

FELONIES:

The greatest increase in crime was in robberies. Downtown merchants reported 75 burglaries totaling more than $450,000. The biggest theft occurred on January 21 at Weisenfarth's Jewelers when three armed robbers stole more than $50,000 in merchandise. (These robbers were apprehended three days later.) Home burglaries accounted for 43 crimes, though the thefts were not confined to any one residential area. We also had 39 car thefts reported.

The number of homicides decreased from last quarter. During the first quarter we had 8 homicides as opposed to 9 last quarter. The battery charges, however, increased to 82—15 more than we had last quarter. There were 5 charges for arson, 11 for carrying a concealed weapon, and 20 for possession of a controlled substance. The number of rapes for this quarter was 8, fewer than last quarter (9). Three of those rapes happened within one week (February 3–8) and have been attributed to the same assailant, now in custody.

TRAFFIC:

Traffic violations for this period compared favorably with last quarter's figures. The 319 citations for moving violations for the first quarter represent a 5 percent decrease over last quarter's 335 violations. Most were issued for speeding (158) or for failing to observe signals (98). Officers issued 45 citations to motorists who were driving while under the influence. These citations point to an impressive decrease over the 78 issued last quarter. The new state

penalty of withholding for six months the driver's license of anyone
convicted of driving while under the influence is an effective
deterrent.

MISDEMEANORS:

The largest number of arrests in this category were for disturbing
the peace—53. Compared to last quarter, this is an increase of 10
percent. There were 48 charges for vagrancy and public drunkenness, a
decrease from the 59 charges brought last quarter. We issued 32
citations for violation of leash laws, which represents a sizeable
increase over last quarter's 21 citations. Fifty citations were issued
for violations of city codes and ordinances; 37 of those 50 citations
were issued for dumping trash at the Mason reservoir.

ious levels of business. Retail stores require a daily sales report in which purchases, coded by clerks on the cash register tapes, are arranged into major categories. Salespersons often submit weekly reports on the types and costs of products sold in a given district. Branch managers write monthly reports based on the figures given to them by their sales force. Higher up the business ladder, the president of a company sends stockholders an annual report assessing the financial health of the business. A report sent to someone at the same level of management as the writer is known as a *lateral report* (branch manager to branch manager). A report sent to a higher executive level than the level of the writer is known as a *vertical report* (branch manager to vice-president of marketing).

Sales reports help businesses assess the past and plan for the future. In doing this they fulfill two functions—financial and managerial. As a financial record, sales reports list costs per unit, discounts or special reductions, and subtotals and totals. Like an accountant's ledger, sales reports show gains and losses. They may also provide statistics for comparing two quarters' sales. The method or origin of a sale, if significant, can also be recorded. In selling books, for example, a publisher keeps a careful record of where sales originate—direct orders for single copies from readers, adoptions for classroom use, purchases at bookstores, or orders from wholesale distributors handling the book.

Sales reports are also a managerial tool, since they help businesses make both short- and long-range plans. By indicating the number of sales, the report alerts buyers and managers as to items or services to increase, modify, or discontinue. The sales report illustrated in Fig. 12.3 guides a restaurant owner in menu planning. Knowing which popular dishes to highlight and which unpopular ones to delete, the owner can increase profits. Note how the recommendations follow from the figures Sam Jelinek gives to Gina Smeltzer. Sales reports can also be the basis for hiring more employees, transferring others, or training new personnel.

Fig. 12.3 A sales report in tabular form.

THE PALACE
Dayton, Ohio 43210

TO: Gina Smeltzer   DATE: June 27, 1982
           Owner

FROM: Sam Jelinek   SUBJECT: Analysis of entree
           Manager   sales, June 10-24

    As you requested at our monthly meeting on June 5, I am supplying a
tabulated analysis of entree sales for two weeks to assist us in our menu
planning. Below is a record of entree sales for the weeks of June 10-17
and June 18-24. I have also compiled a table combining these two weeks'
sales for easier and more valid comparisons.

	Portion Size	June 10-17		June 18-24		2 weeks combined	
		Amount	Ratio	Amount	Ratio	Amount	Ratio
Strip Steak	12 oz	168	12%	198	11%	366	11%
Veal à la Viennoise (2)	8 oz	112	8	182	10	294	9
Shrimp Newburg	8 oz	154	11	217	12	371	12
Brook Trout	12 oz	56	4	70	4	126	4
Prime Rib (1)(2)	10 oz	343	25	413	23	756	24
Lobster Tails	2-4 oz	147	10	161	9	308	10
Delmonico Steak	10 oz	182	13	252	14	434	13
Beef Stroganoff (2)	8 oz	238	17	307	17	545	17
		1,400	100%	1,800	100%	3,200	100%

(1) 14 cuts / 22# rib.
(2) Prepared in advance.

    Based on these figures, I recommend that we

1. order at least one hundred more pounds of prime rib each two-week
   period to be eligible for further quantity discounts at the Northern
   Meat Company.

2. delete the brook trout entree because of low acceptance.

3. introduce a new beef or pork entree to take the place of the brook
   trout item. I would suggest stuffed pork chops.

    Please give me your reactions.

Fig. 12.4   A narrative sales report.

HAMILTON COIN SHOP
Erie, Pennsylvania 17321

```
TO:     Harry T. Udall              DATE:     September 8, 1982
        Owner

FROM:   Jessica Alonzo  J. A        SUBJECT:  August sales
        Manager
```

Our sales were brisk during August. Sales of mint sets and proof sets totaled $1,634. The sale of individual coins came to $2,340. Commemorative coin sales were $521. These sales total $4,495.

The most impressive sales came from our offer to sell pennies by the pound. We placed ads in one local paper and in a trade publication. Our ads over WTOR may also have helped sales. It is hard to determine what portion of our walk-in business came from the radio announcements. Possibly it is as much as a third. The total amount of sales for the pennies by the pound is $5,930.

Sales for the month of August come to $10,425. Detailed breakdowns of these figures will appear in the September 30 quarterly report.

To write a sales report, keep a careful record of order forms, invoices, and production figures. Sales information might be arranged in list form, as in Fig. 12.3, or in narrative form, as in Fig. 12.4. If you use the narrative format, make sure you do not overload your readers with numbers.

▶ Progress Reports

A progress report informs readers about the status of a project. It lets them know how much and what type of work has been completed by a particular date and how close the entire job is to being completed. A progress report emphasizes whether you are keeping on schedule, staying within a budget, using the proper equipment, making the right assignments, and completing the job efficiently and correctly. Almost any kind of ongoing work can be described in a progress report—research for a paper, construction of an apartment complex, preparation of a fall catalog, documentation of patient care.

The progress report is intended for people who are generally not working alongside you, but who need a record of your activities in order to coordinate them with other individuals' efforts and to learn about problems or

Fig. 12.5   A one-time progress report.

REPUBLIC INDUSTRIES
Trenton, New Jersey 08542

TO: Kathy Sands   DATE: September 14, 1981

FROM: Philip Javon   SUBJECT: Preparations for the
                                               Time Management
                                               Workshop

   Following your request of last week, I called the managers of all
departments on Thursday (September 7) to alert them about the time
management workshop we will offer on October 2–3. I also sent follow–up
notices to the managers today.

   I have reserved the cafeteria annex for both October 2 and 3 and
ordered all the supplies we will need. The management kit will have the
company brochures on organization policies, the time sheets used in the
plant, the report forms we used last March, note pads, and ball point
pens. I have also arranged with Ms. Suarez in the audiovisual department
to set up the projector on the morning of October 2. By tomorrow I hope to
have typed a list of all those who will participate in the workshop.

---

changes in plans. For example, since local management or workers at the
home office cannot be in the field or at the construction site, they will rely on
a progress report for much of their information. Customers, too, will expect
a report on how carefully their money is being spent. Health care professionals will consult the progress notes from the previous shift to provide continuity of care for their patients.

The length of the report will depend on the complexity of the project. A
report to a teacher about the progress you are making with a course paper
will not require more than a few paragraphs. A short memo about a time
management workshop, such as that in Fig. 12.5, might be all that is necessary. Similarly, Dale Brandt's assessment of the progress his firm is making in
renovating Dr. Burke's office is easily handled in a few paragraphs, as Fig.
12.6 shows.

Progress reports should contain information on (1) the work you have
done, (2) the work you currently are doing, and (3) the work you will do.

They can be written daily, weekly, monthly, quarterly, or annually. Your
specific job and your employer's needs will dictate how often you have to
keep others informed of your progress. Nurses have to write progress notes

Fig. 12.6 The second of three progress reports.

BRANDT CONSTRUCTION COMPANY
Halsted at Roosevelt
Chicago, Illinois 60608

April 28, 1982

Dr. Pamela Burke
1439 Grand
Mount Prospect, IL 60045

Dear Dr. Burke:

Here is the second progress report about the renovation work at your new clinic at Hacienda and Donohue. As I informed you in my letter of March 31, we had torn down the walls, pulled the old wiring, and removed the existing plumbing. With this gutting work completed, we were able to proceed satisfactorily in April according to plans you approved.

By April 9, we had laid the new pipes and connected them to the main sewer line. We had also installed the two commodes, the four standard sinks, and the utility basin. The heating and air conditioning ducts were installed by April 13. From April 16–20, we erected soundproof walls in the four examination rooms, the reception area, your office, and the laboratory. We had no problems reducing the size of the reception area by five feet to make the first examination room larger, as you had requested.

We had difficulty with the electrical work, however. The number of outlets and the generator for the laboratory equipment required extraduty power lines that had to be approved by both Con Edison and county inspectors. The approval slowed us down three days. Also, the wholesaler, Midtown Electric, failed to deliver the recessed lighting fixtures by April 23 as promised. We are now installing these fixtures and wiring. Moreover, the cost of those fixtures will increase the materials budget by $345. The cost for labor is as we had projected—$49,450.

The finishing work is scheduled for May. By May 10, the floors in the reception area, laboratory, washrooms, and hallways should be tiled and the examination rooms and your office carpeted. By May 15, the reception area and your office should be paneled and the rest of the walls painted. If everything stays on schedule, touch-up work is scheduled for May 18–22. You should be able to move into your new clinic by May 23.

I shall provide you with a third and final progress report by May 15.

Sincerely yours,

Dale Brandt

Dale Brandt

for each eight- or twelve-hour shift; management trainees may have to submit a weekly report of their accomplishments. A single progress report is sufficient for Philip Javon's purpose in Fig. 12.5. On the other hand, contractor Brandt in Fig. 12.6 has found that three separate reports, spaced four to six weeks apart, are needed to keep Dr. Burke posted.

How to Begin a Progress Report

In a brief introduction indicate why you are writing the report. Provide any necessary project titles or codes and specify dates. Help readers recall the job you are doing for them. If you are writing an initial progress report, supply background information. Philip Javon's first two sentences in Fig. 12.5 briefly establish his purpose by reminding Kathy Sands of their discussion last week. If you are submitting a subsequent progress report, show where the previous report left off and where the current one begins. Make sure that the period covered by each report is clearly specified. Note how Dale Brandt's first paragraph in Fig. 12.6 calls attention to the continuity of his work.

How to Continue a Progress Report

The body of the report should provide significant details about costs, materials, personnel, and times for the major stages of the project. Emphasize completed tasks, not false starts. If you are writing to say that the carpentry work or painting is finished, readers do not need an explanation of paint viscosity or geometrical patterns. Omit routine or well-known details ("I had to use the library when I wanted to read the back issues of *Safety News*" in a progress report on a term paper; "I made sure I applied the proper coating first" in a report on a painting contract). Describe in the body of the discussion, too, any snags you encountered. It is better for the reader to know about trouble early in the project, so that appropriate changes or corrections can be made. If you postpone reporting that you cannot meet a deadline, that costs have risen sharply, or that research has lead you down a blind alley, readers will be justly upset.

How to End a Progress Report

The conclusion should give a timetable for the completion of duties. Give the date by which work will be completed. Be realistic. Do not promise to have a job done in less time than you know it will take. Readers will not expect miracles, only informed estimates. Any conclusion must be tentative. Note that the good news Dale Brandt gives Dr. Burke about moving into her new clinic is qualified by the words "if everything stays on schedule." A student writing to a professor about a research paper might likewise emphasize the tentativeness of finishing by pointing out what further reading or laboratory work remains. A recommendation may also find a place in the conclusion, advising readers, for example, of a less costly, equally durable siding than the one originally planned, suggesting that a joint meeting of two committees would expedite production of a college yearbook, or advising that hiring an additional part-time salesclerk would help ease the busy holiday sales period.

▶ Trip Reports

Reporting on the trips you take is an important professional responsibility. Trips can range from a brief afternoon car ride across town to a two-week journey across the country. Trip, or travel, reports serve three functions:

1. They inform readers about activities outside the office, clinic, or plant.
2. They document what you did and saw.
3. They gather information that you and co-workers can use for later reports.

Common Types of Trip Reports

Trip reports can cover a wide range of activities and are called by different names to characterize those activities. Undoubtedly, you will encounter the following three types of trip reports:

1. Field trip reports. These reports, often assigned in a course, are written after a visit to a local plant, military installation, restaurant, garage, hospital, forest, or detention center. Their purpose is to show what you have learned about these places. You will be expected to describe how an institution is organized, the equipment or procedures it uses, the ecological conditions present, or the ratio of one group to another. The emphasis is on the educational values of the trip, as Mark Tourneur's report in Fig. 12.7 demonstrates.

2. Site inspection reports. These trip reports are written to inform readers about conditions at a branch office or plant, a customer's business, or at an area directly under an employer's jurisdiction. Site inspection reports tell how machinery or production procedures are working or provide information about the physical plant, environment (soil, trees, water), and clerical or financial operations. Sanitation and food inspectors, for example, report on conditions at restaurants, processing plants, and hotels and motels. A site inspection report will be written for an employer or a customer who wants to relocate or build new facilities (a fast-food restaurant, a half-way house, a branch office) to assess the suitability of a particular location. After visiting the site, you will determine whether it meets your employer's (or customer's) needs. Figure 12.8, which shows a report written to a manager interested in acquiring land for a fast-food restaurant, begins with a recommendation.

Fig. 12.7   A field trip report.

TO: Ms. Katherine Holmes,   DATE: November 9, 1981
       R.N., M.S.N.
       Director, R.N. Program

FROM: Mark Tourneur *MT*   SUBJECT: Field Trip to Water
       R.N. Student   Valley
                                             Convalescent Center

On Tuesday, November 2, I visited the Water Valley Convalescent
Center, 1400 Medford Boulevard, in preparation for my internship in a
nursing home next semester.

Before the tour started, the Director explained the holistic
philosophy of health care at Water Valley and emphasized the diverse
kinds of nursing practiced there. She stressed that the agency is not
restricted to geriatric patients, but admits anyone requiring long-term
care. She pointed out that Water Valley is a medium-sized center (150
beds) and contains three wings: (1) the Infirmary, (2) the General
Nursing Unit, and (3) the Ambulatory Unit.

My tour began with the Infirmary, staffed by one R.N. and two
L.P.N.'s, where I observed a number of life-support systems—I.V.'s,
oxygen setups, electrocardiograph equipment. Then I was shown the
General Nursing Unit, which has wide halls and doorways for patients
using walkers and wheelchairs. This forty-bed unit is staffed by three
L.P.N.'s and four aides. Patients can have private or semiprivate rooms;
bathrooms have extrawide commodes and sinks suitable for patients using
wheelchairs or walkers. The ambulatory section cares for ninety
patients.

Before having lunch in the main dining room, I was introduced to
Doris Betz, the dietitian, who explained the different diets she
coordinates. The most common are low sodium and restricted calorie.
Staff members eat with the patients, reinforcing the holistic concern of
the agency.

After lunch, Jack Tishner, the pharmacist, discussed the agency's
procedures for ordering and delivering medications. He also stressed
the patient teaching and inservice workshops he does. I then observed
patients in both recreational and physical therapy. Water Valley has a
full-time physical therapist who works with stroke and arthritic
patients and helps those with broken bones regain the use of their
limbs. In addition to a weight room, Water Valley has a small sauna that
most of the patients use at least twice a week. The physical therapist,
Kathy Jansen, works very closely with the nursing staff. The patients'
spiritual needs are not neglected, either. A small chapel is located on
the Ambulatory Unit.

From my visit to Water Valley, I learned a great deal about the
health care delivery system at a nursing home. I was especially pleased
to have been given so much information on emergency procedures,
medication orders, and physical therapy programs. My forthcoming
internship will be much more useful, since I have first-hand knowledge
about the scope of available services.

Fig. 12.8   A site inspection report and accompanying map.

VAIL'S, INC.

Denver, Colorado 87123

TO: Dale Gandy
      District Manager

FROM: Delores Marshack ĐM
       Development Dept.

DATE: July 1, 1982

SUBJECT: New site for Vail's #8

RECOMMENDATION:

    The best location for the new Vail's Chicken House is the vacant
Dairy World property at the northeast corner of Smith and Fairfax
Avenues—1701 South Fairfax. I inspected this property on June 23 and 24
and also talked with Marge Bloom, the broker at Crescent Realty
representing the Dairy World Company.

THE LOCATION:

    See the map below. Located at the intersection of the two busiest
streets on the southeast side, the property can take advantage of the
traffic flow to attract customers. Being only one block west of the
Cloverleaf Mall should also help business. Only two other fast-food
establishments are in a one-mile vicinity. McGonagles, 1534 South
Kildare, specializes in hamburgers; Noah's, 703 Zanwood, serves
primarily fish entrees. Their offerings will not directly compete with
ours. The closest fast-food restaurant serving chicken is Johnson's,
1.8 miles away. Customers can exit or enter the Dairy World from either
Smith or Fairfax, but left turns on Smith are prohibited from 7 A.M. to 9
A.M. However, since most of our business is done after 11 A.M., the
restriction poses few problems.

PARKING FACILITIES:

    There is enough space for 45 cars in the parking lot; the area at the
south end of the property (38 feet × 37 feet) can accommodate another 11
to 15 cars. The driveways and parking lot were paved with asphalt last
March and appear to be in excellent shape. We will be able to make good
use of the drive-up window on the north side of the building.

THE BUILDING:

    The building has 3,993 square feet of heated and cooled space. The
air conditioning and heating units were installed within the last
fifteen months and seem to be in good working order; nine more months of
transferable warranty remain on these units. The only major changes we
would have to make are in the kitchen. To prepare items on the Vail's
menu, we have to add more exhaust fans (there is only one there now) and
expand the grill and cooking areas. There are three relatively new sinks
and ample storage space in the fourteen cabinets. The restaurant has a

seating capacity of up to 54 persons; ten booths are covered with red vinyl and are comfortably padded. The floor does not need to be retiled, but the walls must be painted to match Vail's color decor.

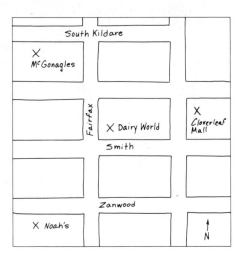

3. Home health or social work visits.   Nurses, social workers, and probation officers report daily on their visits to patients and clients. Their reports describe clients' lifestyles, assess needs, and make recommendations. A report from a social worker to a county family services agency can be seen in Fig. 12.9. The report begins with the information Jeff Bowman acquired from his visit with the Scanlons and concludes, not with a recommendation, but rather with a list of the actions this social worker has taken.

How to Gather Information for a Trip Report

Regardless of the kind of trip report you have to write, your assignment will be easier and your report better organized if you follow these suggestions.

Before You Leave for the Site

1. Obtain all necessary names, addresses, and telephone numbers.
2. Check the files for previous correspondence, case studies, terms of contracts or agreements.
3. Locate a map of the area or a blueprint of the building.
4. Look for brochures, work orders, instructions, or other documents.
5. Make sure you have a notebook and a pen with you. Depending on your job, you may also need to bring a tape recorder or camera.

Fig. 12.9   A social worker's visit report.

GREEN COUNTY FAMILY SERVICE
Randall, Virginia 21032

TO: Margaret S. Walker, Director
           Green County Family Services

FROM: Jeff Bowman, Social Worker

SUBJECT: Visit to Mr. Lee Scanlon

DATE: October 14, 1981

PURPOSE:

   At the request of the Green County Home Health Office, I visited
Mr. Lee Scanlon at his home at 113 West Diversy Drive on Tuesday, October
12. Mr. Scanlon and his three children (ages six, eight, and eleven)
live in a two–bedroom apartment above a garage. Last week, Mr. Scanlon
was discharged from Methodist General Hospital after leg surgery and has
asked for financial assistance.

DESCRIPTION OF VISIT:

   Mr. Scanlon is a widower with no means of support except a monthly
Social Security check of $305 and unemployment compensation totaling
$130 a month. He lost his job at Baymont Manufacturing when the company
went out of business four weeks ago and wants to go back to work, but Dr.
Canning–Smith advised against it for six to seven weeks. His oldest
child is diabetic, and the six–year–old daughter must have a
tonsillectomy. Mr. Scanlon also told me the problems he was having with
his refrigerator; it "was broke more than it was on," he said.

   Mrs. Alice Gordon, the owner of the garage, informed me that
Mr. Scanlon had paid last month's rent but not this month's. She also
stressed how much the Scanlons need a new refrigerator and that she had
often let them use part of hers to store their food.

   Mr. Scanlon's monthly bills and income are as follows:

Expenses	Income
$170 rent	$305 Social Security
65 utilities	130 unemployment
250 food	$435
60 drugs	
80 transportation	
$625	

ACTION TAKEN:

    To assist Mr. Scanlon, I have done the following:

1. Set up an appointment (10/16/81) for him to apply for food stamps.
2. Talked with Mrs. Blanche Derringo regarding Medicaid assistance.
3. Asked the State Employment Security Commission to aid him in finding a job as soon as he is well enough to work.
4. Visited Mr. Robert Adkins at the office of the Council of Churches to obtain food and money for utilities until federal aid is available; he also will try to find the Scanlons another refrigerator.
5. Telephoned Sharon Munez at the Green County Health Department to have Mr. Scanlon's diabetic daughter receive insulin and syringes gratis.

When You Return

1. Write your report promptly. If you put it off, you may forget important items. Also, the interests of your employer and/or customer may be hurt by the delay of your report.
2. When a trip takes you to two or more widely separated places, note in your report when you arrived at each place and how long you stayed.
3. Do not include in your report everything you saw or did on the trip. Exclude irrelevant details, such as whether the trip was enjoyable, where you stayed overnight, what you ate, or how delighted you were to meet people.

▶ Test Reports

Much physical research (the discovery of facts) is communicated through reports. These reports have various names. Depending on your profession's terminology, they may be called experiment, investigative, laboratory, operations, or research reports. They all record the results of tests, whether the tests were conducted in a forest, laboratory, parking lot, shopping center, or soybean field.

Tests in business and industry serve a variety of functions. They help to assess health, ensure safety, accomplish routine maintenance, or develop new products. Medical laboratories examine specimens—blood, urine, sputum, tissue—to determine abnormalities. Safety regulations account for tests done by the Environmental Protection Agency (EPA) or Occupational Safety and

Health Administration (OSHA) to measure, for example, the air for pollutants—asbestos particles, cotton dust, or gasoline fumes. The building industry routinely conducts tests for new developments—examining the soil, for example, to see whether it is dense enough to accommodate a septic tank or firm enough to support a parking lot. Businesses themselves run tests on new products—toys, automobiles, home appliances—to ensure customer safety. They also regularly investigate conditions in their own facilities for employee safety.

Readers want to know abour your empirical research (the facts), not about your feelings (the "I"). A laboratory journal or log book for recording facts is a useful companion when you run tests. When you sign your name to a test report, you are certifying that things happened exactly when, how, and why you say they did. Readers want to know why the test was made, under what circumstances (or controls) it was made, and what the outcome was. The answers to these questions are indicated clearly but briefly in the short report in Fig. 12.10 regarding sanitary conditions at a hospital psychiatric unit. Submitted by an infection control officer, the report does not provide elaborate details about the particular laboratory procedures used to determine if bacteria were present; nor does it describe the pathogenic (disease-causing) properties of the bacteria. Such descriptions are unnecessary for the audience (the housekeeping department) to do its job. Although the results of this test are recorded in memo format, other types of simple tests are printed on forms on which the technologist fills in the appropriate numbers after the test is run.

▶ Incident Reports

All the reports discussed thus far in this chapter have dealt with routine work. They have described events that were anticipated or supervised. But every business or agency runs into unexpected trouble that delays routine work. Employers, and on some occasions government inspectors, insurance agents, and attorneys, must be informed about those events that interfere with normal, safe operations. A special type of report known as an *incident report* is submitted when there is an accident, law enforcement offense, machine breakdown, delivery delay, cost overrun, or production slowdown.

Protecting Yourself Legally

The incident report can be used as legal evidence. It frequently concerns the two topics over which powerful legal battles are waged—health and property. The report can sway the outcome of insurance claims, civil suits, or criminal

Fig. 12.10   A laboratory (or test) report with recommendations.

CHARLESTON CENTRAL HOSPITAL
CHARLESTON, WV 25324

TO: James Dill, Supervisor   DATE: December 3, 1981
        Housekeeping

FROM: Janeen Cufaude   SUBJECT: Routine sanitation
        Infection Control Officer   inspection

As part of the monthly check of the psychiatric unit (11A), the following
areas were swabbed and tested for bacterial growth. The results of the
lab tests of these samples are as follows:

AREA   FINDINGS

1. cabinet in patients' kitchen   1. positive for 2 colonies of
                                         streptococcus pyrogens

2. rug in eating area   2. positive for food particles
                                         and yeasts and molds

3. baseboard in dayroom   3. positive for particles of dust
                                         and fungi

4. medicine counter in nurses'   4. negative for bacteria——no
   station   growth after 48 hrs

5. corridor by south elevator   5. positive for 4 colonies of
                                         staphylococcus aurens

The following action should be taken at once:

1. Clean the kitchen area with K–504 liquid daily, 3:1 dilution.

2. Shampoo rug areas bimonthly with heavy–duty shampoo and clean
   visibly soiled areas with Guard–Pruf as often as needed.

3. Wipe all baseboards weekly with K–12 spray cleanser.

4. Mop heavily traveled corridors and access areas with K–504 cleanser
   daily, 1:1 dilution.

cases. To ensure that what you write is legally proper, follow these three rules:

1. Make sure that the report is full, accurate, and objective. Never omit facts, even if you were at fault; the information may surface later, and you could be guilty of a cover-up. Do not write "I do not know" for an answer. If you are not sure, state why. Also be careful that there are no discrepancies in your report.

2. Give facts, not opinions. Provide an objective account of what actually happened, not a biased interpretation of events. Indirect words, such as "I guess," "I wonder," "There was some apparent injury," "perhaps," or "possibly," weaken your objectivity. Stick to details you witnessed or that were seen by eyewitnesses. Indicate who saw what. Keep in mind that stating what someone else saw will be regarded as hearsay, and therefore be inadmissible in a court of law. State only what *you* saw or heard. When you describe what happened, avoid drawing uncalled-for conclusions.

Wrong: The patient seemed confused and caught himself in his I.V. tubing.

Right: The patient caught himself in his I.V. tubing.

Wrong: The equipment was defective.

Right: The bolt was loose.

Be careful, too, about blaming someone. Saying that "Baxter was incompetent" or that the "company knew of the problem but did nothing about it" are libelous remarks.

3. Do not exceed your professional responsibilities. Answer only those questions you are qualified to answer. Do not presume to speak as a detective, inspector, physician, or supervisor. Do not represent yourself as an attorney or claims adjuster in writing the report.

Parts of an Incident Report

You will use either a memo or a specially prepared form with spaces for detailed comments. Figure 12.11 contains an incident report written in memo format; Fig. 12.12 shows a typical incident report form used to report an accident. Regardless of the format, all incident reports will ask for the following information:

1. Personal details. Record titles, department, and employment identification numbers. Indicate if you or your fellow employees were working alone. For customers and victims, record home addresses, phone numbers, and places of employment. Insurance companies will also require policy numbers. Note that the first four questions in Fig. 12.12 request this kind of information.

Fig. 12.11 An incident report.

THE GREAT HARVESTER RAILROAD

TO: Marge O'Brien   DATE: March 2, 1982
      District Manager

FROM: Ned Roane *NR*   SUBJECT: Derailment of Train #28
      Engineer   on March 1, 1982

DESCRIPTION OF INCIDENT:

At 7:20 A.M. on March 1, 1982, I was driving engine #457 traveling north at a speed of fifty-two miles an hour on the single mainline track four miles east of Ridgeville, Illinois. Weather conditions and visibility were excellent. Suddenly the last two grain cars, #3022 and #3053, jumped the track. The train automatically went into emergency braking and stopped immediately. There were no injuries to the crew. But the train did not stop before both grain cars turned at a 45° angle. After checking the cars, I found that half the contents of their load had spilled. The train was not carrying any chemical shipments.

I notified Supervisor Bill Purvis by AMAX telephone at 7:40 A.M. and within forty-five minutes he and twelve sectionmen arrived at the scene with rerailing equipment—a bulldozer and a derrick. The sectionmen removed the two grain cars from the track, put in new ties, and made the mainline track passable by 9:25. At 9:45 a vacuum car arrived with engine #372 from Hazlehurst, Illinois, and its crew proceeded with the clean-up operation. By 10:25 A.M. all the spilled grain was loaded onto the cars brought by the Hazlehurst train. Bill Purvis called Barnwell Graneries and notified them that their shipment would be three hours late.

CAUSES:

Supervisor Purvis and I checked the stretch of train track where the cars derailed and found it to be heavily worn. We believe that a defective fisher joint slipped when the grain cars hit it, and the track broke.

RECOMMENDATIONS:

We made the following recommendations to the switchyard in Hazlehurst to be carried out immediately:

1. Check the section of track ten miles either side of Ridgeville for defective fisher joints.

2. Repair all such joints at once.

3. Instruct all engineers to slow to five to ten mph over this section of the road until the rail check is completed.

Fig. 12.12   An accident report form.

DIVERSIFIED INDUSTRIES

ACCIDENT REPORT

1. Name of the employee (last, first, middle) _____

2. Employee identification number _____

3. Social Security number _____

4. Home address and telephone number _____

5. Time of injury _____ $\frac{AM}{PM}$ Location _____

6. Type of injury (specify exact body part(s)) _____

   _____

7. What kind of treatment did injured party receive?   Where was treatment given?_____

   _____

   _____

8. Description of what happened (give a narrative of events before,
   during, and after; describe materials or tools involved in accident):

9. Names and addresses of eyewitnesses:

10. What caused the accident?

11. What action should be taken to prevent similar accidents in the future ?

Signature of person filling out form _____

Date form is filled out. _____

Send one copy to Home Office; one copy to Safety Department ; and one to Personnel Department.

---

2. Type of incident.   A short statement should describe the incident: personal injury, fire, burglary, delivery delay, equipment failure. In the case of injury identify the part(s) of the body precisely. "Eye injury" is not enough; "injury to the right eye, causing bleeding" is better. "Dislocated shoulder," "punctured left forearm," and "twisted left ankle" are descriptive phrases. A report on damaged equipment should list model numbers. Note how Ned Roane's report (Fig. 12.11) specifies the grain car numbers. For thefts, supply colors, brand names, quantities, and serial numbers. "A stolen watch" will not help detectives locate the right object; "a seven-jewel lady's Benrus" will.

3. Time and location of the incident.   Follow the advice given at the beginning of this chapter, pp. 358–359.

4. Description of what happened.   This section is the longest part of the report. Some forms ask you to write on the back, to attach another sheet, or to add a photograph or diagram. Put yourself in the reader's position. If you were not present or did not speak directly to witnesses, would you know by reading the report what happened exactly and why, how it occurred, who and what were involved, and what led up to the incident? The two most common errors writers make are that they do not give (1) enough information or (2) the right kinds of information. Recount what happened in the order in which it took place. What you (or eyewitnesses) saw, heard, felt, and smelled are the essentials of your description. Describe what happened before the incident, if that is relevant—for example, environmental or weather conditions for storm damage or an automobile accident, or warning signals for a malfunctioning machine. If you are depending on an eyewitness account, use quotation marks to set off statements by the witness. But delete any emotional reactions of eyewitnesses—how much an object meant or how surprised they were to see something happen. Filter out other irrelevant details. If you are reporting a work stoppage, it is unnecessary to indicate what the employees did while waiting for machinery to be repaired. Do not duplicate information found elsewhere in the report—license numbers, times, employee identification numbers. Wherever necessary, give information about expenses.

5. What was done after the incident.   After describing the incident, be concerned with the action you took to correct conditions, to get things back to normal. Readers will want to know what was done to treat the injured, to make the environment safer, to speed delivery of goods, to repair damaged equipment, or to satisfy a customer's demands.

6. What caused the incident.   Make sure that your explanation is consistent with your description in number 4 above. Pinpoint the trouble. In Fig. 12.11, for example, the defective fisher joint is discussed under the heading "Causes." In the following example causes cited are exact and are helpful in a report of an accident involving a pipe falling from a crane:

1. The crane's safety latch had been broken off and was never replaced.
2. A tag line was not used to guide the pipe onto the truckbed.

7. Recommendations.   Readers will be looking for specific suggestions to prevent the incident from happening again. Recommendations may involve discussing the problem at a safety meeting, asking for further training from a manufacturer, adapting existing equipment to meet customer's needs, modifying schedules, or cutting back on expenses. In the example of the falling pipe in number 6, the writer of an incident report listed two recommendations:

1. Order safety latches to replace the broken latch and have additional spare latches on hand.
2. Have a pipeshop foreman conduct a safety meeting for employees and use a representative drawing of the incident as an aid.

Before going on to consider long reports, let's review the main points about short reports:

1. They are brief.
2. They can be prepared in a variety of formats—memo, letter, or special form.
3. Their content will vary with the type of report—periodic, sales, progress, trip, incident. In all types of short reports, however, the emphasis is on facts and objectivity.
4. They should be organized to include information on the purpose, time frame, and scope of the report; procedures used; results; and recommendations.

▶ Exercises

1. Bring to class an example of a periodic report from your previous or present job or from any community, religious, or social organization to which you belong. In an accompanying memo to your instructor, indicate why such a report is necessary, stressing how it is submitted and organized and what kinds of factual data it contains.

2. Assume that you are a manager of a large apartment complex (200 units). Write a periodic report on how many units are vacant, filled, or ready to become vacant or soon-to-be-leased as of November 1.

3. Write a periodic report to an employer on how you spent company time for any one week. Indicate the times you spent on individual assignments, special duties, or overtime work. Compute a rate of pay for regular, special, and overtime work. Give your employer an itemized account of the pay that is due to you.

4. Write a sales report with a recommendation to the general manager of an automobile dealership based on the following data:

January:	sold 4 full size cars, 32 compacts, and 11 pickups
February:	sold 10 full size cars, 34 compacts, and 10 pickups
March:	sold 5 full size cars, 23 compacts, and 23 pickups
April:	sold 7 full size cars, 41 compacts, and 19 pickups
May:	sold 8 full size cars. 39 compacts, and 17 pickups
June:	sold 11 full size cars, 36 compacts, and 18 pickups

5. Write a progress report on the wins, losses, and ties of your favorite team for last year. Address the report to the Director of Publicity for the team and stress how the director can use these facts for future publicity.

6. Submit a progress report to your writing teacher on what you have learned in his or her course so far this term, which writing skills you want to develop in greater detail, and how you propose doing so.

7. Compose a site inspection report on any part of the college campus or plant, office, or store in which you work that might need remodeling, expansion, or air conditioning or heating work.

8. Assume that you are a social worker, law enforcement officer, or youth counselor. Write an appropriate trip report based on the following information. Make sure to include your reasons for the visit, a description of the visit, and some recommendations based on the visit.

> George Morrow, age 15, was put on probation last August for stealing. He has missed a number of school days this term. The principal at his high school said he also got into some trouble about library books—defacing them or not returning them. George's parents were recently divorced, and he lives with his mother. His mother has requested some help and wants to know what kinds of programs are available. George is very eager to go to technical school and become an electrician. He feels as though his misdeeds will hurt him. George has to report to the court at least once a month for the next year.

9. Write a report to an instructor in your major field about a field trip you have taken in the last twelve months. Indicate why you took the trip, name the individuals you met on the trip, and stress what you learned and how that information helps you in current or past course work.

10. Submit a test report on the procedures, results, and recommendations of an experiment you conducted on one of the following subjects:

(a) soil	(i) computers
(b) machinery	(j) forests
(c) water	(k) food
(d) automobiles	(l) housing
(e) textiles	(m) money
(f) animals	(n) transportation
(g) fingerprinting	(o) blood
(h) recreational facilities	(p) noise levels

11. Write an incident report about a problem you encountered in your work in the last year. Use the memo format or use the form reprinted in Fig. 12.12 (p. 379).

12. Write an incident report about one of the following problems. Assume that it has happened to you. Identify the audience for whom you are writing and the agency you are representing or trying to reach. Include all relevant details in your report.

(a) After hydroplaning, your company car hits a tree and has a damaged front fender.

(b) You have been the victim of an electrical shock because an electrical tool was not grounded.

(c) You twist your back lifting a bulky package.

(d) Your boat capsizes while you are patrolling the lake.

13. Choose one of the following descriptions of an incident and write a report based on it. The descriptions contain unnecessary details, vague words, insufficient information, an unclear cause-and-effect relationship, or all of these errors. In writing your report, correct the errors by adding or subtracting whatever information you believe is necessary. You may also want to rearrange the order in which information is listed. Use the form in Fig. 12.12 (p. 379) or a memo format to write the report.

(a) Joe Williamson is hurt. It took the ambulance about ten minutes to arrive and another five to get Joe on a stretcher headed for St. Paul's Hospital, which is about four miles away. The spot where Joe was installing the light was very close to the employee cafeteria. His right arm may be broken, and his left ankle is twisted. His shirt sleeve is ripped, and so are his trousers. Joe was installing a new high-wattage electric light, and he cut himself when the light broke in the socket. Trying to install that light without someone holding the ladder was foolish, said Cynthia Parker, who saw the whole thing. The plant nurse was called; her name is Mary Noonan, and she told Joe not to move and tried to stop the bleeding in his hand. When Joe got a handkerchief to stop the bleeding when he was still on the ladder, he lost his balance, and that's what led to the fall. The ladder wobbled and gave way. Joe fell quite a distance. It's too bad all this happened so close to lunch. All the employees saw poor Joe, and they felt bad.

(b) After sliding across the slippery road late at night, my car ran into another vehicle, one of those imported Japanese cars. The driver of that car must have been asleep at the wheel. The paint and glass chips were all over. I was driving back from our regional meeting and wanted to report to the home office the next day. The accident will slow me down.

(c) Whoever packed the glass mugs did not know what he or she was doing. The string was not the right type; nor was it tied correctly. The carton was too flimsy as well. It could have been better packed to hold all those mugs. Moreover, since the bus had to travel across some pretty rough country, the package would have broken anyhow. The best way to ship these kinds of goods is in specially marked and packed boxes. The value of the box was listed at $350.

13

Long Reports

Reports can be far more complex and lengthy than the ones discussed in Chapter 12. A long report records weeks or months of research in an attempt to offer a comprehensive discussion of the subject. Unlike a short report, a long report discusses not one or two current events, but rather a large problem (and all the background information about it) whose solution has far-ranging implications for a business, industry, or community. A long report provides a full-scale investigation of a problem and offers a set of detailed recommendations for solving it. A long report is carefully planned, researched, and may take weeks, even months, to write.

What type of large problem requires a long report? Figure 13.1 shows the kind of significant and complex subject investigated in a long report—in this case the ecological conditions at a widely used creek in the Great Smoky Mountains National Park. The findings of the report have important implications for managing the park, protecting visitors' health, and maintaining a natural ecological balance.

In the world of business a long report is not necessarily the work of one employee. Rather, it may be the product of a committee or group effort. Individuals in many departments within the company—art, data processing, engineering, public relations, public safety—cooperate in planning and producing a long report, which may reflect their various skills—drawing, data analysis, interviewing. Even though you may not have coauthors for the long reports you write for class, you still make use of many skills various professionals employ in writing a long report for business and industry.

The audience for a long report differs considerably from that for a short report, too. The audience for a long report is generally wider and goes higher in an organization's hierarchy than that for a short report. Your short report may be read by your fellow workers or a first-level supervisor, but a

Fig. 13.1   An introduction to a test report.

Introduction

Abrams Creek is a major stream in the Great Smoky Mountains National Park (Fig. 1). The headwaters of this stream (referred to as Anthony Creek) drain the north face of Mount Squires, 4,958 feet above mean sea level (MSL), flowing mostly through second growth forest. At an elevation of about 1,900 feet above MSL, the stream, now called Abrams Creek, enters an historical pastoral area—Cades Cove. The stream flows for a distance of about six miles in the cove before flowing again through second growth forest. About 18 miles downstream from the cove, the creek discharges into Chilhowee Lake (874 feet above MSL).

Fig. 1   Great Smoky Mountains National Park, showing Cades Cove, pasture areas, and Abrams Creek.

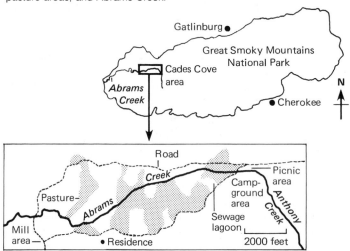

The Abrams Creek drainage is visited by thousands of park visitors each year, mostly in summer. The preponderance of visitor traffic is centralized in the Cades Cove area. People are attracted to the cove because this scenic historical area has pastures, pioneer cabins, a grain mill, picnic area, campground, and other attractions, such as fishing and swimming, which are readily accessible by automobile (Fig. 1). Visitors to the cove are also able to observe an abundance of wildlife, including squirrels, turkeys, deer, wild European boar, skunks, ground hogs, and bear.

The pastures in the cove are still used for cattle grazing and for haying by descendants of the cove settlers. The cattle obtain most of their drinking water directly

Gary L. Larson, Raymond C. Mathews, Jr., and Jacalyn L. Klausmeyer, "A Survey of Bacterial Water Quality in Abrams Creek, Great Smoky Mountains National Park," *Journal of the Tennessee Academy of Science,* 55 (January 1980), 1. Reprinted by permission.

from the creek and tributaries at specific sites. The number of cattle in the cove was reduced from 1,200 to 500 late in 1976.

Owing to the potential environmental impacts from visitor traffic and cattle, the water quality of Abrams Creek in Cades Cove was investigated by Kelly (1974) and Silsbee et al. (1976). The former examined temperature and turbidity, while the latter determined numbers of fecal coliform and fecal streptococcus bacteria in the creek as part of a survey of the backcountry water quality of streams in the park in 1976. The results of both studies showed that the water quality of Abrams Creek deteriorated in the cove.

A management policy of the National Park Service is to conserve, perpetuate, and restore, when necessary, park resources. The basis of this policy is to manage natural processes on the ecosystem level. Although historic areas in parks, such as Cades Cove, depart from this concept, the Service attempts to manage these areas by emphasizing a balance between the resource alterations and the associated changes of natural processes. But the deteriorated condition of Abrams Creek noted by Kelly and Silsbee suggests an imbalance in Cades Cove. In view of the present conditions, an ecological survey of Abrams Creek was conducted in 1977 to assist in the development of appropriate management programs for the cove. Part of this survey included estimates of the numbers of total coliforms, fecal coliforms, and fecal streptococcus bacteria from May to August. These bacterial types are often used to establish water quality (U.S. Environmental Protection Agency 1975).

---

long report is likely to be read by people in the top levels of management—presidents, vice-presidents, superintendents, directors—who make financial and organizational decisions. In addition, copies of long reports may be sent to appropriate department heads for their information and commentary. Governmental agencies, too, sponsor lengthy reports on a variety of topics (see the *Government Reports Announcements and Index,* published bimonthly) by awarding substantial annual grants. Finally, long reports may appear as articles in professional journals. This enables specialists in other agencies and companies across the country or throughout the world to study the findings these reports offer and to apply the recommendations to problems encountered in their own work environments.

The most significant difference between a short report and a long report is in format. The information in a long report cannot be properly or effectively arranged or discussed in a simple memo or letter format. The graphs, charts, and tables in a long report provide readers with extensive background information and documentation. The product of thorough research and analysis of that research, the long report gives detailed discussions of a great deal of data. To present all this information, the long report must contain many sections, headings, and subheadings, which cannot be incorporated into the memorandum or letter format.

▶ Parts of a Long Report

A long report may include some or all of the following twelve parts, which form three categories—front matter, the text, and back matter.

Front Matter

As the name implies, the front matter of a long report consists of everything that precedes the actual text of the report. Such elements introduce, explain, and summarize and help the reader locate various parts of the report.

1. Title page. Generally the first element in the front matter, this page gives the name of the company or agency preparing the report, the name(s) of the report writer(s), the date, any agency or order numbers, and the name of the firm for which the report was prepared. Figure 13.2 shows a typical title page for a long report. Note that the various elements are centered and well spaced on the page.

2. Letter of transmittal. This brief three- or four-paragraph letter states the purpose, scope, and major recommendation of the report. Sometimes the letter of transmittal is bound with the report as part of it; sometimes it comes before the report, serving as a kind of cover letter. Figure 13.3 is a sample letter of transmittal.

3. List of illustrations. This list of all the figures and tables indicates where in the report they are found. Figure 13.4 shows a sample list of illustrations.

4. Table of contents. The major sections of the report (any or all of parts 5–12 below) are listed on the contents page. By looking at the table of contents in Fig. 13.5, for example, the reader sees at a glance how the report "New Directions in Women's Athletics at Coastal College" is organized and the location of the various sections of that report. When preparing a table of contents, use lower-case Roman numerals for front matter elements as in Fig. 13.5. Never list the contents page, and never have just one subheading under a heading.

Incorrect:	EXPANDING THE SPORTS PROGRAM
	Basketball
	BUILDING A NEW ARENA
	The West side Location
Correct:	EXPANDING THE SPORTS PROGRAM
	Basketball
	Track and Field
	BUILDING A NEW ARENA
	The West side Location
	Cost

Fig. 13.2   A title page for a long report.

New Directions in Women's Athletics at Coastal College

Prepared for

Dr. K. G. Lawry
President, Coastal College

by
Barbara Gilcrest

ALPHA CONSULTANTS
Report No. 4202

August 1, 1981

Fig. 13.3 A letter of transmittal for a long report.

ALPHA CONSULTANTS
1400 Ridge
Evanston, California 97213

August 1, 1981

Dr. K. G. Lawry
President
Coastal College
San Diego, California 93219

Dear Dr. Lawry:

I am enclosing the report "New Directions in Women's Athletics at Coastal College" that you asked us to prepare. The report contains our recommendations about strengthening existing programs and creating new ones at Coastal College.

After studying Coastal's sports facilities and the College's plans for expansion, we interviewed the entire coaching staff and many of the women athletes. We also polled the coaching staffs and 100 women athletes at three local colleges—Baystown Community College, California State University of Arts and Sciences, and Central Community College.

Our recommendation is that Coastal should engage in more active recruitment to establish a competitive women's basketball team, start to offer athletic activities in women's track and field by August 1982, and create a new interdisciplinary program between the Athletic Department and the Women's Studies Program.

I hope that you find our report satisfactory. If you have any questions or if you would like us to comment further on any of our recommendations, please do not hesitate to call me.

Sincerely yours,

Barbara Gilcrest

Barbara Gilcrest

Encl. Report

Fig. 13.4 A list of illustrations for a long report.

LIST OF ILLUSTRATIONS

Women's Athletics' Share of the Coastal Sports Budget 2

Floor Plan of the Mendez Sports Arena 15

Awards Won by Coastal's Women Athletes in
Seven Regional Tournaments 19

Faculty Participation in Women's Studies Program 23

Fig. 13.5   A table of contents for a long report.

CONTENTS

5. Abstract. As discussed in Chapter 8 (pp. 246–247) an abstract presents a brief overview of the problem and conclusions; it summarizes the report. An informative abstract is far more helpful to readers of a report than is a descriptive one, which gives no conclusions or results.

Not every member of your audience will read your entire report. But almost everyone will read the abstract of your long report. For example, the president of the corporation or the director of an agency may use the abstract as the basis for approving the report and passing it on for distribution. Thus the abstract may be the most important part of the report.

Abstracts may be placed at various points in long reports. They may be placed on the title page, on a separate page, or on the first page of the report text. Note in Fig. 13.5, for example, that the abstract has been put on a separate page (iii). In Fig. 13.6, on the other hand, the introduction immediately follows the abstract.

Text of the Report

6. Introduction. The introduction tells readers why the report was written. It defines the problem. Therefore, your statement of the problem must be clear and precise.

The following types of information are included in the introductory part of the report text: (a) background details the readers need to understand the report, (b) identification of the problem to be studied in the report, and (c) review of recent research (or a summary of what has been done, what others know, what gaps exist in current knowledge). Note how this information is listed under "Introduction" in Fig. 13.5. Reread Fig. 13.1 to see how the three types of information pertinent to an introduction are effectively incorporated and coherently follow in sequence.

7. Body. The longest part of the report, the body describes how the problem was investigated. This section will contain subheadings such as "Methods," "Population Studied," "Materials Used," "Analysis," "Commentary," and "Discussion." The emphasis is on all the statistical, environmental, and socioeconomic details that have been gathered; particular experiments or interviews will also receive lengthy treatment. Headings, subheadings, and internal summaries should be used extensively in the body of the report to make it easy to follow. These organizational headings and summaries enable someone skimming the report to find specific information quickly, without having to wade through the entire report. The body section may also contain a variety of visuals—tables, graphs, photographs—to condense and emphasize information.

8. Conclusion. The findings of the report are contained in the conclusion—the results of tests and experiments, a summary of opinions surveyed, the outcome of legal proceedings or agency deliberations.

9. Recommendations. After the abstract, the most important part of the report is the recommendation(s) section, which tells readers what should be done about the findings recorded in the conclusion. Some principles of writing effective recommendations are given in Chapter 9.

Back Matter

Included in this section of the report are all the supporting data which, if included in the text of the report, would bog the reader down in details and cloud the main points the report makes.

10. Glossary. An alphabetical list of the specialized vocabulary with its definitions appears in the glossary (see pp. 328–330). A glossary might be unnecessary if your report does not use highly technical vocabulary or if all members of your audience are familiar with the specialized terms you do use.

11. Appendix. All the supporting materials for the report are gathered in the appendix—tables and charts too long to include in the discussion, sample questionnaires, budgets and cost estimates, correspondence about the preparation of the report, case histories, transcripts of telephone conversations. Group like items together in the appendix, as the example in Fig. 13.5 shows.

12. Bibliography. Any source of information consulted for the report must be listed in the bibliography. Articles, audiovisual materials, books, and reviews are all arranged alphabetically by author. Chapter 7 explains how to cite this information.

▶ Stages in Writing a Long Report

A long report is not written in the order in which the parts have been discussed. The body section is written first, for authors must obtain material included here in order to construct the rest of the report. The abstract, which appears very early in the report, is written last—after all the facts have been recorded and the recommendations made or the conclusions drawn. Introductions are written later as well, since authors can then make sure that they have not left anything out.

▶ Report Formats

Not every report will contain all twelve parts or present them in the sequence given here. The various parts may be rearranged, combined, or omitted. A report's format—the number and sequence of its parts—is determined by the purpose of the report and what the audience wants to learn from it. A *feasibility report*, for example, helps determine whether a project can be accomplished or whether it is worthwhile to even try—for example, adding an extra floor to a building, establishing a new credit policy at a lending institution. Thus the readers of a feasibility report will expect to see information about and headings pertaining to costs, schedules, and benefits. Readers will be looking for recommendations to help them decide if and when specific changes should be made. A *self-study report*, by contrast, assesses the current operation of an institution and the performance of its personnel and indicates the changes that must be made to build up strengths and eliminate weaknesses. Readers of a self-study report will expect detailed sections on company goals and ways of achieving them. A *physical research report*, to cite another example, records the procedures and results of a scientifically controlled experiment. The emphasis is on what happens to an object or a phenomenon under certain conditions. The physical research report is concerned not so much with recommendations as with results.

Figure 13.6, a physical research report, shows how the twelve parts of a

(Continued on p 407)

Fig. 13.6   A long report.

Assessment of Ventilation Characteristics of Standard and Prototype Firefighter Protective Clothing[1]

Uwe Reischl

Program in Industrial Health and Safety, Oakland University, Rochester, Michigan 48063

and

Alfred Stransky

Department of Physical Education, Oakland University, Rochester, Michigan 48063

Abstract

Specialized clothing is an integral part of a firefighter's protective system. However, existing firefighter clothing, which attempts to protect against environmental hazards, also restricts dissipation of metabolic heat. This restriction can lead to severe heat stress and may result in subsequent hazards to the health and safety of the firefighter. A new prototype design has been developed that exhibits some improved heat-dissipation characteristics under controlled laboratory settings. Two versions of the prototype design were tested for ventilation and compared with the ventilation of standard turnout gear. Laboratory information was obtained using one male and one female test subject participating in a series of treadmill exercise tests. Biophysical data collected show that the prototype design provides improvements in clothing ventilation over the standard turnout gear presently in use. Analysis of results suggests that reduction in firefighter

Reprinted by permission from *Textile Research Journal*, March 1980, pp. 193–201.

heat stress can be achieved, and continued development of the prototype design is recommended.

Introduction

The human body is a heat-producing system with a complex thermoregulatory mechanism that maintains a balance between heat loss and heat gain. This insures a relatively narrow range of internal body temperatures. To keep the normal internal body temperature constant, it is necessary to cool the body at a controlled rate. This cooling process is dependent upon air temperature, moisture content, velocity of the surrounding air, and heat radiation. The amount of heat energy involved in maintaining thermoequilibrium can vary considerably, depending upon energy expenditure and environmental conditions. Ultimately, the amount of heat exchanged between the body and the environment depends upon the differences between temperature and the vapor pressure existing between the skin and the ambient environment.

Clothing complicates the process of heat exchange between a person and the environment. Although the same biophysical processes are involved, the properties of clothing (*i.e.*, porosity, permeability, flexibility, elasticity, design and fit, thickness, number of layers, color, texture, and weight) and the properties of various fibers such as size, stiffness, behavior towards water, etc., influence the radiative, convective, and evaporative heat exchanges. Because of this complexity, it is necessary to perform controlled testing with human subjects to understand the final impact of a total protective-clothing system on firefighters.

Specialized clothing is an integral part of a firefighter's protective system. Protective clothing provides a barrier against toxic chemicals, traumatic injury, exposure to flames, hot gases, steam, and heat radiation. However, protective clothing currently in use accumulates metabolic heat. A major factor contributing to this heat build-up is insufficient clothing ventilation. The lack of air exchange between the clothing air spaces and the ambient environment generates humid conditions leading to increased temperatures by reducing the sweat evaporation near the skin. Furthermore, reduced air flow prevents significant heat transfer by convection. Improvements in the ventilation characteristics of protective clothing must be achieved without sacrificing the protection afforded against heat radiation, flames, hot gases, and toxic chemicals.

Clothing Systems

Of special interest in this study is the heat build-up generated by protective clothing designed for firefighters engaged in structural fire-suppression activities. A structural firefighter's protective clothing is a suit normally worn over a standard station uniform. This suit is sometimes termed "turnout gear" or "bunker clothing." The standard turnout gear (STG) is of multilayer construction with a durable fire-retardant outer shell fabric. The outer shell may or may not be air- and/or water-permeable. Furthermore, the turnout system may or may not incorporate a detachable vapor barrier or insulative liner. In general, the outer shell is designed to provide flame resistance, protection against heat radiation, and resistance to water, while the inner liner acts as an insulating medium against heat conduction. The vapor barrier is intended to protect the firefighter from steam and harmful chemicals. Typical turnout gear meeting the National Fire Protection Association (NFPA) #1971 requirements is illustrated in Figure 1.

The NFPA #1971 standard for turnout gear is based primarily on the philosophy that maximum protection from radiant and conductive heat should be achieved. Protec-

Fig. 1   Photograph of standard turnout gear (STG) tested for ventilation characteristics.

Fig. 2   Photograph of new prototype protective clothing. This design has two versions, PT1 and PT2, and each version has two possible configurations; open and closed.

tion against hot and cold liquids, steam, and harmful chemicals is to be achieved by an impermeable vapor barrier installed underneath the outer shell. Unfortunately, this standard does not adequately address the evaporative and convective cooling needs of firefighters working under warm and humid climatic conditions. As a result of inadequate ventilation, existing turnout gear may lead to excessive metabolic heat build-up and jeopardize the health and safety of the firefighter.

To improve the occupational health and safety of firefighters, a new prototype firefighter protective suit has been developed. This prototype is designed to enhance metabolic heat dissipation while providing equivalent protection against the fire environment. The new prototype protective suit is illustrated in Figure 2.

The new design features of the prototype protective suit are summarized below.

Coat: The collar opening (neck) is 40% larger than is normal for standard turnout gear. Ventilation spacers are placed around the neck opening in a spoke-hub configuration. The spacers extend into the shoulder area of the coat and over the collar of the coat.

Collar: The collar is designed to be twice the height in the rear (back of collar) as in the front. The design provides protection to the back of the neck and head, while the front does not interfere with the use of a breathing apparatus.

Sleeves: The sleeves of the coat are designed to act as bellows. There are vent openings provided under the arm areas. The vents are zippered and can be opened and closed easily.

Front: The coat is opened and closed by both a zipper (break-away) covered by a storm flap and by a velcro closure.

Back: Ventilation spacers extend from the top of the shoulders to slightly below the shoulder, ending at the base of the shoulder blades. The lower portion of the back of the coat has an experimental "bellows" design, which is weighted with sand. The bellows are intended to move counter to body motion, thus creating air movement in the back area. The outseams of the coat have zippered vents.

Coverall (Pants): The coverall design incorporates zipper vents and vertical ventilation spacers. The vents are located on both the inner and outer seams of the pant legs.

The new protective clothing system is designed to be "modified" in the field as required by tactical and environmental conditions. In contrast to the STG, the new prototype can be "opened" and ventilated or "closed" by selective use of the zippers and velcro closures. Thus, the new prototype is intended to be a versatile protective clothing system capable of substantially increasing firefighter comfort and safety in the field. Figure 3 illustrates the location of ventilation openings on the prototype system.

Experimental

Ventilation Measurements

Several studies have investigated the impact of clothing and protective equipment on human performance [2, 3, 5–8], but the effects of ventilating the clothing have not been

Fig. 3 Photograph of new prototype protective clothing. Arrows point to location of zippered vent openings.

directly documented. Physiological testing of protective clothing has generally focused on parameters not sensitive to small or moderate changes in clothing configuration. Pulse-rate, rectal-temperature, and skin-temperature measurements have been used as physiological indicators of strain [3, 4]. Measurements of oxygen consumption have also been used in an effort to quantify the effects of protective clothing and rescue gear on the physiological burden placed upon firefighters [1]. However, these indicators were not sufficiently sensitive to changes in uniform ventilation tested in our laboratory under moderately stressful conditions.

An effective method of assessing ventilation in firefighter protective clothing is to monitor changes in air temperature inside the clothing system during exercise. Since the body is a continuous heat source, with its heat production proportional to the level of physical exertion, air exchange between clothing and the ambient environment will moderate increases in inside clothing air temperature. The effects of ventilation can be observed most clearly when the ambient air temperature is significantly lower than the body skin temperature.

Ten fast-responding thermister-type temperature sensors were used in monitoring air temperature inside the protective clothing used in this study. The position of each temperature sensor is illustrated in Figure 4. Each temperature sensor was enclosed in a wire "cage" so that the thermister at no time made contact with clothing material or the skin. Each temperature sensor was pinned to the inside of the protective clothing, and the leads passed through the collar opening to the temperature monitor located in the laboratory. The laboratory air temperature was maintained at 72°F ±°F (22°C). The relative humidity fluctuated between 25 and 40%. The air velocity ranged from 20 to 40 fpm (100 to 200 mm/s).

Fig. 4   Illustration of air-temperature sensor locations inside protective clothing. Location of sensors were the same in all systems tested.

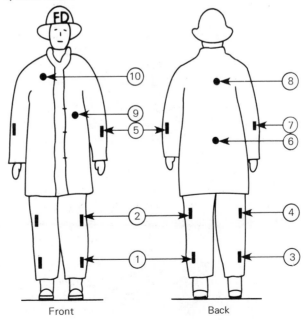

Front   Back

Test Facilities

All experiments were conducted in a temperature-controlled laboratory. A motorized treadmill with variable speed and grade control was used to generate physiological stress (exertion). Electrocardiograph (ECG) data were obtained using a 5-lead electro-cardiograph. Oxygen-consumption data were obtained using open-circuit spirometry. Ambient and clothing air-temperature measurements were made with a 12-channel telethermometer.

Test Subjects

One male and one female student volunteer test subject participated in this study. Prior to experimentation, both subjects were given a medical examination and a maximal treadmill stress test. Both were nonsmokers. Relevant test-subject data are listed in Table I.

Table I. Volunteer test-subject data.

Sex	Age, years	Height, in. (cm)	Weight, lb (kg)	Max VO$_2$, (ml/kg/min)	Max H.R.[a]
M	18	73 (185)	141(64)	57.27	204
F	21	66 (168)	160 (73)	42.55	187

[a]H.R. = heart rate (beats per min).

Exercise Protocol

To produce work-stress (exertion), an exercise protocol was employed that involved a treadmill speed of 3.3 mph (1.5 m/s) with 0% grade during the first 3 min. After the first 3-min period, a grade increase of 3% was administered while speed was held constant. A 6-min standing-recovery period followed each test. Subjects completed only one test per day. The male subject followed a regimen requiring 15 min of treadmill walking, while the female test subject followed a regimen requiring 9 min of treadmill walking. The exercise protocols are illustrated diagramatically in Figure 5. The difference in the male and female protocols was due to the different physical-fitness levels of the subjects. Both test subjects reached 70 to 75% of maximal exertion (as measured by percent of maximum oxygen consumed: % max. VO$_2$) at the end of each test. Therefore, subjects were exposed to similar stress levels. Subjects were tested three times using the standard turnout gear. Each of the two prototype clothing systems was tested three times in the closed configuration and three times in the open configuration.

Clothing

The protective clothing tested included the STG illustrated in Figure 1 and the new prototype system illustrated in Figures 2 and 3. Two versions of the new prototype (PT1 and PT2) were monitored. The fabric materials used in the construction of each of the protective clothing systems are listed in Table II. PT1 is constructed with an outer shell, vapor barrier, and a liner similar to the STG pants. This included a 7.5-oz (113-g), 100% Nomex III Aramid shell, a 7.0-oz (198-g), 100% cotton coated with neoprene vapor barrier, and a 7.5-oz (213-g), 100% Nomex III Aramid liner. PT2 is constructed with fabric material using natural fibers only. PT2 was constructed of a 9.5-oz (270-g), 100% wool shell, a vapor barrier of 6.0-oz (170-g), 100% cotton GORETEX™ fabric, and a 9.5-oz (270-g), 100% wool liner. All clothing systems were tested under full suit-up con-

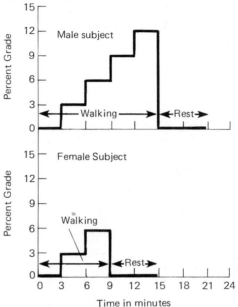

Fig. 5 Treadmill exercise protocol for male and female test subjects wearing firefighter protective clothing. Treadmill speed was held constant at 3.3 mph (1.5 m/s).

ditions. Helmets, boots, and gloves were included. Underneath the uniform, test subjects wore standard underwear, trousers, and a shirt/blouse.

Results and Discussion

Biophysical data obtained during initial maximal stress tests were used as "controls" in this study. During the maximal treadmill stress tests subjects wore gym clothing—*i.e.* tennis shorts and tennis shoes. Air-temperature measurements were obtained at the ten previously-described locations. Measurements for the controls demonstrated that temperatures adjacent to the skin remained relatively stable and varied between 77 and 73°F (23 to 25°C). However, as illustrated in Figures 6 and 7, temperatures inside the protective clothing increased during exercise. For both the male and female subject, heat build-up was less severe for PT1 (open), PT2 (open), and PT2 (closed) than for the STG or PT1 (closed configuration). It should be noted, however, that heat build-up inside the protective clothing systems always increased as exercise intensity increased, and it continued to increase during the recovery periods.

Although overall temperature measurements demonstrate differences among the clothing systems tested, a more comprehensive analysis was needed to identify design features that contributed to the performance of each suit. To accomplish this, data of both test subjects were combined. This was achieved by relating each clothing-temperature measurement to an exertion level—*i.e.* % max VO_2. Temperature measurements were then related to specific regions of the body—*i.e.* legs, arms, chest, and back.

Figure 8 illustrates the heat build-up in the leg regions in relation to exertion exhibited by the subjects (% max VO_2). Air-temperature conditions inside PT2 were lower

Table II. Material composition of garments tested for ventilation characteristics.

Garment		Shell	Vapor barrier	Liner	System weight
Standard Turnout Gear (STG)	Coat	7.5-oz, 100% Nomex III Aramid, Duck Weave	7.0-oz, Nomex III Aramid, 10-oz Neoprene Coating	Needle-Punch Weave,	10 lb, 0 oz (4.5kg)
	Pants	7.5-oz, 100% Nomex III Aramid, Duck Weave	7.0-oz., 100% Cotton, FR, Neoprene Coated	7.5-oz, 100% Nomex III Aramid, Batting Quilted with Nomex III Aramid Scrim Stabilizer	
Prototype 1 (PT1)	Coverall and Coat	7.5-oz, 100% Nomex III Aramid, Duck Weave	7.0-oz., 100% Cotton, FR, Neoprene-Coated	7.5-oz, 100% Nomex III Aramid, Batting Quilted with Nomex III Aramid Scrim Stabilizer	10 lb, 12 oz (4.85 kg)
Prototype 2 (PT2)	Coverall and Coat	9.5-oz, 100% Wool, Zipro-Treated	6.0-oz, 100% Cotton Flannel, FR, Single Napped, Coated with GORETEX™	9.5-oz, 100% Wool, Zipro-Treated	11 lb, 12 oz (5.3 kg)

Fig. 6   Clothing air temperature changes monitored inside STG, PT1, PT2, and gym clothing for the male test subject walking on the treadmill.

Fig. 7   Clothing air temperature changes monitored inside STG, PT1, PT2, and gym clothing for the female test subject walking on the treadmill.

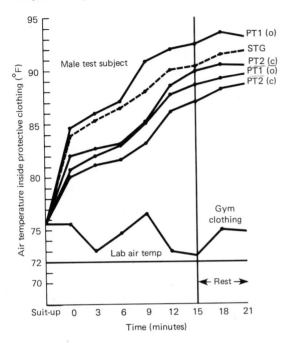

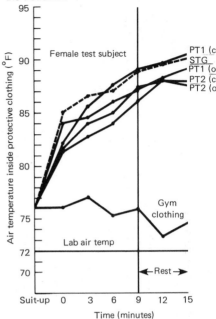

than the air-temperature conditions inside the STG. While the air temperature in the STG was 84.0°F (29°C) at 10% max VO_2 and reached 91.3°F (33°C) at 70% max VO_2, the PT2 (open) was 79.4°F (28°C) at 10% max VO_2 and reached 86.2°F (30°C) at 70% max VO_2. Figure 8 also shows that the performance of PT1, both open (o) and closed (c), is less favorable than PT2—*i.e.* temperatures were higher in PT1 than in PT2.

The differences in temperature build-up monitored inside PT1 and PT2 may be attributed to the use of Nomex III, batting, and neoprene vapor barrier in PT1 and the use of wool and GORETEX in the construction of PT2. The differences in heat build-up observed for open and closed configurations in both systems can be attributed to ventilation enhancement produced by the zippered openings located on the inside and the outside seams of the pants.

Figure 9 illustrates the heat build-up in the arm regions of the protective clothing systems. It can be seen that the air temperatures inside PT1 and PT2 are considerably lower than in the STG. At 10% max VO_2 the air temperature for PT2 was 81.1°F (27.3°C) and at 70% max VO_2 it was 84.1°F (29°C). PT1 (o) produced a temperature of 84.1°F (29°C) at 10% max VO_2 and 85.6F (29.8°C) at 70% max VO_2. Again, the differences in temperature build-up inside PT1 and PT2 may be attributed to differences in construction materials. The differences in heat build-up observed for open and closed configurations in both systems can be attributed to enhanced ventilation produced by the zippered openings located under the arms, and the opening of velcro closures at the wrists.

Fig. 8   Clothing air temperature conditions in the leg regions of STG, PT1, and PT2 at various exertion levels. Each data point represents the average value of six experiments.

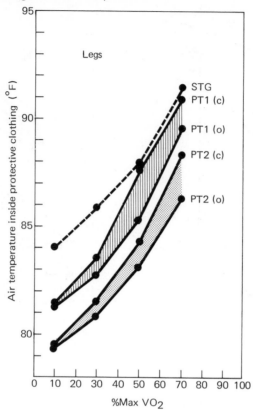

Figure 10 shows the temperature changes occurring in the chest region. The changes in temperature inside the STG are small between low and high exertion levels. At 10% max VO_2 the air temperature was 84.3°F (29°C) and reached 85.0°F (29.4°C) at 70% max VO_2. PT2 (o) generated relatively low air-temperature conditions (81.5°F (27.5°C) at 10% max VO_2 and 84.0°F (29°C) at 70% max VO_2). However, PT2 (c) demonstrated air temperature of 82.6°F (28.1°C) at 10% max VO_2 and 86.4°F (30.8°C) at 70% max VO_2. This maximum exceeded the STG conditions by 1.4°F. PT1 (o) had an air temperature of 82.5°F (28°C) at 10% max VO_2 and reached 85.0°F (29.4°C) at 70% max VO_2. This was identical to the air temperature of STG. PT1 (c) started at 84.4°F (29.1°C) at 10% max VO_2 and increased to 90.0°F (38°C) at 70% max VO_2. This temperature condition is 5°F above the condition reached in STG.

The relatively better performance in the chest region of PT2 under an open configuration is the result of zipper and velcro openings in the front, as well as the fabrics used in its construction. This condition enhances ventilation. However, under a closed configuration, ventilation is severely limited, especially due to the "tight" collar closure (Fig. 2). This closure restricts air circulation from the chest through the neck area.

The performance differences seen in PT2 for open and closed configuration also were observed for PT1. However, the temperature conditions in PT1 were higher than

Fig. 9 Clothing air temperature conditions in the arm regions of STG, PT1, and PT2 at various exertion levels. Each data point represents the average value of six experiments.

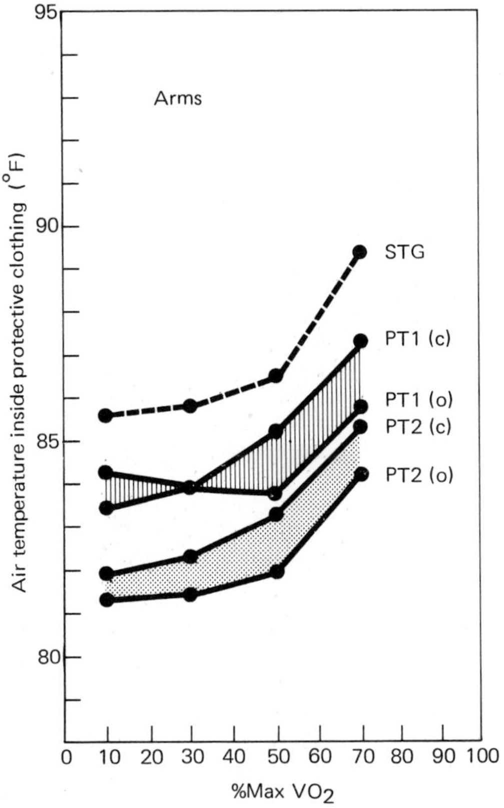

Fig. 10 Clothing air temperature conditions in the chest region of STG, PT1, and PT2 at various exertion levels. Each data point represents the average value of six experiments.

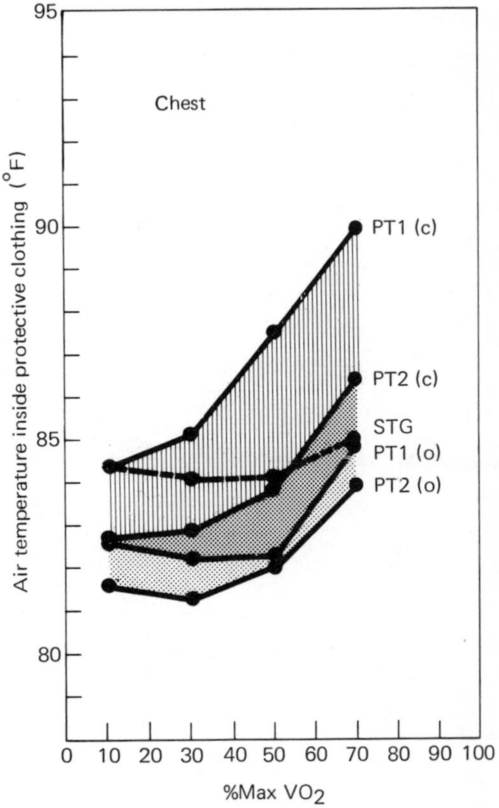

those in PT2. The differences between PT2 and PT1 again can be attributed to differences in construction. However, the differences seen between PT1 and STG appear to be the result of differences in air circulation through the neck openings of the coat, the coverall/coat overlap in the prototype, and differences in construction (batting). Figure 11 shows the temperature changes that occurred in the back region of the three clothing systems tested. Temperatures in the STG ranged from 84.3°F (29°C) at 10% max VO_2 to 89.7°F (32°C) at 70% max VO_2. Temperatures in the PT2 were lowest at the 10% max VO_2 levels. PT2 (o) demonstrated a temperature of 82.1°F (27.8°C) and 80.6°F (27°C) at 10% max VO_2 for PT2 (c). However, the 70% max VO_2, PT2 (o) reached 89.4°F (32°C), and PT2 (c) reached 90.2°F (32.3°C). PT2 (c) exceeded the temperatures of STG by 0.5°F, and FPT2 (o) was lowest by 0.3°F. PT1 (o) produced a temperature of 84.2°F (29°C) at 10% max VO_2 and 90.2°F (32.3°C) at 70% max VO_2. PT1 (c) produced a temperature of 84.6°F (29.2°C) at 10% max VO_2 and 92.5°F (33.6°C) at 70% max VO_2.

The differences in air-temperature build-up between PT1 and PT2 may be attributed to differences in construction. Also, the very large heat build-up observed for PT1 under a closed configuration was probably the result of restrictions in air circulation through the collar. Opening the neck area could reduce this air temperature.

Fig. 11 Clothing air temperature conditions in the back region of STG, PT1, and PT2 at various exertion levels. Each data point represents the average value of six experiments.

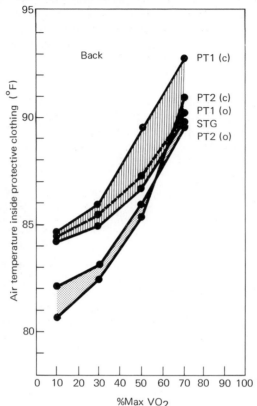

The air-temperature build-up in the chest and back regions of PT1 and PT2 was not only the result of limited ventilation, but probably also a result of the "fit" of the coverall pants. It is likely that the overlap between the coat and the coverall pants on the chest and back, and the bellows design on the back, contributed to an increase in chest and back temperatures.

Information obtained in this study suggests that the prototype design PT2 has improved metabolic heat-dissipation characteristics when compared to the STG. Reductions in heat build-up were most evident in the leg and arm regions of the protective garment. Performance of the prototype design PT1 failed to produce an advantage over the STG. The effectiveness of the zippered vents in the leg and arm regions of the prototype design could be seen in reductions of clothing air temperatures. The concept of "opening" and "closing" selected parts of the protective suit to enhance ventilation during firefighting may prove to be a feasible approach to improving firefighter health and safety.

Conclusions

Monitoring air-temperature conditions was a sufficiently sensitive technique for identifying contributing factors in clothing ventilation inside STG and inside PT1 and PT2. Based on the data collected in this study, PT2 generated less metabolic heat build-up than the standard turnout gear. Furthermore, improvement may be the result of design characteristics as well as the fabric material used in the uniform construction. Continued development of the PT2 is recommended.

Acknowledgments
The prototype design of the new firefighters protective clothing was developed by Ralph Travis of the United Fire Fighters of Los Angeles, California. The clothing systems tested in this research program were supplied to the University by Morning Pride Mfg. Co. of Dayton, Ohio. Financial support for this project was received from W. L. Gore and Associates, Inc., in Elkton, Maryland.

Literature Cited

1. Barnard, James, R., Gardner, G. W., and Duncan, H. W., "Physiological Testing of Firefighter Uniforms," School of Medicine, University of California, Los Angeles, California, 1978.
2. Burton, D. R., "The Thermal Assessment of Personal Conditioning Garments," Curr. Pap. Aeronaut. Res. Count. No. 953, 1971.
3. Givoni, B. and Goldman, R. F., Predicting Metabolic Energy Cost, *J. Appl. Physiol.* **30**, 429–432 (1971).
4. Givoni, B. and Goldman, R. F., Predicting Rectal Temperature Responses to Work, Environment, and Clothing, *J. Appl. Physiol.* **32**, 812–822 (1972).
5. Martin, H. V. and Goldman, R. F., Comparison of Physical, Biophysical and Physiological Methods of Evaluating the Thermal Stress Associated with Wearing Protective Clothing, *Ergonomics* **15**, 337–342 (1972).
6. Martin, H. V. and Callaway, S., An Evaluation of the Heat Stress of Protective Face Mask, *Ergonomics* **17**, 221–231 (1974).
7. Reischl, U. and Reischl, P., Safety Limits of a Firefighter Proximity Suit, *Am. Indust. Hyg. Assoc. J.* **39** (July 1978).
8. Welch, R. B., Longley, E. O., and Lomaev, O., The Measurement of Fatigue in Hot Working Conditions, *Ergonomics* **14**, 85–90 (1971).

---

report can be modified for its specific audience, purpose, and scope. The purpose of the report in Fig. 13.6 is to discover ways of making firefighters' clothing safer and more comfortable, a significant and practical project. The writers conducted experiments involving three kinds of clothing—a standard type of gear and two prototype models—to determine the effectiveness of each in offering proper ventilation. Because it was published in a journal, this report needs no title page, letter of transmittal, or table of contents. Nor does it have a glossary, since all the readers of the journal are specialists and are familiar with the technical vocabulary and abbreviations used.

Readers will expect the parts and emphases of this report to reflect the phases of the experiment. The writers stress the conditions, procedures, and results of the experiment in the various sections of their report. They provide detailed information on everything from the clothing (both control and experimental models), measuring devices, and the subjects' health statistics to an analysis of the data with scientific accuracy and graphic support. Such faithfulness to detail is an essential characteristic of the long report. Readers may want to test or duplicate the results themselves; without the authors' accurate and complete documentation, readers could not do so.

Figure 13.6 is organized as follows: *front matter* (abstract), *text of the report* (introduction, body—materials, methods, results, discussion—conclusion), and *back matter* (acknowledgments, references). More specifically:

1. *Abstract.* An informative abstract states important conclusions of the report.
2. *Introduction.* Background information on the human body as a "thermoregulatory mechanism," problem identification and significance, and relationship of problem (protective clothing and the body thermoregulation process) to specific circumstances and audience (the conditions firefighters are placed in) is given.
3. *Materials* ("Clothing Systems"). The three kinds of gear being tested are summarized and compared. Note how the functions of the prototype allow the authors to claim its "improvement" over other suits.
4. *Methods* ("Experimental"). Test procedures in the selection and gathering of data from facilities, subjects, exercise techniques, and clothing are reviewed. The conditions of the experiment and the ways data were gathered are outlined carefully.
5. *Results* and 6. *Discussion.* The data are analyzed, and further comments are made on procedures ("a more comprehensive analysis was needed to identify design features that contributed to the performance of each suit"). Note how the last paragraph in this section interprets the results of the experiment.
7. *Conclusion.* The experiment is summarized, results are assessed, and the success of the experiment is asserted ("Continued development of the PT2 is recommended").
8. *Acknowledgments.* Credit to designer and test facilities is given, and thanks for financial assistance are expressed.
9. *References* ("Literature Cited"). The authors' references are listed according to an alphabetical reference list similar to the one described in Chapter 7, p. 212.

Physical research reports also contain information on literature searches, on research that has been conducted on the problem under discussion, and conclusions needing further study. This can be a separate section placed after the introduction or can be incorporated into the report wherever it is most appropriate, as was done in Fig. 13.6.

So far we have considered the parts and functions of a long report as separate elements. The following list provides a thumbnail sketch of the material presented in this chapter:

1. The problem: the reason why the report has been written.
2. The purpose: what will be done about the problem.
3. The background of the problem.
4. What was done about the problem:
   (a) Where
   (b) To whom
   (c) When
   (d) How
5. What was discovered.
6. What it all means.

▶ Exercises

1. Write a one-page memo to your instructor in which you describe the major differences between a short report (Fig. 12.10) and a long report (Fig. 13.6). Concentrate on format and scope. Also indicate the similarities between the two reports.

2. Study Fig. 13.6 and answer the following questions:
   (a) Why can the abstract be termed informative rather than descriptive?
   (b) Which sentence in the introduction states the problem and its significance for investigation?
   (c) Which sentence in the body describes the new prototype that is the subject of the report?
   (d) What are the advantages of the new prototype?
   (e) Under the subheading "Ventilation Measurements," what do the numbers in brackets refer to?

3. Write a letter of transmittal for the report in Fig. 13.6, as if the report were being submitted to the fire chief of a large city.

4. What kinds of visuals does the long report in Fig. 13.6 use, and how effective are they?

5. Construct a flow chart showing the stages of writing a long report.

6. Come to class prepared to discuss at least two major problems that would be suitable topics for a long report. Consider an important community problem—traffic, crime rate, air and water pollution—or a problem at your college. Then write a letter to a consulting firm or other appropriate agency or business, requesting a study of the problem and a report.

7. Write an outline of the report appropriate for one of the problems listed in question 6. Use major headings and include the kinds of information listed in Fig. 13.5.

8. Have your instructor look at and approve the outline you prepared for question 7. Then write a long report based on the outline.

14
Oral Reports

It is difficult to say how much of your job will be devoted to speaking with people—employers, colleagues, customers, or patients. Of one thing you can be sure, though. You will communicate orally with those individuals more often than you will in writing. For that reason, a chapter on oral communication in business and industry is included in this book. This chapter is not intended as a substitute for a course in speech communication or public address, but rather as a supplement to the discussions of written communication found in the preceding chapters.

Every job requires employees to have carefully developed speaking skills. In fact, in order to get hired, you had to be a persuasive speaker at your job interview. On the job you will have several oral communication responsibilities that will vary in the amount of preparation you have to do for them, the time they last, and the audience and occasion for which they are intended. Five types of communication situations will be discussed in this chapter:

1. Telephone conversations
2. Impromptu conversations
3. Nonverbal communication
4. Informal briefings
5. Formal speeches

This chapter offers practical advice on how to become a better, more assured communicator—both verbally and nonverbally.

▶ Telephone Conversations

Much of your time at work may be spent using the telephone, an indispensable communication tool in almost every occupational setting. Ask yourself this basic question: "When should I use the telephone rather than write a letter or make a visit?" It is not economical to use the telephone every time you must communicate with someone. Moreover, calls may represent an unwarranted intrusion for routine messages. You should telephone rather than write or visit when time is essential—when you must obtain or give an answer within a few minutes or hours. Your employer will give you guidelines to follow on telephone policy. Sometimes you may not be able to reach an individual by telephone, or perhaps you have to notify ten people, all of whom cannot be telephoned in a short time. Then your employer may instruct you to send telegrams or night letters, the latter guaranteed to arrive at their destination overnight, according to the U.S. Postal Service.

Even after making a telephone call, you may still have to write a summary of the call or send a follow-up letter. Written confirmation of information given over the telephone is mandatory for legal and financial reasons. A letter or memo written right after the call will substantiate the details of a conversation which, unless it was taped, may be lost except for your written reminder.

Telephone Etiquette—Some Basics

Telephone etiquette refers to the way you treat the person (or persons) on the other end of the line. For years, the telephone company has advised customers to have a pleasant telephone voice. A pleasant voice conveys an "I want to help you" attitude. Your voice—its volume, tone, and clarity—will tell the listener about your attitude. Crucial to your call, your voice is the only medium, just as words are in a letter, by which a listener can evaluate your sincerity and professionalism. Neither shout nor whisper on the telephone. Do not hold the speaker against your lips, for this will give your voice a raspy quality. Instead, place the speaker about an inch or two from your mouth. Talk slowly and enunciate clearly. Do not respond to questions with "Yeah," "Nope," "I dunno," or "Whatjasay." Also avoid stringing out a series of "Um, um, um's," which signify only your boredom, not your interest.

Prevent any distracting sounds from competing with your conversation. Munching, blowing, or tapping sounds show lack of attention and impoliteness. Equally discourteous are any background noises coming from radios, televisions, C.B.'s, or typewriters. Turn them down when you are on the phone. Also, never try to carry on two conversations at once—one on the telephone and another with any individual in the room with you. Politely excuse yourself from any ongoing conversations when someone calls you on the telephone.

If at all possible, answer your telephone on the first or second ring. Begin each call with a courteous "Hello." Never start a call with a gruff "Who is this?" or "Yeah, what do you want?" When you ask the party "How are you?" give the individual a chance to respond before you launch your conversation. If you should get a wrong number, do not just hang up without saying anything or breathe heavily while wondering what to say. Say that you have a wrong number and apologize. When talking on the telephone, remember that a successful conversation requires both clear speaking and attentive listening. Do not interrupt or, worse yet, "talk over" the other person's words. Conclude your call with a pleasant "Goodbye."

Making a Call

Each business call should be planned and prepared just as carefully as a letter. First of all, make sure that you have the individual's correct name and telephone number, including, whenever possible, the extension number. If you call a number frequently, keep a handy and permanent record of it. Call people at a time convenient for them, allowing for time changes from one time zone to another. It may be 9:00 A.M. in your New York office, but only 6:00 A.M. in the Los Angeles household or 7:00 A.M. at the Denver hotel you are trying to reach.

Before actually making your call, collect appropriate materials. A supply of pens and paper is a must. No one likes to wait while a person searches for "something to write with" or "something to write on." Also obtain any files, bills, orders, catalogs, or charts relevant to your call.

Your call should begin with answers to these three questions:

1. Who are you?
2. Why are you calling?
3. What do you want the individual to know or to do?

After a courteous "Hello," identify yourself clearly and fully. Do not just say "This is Sarah" or "This is Steven." Give your first and last names and, if relevant, your title and department or floor. Mention your company or agency name. If the person you are calling does not know you, say "This is Fran Brown, the Service Manager at Madison Motors." After this brief introduction, state exactly why you are calling: "I need to verify your reservations" or "Our firm would like to invite your company to participate in our annual fair." If you have several items of business to discuss, you might want to mention each briefly or state the number of questions or topics at the beginning of your conversation so the listener will know what kinds of information you are seeking and how various parts of your conversation may be related. "I am calling to discuss delivery schedules for three recent orders we placed with you—orders placed on May 2, May 4, and May 8." "Dr. Margot, I am calling about your recently admitted patient, Ms. Hodgson. I need to know if she can have a regular diet and also something for the pain in her right leg." Always specify what you want the listener to do—whether it is to send you materials in the mail, call you back in an hour or a week, check on a request while you are still holding on the telephone, or call a third party and inform you in writing of the results of that call.

Receiving a Call

Identify yourself and the company or department you work for. Unless your employer requests you to do otherwise, do not give a shortened or incomplete name for your place of employment. By answering a phone with the words "This is NORDA. May I help you?" you may mislead a caller who does not know that these letters stand for the *N*ational *O*ceanographic *R*esearch and *D*evelopment *A*dministration. Never give only a part of your organization's name. Rather than telling a caller that she has reached "Fisheries," state that she is talking with the "Wildlife and Fisheries Bureau." If interested in only a wildlife issue, for example, that caller, thinking that another office handles it, may say that she has reached the wrong number and hang up.

If you handle a switchboard, do not transfer a call until the individual has finished a sentence and has stated a request. And never begin talking before you answer a call (press a switchboard button), for the caller will miss part or all of the company name and possibly your offer of assistance.

Before putting callers on hold, ask if it will be all right, or if they would prefer to have you call back. When you put someone on hold, press the correct button on the telephone. Should your phone not be equipped with a hold button, gently lay the receiver down on your desk or on the special ridge on the top of a wall phone. The telephone company recommends that when you put someone on hold, you come back every thirty or forty seconds with a brief progress report: "Thank you, Ms. Lucas, for waiting. I'm still checking that information for you." "Rose Tullos is still on the other line, Mr. Sanders. Do you still want to hold, or shall I have her call you?" "We appreciate your waiting for those confirmation numbers. We'll have them for you in a moment." Not very courteous is a question such as "Are you still there?" asked with a definite tone of amazement in the speaker's voice. If you know that you will have to place individuals on hold for more than a few minutes, inform them of this fact right away. Never leave a caller on hold for four or five minutes without reporting promptly and often about your efforts.

If you are answering a telephone for a fellow employee, let callers know that they have reached the right number if not the exact person to whom they want to speak. "Tom Traverse's desk. Pablo Nelda speaking." "Ms. Gloria Massey's office, Barbara Janecki, her secretary, speaking." Do not bluntly state that the individual is "out to lunch," "hasn't made it in yet," or "is in the washroom." If someone is at work but not available, you might give one of the following explanations: "Ms. Pell is away from her desk for a moment. May I take a message or have her call you?" "Mr. Friendenreich is in another office for a few minutes. Would you like me to have him call you when he returns?" Of course, when the individual is at a meeting, out of town on business, or on vacation, inform callers so that they will not expect a return call in the next hour.

Avoid using telephone clichés that have potentially embarrassing implications. "Mr. Lott is tied up at the moment." (Who would do such a terrible thing?) "Marsha Loeb is being detained right now." (Has she been arrested?) "Terry Wilson is not on the floor right now." (Thank God, she's able to walk.)

Preferable alternatives to such lame explanations are "Mr. Lott is at a buyer's meeting until 4:30 today," "Marsha Loeb's airplane will not arrive for another forty-five minutes," or "Terry Wilson is not on duty now." To ensure that the caller receives courteous treatment, always stress your willingness to take a message or have the call returned.

If you have to transfer a call, tell the individual why and ask if it is all right to do so. Callers deserve an explanation so that they will not feel as if they are getting the run around. Try to be as explicit (and brief) as possible. Do not say "I cannot help you. You'll have to call extension 4212." Indicate why: "Mr. Monroe at extension 4212 handles insurance claims for the doctor. May I transfer your call to him?" You may receive a call from someone who already has been transferred two or three times and now is frustrated and angry. Rather than passing the buck, ask if you could take pertinent information and have the appropriate office or employee call back.

▶ Impromptu Conversations

The word *impromptu* means "unannounced, not prepared" and characterizes those speaking occasions for which you will not have an opportunity to prepare—that is, when you are caught off-guard. Such occasions are frequent in any business or industrial setting.

Clearly there is no way to foresee every time you will be asked for information or invited to give your opinion. The best that you can do is to stay on top of your work—read memos and act on them promptly, review a steady customer's file periodically, study patients' charts, attend company meetings, look through policy books and warranty statements, or ask questions. If you are unsure of an answer or need more time, diplomatically arrange to speak to the individual after you offer to check files, make a telephone call, or otherwise acquire the desired information. Should someone stop you when you are busy or on your way to a meeting, give a polite explanation and, again, offer to get back to the individual.

▶ Nonverbal Communication

Remember that the way you speak face to face will also influence the way people respond to your message and to you. Body language is as important as the words you speak. Be conscious of two things: (1) how close you stand to the person or persons with whom you are speaking, and (2) how often you touch these people. We have all known individuals who have made us feel uncomfortable by standing too close to us as they talk, as if they have taken over our talking room. While there are no hard-and-fast rules about how much distance to maintain, keep about two feet away from the person with whom you are talking. Of course, if you sense that this amount of space is not appropriate, move back a bit more or a little forward.

A basic rule about touching someone with whom you are conversing is this: Keep your hands off. Of course, if you know the individual well and realize that a pat on the arm or on the shoulder is an acceptable thing to do, that's all right. If you do not know the individual well or sense that the person does not welcome this kind of familiarity, keep your hands to yourself. Back slappers, elbow knockers, rib punchers, knee patters, or lapel thumpers cannot carry on a conversation unless they touch their audience periodically and sometimes vigorously. These gestures may signal insincerity and discourtesy.

▶ Informal Briefings

If you have ever given a book report or explained laboratory results in front of a class, you have given an informal briefing. Such semiformal reports are a routine part of many jobs. Nurses and law enforcement officers, for example, give their colleagues or supervisors end-of-shift reports, summarizing major activities for the previous eight or twelve hours. During "walking rounds," the nurse leaving one shift identifies pertinent patient data for the nurse starting the next shift as the two of them go from one patient room to another. The nurse giving the report summarizes from patient care cards, while the nurse taking the report listens, asks questions, or takes notes—possibly on a clipboard.

Another kind of briefing involves explaining a new procedure or policy to other departments. As a personnel officer, you may have to inform plant employees of extended coverage on an insurance policy. If your company has just purchased a new piece of equipment, you may have to demonstrate it. Or you may be called on to introduce a speaker, a visitor to your agency, or a new employee or to report on a convention you attended at company expense. Finally, you may give a brief report at a public hearing—before a school board, group of county supervisors, or government agency.

These informal reports are short (one to seven minutes, perhaps), and you always will be given advance notice that you are expected to report. Your comments should be brief and to the point. When the boss tells you to "say a few words about the new Minivac (or the new parking policy)," she does not expect a lengthy formal speech. For example, the nurse reporting to a colleague about a patient should not mention every detail about medications, temperatures, or diet; only something special or unusual that occurred during the shift needs comment. The personnel officer informing employees about extended insurance coverage should not read the fine print in the policy, but rather cover its key points, saving detailed personal questions for a private conference.

Rather than writing down all your comments in full sentences, make a few rough notes and jot them down on a three-by-five or four-by-six inch note card you can easily hold in the palm of your hand or attach to a piece of equipment as you talk. Your notes should consist of only the major points you want to mention, preferably in chronological order or from cause to effect. A note card with key facts used by an employee who is introducing Ms. Rizzo, a visiting speaker, to a monthly meeting of safety directors might include the following items:

- Ms. Diana T. Rizzo, Chief Engineer of the Rhode Island State Highway Department for twelve years.

- Experience as both a civil engineer and safety expert.

- Consultant to Secretary Volpe, Department of Transportation.

- Member of the National Safety Council and author of "Field Test Procedures in Highway Safety Construction."

- Designed specially constructed aluminum posts used on Rhode Island highway system.

- Advocate of standardized gradings.

Similarly, a note card used by a personnel officer to inform employees about new insurance coverage might list the following major points:

- American Democratic Insurance has changed some of the coverage on employees' policies.

- If you are hospitalized, American Democratic will pay up to $121.75 per day on your room. This is an increase of $11.35 per day from the old policy.

- Outpatient lab benefits are also increased. American Democratic will now pay $100 a year rather than the $75 under the old policy.

- Premiums will also increase by about $1.40 a week, but Mr. Dobbs, the employer, will pay 75¢ of that increase, meaning employees will have 65¢ more deducted from weekly checks.

- Currently we are exploring a dental rider on the American Democratic policy.

- If any questions, can call me or Ms. Blackwell at extension 3452 or drop by the Personnel Office, in the Administration Building, Monday through Friday, 8:00 A.M. to 4:30 P.M.

▶ Formal Speeches

Whereas an informal briefing is likely to be short, generally conversational, and intended for limited numbers of people, a formal speech is likely to be longer, less conversational, and intended for a wider audience. Therefore, it involves more preparation and less interaction between speaker and audience; it is, in other words, more "formal."

Most of us are uncomfortable in front of an audience because we feel frightened or embarrassed. The very formality of the situation makes us uneasy. Much of this fear and anxiety can be eased, though, if you know what to expect. The two areas you should investigate thoroughly before you begin to prepare your speech are (1) who will be in the audience and (2) why they are there. Thus the formal speech is like a sales letter (see Chapter 6) in that you must identify your audience and determine what its needs are.

Analyzing the Audience

The more you learn about the members of your audience, the better equipped you will be to give them what they need and want to hear. Your goal as a speaker is to communicate as effectively as possible with your audience. In order to win your listeners over or to explain something to them, find out whether anything unites them as a group—search for a common denominator. For example, are they all members of one profession (architecture, computer programming, mechanical engineering, secretarial science), or are they a group of individuals who have similar professional interests (court reporters, legal assistants, legal secretaries, police officers)? Perhaps your audience will consist of all the students at your school majoring in your field of specialization. Or, your audience may be linked not by professional training, but by place of employment: all the employees—mechanics, bookkeepers, salespeople—in a car dealership. Other bonds, too, may unite an audience: ethnic background, hobbies, membership in clubs, age, sex, or religion.

Once you have defined your audience, you have to assess how much they will know about the topic you are discussing. Everything depends on what your audience will understand and need—the terms you use, how many details you have to give, the number of explanations and definitions you supply, and the amount of background information required. Obviously, you would not want to use technical terms or sophisticated explanations, expected by professionals in your field, in front of an audience unfamiliar with your profession. For example, terms taken for granted in one group must be explained or never used with another group. If you were speaking about a new type of fire wall to an audience of fire safety specialists, your approach to the topic would differ from that for a group of homeowners. Similarly, in talking about CPR (cardiopulmonary resuscitation), you would use technical terms, provide physiological explanations, and expect fewer questions about procedures when addressing a group of respiratory therapists than when speaking to the local PTA. Draftsmen know the meaning of *hidden lines;* a group of nondraftsmen would not. If you were addressing a group of real estate agents about housing values in your area, you could use a phrase like *wraparound mortage* or an abbreviation such as PMI (or private mortgage insurance) that might require a clear translation for a cross section of homeowners.

Your audience will also determine the approach you take toward the material. The facts you select about the hotel you work for and the emphasis you give these details may vary considerably if you are talking to a group of young singles as opposed to retired couples.

Speaking for the Occasion

Understanding why your audience is assembled before you will help you deliver a successful speech. An audience may be there for a variety of reasons—for a social gathering, a business meeting, or an educational forum. Shape your remarks to fit the occasion. At a social occasion—a retirement party, a community center dedication, an awards dinner—a humorless speech over-loaded with statistics and details will not be well received. At a retirement party, a light speech is in order. At a monthly sales meeting, on the other hand, jokes, anecdotes, and friendly personal observations would not supply the audience with what it must have—hard facts about costs, dates, and finan-cial analyses.

In addition to selecting material appropriate for the occasion, consider both the time allotted for your speech and whether you are the only speaker scheduled to address the audience. It makes a big difference in your prepa-ration if you are the first speaker at an 8:00 A.M. breakfast meeting or the last of four speakers at an evening meeting. Take into account what will happen before you speak and what will follow. If you are the only speaker, will the meeting be devoted entirely to your speech? If so, then your remarks need to be more than just five or ten minutes long, and you will have to do consid-erable research. If others are scheduled to speak, try to coordinate their ef-forts with yours. For example, if you are one of three speakers on community affairs, confer with the other two speakers so that you do not repeat what they are saying.

The number of people you have to address is also a significant factor. A formal presentation to a small group—five or six supervisors or buyers—seated around a conference table can nonetheless be made more intimate; you can walk around, perhaps leave more time for questions, or stop your talk a few times to ask if there are any questions. You will have much less flexibility when addressing a large group—seventy or eighty people—in an auditorium.

Above all, study why your audience is present. Is it because its members have to attend (students in your speech class) or because they have paid to be entertained?

Ways of Presenting a Speech

The effectiveness with which you deliver your speech depends directly on the extent of your preparation. Of the four approaches we will consider, the ex-temporaneous is best suited to most individuals and occasions. But first we will examine three other possibilities and their advantages and disadvantages.

1. Speaking off-the-cuff. The professional speechmaker may be com-fortable with an off-the-cuff approach, but for the average person, there are no advantages to off-the-cuff speaking, for the worst way to deliver a speech is to speak without any preparation whatsoever. You may know a subject very well and feel that your experience and knowledge qualify you for an on-the-spot performance. But you will only be fooling yourself if you think you have all the details and explanations in the back of your head. It is equally dan-gerous to believe that once you start talking, everything will fall into place smoothly. The "everything works out for the best" philosophy, unaided by a lot of hard work, does not operate in public speaking. Without preparation, you will be at the mercy of your memory. Once on stage, you are likely to forget or to confuse important points entirely or to annoy your audience by returning to an earlier point with a vital fact that has just popped into your mind. Without notes in front of you, you will be at a distinct disadvantage if someone asks you a question, and your talk can easily become a series of repetitious (and possibly contradictory) statements. Nor is the unprepared approach likely to make you sound professional and relaxed. You will probably stumble and pause, groping for things to say, hemming and hawing nervously in front of your audience. Mark Twain's advice is apt here: "It takes three weeks to prepare a good impromptu speech."

2. Memorizing a speech. This type of public speaking is the exact opposite of the off-the-cuff approach. A memorized speech does have some advantages, but only for certain individuals—tour bus drivers, guides at museums or amusement parks, or salespeople—who must deliver the same speech many times over. But for the individual who has to deliver an original speech just once, a memorized speech contains pitfalls. First, it is difficult to do. You might spend hours memorizing exact words and sentences—time that would be better spent in organizing your speech or gathering information for it. Second, if you forget a single word or sentence, you may forget the rest of the speech. It is easy to lose the whole speech when you are panic-stricken over one small part, for that one small part suddenly becomes your entire speech. Third, a memorized delivery can make you appear mechanical. Rather than adjusting, second by second, to an audience's reactions to your speech, you will be obligated to speak the exact words you wrote before you saw your audience. The chances are good, too, that you will be so concerned about remembering what words come next that you will not notice if the audience approves of or understands what you are talking about. Fourth, and finally, a memorized speech may be an albatross around your neck if you have less time than you thought you did to address your audience. Perhaps the speaker before you went overtime and your time is shortened by five or ten minutes. What would you do with a memorized speech? Where would you stop or what would you cut?

3. Reading a speech. Reading a speech to an audience may, in some circumstances, be appropriate. If you are presenting information on company policy or legal issues on which there can be no deviation from the printed word, reading a speech might be a wise idea. Most of the speeches you have to make, however, will not require this kind of rigid adherence to a text. Your speeches will be more personal and acceptable, socially and professionally, when you interact with the audience; reading from a prepared text does not permit such interaction. When you read rather than present your speech, you set up a barrier between yourself and the audience. With your head in your notes, you will not establish eye contact with your audience, for you will probably be too concerned about losing your place. Moreover, the tone of your voice will be too formal, even mechanical. Of course, broadcasters and other experienced speakers can move almost effortlessly from the text to the audience, but that kind of switching ability requires a lot of practice and a carefully trained memory.

4. Delivering a speech extemporaneously. An extemporaneous delivery is the best way of giving a speech for the widest variety of occasions. Unlike a speaker using a memorized or written speech, you do not come before your audience with the entire speech in hand. By no means, though, is an extemporaneous delivery an off-the-cuff performance. It requires a great deal of preparation. But what you prepare is an outline of the major points of your speech, as discussed later in this chapter. You will rehearse using that outline, but the actual words you use in your speech will not necessarily be those you have rehearsed. Your words to the audience should flow naturally and knowledgeably. You should stand confidently in front of the audience with your outline reminding you of major points but not the precise language to express them. In this way you can establish contact with the audience rather than presenting a programmed, robotlike appearance.

The rest of this chapter will discuss various effective ways of preparing and delivering an extemporaneous speech.

Preparing the Parts of a Speech

The Introduction

The introduction is the most important part of your speech. Its goal is to capture the audience's attention. If you fail to do so, you may soon put your listeners to sleep and lose them completely. An effective introduction answers these questions for the audience: (1) Who are you? (2) What are your qualifications? (3) What restricted topic are you speaking about, and how is that topic restricted? and (4) How is that topic, and your presentation of it, relevant? An effective introduction is proportional to the length of your speech. A ten-minute speech requires no more than a sixty-second introduction; a twenty-minute speech needs no more than two minutes of the speaker's time to introduce it.

You will probably begin by introducing yourself, emphasizing your professional qualification. "I'm Felicia Manheim, and I've been a riveter at Gibson Steel Works for six years." "My name is Charles Constantine, and I have worked as a nurse in the Emergency Room at St. Barnabas Hospital for the last two years." (This self-introduction may be unnecessary if someone else introduces you or if everyone in the room knows you.) Never apologize for wasting your audience's time or for your limitations as a professional speaker.

Thank the audience for the opportunity of addressing the group and indicate at once what your topic is and how it is divided. The most interesting speeches are the easiest to follow. By restricting your topic, you will help to ensure that it will be organized carefully. Focus on one major (and restricted) idea—home health programs for the aged in Niles, Illinois; a new word processor model; a tasty diet under 1,200 calories a day; a course in canoeing. Tell your audience what you will do with the topic and how you will divide it: "I believe there are three reasons why gasohol is preferable to gasoline for our mass transit system: it is cheaper, it is more fuel-efficient, and it makes us less dependent on foreign suppliers." Or, "Tonight I will discuss the three problems a foodstore manager faces when deciding to stock inventory: (1) the difficulty in predicting future needs, (2) the inability of the production department to record current levels of stock accurately, and (3) the uncertainty of marketplace conditions." Give your listeners a road map at the beginning of your talk so that they will know where you are, when you are there, and what they have to look forward to or to recall.

Moving from your announcement of the topic to your presentation of it requires skill at inducing an audience to listen. After introducing yourself and the topic, concentrate on how you will get the audience to "bite" on the "hook" you offer. There are a variety of tactics you can use to get the audience's attention. Perhaps the simplest way is to ask a question—"Do you know how much actual meat there is in a hot dog?" "How many of you have taken Graphics 201?" "How serious is a nosebleed?" Choose a question closely linked to your topic. By getting the audience to think about the answer to your question, you start your listeners on a trail you hope to blaze for them. The implication is that this is a question the listeners should ask themselves.

Another often-used technique for beginning a speech is to cite some interesting statistics. Listeners' curiosity should be so excited that they will stay tuned in for an explanation or description: "In 1980 there were two million heart attack victims in America who lived to tell about it." "Seventy-five percent of those taking the sales refresher course pass their state board examination." "By 1990, more than half of America's population will be over thirty-five." Of course, you can combine techniques, as the following opening does with a question containing statistics: "Did you know that 40 percent of all house pets get lost in a one-year period?"

You might also begin with an anecdote, or brief story, that illustrates the main points of your speech. With a fast-paced story, especially one of human interest, you pull your listeners into your speech. Sometimes effective speakers start with something humorous. But be careful about using jokes to get the audience in a good mood. Others may not find your joke amusing, in good taste, or relevant to your speech. You will have lost your audience before you start.

In addition to employing these attention-getters (questions, statistics, anecdotes), your speech may also begin with background information or definitions. If no one of these approaches seems appropriate or if you just cannot think of an effective introduction, try talking about yourself, emphasizing those interests or professional duties you have in common with your listeners. If you are addressing the local PTA, tell them about a situation involving your own child. Many of the parents before you doubtless have had the same experience. Your main goal is to establish a bond with your audience.

The Body of the Speech

Coming between the introduction and the conclusion, the body is the longest part of your speech. The body supplies the substance of your speech, for it contains the subject matter your audience must have in order to consider you a credible and well-informed speaker. Specifically, the body of a speech can (1) explain a process, (2) describe a condition, (3) tell a story, (4) argue a case, or (5) do any or all of the previous four tasks.

To get the right perspective about the body of a speech, recall your own experiences as a member of an audience. How often did you feel bored or angry because a speaker tried to overload you with details? The Peanuts cartoon in Fig. 14.1 bluntly points out the consequences of boring an audience. Conversely, what kinds of details made you sit up and listen attentively? Your answers to these questions will almost certainly point to the speaker's ability to choose just the right amount of information to share with an audience.

When you prepare the body of your speech, consider your audience as a group of listeners, *not readers*. Readers will have more time to digest the ideas in your work. They can read as slowly or as quickly as they want, reread and

Fig. 14.1   How to find out if you are a boring person.

© 1980 United Features Syndicate, Inc.

double-check details, or skim wherever they want. Those listening to your words, however, cannot absorb nearly as much as readers can. The speaker's audience has a shorter attention span. In fact, a good rule to follow in preparing the body of your speech is to be direct and relevant. You cannot include every available detail. The body of your speech should be lean and attractive, not swollen with every fact you gathered in preparing the speech. Select details that are relevant to your audience, not simply because you went to the trouble to find these details or because you thought they were amusing. If you must include statistical data, do not rely exclusively on a verbal presentation. Select an appropriate visual—a bar graph or pie chart—and correlate the visual with a brief verbal analysis. An audience will remember a shape longer than it will recall a string of numbers. (The use of visuals in a speech will be discussed later in the chapter.)

There are a few helpful ways you can present and organize information in the body of your speech. In writing a report, you can assist readers by supplying them with headings, labels, underscorings, and bullets. In a speech, switch from purely visual devices to aural ones. Here are some examples:

1. Give signals (directions) to show where you are going or where you have been. These signals will help convince an audience that your speech does not ramble. Enumerate your points: "first," "second," "third." Tell the audience which way your description is moving by reminding listeners of their position in your speech. In describing a piece of property to prospective buyers, for example, say "from the inside of the house" or "looking at the northeast corner of the building." When you tell a story, follow a chronological sequence and fill your speech with signposts—*before, following, next, then.*

2. Comment on your own material. Tell the audience if some point is especially significant, memorable, or relevant. "This next fact is the most important one in my speech." "Please remember that the current law expires in June." "The best determiner of pressure is the amount of liquid present in the chamber."

3. Repeat key ideas. You can repeat a sentence or a word for emphasis and to help the audience remember it. But do this sparingly; repeating the same point over and over again will bore your audience. Here is an example of the effective use of repetition. "The mayor-council form of government is our best financial investment. Yes, our best financial investment. Here's why."

4. Provide internal summaries. These are "minisummaries" supplied after you finish one point but before you move to another. Spending a few seconds to recap what you have already covered will reassure your audience and you as well. These summaries are bridges between the material and the listeners. For example, "We have already discussed the difficulties in establishing a menu repertory, or the list of items that the foodservice manager wants to appear on the menu. Now we will turn to ways of determining which items should appear on a menu and why."

The Conclusion

Plan your conclusion as carefully as you do your introduction. Stopping with a screeching halt is as bad as trailing off in a fading monotone. An effective conclusion leaves the audience with a good feeling, satisfied that you have come full circle and accomplished what you promised. Your last words should echo in your listeners' ears, not fall limp to the ground. This does not mean that you have to leave them laughing, which may be inappropriate. It does mean that you should emphasize how important your findings are. You have to do all this quickly. Conclusions, even for long speeches (twenty minutes), should never run more than sixty to ninety seconds. Moreover, you should clearly inform your audience when you are approaching the end of your speech: "finally," "in conclusion," "to summarize," "to wrap up." Nothing is more embarrassing for a speaker than to finish and not convey this fact unequivocally to an audience still expecting to hear more. But be careful not to give the audience false signals. To keep talking for another four or five minutes after saying "in conclusion," "to repeat one last time what I said before," or "to summarize" is unforgiveable.

What belongs in a conclusion? A conclusion should contain something lively and memorable. Under no circumstances should you introduce a new subject in a conclusion; nor should you simply restate your introduction. A conclusion contains a restatement and reemphasis of your most important points (or the conclusions you reached about them). For example, "The installation of the stainless steel heating tanks has, as we have seen, saved our firm 32 percent in utility costs, since we do not now have to run the heating system twenty-four hours a day." If you are delivering a persuasive speech, issue a call for action, just as in a sales letter (see Chapter 6). Your purpose may be to have your listeners buy a product, join a community organization, write their congressional representative, review a policy, or take a course. State the purpose in terms that an audience can translate into action. Stress what you want your listeners to do and why it is beneficial for them to do it or harmful (or less desirable) if they do not follow your advice. For example:

> In two weeks, you will graduate and become alumni of Holmes College. As a student you profited from the alumni's financial contributions to the sports program. Shouldn't you join the alumni club to carry on the Holmes tradition and help other students coming after you just as you were helped?

> Have your blood pressure checked at least once a year to reduce chances of falling victim to kidney disease, stroke, or heart attack. Protect your body against a killer that gives little or no warning.

Think of a conclusion as not closing doors but opening avenues. Make your listeners feel as though they are partners or participants with you. If a question-and-answer period has been planned, remind your audience at the conclusion of your speech that you are ready for questions.

The Speech Outline

Construct a speech outline to represent the three parts of your speech—the introduction, the body, and the conclusion. As was pointed out earlier in this chapter, in an extemporaneous speech you do not write out the entire speech you are going to deliver. But you must have some speaking notes to guide you; you cannot appear empty-handed before your audience. The speech outline has great psychological value in that it gives you enough facts to handle your speaking engagement confidently, yet it is not so detailed that it places you in a straitjacket.

The speech outline illustrated in Fig. 14.2 contains the right amount of detail to represent the introduction, body, and conclusion of Tim Phalen's speech. A Roman numeral designates each major point; capital letters indicate appropriate supporting facts. Be careful about crowding too much into a speech outline; in other words, you do not need an outline as highly structured as the following:

  I.
    A.
      1.
        a.
          (1)

Your talk will not be taking an hour, which is what such a detailed outline suggests. Not every point will require four or five capital letters. But each point, whether indicated by a Roman numeral or a capital letter, should be written as a complete sentence. Since your outline must be easy to read and follow, leave wide margins and triple space between your points. Mark, perhaps with a red pen, a red typewriter ribbon, or capital letters, the places where visuals appear in your speech. Thus you will not forget them in your concern with moving to the next point in your talk.

Using Visuals

You may use a number of different visuals during your talk: photographs, maps, chalkboards, models, pasteboards (a large, two-by-three-foot, stiff piece of white cardboard), diagrams, tables, or projector slides. Visuals are used in a talk for the same reasons as in a report. They explain quickly, condense information, and add interest and variety to your speech. But visuals used in an oral presentation must be constructed even more carefully than for a written report. Unlike a reading audience, a listening audience cannot refer to a visual again; nor does this audience have the time to study the visual in detail.

The size and shape of your visuals are all-important. If they cannot be seen clearly from a distance and understood at once, they are not very useful.

Fig. 14.2   A speech outline.

SPEAKER: Tim Phalen, Assistant Vice President, Madisonville Savings
and Loan

AUDIENCE: Madisonville Optimist Club

PURPOSE: To encourage members of the Optimist Club to do business with
Madisonville Savings and Loan

INTRODUCTION:

   I. Is there a secret to financial success?

      A. Authors of books on "how to make a million dollars" say that read-
ers will profit from their advice.

      B. Fashion designers claim that the way we dress determines our
success.

      C. Psychologists maintain that the key to success rests with how well
we manipulate people.

      D. Real success is knowing how to turn your dreams into reality.

      E. Madisonville Savings and Loan can show you how to make your dreams
of financial success come true. SHOW POSTER WITH WORDS "MADISON-
VILLE SAVINGS AND LOAN," "DREAMS," AND "REALITY" TO EMPHASIZE RE-
LATIONSHIP FOR AUDIENCE.

BODY OF THE SPEECH:

  II. Madisonville Savings and Loan will help you find the best way to save.

      A. We have the highest interest rates payable by law.

      B. Our staff of financial counselors will assist you in selecting
the right savings account.

      C. Madisonville Savings and Loan currently offers customers five
different types of savings accounts.

          1. The Basic, or Standard, Account is the most flexible; it pays
interest daily from the day of deposit and requires no minimum
balance.

2. A Payroll Savings Account automatically deposits money into your account.

3. An Ambassador Account allows you to get money away from home when you need it.

4. A Certificate Account pays more interest than the Basic Account but requires a $500 minimum.

5. A Money Market Account, requiring a $10,000 balance, pays the highest interest rates.

D. Our Retirement Plan assures you of trouble–free years to travel or to do anything else you wish knowing that you will have a steady income when you need it.

E. All savings accounts and retirement plans are insured by the Federal Savings and Loan Insurance Corporation.

F. With any account you select, you will receive a quarterly statement showing the interest earned and, where appropriate, maturity dates.

III. Madisonville Savings and Loan will help you to borrow as well as to save money.

A. Savings and loans have been in the lending business for 100 years.

B. Madisonville Savings and Loan is dedicated to strengthening the community.

C. Madisonville Savings and Loan is a leader among local financial institutions in giving home owners and businesses long–term loans. SHOW GRAPH.

D. Most of our savings are invested in mortgages.

E. In fact, 70 percent of all houses in Madisonville in the last fifty years were built or bought with mortgage money obtained from Madisonville Savings and Loan.

F. Madisonville Savings and Loan offers customers three types of mortgages.

1. VA loans give veterans interest rates fixed by the U.S. government, no closing costs, and no down payments.

2. FHA loans, another federally assisted program, also offer fixed interest rates below the conventional market, but buyers must purchase insurance to protect an FHA loan.

3. Conventional mortgages allow buyers to obtain their money in Madisonville; on a month-to-month basis they are cheaper than FHA loans.

IV. Our new Fast Account gives you checking benefits you have not had before.

A. You can write checks and earn interest on the same account.

B. You can pay your bills by telephone—no postage or envelopes to worry about.

C. You receive a monthly statement of all transactions, including the interest your money has earned.

D. If your checking account has ever been overdrawn, you will like the automatic line of credit a Fast Account gives you.

CONCLUSION:

V. Let Madisonville Savings and Loan help you to find your most successful financial opportunities.

A. The three services we offer—savings, loans, and checking—are interrelated. SHOW TRIANGLE DEPICTING RELATIONSHIP.

B. Come to Madisonville Savings and Loan and allow us to show you how to take advantage of all our services.

C. We are open during the hours that are most convenient for you.

1. We stay open until 6:00 P.M. two nights (Thursday and Friday) a week.

2. We are here until noon on Saturday.

Thank you for your attention. I will be happy to answer any questions.

If possible, before using any visual, mount it in the front of the room and sit in the last row of chairs in the room in which you will speak to see if your audience will be able to decipher it. After this experiment, you might decide to increase the size of your visual (blow up a picture, for example), hold it up higher, or show it to different sections of your audience by walking from one side of the room to another. Or you might want to change color schemes for greater visibility.

Determining How Many Visuals to Use

Your speech may not require any visuals. A very brief presentation (two to four minutes) may not. But even a very long speech may need only two or three visuals. Use visuals sparingly. Their purpose is to clarify (or supplement), not to compete with what you say. (Note in Fig. 14.2 the limited use of visuals.) If you use too many visuals, your audience will not pay strict attention to what you are saying, but will instead be trying to watch each new visual that comes along. For a ten-minute speech, two or three visuals are probably adequate; seven or eight would be excessive. Too many visuals will interfere with your speech; you will be using time setting up and removing visuals, time that should be reserved for your speech. Moreover, your audience will fail to attach much emphasis or importance to visuals after the first few if you bombard the group with pictures, diagrams, or slides. Ask yourself: "What will a visual tell an audience that my words cannot?"

Getting the Most from Your Visuals

The following points are practical suggestions on how to get the most from your visuals:

1. Do not set up your visuals before you begin speaking. The audience will try to determine what they mean or how you are going to use them and so will not give you full attention.
2. Make sure that any maps or illustrations are firmly anchored. Having a map roll up or a picture fall off a stand during your presentation is an embarrassment you can prevent by checking equipment ahead of time.
3. Never obstruct the audience's view by standing in front of the visuals you are explaining. Also, when you finish with a visual, do not leave it standing to block the audience's view of you or of other visuals for the rest of your talk. Unobtrusively roll maps up, set pictures down on a desk or the floor, or put the visual out of your way so you do not trip over it.
4. Avoid crowding three or four visuals onto one pasteboard to save space or time. Use different pasteboards instead.
5. Do not put a lot of writing on a visual. Elaborate labels, markings, or descriptions defeat your reason for using the visual. Your audience will spend more time trying to decipher the writing on your visual than attempting to understand the visual itself.
6. Be extra cautious with a slide projector. Check beforehand to make sure that all your slides are in the order in which you are going to discuss

them and that they are right side up. A slide out of sequence can ruin a large section of your speech. Test the equipment a few times before you make your delivery. It's wise to carry an extra light bulb with you in case the bulb in a projector burns out while you are talking. Make sure, too, that you turn a projector off when you are finished with it, so the noise of the projector will not disturb the audience as you continue speaking.

Rehearsing a Speech

An efficient writer never submits a rough draft of a paper or report to an employer. Rather, the rough draft is edited and carefully checked before it is typed to produce the final copy, and that final copy is carefully proofread before it goes to the boss's desk. Similarly, an effective speaker does not write a speech and march off to deliver it. Between the time you write a speech and deliver it, rehearse it several times. You will gain self-assurance by becoming familiar with your material—knowing your subject very well and recalling the order in which certain points are made. Going over your ideas aloud may help you to spot poor organization and to correct insufficient or inaccurate content. An intimate knowledge of your material will, furthermore, reduce the risk of having to search frantically for ideas should something go wrong at your presentation, since you will have gone over the material so often as to be well aware of your information.

Rehearsing will also help you to acquire more natural speech rhythms, pitch, pauses, and pacing. Try speaking in front of a full-length mirror for at least one of your rehearsals to see how an audience might view you. At another time, speak into a tape recorder or in front of someone to determine if you sound friendly or frantic, poised or pressured. You can also catch and correct yourself from going too quickly or too slowly. Time yourself so that you will have a fairly accurate idea if your talk falls within the time allotted you. Practice with the visuals or equipment you intend to use in your speech, for this kind of "hands-on" experience will make you aware of how and when to use them.

If possible, go to the room in which you will give your speech to find out as much as you can about it. How large is it, and how many entrances does it have? Are there any special acoustical problems? Are there posts or counters that might block an audience's view of you? Where is the blackboard, how large is it, and is there an ample supply of chalk? Where is the light switch and electrical outlet? These are essential questions if you are using a slide projector. Where will the audience sit? In rows before you, in a semi-circle, upstairs and downstairs? Where is the lectern (a desk or stand with a slanted top, used to hold books or other reading material) placed? Does it have a shelf for your materials? What is the easiest way to get to the lectern from where you will sit or be introduced? Is there a place to leave your coat? Simulate the conditions of the room as much as possible in your rehearsals. Every unknown you can erase will make you feel more secure.

In rehearsing your speech, pay special attention to your pronunciation. Mispronouncing a word is embarrassing—the audience might laugh and break the flow of your speech. Double-check your dictionary for the correct pronunciation of any word about which you are unsure. Or you might wish to consult such pronunciation guides as Abraham and Betty Lass's *Dictionary of Pronunciation* (Quadrangle, 1976) and Samuel Noory's *Dictionary of Pronunciation,* second edition (A. S. Barnes, 1971). Always check the pronunciation of proper names carefully. You will quickly offend your audience if you mispronounce their hometown. It is Reading (red + ing) not (read + ing), Pennsylvania. The "s" is silent in Illinois (Illin + oi), and someone from Arkansas is an Ark + Kansan. If you are unsure about how to pronounce an individual's name, ask long before you deliver your speech. Is Patricia's last name Le + viche or Lev + iche? Is Bob's last name pronounced Cut + tone or Cut + toni? Ask ahead of time.

Delivering a Speech

A poor delivery can ruin a good talk. When you speak before an audience, you will be judged on more than what you have to say; you will be evaluated on the type of image you project. That image will depend on how you look, move, and talk—your body language. Do you mumble into your notes, never looking out into the audience? Do you clutch the lectern as if to keep it in place? Do you shift nervously from one foot to another? All these actions betray your nervousness and detract from your presentation.

Physical appearance and speaking skills correspond to format and neatness in your written work. In both mediums strive for clarity and attractiveness. The following suggestions on how to present a speech will help you to be a well-prepared speaker.

Before You Speak

Your name is called, and within a minute or two you will have to begin addressing the audience. You will be nervous. Accept the fact and even allow a few seconds for a "panic time." But then put the nervous energy to work for you. Chances are, your audience will have no idea how fearful you are. The audience cannot see the butterflies in your stomach. If you have to go to a lectern, walk slowly so you do not trip. Watch carefully for any steps you may have to make if the lectern is on a platform. If you have applications, brochures, or handouts to share, distribute the material before you reach the lectern.

Once you are on the podium or dais (raised stage) or before the lectern, remove any pitchers or glasses of water if you are worried about spilling them. Always have a wristwatch with you. Before speaking, lay it on the desk or lectern so that you can occasionally glance down to see how much time you have left. This unobtrusive act is far preferable to reminding the audience that you are running out of time by noticeably raising your arm to look at your watch. If you are the first to speak into a microphone, you might want to test it by beginning "Can everybody hear me?"

You are ready to start. But before you utter the first word, take a quick look at your listeners. Let them know that you are concerned about them. View your audience as a group of friendly people who are sincerely interested in what you have to say. Otherwise, they would not be there. They are people with whom you work or have a great deal in common. Convince yourself that what you have to say is valuable. Now you are ready to start.

Giving Your Talk

Begin your speech slowly. You have to give your listeners a chance to sit back in their chairs, adjust themselves, and establish a mental connection with your topic. Rushing into your speech may be startling, causing you to lose the audience from the start. To speak effectively, pay attention to the following four points.

1. By establishing eye contact with your listeners you form a special relationship with them. If you do not look into their faces, they will rightfully think that you are not interested in them. Burying your head in notes signals your lack of interest in the audience or your fear. Some timid speakers think that if they look only at some fixed place or object in the back of the room, the audience will still regard this as eye contact. But this kind of cover-up does not work. Another tactic poor (or frightened) speakers use is to look at only one member of the audience or to focus, with frequent sidewise glances, on the individual next to them on the stage, perhaps the person who has introduced the speakers. Again, this approach slights the audience.

Establish a pattern of gazing at your notes and then looking up at various individuals in the audience. If the group you are addressing is small (ten to twenty people), you should look at each person in the course of your talk. When you speak to a large audience (forty or fifty or more individuals), visually divide this group into four or five sections, and look at each section a number of times as you speak. If you have to use a blackboard during your speech, do not turn your back to the audience and talk to the blackboard; rather, try to look at the audience as much as possible. To see examples of effective eye contact with an audience, watch how professional newscasters or experienced lecturers focus their eyes on an audience, visually linking themselves to their listeners.

Eye contact with your audience will also give you valuable feedback about your performance. An audience's reactions to your speech (content as well as delivery) can tell you to speak slower or faster, use fewer illustrations, vary your pace, or modify your gestures. Watch your listeners' faces for smiles, frowns, or yawns. If they sit there with puzzled looks on their faces, your material may be too technical or not relevant for them. Reduce the amount of detail and concentrate on the main points clearly. If many people in the audience are sitting with their arms folded, their body language signals that they are not receptive to what you are saying. In this case you may have to deviate from your prepared outline and supply a more convincing example.

If members of the audience yawn or turn their heads to look out the window or across the aisle, change your tempo, try a louder voice to emphasize points, or use an appropriate gesture to bring the audience's attention back to you.

2. Make the volume, tone, and rate of your delivery a favorable part of your image.   Speak in a natural, conversational voice. But avoid such "verbal tics" as "you know" or "I mean," repeated several times in every sentence. Such nervous habits will make your audience nervous too and will make your speech less effective. Many inexperienced speakers feel as though they have to be something they are not when they address an audience. Be yourself, someone your community or business knows and expects to hear. Talk slowly enough for your audience to understand you, yet quickly enough so that you don't sound as if you were emphasizing each word. By going too quickly, you will lose your audience and sound as though you are in a hurry to finish.

Your voice should be easy and pleasant to hear. Talk loudly enough for everyone to hear, but be careful if you are using a microphone. Your voice will automatically be amplified, so if you are already speaking loudly, you will boom rather than send messages pleasantly to your audience. Watch the other extreme—speaking so softly that only people in the first two rows can hear you. Vary both the volume and the emphasis of your voice to sound realistic and interested in what you are doing. Speaking in a monotone will put your audience to sleep. If you have to interrupt your speech to sneeze or cough, politely excuse yourself and go on.

3. Watch your posture.   If you stand motionless, looking as if rigor mortis has set in, your speech will be judged as cold and lifeless, no matter how lively your words are. Be natural, move, and let your body react to what you are saying. Smile, frown, nod your head, move your arms, point your fingers at an object, stand back a little from the lectern. This is not to say that you should be a moving target. Never sit on a desk or lean on a lectern in front of your audience. You may want your listeners to believe that you are trying to get closer to them, but they will be waiting to see if you fall off your newly discovered prop.

4. Let your gestures be a help, not a hindrance.   They should be natural and consistent. If your own style of delivery is calm and deliberate, you will startle, not enlighten, an audience by suddenly pounding on the lectern for emphasis. Any quick, unexpected movement will detract from what you are saying. Let your material suggest appropriate movements. If you are itemizing four or five points, hold up the appropriate number of fingers to indicate which point you are discussing. Using your hands and arms to indicate direction, size, or relationships is also a way to use body language to comment on your material. But do make sure that each gesture is well timed and meaningful.

You do not want to be all hands and arms in front of your audience, however. Use gestures only when they emphasize or help explain a point. Not every sentence calls for a smile or an arm movement. Do not try to rehearse every gesture you want to use. You will be too animated for the actual presentation.

Avoid any gesture that will distract your audience. You do not want to provide your own sideshow. The following nervous habits, engaged in frequently during a speech, can divert the audience's attention: scratching your head, rubbing your nose, pulling your ear, twirling your hair, pushing up your glasses, fumbling with your notes (bending corners, shuffling note cards, straightening edges), tapping your foot, or moving your finger back and forth across the top of the lectern.

When You Have Finished Your Speech

Don't just smugly sit down, walk back to your place on the dais or in the audience, or, worse yet, march out of the room, your notes grasped firmly in your hand. Thank your listeners for their attention, and stay at the lectern for them to applaud, ask questions, or perhaps give the person who introduced you a chance to thank you while you are still in front of the group. If a question-and-answer session will follow your speech, give your audience a time limit for questions. For example, you might say, "Ladies and gentlemen, I'll be happy to answer any questions you may have now before we break for lunch in fifteen minutes." Or you might say, "Ladies and gentlemen, I have set aside the next ten minutes for questions." By setting limits, you reduce the chances of engaging in a lengthy debate with particular members of the audience, and you also can politely leave after your specified time elapses.

Answer questions honestly, even if it means admitting that you do not know the answer. When you receive a question you cannot answer, say that you do not have the answer and, if possible, refer the individual to an appropriate source. You might even share your sources with your listeners. A question-and-answer period may try your patience and diplomacy, but you can defuse potential conflicts by responding to all questions courteously and respectfully, regardless of the tone of voice used by the individual asking the question. Also, don't entertain questions from only one or two people. Give as many of your listeners as possible a chance to ask questions.

▶ Speech Evaluation

A large portion of Chapter 14 has given you information on how to construct and deliver a speech. As a way of reviewing that advice, study Fig. 14.3, an evaluation form similar to those used by instructors in speech classes. Note that the form gives equal emphasis to the speaker's performance and to the organization and content of the speech.

Fig. 14.3   A speaker evaluation form.

Name of speaker _____   Date of speech _____

Title of speech _____   Length of speech _____

PART I—THE SPEAKER   (circle the appropriate number)

1. Appearance:	1 sloppy	2	3	4	5 well groomed
2. Eye contact:	1 poor	2	3	4	5 effective
3. Voice:	1 monotonous	2	3	4	5 varied
4. Posture:	1 poor	2	3	4	5 erect and natural
5. Gestures:	1 disturbing	2	3	4	5 appropriate
6. Self-confidence:	1 nervous	2	3	4	5 poised

PART II—THE SPEECH   (circle the appropriate number) 1=poor; 5=superior

A. Overall performance:

    1. Speaker's knowledge of the subject—carefully researched; factual errors; missing details:

        1   2   3   4   5

    2. Relevance of the topic for audience—suitable for this group:

        1   2   3   4   5

    3. The speaker's language—too technical; filled with cliches or slang expressions; or crisp and descriptive:

        1   2   3   4   5

Fig. 14.3   (continued)

4. Use of visuals—too many or too few; well placed; appropriate size; handled with care; interfered with speech:

1   2   3   4   5

B. Parts of the speech

5. The introduction—brief and attention getting; informative about division and presentation of topic:

1   2   3   4   5

6. The body—carefully organized and easy to follow; appropriate amount of information; message developed and conveyed clearly:

1   2   3   4   5

7. The conclusion—brief, effective summary of the main points:

1   2   3   4   5

PART III—FINAL REACTIONS   (briefly complete the following)

1. Of all the speakers on the platform today, this speaker should be ranked: _____

_____

2. The speaker's main strengths were: _____

_____

_____

_____

3. The speaker needs to improve on: _____

_____

_____

_____

_____

▶ Exercises

1. List five or six examples of poor telephone etiquette that you have witnessed. Write a memo describing these mistakes and provide recommendations on how to correct the errors.

2. In two or three paragraphs explain some of the fears you have had about delivering a briefing or speech. Be very specific about anything that caused you anxiety. Then, in another two or three paragraphs, describe how what you learned in this chapter (analyzing your audience ahead of time, preparing a speech outline, using visuals) can help calm your fears.

3. Prepare a three- to five-minute talk explaining how a piece of equipment that you use on your job works. If the equipment is small enough, bring it with you to class. If it is too large, prepare an appropriate visual that you can use in your talk.

4. You have just been asked to talk about the students at your school. Narrow this topic and submit a speech outline to your instructor, showing how you have limited the topic and supplied appropriate evidence. Use two or three appropriate visuals (tables, photographs, etc.).

5. Prepare a ten-minute talk on a controversial topic that you would present before some civic group—a local PTA, Lions' Club, local chapter of the American Heart Association, a post of the Veterans of Foreign Wars, a church club. Submit a speech outline to your instructor, along with a one-page statement of your specific call to action and its relevance for your audience.

6. Using the evaluation form contained in Fig. 14.3, evaluate a speaker; this person can be someone in a speech class, a local politician, or perhaps someone delivering a report at work.

Index

what to exclude, 88-89
what to include, 89
Robert's Rules of Order, 242
Rough draft, of summary, 235-236

Sales reports, 361, 363-365
Salutation, 61-62
Sampling
  quota, 273-274
  stratified random, 273
  systematic random, 272-273
"See also" card, 180
Semiblock format, for letters, 55, 57-58
Sentences, 31-46
  appropriate context, 36
  in business letters, 62
  definition of, 31
  in descriptive abstracts, 246
  fragments, 32-33
  graceful and positive, in letters, 69-70
  imperative, 340-341
  lead-in, for visuals, 299
  length of, 37-38
  logical, 35-36
  in instructions, 341
  in sales letters, 136
Short reports
  definition of, 357-358
  how to write, 358-359
Signature, 63
Slang, 27-28
Slide projectors, 431-432
Special mailing instructions, 65-66
Speaking off-the-cuff, 419-420
Speech outline, 426-429
Spelling correctly, 19-21
State names, abbreviations for, 61
Stransky, Alfred, 395-407
Stratified random sampling, 273
Stub, part of a table, 301, 303
Style
  nontechnical, 9
  technical, 8
Subject card, 179-181
Subject line, 62
Summaries. *See also* Abstracts
  contents of, 225-226
  definition of, 223-225
  evaluative, 238-240

internal, in formal speech, 424-425
length of, 225
preparation of, 226-238
of questionnaires, 277
usefulness of, 223-225
Suppressed zero, 305, 307
Systematic random sampling, 272-273

Table of contents, 388, 392
Tables, 300-303
Taking notes, 196-199
Talks. *See* Oral reports
Tape recorder
  in rehearsing a speech, 431
  for a trip report, 372
Technical audience, 4-6, 8, 266, 385
Technical language, 6, 8, 71, 340, 418
Telephone conversations, 411-415
  etiquette for, 412-413
  making a call, 413
  receiving a call, 414-415
Telephone messages, 126, 128
Test reports, 374-376
Thank-you letters, 113-114, 142, 144-
  146
Thompson, Edward T., 43-46
Tick marks, 305
Title card, 178-179
Title page, for long reports, 388-389
Titles, underscoring, 105
Transmittal letter, for long reports, 388,
  390
Trip reports, 369-374
Typewriter maintenance, 249-250
Typing
  of business letters, 54-57, 58-64
  of envelopes, 64-66
  of résumés, 89-98

Underscoring, 12, 105

Vague pronoun reference, 25
Vague words, 24-25
Validity
  of questions, 263, 268
  of questionnaires, 285
Vertical axis, of graph, 304
Visuals, 295-330
  charts